AF600683

DISRUPTIVE POWER

Catholic Women, Miracles, and Politics in Modern Germany, 1918–1965

GERMAN AND EUROPEAN STUDIES

General Editor: Jennifer J. Jenkins

MICHAEL E. O'SULLIVAN

Disruptive Power

Catholic Women, Miracles, and Politics in Modern Germany, 1918–1965

UNIVERSITY OF TORONTO PRESS
Toronto Buffalo London

Toronto Buffalo London
utorontopress.com

ISBN 978-1-4875-0343-7

(German and European Studies)

Library and Archives Canada Cataloguing in Publication

O'Sullivan, Michael E., 1977–, author
Disruptive power : Catholic women, miracles, and politics in modern Germany, 1918–1965 / Michael E. O'Sullivan.

(German and European Studies; 31)

Includes bibliographical references and index.
ISBN 978-1-4875-0343-7 (hardcover)

1. Catholic Church – Germany – History – 20th century. 2. Miracles – Social aspects – Germany – History – 20th century. 3. Neumann, Therese, 1898–1962. 4. Religion and sociology – Germany – History – 20th century. 5. Church and state – Germany – History – 20th century. 6. Christianity and politics – Germany – History – 20th century. 7. Women and religion – Germany – History – 20th century. I. Title. II. Series: German and European Studies; 31

BX1536.2.O88 2018 282'.430904 C2018-903133-6

University of Toronto Press acknowledges the financial assistance to its publishing program of the Canada Council for the Arts and the Ontario Arts Council, an agency of the Government of Ontario.

Funded by the Government of Canada | Financé par le gouvernement du Canada

To my Dad – my first and most beloved history teacher

Contents

Illustrations

Acknowledgments

After several years of archival work, conference travel, and writing, this book owes much to a variety of institutions and people. First among these are my mentors in the field of modern German history. Larry Eugene Jones motivated me to enter this profession through his example and steadfast encouragement and stimulated my initial interest in German Catholics. My dissertation director Konrad H. Jarausch graciously cultivated my interest in religious history and Christopher Browning has been a source of great counsel. Thanks also to Jay Smith, Lloyd Kramer, Karen Hageman, and other faculty who nurtured me at the University of North Carolina–Chapel Hill. I was fortunate to enjoy dissertation funding from the DAAD in 2003–4 when conducting the earliest research for this project. I also received the Dr Richard M. Hunt Fellowship for the Study of German History, Politics, Society, and Culture from the American Council on Germany in 2013, which permitted extensive archival work. The Office of the VPAA at Marist College awarded three summer research grants for trips to Washington, DC and Germany; multiple grants for conference travel; an annual professional development budget for acquisition of rare books and archival copies; and a sabbatical. I am grateful to the staffs of the archives and libraries where I worked. Although countless people helped at the facilities cited in this book, I would single out Hans Ammerich at the diocesan archive in Speyer and Rudolf Fritsch at the state archive in Amberg for special praise. This project would not have been possible without the generous assistance of Maria Anna Zumholz and the access she granted to archival copies at her home in Münster.

A number of people read sections of this manuscript and provided valuable feedback. The two anonymous readers recruited by University of Toronto Press improved this book immensely. They went beyond what was expected and I am truly in their debt. Thanks also to Jeff Zalar who read parts of the manuscript and to James Chappel who shared feedback on my book proposal. Richard Ratzlaff expressed enthusiasm and imparted wise advice from our first meeting about this manuscript and I am appreciative to all at the University of Toronto Press who guided the book through the process of publication.

The book improved due to interactions with several other scholars. I owe a particular debt to Mark Edward Ruff and Thomas Großbolting for organizing a series of seminars at the German Studies Association on the history of religion. The ideas exchanged at these events sustained me as I wrote. Others who provided collegial support include Paula Kane, Maria Mitchell, Michael Gross, Martin Menke, Christoph Kösters, Anthony Steinhoff, Suzanne-Brown Fleming, Raymond Sun, Benjamin Pearson, Till van Rahden, Martina Cucchiara, Kevin Spicer, Thomas Brodie, Edward Snyder, Monica Black, Jan-Holger Kirsch, Eric Kurlander, Bernard Schneider, Monique Scheer, and Helena Tomko. Skye Doney and Cassandra Painter kindly permitted access to their promising work prior to official publication. Georg Schwager and Toni Siegert were warm and welcoming when I interviewed them about Therese Neumann. I am thankful for Joachim Kuropka's invitation to Vechta in 2013. I am indebted to Adam Seipp and Laurence Hare for suggesting I work with University of Toronto Press and for their enduring friendship.

Marist College served as my professional home as I pursued research about German Catholicism over the last decade. My colleagues in the School of Liberal Arts formed a vibrant community of teacher-scholars while I wrote this book. I am especially thankful to the Department of History. Were it not for the friendship and collegiality of Kristen Bayer, Steven Garabedian, Robyn Rosen, Janine Larmon Peterson, Nick Marshall, David Woolner, Artin Arslanian, James Johnson, and the late Jerry White, I would never have had the persistence to finish this project. Sally Dwyer-McNulty contributed comments to part of the manuscript and Juris Pupcenoks encouraged me about the project during our regular lunches. The enthusiasm of the History majors at Marist sustained me whenever I became frustrated with the writing process.

I am grateful to the editors at Camden House and *Zeithistorische Forschungen* for permitting me to use material in chapters 5 and 6 respectively. Some of the findings discussed in chapter 5 originally appeared as "Disruptive Potential: Therese Neumann from Konnersreuth,

National Socialism, and Democracy," in Monica Black and Eric Kurlander, eds., *Revisiting the Nazi Occult: Histories, Realities, Legacies* (Rochester, NY: Camden House, 2015), 181–201. I also first published some research from chapter 6 in "West German Miracles: Catholic Mystics, Church Hierarchy, and Postwar Popular Culture," *Zeithistorische Forschungen/Studies in Contemporary History* 6, no. 1 (2009): 11–34.

Research for this manuscript required several long stays in Germany. I am forever appreciative for the friendship and hospitality of the Kolbe family. Dietrich, Bärbel, Nina, Maren, Jörg, and Eicke helped me learn German long before I dreamed of this project and became my family away from home for several years. Thanks also to Horst Martin for his camaraderie as I started research on this topic in Cologne.

It is hard to express the gratitude I feel for my family. My parents, Wayne and Mary Jo, gave everything they could have to my education and development. They each read and copy-edited some sections of this book. My mother's persistence, faith, and grounded advice and my late father's passionate humanism are an inspiration. I thank my in-laws, Charles and Ellen, for loving support and helping with childcare while I travelled for this endeavour. My gratitude to Mike, Ashley, the O'Sullivans, and the Edmonds for bringing happiness to life outside the workplace. The Rosenbergs offered doting hospitality from the Chapel Hill years to our reunion in the Hudson Valley. My two sons, Sam and Jack, tolerated this work when it kept me from the most important job of all – being their father.

To Meg, my brilliant, inspirational, and feminist life partner: my deepest gratitude and love. Without your patience, feedback, and copy-editing, this book would not have been possible. Without your love, faith, and sharp humour, I would have far less joy in my life.

DISRUPTIVE POWER

Catholic Women, Miracles, and Politics in Modern Germany, 1918–1965

Introduction

On 22 September 1963, forty thousand people travelled to the tiny town of Konnersreuth near the German border with Czechoslovakia. Their destination was the consecration of the "Convent of Adoration," which was to be the new home for nine Carmelite nuns. Such an event might seem an unlikely source for a crowd usually reserved for football matches in post-war West Germany. It also formed a contrast with the ongoing Second Vatican Council where leading theologians fiercely debated the relationship of the church to modernity. At a time when many Catholic leaders sought distance from the emotive approaches to piety of the past, rural Catholics from Bavaria and around Europe oversaw the completion of stigmatic Therese Neumann's final project one year after her death. The crowd to honour a German mystic illuminated the enduring faith in the miraculous by a group of powerful non-conformists who spent decades trying to reshape the Catholic Church in their own image.

The case of Therese Neumann (1898–1962) represents the most sensational instance of stigmata in the German-speaking world during the modern age. She became a religious visionary from 1926 until her death, hearing heavenly voices and bleeding from her eyes, feet, and hands before devoted followers for thirty-five years. She also allegedly spoke archaic languages during her trances, purportedly possessed clairvoyance, made prophecies, suffered vicariously for others, experienced miraculous cures, and subsisted exclusively on communion hosts. Although accused by many of fraudulence, she developed a group of advocates known as the Konnersreuth Circle and her beatification process began in 2005 after church authorities received forty-five thousand letters of support. Neumann became something of a media celebrity as her wax statue featured for several years at Oktoberfest tents in Munich, while stories about her appeared in the German tabloid press for decades.[1] The sensational events of this woman's life form a seemingly ideal field of inquiry for historians examining religion during the rise and fall of democracy and dictatorship in Germany.

Therese Neumann represented only the most famous of numerous largely female mystics, visionaries, and seers who captured the popular imagination of German Catholics at the time. She was one of at least seven German stigmatics who gained popular acclaim during the first three decades of the twentieth century. Furthermore, Germany underwent a major proliferation of Marian apparitions, starting with visions in the town of Heede that attracted twenty thousand pilgrims in one day in 1938. From 1945 to 1954, the Virgin Mary appeared in at least twelve different West German locations in the Rhineland, the Palatinate, and Bavaria.[2] In sum, German Catholicism experienced a massive revival in miraculous faith from the aftermath of the First World War until the onset of the Cold War that most of the academic world has disregarded.

With Therese Neumann of Konnersreuth as a centrepiece, but not its exclusive focus, this book argues that these twentieth-century German Catholic miracles constituted both an upsurge in devotion and a revolt by traditionalists against mainstream religious and political leaders that ultimately contributed to the church's fragmentation and the transformation of Christianity's role in politics. By increasing the level of religious intensity around holy women and makeshift apparition shrines, conservative heretics challenged the orthodoxy and exclusive power of the clergy, the hierarchy, and many lay leaders just as the church balanced efforts to fight secularism and integrate into the modern nation state. Miracle towns became sites where peripheral seers, sophisticated theologians, and pious pilgrims contested the fraught place of Catholicism through decades of turbulent war and upheaval.[3]

Furthermore, these miracles disrupted three major elements of German history: religious secularization, Christian politics, and patriarchal gender roles. First, movements surrounding cures, stigmata, bleeding pictures, and visions of the Blessed Virgin highlighted the hybrid nature of German secularization. This reinvention of Catholic mystical customs tapped a vein in German popular culture, making increased religious devotion possible with an active set of believers. However, these zealous Catholics also unintentionally weakened elements of their church, acting as a catalyst for a personal spirituality independent of priests and bishops whom they perceived as overly modern. Second, these miracles threatened Catholic political elites by challenging the unity of their electorate during the unstable aftermath of both world wars, providing a cultural counterpart to histories of the fall of the Centre Party and the fragile rise of Christian Democracy. Finally, the women at the centre of these popular visions endangered the exclusive control of men over the faith and women's bodies. They and their male advisors offer rich examples about how Catholics negotiated femininity, masculinity, and sexuality during decades of crisis in Germany.

The surprisingly ubiquitous twentieth-century miracles suggest that German Catholicism followed a "braided" and twisting rather than teleological course of secularization. A term with many meanings, secularization continues to cause enormous disagreement. This book defines it as the process by which religion became less central to the world views, mentalities, and institutions that shaped the everyday lives of modern historical subjects. Nonetheless, it also maintains the view that religion serves necessary communal functions by assisting the production of cultural meaning and orienting people socially. I will support those theorists who believe that secularization followed a hybrid path in the modern age where the secular and sacred existed side by side. While some aspects of devotion declined in twentieth-century Germany, other types of faith simultaneously thrived.[4]

Using occult phenomena to complicate the history of Catholicism in Germany, I depict calls for reform from religious conservatives that heightened piety at the same time that other Catholic elites sought either a secular or more mainstream confessional identity. The intensity of the revival described in this book and the persistence of worship at places like Konnersreuth indicate the slippery nature of historical accounts of religion. While many Catholic regions of Germany experienced decline in communion statistics, reductions in church association memberships, and an increase in interfaith marriages, the following of Therese Neumann and a series of Marian apparitions spiked. The latter of these developments strengthened faith among already devout Catholics – primarily from rural areas – who increasingly demanded a more parochial church with fewer accommodations to modern nation states and a less hierarchical faith community in which believers could initiate doctrine and have direct access to God. While the ensuing power struggle between mystical pilgrims and mainstream institutional elites led to a revival of early modern Catholic piety that contradicted secular developments, it also paradoxically added to the secularization process by creating a more individualized sense of spirituality that depended less on priests and bishops than in the past. The tumultuous debates about these miracles within the Catholic Church's leadership and among the laity also reveal the fissures within a national religious community sometimes presented as a monolith. While some viewed the miracles as a sign of salvation in the midst of what they understood to be apocalyptic conditions, others devoted their lives to combatting a type of faith they felt inhibited the church's modernization and integration into a largely Protestant or secular national community. This exploration of Catholic mysticism illustrates the endurance of faith in a period where other indicators showed a decline of religiosity, but it also examines how the grass-roots nature of this religious passion unsettled the institutional power of the church during the already uncertain era of the world wars. Although many histories of the Catholic Church feature progressive change agents who served as antecedents to Vatican II, this study highlights the role of largely conservative reformers who frequently opposed efforts by church leaders to rationalize and modernize Catholicism.

While this cultural history of miracles relates to how Germany became pervasively secular, it also contributes to the remarkably impactful history of twentieth-century Catholic politics. While political Catholicism paradoxically both made and unmade Germany's first republican experiment after the First World War, Catholic politicians' ambiguous relationship with Nazism both facilitated the dictatorship and the dynamic democracy that followed in the West. With linkages to political Catholicism during the Weimar and Adenauer eras, the microhistories of these miraculous movements unveil some features of the downfall of the Bavarian People's Party (BVP) and Centre Party in 1933 and the rise of the Christian Democratic Union / Christian Social Union (CDU/CSU) alliance during the early years of the Cold War. Groups like the Konnersreuth Circle intermingled with the larger Christian political establishment, sometimes repeating the tropes outlined by their leaders and occasionally innovating new directions that Catholic politicians would eventually adopt. Church reformers from the mystical movement contributed to the downfall of political Catholicism by adding to the fragmentation within the precarious alliance that held together the coalitions of the BVP and the Centre Party. These fervent provocateurs, however, provided an unlikely source of dissent against National Socialist principles during the Third Reich. After the war, the mixture of support for and rebellion against the new Christian

Democratic consensus highlights the inherent frailty in the CDU/CSU's rise to power and of the new Federal Republic.

Finally, the stories of these seers and mystics illustrate the complexity of gender within religious networks. Rural women and girls formed a majority of Catholic visionaries, posing a potential problem for a patriarchal church. They positioned themselves in relation to usually wealthier and more educated fathers, brothers, priests, and spiritual advisors, subtly seeking avenues to power through their spiritual gifts and popularity with predominantly female pilgrims. An analysis of how these women interacted with their male counterparts in the church and sometimes evaded sexual predators uncovers much about how pre–Vatican II constructs of femininity and masculinity shaped struggles for influence within spiritual communities. While female seers usually faced stern discipline from the men whose power they undermined, Therese Neumann illustrates how pious women negotiated spheres of power while embracing strict moral codes and paternal hierarchy. Simultaneously men of the Konnersreuth Circle and other mystical communities experimented with different models of masculinity that reconciled some of the dissonance between gendered expectations and their emotive brand of spirituality.

The Asymmetric Path to a Secular Germany

A visit to Germany today reveals a remarkably secular society. Great cathedrals serve more as tourist attractions than houses of worship and the large Catholic minority seems to share the Protestant majority's apathy about weekly religious devotion and Christian doctrine. In fact, the greatest focal point for religious dynamism in the Berlin Republic is Germany's Muslim minority rather than its Christian majority. The situation for German Catholics could not have been any more different in the first decades of the twentieth century when they boasted a king-making political party, a vast spectrum of professional, political, and devotional associations, and a vibrant youth movement.[5] The German historical profession has understandably devoted much research to explaining this stunning transformation of the country's Catholic Church, especially given the disproportionate political impact of Catholic politicians on the fates of the Weimar Republic and the early Federal Republic of Germany.

In the last three decades, historians of Germany have discredited notions that faith disappeared from the modern world and many advance the idea of a Catholic "milieu" to explain the institutionalization of power by the nation's largest religious minority.[6] The milieu concept reached its highpoint in the 1990s when several scholars suggested that regionally fragmented religious cultures experienced a unique period of unity from the 1840s until the 1950s as a result of modern uses of organization, transport, and communication. These elements of modernity, however, paved the way for lay people to eventually seek even greater independence from the clergy by the 1960s.[7] Therefore, these social historians also examined the Catholic milieu as a transitional phase in the modernization process where "elements of traditional society mixed with modern forms of production in bourgeois industrial societies."[8] Mark Edward Ruff summarized the mainstream understanding of sheltered Catholic communities at their height in the early twentieth century in his renowned book about West German youth after 1945: "From the cradle to the grave, daily life in many southern and western regions of Germany was steeped in religion – in prayers, blessings, pilgrimages, festivals, and processions."[9] Much recent work on the social history of Catholicism reinforces the hegemony of the milieu model and its new narrative of secularization.[10]

Some recent researchers either encourage a more flexible version of the milieu model that incorporates linguistic and gender analysis or argue for a complete break from the paradigm.[11] For example, Christian Schmidtmann's somewhat postmodern monograph about West German university students rejects exclusively structural histories of Catholicism and focuses on the competing cultural values and conflicting identities of diverse post-1945 students. Other work on the post-1945 era also creates a new narrative about the personalization of devotion by examining the ways in which Christian values persisted even after church attendance declined and Germans ceased adherence to doctrines and moral teaching.[12]

Robert Orsi's concept of "lived religion" for secularization in the United States provides an interesting alternative for Germany. Orsi opposes accounts that view religious worlds, subcultures, and mentalities as isolated and separate from other aspects of society and experience.[13] He discourages religious narratives that only depict religious conformity to a "normative trajectory toward the modern." Instead, we should look beyond the gradual subordination of belief in the supernatural to see how "the children and grandchildren of the modernizing generation rediscovered old devotional practices." This method would be especially useful for examining German Catholicism after it went into formal decline. The notion of a "braided narrative" does not eliminate the possibility of secularization. Rather, it draws attention to "improbable intersections, incommensurable ways of living, discrepant imaginings, unexpected movements of influence, and inspiration existing side by side."[14]

The example of Bavarian visionary Bärbel Reuβ illuminates how this multidimensional methodology makes room for the miracles studied in this book. As a sixteen-year-old in the village of Marienfried, Reuβ first saw the Virgin Mary in 1940 at the start of the war, which encouraged her devotion to the rosary and prayers for the well-being of her "Fatherland." When Mary appeared again in 1944, she offered Reuβ hope for peace in war-torn Germany if its residents followed her instructions for prayer. Reuβ became immersed in a women's group devoted to the veneration of Mary inspired by the Rhineland's so-called Schönstatt Movement. Building on this local following, she attracted many pilgrims at the end of the war and the start of the occupation.[15] This vignette demonstrates how the religiosity of such visions occurred against the backdrop of the lived experience of war. It also highlights how a small-town Marian circle countered the decline of formal Catholic social and political life under Nazism with a less institutionalized form of devotion. With millions of pilgrims, widespread press coverage, the interest of powerful theologians, and international relevance, the movements around Catholic ecstasy represent a dramatic counterpoint to the waning of confessional associations and church attendance documented by other studies.

The eccentricities of historical subjects such as Reuβ prevented their complete penetration of the mainstream. They neither shaped the daily life of all Christian Schmidtmann's Catholic students nor halted the rejection of Catholic organizational life by Mark Ruff's young subjects after the war. Nonetheless, the lived religion approach to secularization seems especially suited to such phenomenon. If we interpret Orsi's narrative as a long rope with numerous braids of various sizes and volumes, it seems a useful way to integrate religious movements that existed outside the primary structures of power, yet achieved a significant cultural impact.

The study of twentieth-century German miracles highlights an upsurge of piety among a group of conservative rebels who simultaneously mobilized mass expressions of Catholic faith and weakened church orthodoxy and clerical authority. These events indicate a deeply ambiguous secularization process that created a pluralistic society where Christian ideals competed indefinitely with other religious and secular beliefs and viewpoints.[16] This book argues that Catholic mystics and their adherents demonstrate this uneven and twisted path towards secular modernity. They provide empirical evidence of uniquely Catholic practices and world views that persisted, adapted, and created modern meaning in the most tumultuous moments of German history. The devotion of hundreds of thousands and sometimes millions of Catholics to relationships with heavenly figures contrasted sharply with the decline in male voters for Catholic parties and memberships in Catholic associations and youth groups. Despite showcasing the perseverance of an exclusively Catholic mysticism, Therese Neumann and other seers also unintentionally contributed to the fragmentation of Catholic doctrine, authority, and influence. By promoting a deeply personal piety and spiritualties that openly rejected the mediation of church institutions, these modern visionaries foresaw Germany's future devotion to new age religions, ecumenical experiments, and individual faiths that no longer adhered to the doctrines of one specific religious tradition.[17]

Miracles and Catholic Politics: From Centre Party to Christian Democracy

After the First World War, the Centre Party and BVP simultaneously reached their zenith and started a rapid descent. These Catholic parties became the powerful coalition lynchpins of the Weimar parliamentary system. Germany's first republican democracy could not form governing coalitions without this steady Catholic voting block because the Social Democratic Party (SPD), the German Democratic Party (DDP), and the German People's Party (DVP) did not usually command a large enough share of the vote to pass legislation on their own. The nationalist parties of the right, which became more prominent at the end of the republic, also required help from the Centre Party up until their decision to work with the National Socialists in January of 1933. Despite their importance, the Centre Party and BVP watched their share of the national vote stagnate and decline throughout the 1920s. Suffering from immense internal diversity, the Centre Party in particular struggled to unite its working-class voters with its nationalist supporters, causing an exodus of male members to more secular alternatives. The internally fragmented parties finally ended their own existence by voting for the Enabling Act in 1933.[18] After such a contradictory past as both democratic cornerstones and abettors of totalitarianism, Catholic politicians entered a similarly paradoxical phase after the Second World War. Numerous Catholic elites, led by West Germany's first chancellor, Konrad Adenauer, created the Christian Democratic Union and the Christian Social Union, both of which became the dominant right-of-centre parties based on confessional unity between Protestants and Catholics. However, these parties ultimately became very secular over time, abandoning many of the Christian principles upon which they were founded.[19]

Most existing studies of German Catholicism either analyse the realm of religious practice or Catholic politics but seldom combine the two in one book. The case studies of stigmata and visions of the Virgin Mary in this monograph provide a unique opportunity given the political activism of many advocates and opponents of these events. In order to bridge the gap between Catholic faith and politics, one must examine how everyday congregants incorporated the values of the church into their everyday lives and eventually their political behaviour.

Applying Pierre Bourdieu's ideas about a "religious field" of competition between representatives of religious institutions and members of the laity over legitimation and the "goods of salvation," this book uses miracles as a vehicle to better understand the transition of political Catholicism in Germany into Christian Democracy after the war.[20] First, several chapters connect the struggle between proponents and opponents of miracles to the decline of the Centre Party and the Bavarian People's Party during the Weimar Republic. The book presents adversaries of miracles as Catholics pursuing a rationalized faith to better integrate into the nation and facilitate the necessary compromises in a tenuous parliamentary political system. It portrays advocates of mysticism as seeking a Christian political utopia. This battle over how to be a modern Catholic damaged an already delicate political Catholic establishment at the end of the Weimar Republic. The political desires of Neumann's Konnersreuth Circle and the supporters of other stigmatics highlight the impossibility of creating a uniformly Catholic vision in a parliamentary system where Protestants constituted a majority and many Christians supported secular variants of liberalism, socialism, communism, and nationalism. Second, the book illustrates the difficulties between devout Catholics and National Socialism. For example, Barbara Weigand of Schippach, a seer close to death during the war, famously referred to Hitler as a "monster vomited from hell."[21] However, the monograph illuminates the inability of pre–Vatican II Catholics to oppose the imperial, racial, and anti-Semitic underpinnings of the Nazi state as well. Tracing subaltern movements in favour of Marian worship and the resistance of many members of Neumann's Konnersreuth Circle against the Third Reich, my research also indicates the limits to dissent by miracle supporters who perpetuated the religious anti-Semitism of their church. Finally, the book examines how some of Konnersreuth's Weimar supporters anticipated Christian Democracy as a future political alternative and how the Cold War helped devotees of apparitions and stigmata after the Second World War to integrate their anti-communism, war trauma, and anti-consumerism into support for a more mainstream Christian rather than exclusively Catholic politics. Konnersreuth became a powerful place of German-American reconciliation during the 1950s and Neumann's brother pursued a career within the rising Christian Democratic wave, making these miracles case studies where one can assess the Catholic role in the erecting the post-1945 NATO consensus.

The Empowerment of Catholic Women

Work about German Catholics frequently employs the "feminization of religion" narrative, which argues that the Christian churches combatted secularization by successfully recruiting women who in turn used the churches as tools for their own emancipation. While this concept attracted attention to the importance of marginalized female worshippers, it limited how we view the agency of religious and conservative women. Several academics concur that the Catholic minority in Germany became feminized. They suggest that nineteenth-century gender norms helped mothers and wives form a majority among practicing Catholics. As the bourgeois ideal of female domesticity became dominant, religious piety and instruction for children became a responsibility for the private sphere. Post-Enlightenment men with active professional lives had less time or desire to participate in religious life.[22] Bishops and priests emphasized "emotional" elements of Catholic piety, such as the cults of the Virgin Mary and Sacred Heart, which they believed would attract female congregants and prevent their participation in the women's movement.[23] Scholars of German Catholicism, however, disagree about whether the feminization of Christianity provided women opportunities for emancipation. While some research suggests that clergy maintained strict control over female associations and used them to inhibit women's engagement with progressive social forces, other work highlights access to new professional opportunities in charities, health care, and education as well as the relatively egalitarian structure of convents.[24] Besides nuns, religious visionaries are also viewed as powerful figures who "inverted" the usual power relationship with men and priests in the village. Some academics even interpret them as "popular theologians" who introduced new elements to church teaching and practice.[25] Several convincing critiques challenge the feminization of religion thesis. For example, Patrick Pasture suggests it is "narrative fiction," arguing that the increase in female participation in the nineteenth century was largely a cultural construct and that women experienced only minimal empowerment through the churches.[26]

On the surface, the life of Therese Neumann and the other mostly female seers of this book appear to confirm rather than contradict the feminization thesis. Building on institutional teaching about the Virgin Mary, the church sanction of the Portuguese Fatima apparitions from the First World War, and the canonization of Therese of Lisieux (Neumann's favourite saint), these women apparently adopted the emotional and sentimental forms of piety prompted by the Vatican and its hierarchy. Furthermore, it would seem that they gained favoured status as religious figures, granting them power through their embrace of Catholicism. However, several factors complicated this narrative.

First, all of these religious women possessed dominant male spiritual mentors. This strong male presence in the immediate following of female mystics contradicts any notion of women exclusively dominating Catholicism in a realm presumed to be more effeminate than most. In fact, the supporters and opponents of Catholic miracles performed multiple competing ideals for religious masculinity. Critics of miracles presented the Catholic man as a beacon of scientific rationalism, meant to restrain the hysteria of feminine piety. Supporters espoused a mixture of emotional, muscular, and militaristic imagery in support of a direct relationship with heavenly figures but a necessarily less hierarchical church.

Within this context of rural patriarchy and hierarchical Catholicism, these female visionaries subtly negotiated restricted areas of authority, but this path to agency required an embrace of normative gender roles. This more complex route towards self-assertion illustrates the balancing act religious visionaries needed to perform in order to retain their spiritual power and still find room for their own autonomy. A natural tension existed in the relationship between female mystics and bishops that was not restricted to the twentieth century. Throughout the Middle Ages, the early modern era, and the nineteenth century, European religious women claimed special status because of their visions and very few of them gained recognition. Only rare figures, such as Hildegard of Bingen, Gemma Galagni, and Bernadette Sourbirous, gained formal sanction for their experiences. Bishops and sometimes clergy resisted when piety became miraculous because they viewed the stewardship of a coherent and consistent doctrine as a sacred duty. They needed to protect the church from fraud and the pagan rituals that mixed with everyday religion. They often doubted cases of miracles because they threatened both ecclesiastical authority and the well-being of the faith. Therefore, the numerous sacred women of the twentieth century risked harmful discipline from church authorities if they became too transgressive. Ursula Hibbeln of Bochum demonstrates this situation well. The wife of a streetcar conductor in the industrial *Ruhrgebiet* (Ruhr region), she lost eight of her nine children, and suffered regularly from medical ailments. This woman became empowered when she started to have visions and to communicate with dead souls in purgatory. She often expressed an excessive amount of respect for clergy, bishops, and the religious hierarchy. Despite her threat to priests' roles as mediators between God and worshippers, many church figures permitted her status as a local figure of reverence even if church officials never formally endorsed her miracles. This leniency allowed Hibbeln to become a community spiritual leader who provided comfort for the sick and grieving. Her small apartment a hub of activity for Catholics in her area, Hibbeln gained vocational fulfilment and spiritual power by submitting to the norms of Catholic patriarchy.[27] The interactions and unconscious struggle for power between female seers, female pilgrims, male spiritual mentors, and male admirers created a malleable dynamic that is too complex for the static feminization of religion thesis.

This study proposes a spectrum of strategies by religious women negotiating overlapping rural, religious, and political subcultures dominated by men. A few of these women submitted almost entirely to a combination of male advisors and ecclesiastical authorities – usually with disastrous results for the acceptance of their sanctity. Another handful of famous mystics became outspoken critics of male privilege, denouncing rules that prevented the ordination of women. This risky approach frequently ended in harsh church discipline or public humiliation. In the most sophisticated cases, Catholic visionaries worked from within existing gender norms that they reaffirmed to seek influence. The power they strived for could take different forms. Sometimes they used male elites interested in their spiritual gifts to improve the standing of their family. Most of them sought a fulfilling spiritual vocation and official recognition of their status by the church. Through a direct connection with God, these women, who almost always suffered long-term illness before their visions, went from sick dependents to valued community leaders that were consulted by the suffering, the dying, and those in crisis. By ministering to a following they naturally threatened the clergy who usually filled these roles. Women like Therese Neumann gradually accumulated power and influence, spreading their interpretation of Catholic traditionalism and shaping the political and religious outlook of their localities. They were emboldened by the sense of purpose their religious mission provided them and the ability to mould society according to their values.

Finally, the stories and disputes surrounding the Catholic miraculous placed male and female sexuality in a central position. While strict morality became a common theme among all movements studied by this book, ambiguities persisted. Therese Neumann used her own lay celibacy as a compelling weapon in pursuit of power within a Catholic subculture and against the danger of sexual assault, but rumours of sexual perversion provided a consistent tool in rhetoric by both advocates and critics as they attacked one another in debates about miracles. This study highlights the role of gender in the struggle for power surrounding twentieth-century German miracles. It subverts depictions of piously Catholic women as anachronisms and instead presents them as empowered agents negotiating a perilous but evolving patriarchal power structure.

Catholic Miracles and Modern Germany

Although European Catholic miracles have featured in much work about the medieval and early modern periods, they have gradually attracted more studies by historians of the modern era. Research about the visions of the Virgin Mary in the small French village of Lourdes by Bernadette Soubirous in 1858, and their ensuing popularity, depicts them as a symbol of Catholic resistance against liberal, socialist, and secular ideals. In fact, the Marpingen visions in Germany occurred in the context of a contentious *Kulturkampf* (culture war) over the place of the church in the newly unified state. Such miracles form the first half of what many scholars of religion call the Marian century from 1850 to 1950 to indicate a time when European clergy and congregants showed particular enthusiasm for veneration of the Virgin Mary.[28]

The Vatican revived the cult of the Virgin Mary in the late nineteenth century to mobilize support against secularization. As a result, rural girls throughout Europe claimed to see the Virgin Mary and sometimes the Vatican recognized the visions as legitimate if enough evidence indicated supernatural activity. Church leaders used famous and officially sanctioned apparitions in Fatima (Portugal, 1917) and Lourdes (France, 1858) to encourage devotion until the Second Vatican Council reforms of the 1960s.[29]

A broad and varied source base exists for this new history of twentieth-century German miracles. Many collections related to Therese Neumann and other visionaries are closed due to ongoing beatification processes. However, rich archival material remains available to researchers.[30] Several other dioceses contain open collections about ecclesiastical investigations of Neumann and other mystical phenomena. In addition to these church records, a voluminous public discourse existed in several popular books, periodicals, and newspapers. Finally, the state kept records about many of these movements. There are materials from police surveillance reports as well as documents from trials regarding the miracles. Finally, the personal papers of opponents of apparitions and stigmata from this age provide another interesting perspective. Such a rich source base creates an opportunity to contribute to the growing literature about Catholic miracles.

This book introduces three fresh interpretations to the existing work about German Catholicism and European miracles. First, it argues that Germany experienced a generally overlooked revival of faith in the miraculous from the 1920s until the 1960s. Corresponding roughly to Therese Neumann's life as a public figure, this period of intense supernatural faith by millions of usually traditionalist Catholics from Bavaria, the Rhineland, the Emsland, and the Palatinate presents an institutional church that was anything but monolithic. Rather the social and political upheaval of this era in modern German history splintered the Catholic population in a manner highlighted by faith in the miraculous. Furthermore, the present persistence of pilgrimage to places like Konnersreuth and Heroldsbach, albeit in much smaller numbers than before, suggests that a braided narrative of secularization functions well in the German Catholic context. A national and transnational movement in favour of the miraculous simultaneously perpetuated distinctly Catholic spiritualties while also damaging the strength of the bishops' authority through the promotion of personal piety that relied less on mediation by church elites. Second, this book depicts female seers and their male supporters as equally divergent from typical academic portrayals of Catholic gender roles. Female visionaries and their pilgrims conformed neither to stereotypes of antimodern religious women at the beck and call of their priest nor to the depictions of Catholic feminist nuns who used the church for their own emancipation. Balancing a massive following made possible by modern media, cadres of patriarchal male advisors necessary for religious legitimacy, and their own self-interested desire for influence, these women charted a complicated and sometimes limited course for spiritual and cultural power. Their male followers also provide alternate examples of Catholic masculinity that competed with other more hegemonic models for manliness and laid the groundwork for the ascension of Catholic men to political leadership after 1945. Finally, the book affirms the central place of Catholic miracles to the politics of modern Germany. Contributing to the fall of political Catholicism, groups surrounding miracles became particularly important during the Third Reich. Although not well documented in the secondary literature, these mystics attracted negative attention from the National Socialist German Workers' Party (NSDAP or Nazi Party) and their interplay with the regime highlights the deeply ambiguous relationship between Catholicism and Nazism. Therese Neumann and a wave of Marian apparitions also became central to the German-American relationship and the Catholic encounter with the Cold War. Interacting with debates about the Nazi past, the nuclear age, the post-war refugee crisis, and the rise of American consumerism, movements surrounding Catholic miracles helped define the nature of Christian Democracy and Western integration.

While the book uniquely emphasizes the enduring popularity of Therese Neumann from 1926 to 1962, it also places her case in context by scrutinizing faith in Catholic miracles more broadly. Chapter 1 investigates the existence of numerous now-forgotten miracles in the aftermath of the First World War. It surveys the rise of several stigmatics from the 1920s, focusing especially on Anna Maria Goebel from Bickendorf (near Trier), who emerged amidst the ruptures caused by the First World War. The chapter also studies the so-called "Aachen Blood Miracle," which converged with the series of miracles in France, Germany, and Belgium where believers claimed paintings of Jesus cried tears of blood. It closes with an in-depth assessment of eighty-three documented cures claimed by sick pilgrims to the Holy Shroud of Trier in 1933. Exploring debates within the church about unsanctioned miracles and gender relations in each case, the chapter illustrates that

Therese Neumann was far from exceptional when she burst into the public sphere in 1926.

Chapter 2 traces the meteoric rise of Therese Neumann from an unknown rural woman stricken with health problems to a religious superstar. It analyses the formation of her Konnersreuth Circle, her intimate relationship with the parish priest, Father Joseph Naber, and the press war over her alleged sanctity. With deep ties to the BVP, famous theologians, aristocrats, and journalists, Neumann became a central but controversial figure to the church and the political Catholic establishment at the end of the Weimar Republic. Her case sparked a wide-ranging debate about the nature of modern Catholicism and factionalized church elites as they reconciled the frightful destruction of modernity with long-standing religious values. Chapter 3 and chapter 4 analyse the importance of Therese Neumann's miracles to the history of politics and gender during the Weimar Republic. They examine the relationship of the Konnersreuth Circle to political Catholicism, social democracy, and communism in the waning years of the Weimar Republic and situate the seer's activism and fame within the history of femininity, sexuality, and masculinity during the same era. Chapter 5 assesses the fragile and at times tragic fate of supporters of Catholic miracles during the Third Reich. Focused mainly on the Konnersreuth Circle, the chapter illustrates how Neumann balanced her potential to disrupt both the church and the totalitarian state through her unfettered access to God with a desire to avoid either excommunication or imprisonment.

Chapter 6 investigates the outbreak of Marian apparitions in Germany after 1945, focusing especially on the towns of Heroldsbach, Fehrbach, and Rodalben. Linking these events to struggles for power within the church, gender relations, memory of the Nazi past, and confrontation with the Cold War, the chapter illustrates how Catholic miracles shed light on the formation of Catholic identities during the era of Konrad Adenauer. Many German refugees, former POWs, and traumatized Catholics sought comfort in the Virgin Mary's stern warning and promises of salvation as the spectre of nuclear war emerged. Supporters of Marian apparitions clashed with leaders of the CDU, CSU, the Catholic hierarchy, and other aspects of the laity during a failed struggle for power within a reconstituted Catholic community in West Germany. Finally, chapter 7 depicts the revival of Konnersreuth as a site for religious pilgrimage after 1945 and illustrates how Therese Neumann became a controversial figure of German-American reconciliation through the pilgrimage of 500,000 American GIs to her town.

In these trans-Atlantic encounters she emerged as a centrepiece for how Bavarian Catholics encountered the Cold War. She used connections with the American military, the new Christian Social Union (CSU), and the emerging economy to pursue several building projects to benefit the Catholic Church, Konnersreuth's economy, and her own legacy.

This monograph demonstrates the disruptive influence of Catholic miracles to the religious, gendered, and political narratives of modern Germany. The spectre of Konnersreuth, Heede, Bickendorf, and Heroldsbach as well as other miracle sites poses a counternarrative to the mainstream depictions of German secularization, while the men and women who made these movements complicate common notions about gender in Catholic Europe. Advocates of miracles also reflected and even shaped Catholic politics as they evolved from the Weimar Republic to the Cold War. Creating hope for salvation in times of great anxiety but also splintering the Catholic community with their fervent approach to the faith, the pilgrims and seers of Germany embodied the "shattered" narrative of their nation's history in the twentieth century.[31]

Chapter One

Germany between Apocalypse and Salvation: Bloody Images and Miraculous Cures

On 8 May 1927 Margareta Lippert suffered a debilitating stroke that left her unable to walk, sit down, or use her left arm without assistance. When she heard the diocese of Trier would display the holy coat of Jesus for the first time in over forty years, she registered with pilgrimage leaders for a special blessing at the cathedral. She journeyed from Camberg to Trier and touched the relic in the middle of the night on 25 August 1933. She said, "I touched the holy coat and said: 'Dear God, if it is your will and good for me, please help me and make me healthy again' … First when I was back in the car and sat in my place I began to feel a deep discomfort that I would compare to an electric storm. I turned to the nun who escorted me and said, 'Sister, I believe I can stand.'" From that moment forward, she could walk without a cane or crutches. When reflecting on her good luck, she uttered, "Dear God, am I worthy of your goodness to me?"[1]

This recollection of direct intercession by God constitutes just one of eighty-three people seeking recognition of a cure in the summer of 1933. Furthermore, these miracles came after several ubiquitous holy men and women rose to local and sometimes national prominence in the aftermath of the First World War. This wave of miraculous mysticism in Western Germany contributed to an upswing in personalized piety that weakened the formal political and religious institutions of the church; strengthened informal elements of spirituality; and highlighted regional, political, and gendered divisions among German Catholics.

In his landmark study about apparitions in Marpingen during the *Kulturkampf*, David Blackbourn suggests a major resurgence of German Catholic miracles after the First World War.[2] Research on the western front also highlights how soldiers at the front developed "spiritualism" to cope with their hardships. For Catholics, this meant deeper devotion to the saints and local traditions from their home regions.[3] After a review of how Catholic leaders encouraged some controlled forms of mysticism through Marian worship from above, this chapter then assesses the rise of multiple visionaries unsanctioned by church authority. It explores the Aachen "blood miracle" of 1920 inspired by the excommunicated French priest Abbé Vachère; a Belgian stigmatist, Rosalia Putt, with numerous German admirers; the following of Barbara Weigand of Schippach; and the stigmata of Anna Maria Goebel of Bickendorf. The chapter concludes with the uneasiness created by the widespread faith in miracles articulated at the institutionally planned Trier pilgrimage of 1933. Comparing and contrasting the promotion of mysticism by the church with instances of personalized and therefore unsanctioned piety, these examples illustrate the tension of a splintering but dynamic religious community during the Weimar years.

Most of these events occurred in Western Germany in the dioceses of Trier and Cologne, which distinguishes them from the Bavarian context of Therese Neumann. The seers of the Rhineland and the Eifel received remarkable support from thousands despite condemnation by the institutional church. The regional location is significant given the prominent Centre Party figures and the dense network of confessional associations popular in the area. The home of powerful politicians and theorists, such as Wilhelm Marx, August Pieper, and Heinrich Brauns, the Rhineland, *Ruhrgebiet*, and Eifel contained a male-dominated laity that supplemented and sometimes challenged the institutional power of the bishops. While the Centre Party possessed much infrastructure in this region, it also relied on support from the *Volksverein für das katholische Deutschland*, Christian Trade Associations, associations for male youth and the working class, and lay organizations for women and girls. Many of these groups sought to integrate the Catholic minority into the nation while maintaining religious identity and values. No matter the make-up of these groups' memberships, either bourgeois male laity or clergy claimed the most important leadership positions. Although powerful, this masculine elite faced deep uncertainty during the Weimar era. Anxiety increased as the Centre Party's share of the national vote lingered between 11 and 13 per cent, well below its pre-war results. The party largely lost its working-class male support and relied heavily on recently enfranchised women to remain relevant, an uneasy proposition for a faith with strict gender hierarchies. Furthermore, political Catholicism faced a test of authenticity in the eyes of its members as it negotiated coalition arrangements with the Social Democratic Party, which it frequently vowed to defeat, and the German National People's Party (DNVP), which offended the left wing of the Centre Party. Ultimately, the multiplicity of Catholic associations engendered competition for financing, membership, and ideological space and sometimes led to revolts against the bishops over power within the country's Catholic subculture. The growing enthusiasm for the miraculous in this part of Germany threatened its powerful but increasingly disconcerted male elite. The worry that rural women with few economic resources could upend the patriarchal hold upon theology and confessional organization in predominantly Catholic towns threatened lay politicians and bishops already concerned with a wavering and divided base.[4]

Despite a regional elite that limited the scope of their power, this interconnected circle of religious seers and devout pilgrims dramatically illustrates the surge of interest in the miraculous in the 1920s, a phenomenon that merits a more central place in the history of German Catholicism. Using the methods of Robert Orsi, this chapter understands "religion as a network of relationships between heaven and earth involving humans of all ages and many different sacred figures together" because this approach "frees us from any notion of religious practices as either good or bad."[5] Examining reports from sick pilgrims, ailing visionaries, and zealous devotees, this analysis of post-1918 miracles captures the vivid presence of heavenly figures in the lives of many Catholics as they endured their personal struggles as well as the angst of a nation in crisis.

Beyond describing the lived experience of Catholic believers in religious ecstasy, this evidence also illustrates many other points of tension in German Catholicism. By analysing the Rhineland and the Eifel, one senses the intense opposition between bishops and political leaders on the one hand and the web of holy figures worshipped by rural communities on the other. While seers balanced their attack on what they viewed as a worldly church with the desire for official legitimacy from the hierarchy, the bishoprics and the Centre Party feared the threat to their power and the consistency of the faith posed by upstart seers in already turbulent times. This concern was not without cause. Miracle supporters and seekers who actually understood their rebellion as one that would revive traditional religiosity unconsciously developed a more personal relationship with God that partially undermined the church institutions, doctrines, and houses of worship they revered. This development threatened the entrenched power structures as well as the ability of Catholicism to maintain its immense social, cultural, and political influence in Germany. Finally, this chapter argues that male and female visionaries adopted different strategies in their struggle for the spiritual goods of salvation. With men attacked as frauds and women declared hysterical, they each crafted personas that converged with accepted Catholic gender norms to defend themselves. The contradictions in these gendered tropes frequently hindered the durability of mystic movements whose popularity lasted only a few years.

Church-Sanctioned Marian Devotion

The church hierarchy promoted mysticism yet struggled to control it during the aftermath of the First World War, especially in the promotion of the Fatima miracles. With the visions deemed authentic in 1930, Fatima became a paradigm for German faith in the Virgin Mary.[6] Even before this verdict, much evidence indicates efforts by local clerics to champion early modern Marian pilgrimages and rituals as their congregations coped with the trauma of war and depression. The popular response to such efforts indicated the widespread and unpredictable connection between German Catholics and heavenly personalities.

In Western Germany, the pilgrimage sites at Neviges (*Ruhrgebiet*) and Kevelaer (Rhineland) teemed with unprecedented numbers of pilgrims after the First World War. With origins in apparitions of the Virgin Mary during the seventeenth century and links to several miraculous cures, the chapel of Kevelaer experienced revival during the twentieth century.[7] With interest already surging on the eve of the First World War, the site's total of 500,000 pilgrims in 1915 eclipsed any previous number as calculated by the shrine's monks. Modern means of transportation, activism by the Rhineland's labyrinth of confessional associations, and a grass-roots interest in Marian worship caused an even greater surge in the aftermath of war and during the rise of National Socialism. In 1932, Kevelaer received 520,000 pilgrims, forcing the town of 9,800 to entertain as many travellers as a "world city like Berlin."[8]

The most important pilgrimage site in the archbishopric of Cologne, Neviges became religiously significant in the seventeenth century when it received a small picture of the Virgin Mary credited with medieval miracles. Starting in the nineteenth century it welcomed numerous visitors from the surrounding industrial cities of Essen, Dortmund, Bochum, and what would become Wuppertal.[9] Attendance at Neviges surged after 1925 receiving over 60,000 pilgrims in 1926 and 1927 and over 150,000 in the year of its 250th anniversary in 1931.[10] From 1934 to 1936 Neviges received its highest totals ever, drawing over 300,000 pilgrims every year from mostly working-class areas in the *Ruhrgebiet*. Referring to a pilgrimage of 10,000 men, one worshipper wrote, "It is our responsibility to undertake this procession with a serious and pious disposition and God will certainly help us get over these difficult days and soon lead us to a better future once again."[11] These examples indicate not only the enthusiasm of Catholics for the pilgrimage site but a common theme emphasized in Catholic mysticism during the 1920s. Catholics viewed the Depression as punishment for sin and they sought forgiveness and renewal through prayer to the Virgin Mary.

The fight against a perceived "godlessness" during the rise of Weimar democracy and liberalism constituted perhaps the greatest motive for pilgrimage as articulated by the church hierarchy. Commenting on a Catholic pilgrimage of 1,300 people from Dorsten, a Catholic newspaper wrote: "Everywhere we look today … old moral values are overthrown and new ones are put in their place … This time, sent to us from Providence, demands great people from our side, who love their faith and their church, people who are prepared to live by the example of the Gospels, people who are confident enough to think and act Catholic, people who are entirely convinced of the Catholic truth. That this is possible today, even within narrow confines, was shown in the pilgrimage to Neviges."[12] The imagined triumph of liberalism and rationalism by Catholics caused appeals to mystical piety as a way to wage the battle against secularism. While popular, these sentiments placed the Centre Party in an awkward position as it frequently cooperated with these very liberal democrats to achieve political influence during the Weimar Republic.

These pilgrimage sites indicate the ways in which faith in the miraculous confounds typical depictions of religious habits. At a time when mass attendance and confessional membership lagged among the working class, a *Ruhrgebiet* shrine prospered more than ever before with visits from workers and their families.[13] Catholic clergy encountered numerous difficulties in industrial regions, but these problems did not dissuade legions of *Ruhrgebiet* Catholics from travelling to a worn picture of the Virgin Mary to pray.

This upswing in officially sanctioned Marian worship also contradicts notions of a feminized church. Women undoubtedly formed a cornerstone of the pilgrimage movements. At times the Franciscans running the shrine in Neviges noted that many pilgrimages only included elderly men, despite the participation of many young women.[14] However, efforts by these same Franciscans also masculinized the piety at places like Neviges and Kevelaer. In the late 1920s and 1930s, Neviges boasted several pilgrimages with strong participation from working-class men and boys. A newspaper from Cologne reported on a pilgrimage to Neviges from parishes in Cologne, Bochum, and Essen: "What struck the Cologne participants was the large throngs of men; men of all ages. At the main mass, at the steps of the main altar, and at the prayers, one saw almost only men." In 1932, a pilgrimage attracted 1,200 men from a working-class parish in Bochum and its papers boasted: "Men of Holy Family! Upstanding, handsome, manly! You have rescued the honour of Bochum once again."[15]

The attraction of Neviges resulted in part from the introduction in 1932 of "*Sturmandachten,*" a mass where believers "stormed" the heart of the Virgin Mary and took part in emotional prayer and fervent devotion.[16] These rituals included assertive hymns of Catholic identity as well as organized chants and structured communal prayer. Pilgrims chanted rhyming prayers rhythmically, imploring the Virgin Mary for assistance in the midst of Depression-era suffering. The aggressive nature of this worship bore some similarities to the militaristic language of the Catholic Youth Movement and the Catholic Workers' Movement. Martial codes of masculinity engulfed much of Europe by the late 1920s and German Catholic groups used military symbols and rhetoric to attract men with some success.[17]

These examples of institutionally organized Marian veneration successfully combatted secular trends but reawakened an old conflict between church leaders and local congregants that had been particularly acute after the Reformation. The Catholic Counter-Reformation in Germany attempted to both solve some of the problems raised by the Protestant critique and revive enthusiasm for Catholicism. Throughout the sixteenth and seventeenth centuries Jesuits and bishops circulated propaganda that encouraged veneration of the Virgin Mary and emotional piety but tried to simultaneously restrain such practices within the umbrella of doctrinal Catholicism. Reformation leaders excoriated the superstition of the church. In response the remaining Catholic territories disciplined residents who adhered to local pagan traditions instead of legitimate devotion. These efforts achieved mixed success as people in regions that lacked centralized state authority resisted against such conformity.[18] Although this conflict lasted well into the nineteenth century, the First World War plunged German Catholicism into a particularly difficult phase where bishops felt it was necessary to reign in religious practices that tested the borderline of what the church could accept. Soldiers used amulets for protection, constructed makeshift Marian chapels at the front, and claimed to see Mary while in battle. Such beliefs originated with the Vatican's own promotion of the communion of saints, yet some chaplains discouraged the practices that leaned more upon illicit local traditions than church teaching.[19] When such spiritualities spread to the home front and extended to civilian life after the war, many bishops felt determined to restore order. Episcopal authorities and most Catholics of the northwest wanted vigorous devotion to the saints, but pursued safeguards against spiritual transgressions embarrassing to the church or creating inconsistencies that would threaten the stable system of beliefs needed for the faith to retain legitimacy. Much like the Jesuits of the Counter-Reformation, the bishops of Cologne and Trier faced a challenging balancing act after the First World War. They had to maintain enthusiasm for sanctioned pilgrimage sites of past Catholic miracles to fend off secular impulses, while also discouraging new seers who threatened to confuse and possibly anger congregants by promoting a wave of new miracles they felt would supernaturally resolve the challenges of a profane continent and heal the spiritual wounds of a population traumatized by war.

Blood Miracles in Germany

As the parishes and dioceses promoted mysticism during and the after the war, the number of unsanctioned examples of religious ecstasy increased throughout Germany. Multiple seers with pre–First World War roots enjoyed an increasing number of advocates. This interest in the supernatural spawned new instances of stigmata and religious visions that transcended regional boundaries and drew the types of disciplinary measures from the institutional church typical since the Council of Trent in the early modern era. The power struggle between bishops and Catholics consumed with the corporeal visions emerged at a uniquely vulnerable moment for the faith during the Weimar years. Conflicts between renegade Catholics propagating sensational beliefs and their bishops were nothing new for church history. However, a revolt from a traditionalist wing of the faithful was most unwelcome for ecclesiastical authorities already overwhelmed by the post-war situation and the prospect of working with anticlerical forces in a new republic.

The so-called Aachen blood miracle (*Aachener Blutwunder*) became the first popular incident of the period, illustrating the linkages between German, French, and Belgian movements in favour of the miraculous. In 1920, a handful of men and women witnessed streaming blood on a picture of Jesus in an Aachen apartment on the occasion of a visit by the excommunicated Abbé Argence Vachère of Mirebeau, France. Vachère claimed for ten years to have seen four pictures of Jesus and nineteen communion hosts bleed on several occasions and he viewed the Aachen events as his latest and most important revelation. Having long possessed deep connections with German Catholics, Vachère travelled to Aachen to say mass and meet the witnesses in the apartment of a widow who supported him. Vachère's presence in this apartment on 6 June 1920 allegedly caused a statue and a copy of the so-called Mirebeau picture to bleed from the forehead and heart for days. The press claimed one hundred thousand people visited the picture in less than one week even though the method of tracking such numbers is unclear. Dr Henri Birven, a secular but enthralled parapsychologist wrote: "An immense commotion developed in the city. Tumultuous masses of people stood before the house where the picture bled. For days long after the departure of the Abbé, the discussion among the residents of Aachen lingered on the 'blood miracle.'" Pilgrims reported three people healed by the Aachen picture in August of 1920, including one woman who had cancer.[20] Numerous Catholics confirmed the event, including initially sceptical priests, and some of them took the red substance from the painting to labs for tests. While results suggested the blood came from a human and in the eyes of many proved the authenticity of the miracle, the church quashed its popularity. Cardinal Karl Joseph Schulte, archbishop of Cologne, condemned the event without investigation due to the involvement of the excommunicated Vachère and tried to silence those who publicized it.[21] He and his clergy prevented the distribution of a book on the blood miracle by Bruno Grabinski, a future Therese Neumann supporter, and threatened clergy and laity who supported its legitimacy with excommunication. The Aachen Catholics most associated with the miracle were to be denied communion.[22] These measures aligned with the church's long-standing policy when emotive piety became transgressive. Hoping to safeguard a stable and coherent system of beliefs, Schulte wanted to protect believers from potential fraud. He would eventually consider the opening of a new seminary as one of his greatest accomplishments as archbishop, indicating how he prioritized an orderly pastoral system. For these reasons, Schulte had little patience for an extremist like Vachère.

Several advocates rejected the church's teaching and maintained their faith in the blood miracle, indicating how they felt such an event could defend a pure form of their faith from secular impulses. Sermons warning against the Aachen events resulted in multiple letters to the archbishop of Cologne. Victor Krebs criticized the cardinal for "robbing" the faith of its honour by threatening people with excommunication without investigating the nature of a true sign from God. He argued that Europe witnessed numerous "signs" from heaven in the aftermath of war, including stigmata in Garango, Italy; a bleeding statue in Templemore, Ireland; and the bleeding paintings of Jesus in Mirebeau. He lamented that both clergy and other members of the congregation insulted those discussing the Aachen events. He complained: "Yes, people mock the individuals, subject the 'alleged' miracle to ridicule and scorn in songs and satires, and more or less doubt the supernatural intervention of God in nature even in circles of modern priests and Catholic publications." This quote imagined a utopian dichotomy between an overly modern clergy and the genuine faithful who believed in events like the blood miracles. Krebs blamed the spread of sin for the country's disastrous state and held the clergy responsible for discouraging a sign from God that might turn the tide in favour of earnest Catholics.[23]

Krebs's letter owes much influence to Vachère's broader Mirebeau movement. Vachère proclaimed the primary purpose of his bleeding pictures and the voices he heard from heaven to be the reconversion of sinners and the fight against secularism in France. These notions of apocalypse and salvation became more pronounced during the war, as the voice of God ordered him to build a large basilica and construct the Stations of the Cross in Gâtine to become a site of pilgrimage and repentance. Despite his excommunication in 1914, he campaigned to have General Joseph Joffre parade his bleeding picture in the trenches as a way to end a war brought by God to punish a sinful French nation. To demonstrate the connection between French sin and God's wrath, he and his supporters suggested that Vachère's pictures and host bled more thickly just before major battles that produced high casualties. After the war, Vachère blamed the violent outcome on the bishops' inattentiveness to his cause and his persecution by the state. His connection with German Catholics and the financing of his Stations of the Cross by a wealthy German woman led the state to seize his property. A subculture within German Catholicism echoed Vachère's accusations against church and state for their failure to appease an angry God.[24]

Both Vachère and the Aachen blood miracle possessed roots in church-sponsored piety from the nineteenth century. In hopes of defending Catholic influence in a rapidly secularizing France and a freshly unified Germany, clergy formed numerous lay associations around worship of the Sacred Heart. A mystical faith in the physical heart of Jesus as a source of encompassing love for all Catholics, this Christ-centred worship was associated with numerous miracles. The clergy hoped that a controlled revival of such traditions would shelter the faithful from the secularization that seemed to accompany industrialization, nationalization, and urbanization.[25] By the outbreak of the First World War, however, a series of visionaries emerged who pushed this worship of the Sacred Heart beyond the control of the hierarchy. Claire Ferchaud, who lived in Vachère's region, became more famous than the Abbé by promoting the addition of the Sacred Heart to the French flag in order to bring a peaceful end to the war.[26] German bishops worried that events like those in Aachen and Mirebeau would jeopardize Catholic attempts to integrate nationally. Cardinal Schulte, other bishops, and Catholic politicians used the war as a rallying cry to overcome Catholic marginalization and hoped that they could better assimilate their congregants into German society by participating vigorously in the national cause.[27]

The Aachen miracles illustrate the struggle of a church committed to a tenuous balance of grass-roots religiosity, clerical oversight, and national integration against Catholics seeking comfort in visionaries with an unmediated connection to a higher power. Schulte and other male elites correctly feared this personalization of piety could derail their centralized control of modern Catholic organizations and world views. Vachère unapologetically attacked and condemned church authorities both before and after his excommunication, to the delight of many German adherents. He wrote to the Vatican in 1920 renouncing his excommunication, rejecting the "slave obedience" demanded of priests. Furthermore, he scathingly addressed Schulte over the refusal to examine the Aachen picture. He referred to him as a "portrait of a modern prelate" overly consumed with pride and ignorant of an inner life of prayer.[28] German aristocrat Friedrich Ritter von Lama joyfully praised many of Vachère's outbursts against the clergy through the years. For example, he highlighted Vachère's message from God that he "cried for his priests, who are not what they should be; they do not do enough to spread my name."[29] Advocates of the blood miracles assailed clergy for "materialist" outlooks. Deeply conservative insurgents hoping for a restoration of past values, von Lama and others viewed the church as compromised from within. They sought official acceptance and reform based on their ideas, but posed a major threat with their extremist rhetoric and Vachère's more individualized spirituality. The power of the hierarchy overcame their grass-roots movement as the enthusiasm for the Aachen events flickered after a few years of official condemnation.

The "blood miracles" of Mirebeau and Aachen also exemplify the masculine presence among miracle seekers of the twentieth century. Based on a more Christ-centred piety, the cult of the Sacred Heart attracted many female followers yet also provided a model for male piety. The antagonism towards Vachère differed from the allegations that typically challenged female religious figures. While critics rarely discussed his mental health, they frequently charged Abbé Vachère (perhaps correctly) with fraud. For example, Everard Feilding, an associate of the British Society for Psychical Research, implied that Vachère poured water from a nearby vase onto his bleeding painting when observers looked away.[30] German newspapers argued that a sophisticated use of chemicals caused the bloody reaction while parapsychologists claimed a telepathic connection with a stigmatic was to blame.[31] Finally, the German clergy contended that Vachère's activities in Aachen both before and after the events of 1920 resulted exclusively from profits to be made through selling copies of his bloody Mirebeau pictures.[32] Either way, Vachère escaped the label of hysteria that usually dogged female visionaries and instead was endowed with manly shortcomings by his critics. His forceful defence against his adversaries, especially within the hierarchy, also distinguished him from female seers of his time. His obstinacy and flouting of official decrees illustrated a lack of concern for obedience to authority. As a man with strong connections to the Vatican in the past, he felt little compunction to demonstrate his submission to an earthly authority. Finally, the proclaimed suffering of the Abbé Vachère that was typical of modern visionaries shaped his life in the public sphere rather than his body. His excommunication destroyed professional ambitions and the seizure of his property inhibited a material and economic manifestation of his faith. However, he suffered no physical hardship like female stigmatics who bled and endured enormous health problems or other female visionaries who experienced tortuous pain when hearing God's voice.

Tine van Osselaer's work on gendered expectations for male visionaries in Belgium also sheds light on why Vachère and his miracles in Aachen lacked the lasting influence of other mystics from the era. Despite the "feminization of religion" thesis, men became accepted visionaries. In order to achieve this status, they blended raw expressions of emotion during states of ecstasy with assurances of cool rationality when not in a religious trance.[33] They required the former in order to match the qualities expected of a modern Catholic seer and the latter to assure followers of their masculine strength and sanity. Vachère's lack of emotional rapture during his trances might have limited the enthusiasm of miracle advocates and his unchecked outbursts against church authority contradicted the rationalism sought from hegemonic masculine norms within Catholic Europe.

The Aachen blood miracles maintained connections to other advocates of mysticism both during and after the First World War. The case of stigmatic Rosalia Putt in Belgium began before 1914 and attracted intense interest from the Abbé Vachère himself. Putt also held the attention of pilgrims from Western Germany during the war, including Vachère's wealthiest patron from Essen. Putt, a working-class Belgian woman from Lummen, claimed to have stigmata. She cultivated a band of followers who visited her for advice. For example, Vachère frequently sought counsel about the future, relying on her responses to assert the validity of his own miracles. German pilgrims visited her in droves on Fridays when she displayed the wounds on her hands and feet and dramatically performed scenes from the crucifixion of Christ. She would typically fall out of her bed and emulate Jesus when he fell three times with the cross and then lie "motionless" for hours. Unlike Vachère, she exhibited the physical suffering typical of modern female stigmatics, such as Louise Lateau of late nineteenth-century Belgium.

Putt had already attracted German followers before the war. A Belgian bishop wrote to the parishes of Cologne in 1910 complaining that "numerous inexperienced and gullible" Germans believed the visions of the Belgian and flocked to her bedside. The church refused to recognize her stigmata, calling it an instance of mental illness. The war, however, increased the intensity of belief in this miraculous visionary and the tension between the religious leaders and their followers. In 1915 and 1916 an Essen church bulletin claimed the wave of German visitors to Putt had become a "true procession" and attacked the pilgrims for trusting their own "insight" over formal teaching of the clergy. Catholic publications generated several letters of protest, including one from a man who also wrote to Cardinal Hartmann of Cologne. He attacked the church for ignoring acts of devotion valued by Catholic congregations. He blamed parish priests for the rise in mixed marriages and the loss of the working class because they were out of touch with the piety of the masses, echoing von Lama's belief that church materialism compromised it from within during the battle against secularism. He encouraged bishops to recognize the "signs" of God through the stigmata of Rosalie Putt as well as cures at the pilgrimage shrine in Neviges. Many of Putt's followers requested her clairvoyance regarding war issues. For example, women visited her hoping to communicate with loved ones lost in the war. The Essen church bulletin asserted that the "uncertainty" of war caused some congregants to reject official doctrine and accept all sorts of "prophecies," including those of Rosalie Putt.

Despite her popularity, the church remained adamant in its opposition to Putt. A Catholic schoolteacher wrote, "It is a scandal for our holy religion and it is a true disgrace that some people, that one would like to think of as more intelligent, believe in it." This teacher, who given his profession was likely ensconced in mainstream Catholic associational and political life, accused Putt and her mother of carrying on with the episode in order to make money from Germans in a time of war. The church remained at odds with those devotees of ecstatic faith who perceived themselves as more genuinely Catholic than the church itself. It condemned her as hysterical.[34] Putt's case deepened the conflict between those who placed their faith in such dramatic visions and those for whom the miracles could only occur within the context of official faith. While bishops, clergy, and mainstream male lay leaders discouraged contact with Putt, many sought salvation in her visions in the midst of intense war trauma. Her death in 1919 and the failure of some of her predictions created a personal crisis for Vachère that was resolved only by the Aachen miracles of 1920. The intense German interest in both Putt and Vachère came from similar circles of Catholics in the Rhineland and other parts of Western Germany, illustrating a relatively broad basis for faith in the miraculous.

Besides the Abbé Vachère and Rosalia Putt, the Aachen blood miracles also partnered with a popular German movement surrounding the well-known Barbara Weigand of Schippach. Weigand published her visions and communications with Jesus and other heavenly figures, which commenced in 1894, and founded an organization of followers known as the *Eucharistische Liebesbund des göttlichen Herzens Jesu* (Eucharistic League for Veneration of the Sacred Heart of Jesus) in 1900. The organization enjoyed significant strongholds in the Rhineland, Baden, Hessen, and Franconia and highlighted the fluid frontier between sanctioned and unsanctioned piety. Although initially endorsed by clergy members in Mainz, who were eager to promote the official cult of the

Sacred Heart, the bishop of Würzburg banned the organization and the devotion to Weigand in 1916. Weigand's brand of religiosity possessed roots in official theology and emphasized similar themes to the associations committed to the Sacred Heart. However, she crossed boundaries through the fervency of her own devotion and the high expectations of piety she demanded from other Catholics, including even priests.[35] The more Weigand's following questioned the authority of the clergy and the more her spiritual following grew, the greater her threat to the institutional church and the coherency of the faith that bishops and priests had to safeguard. Like Vachère and Putt, Weigand also unintentionally fractured the unity of German Catholics and weakened the institutional church by advancing a deeply personal brand of spirituality that achieved a degree of separation from the authority of the clergy and confessional associations. Like the other seers discussed in this chapter, Weigand wanted a place of prominence within the church for her movement but increasingly undermined the leadership of the very institution she thought her visions could save when approval was not forthcoming.

Local clergy noted the involvement of Weigand's *Liebesbund* in the Aachen miracles with concern. A woman referred to as Frau Hilker of Essen financially supported Vachère, visited Putt, advocated the Aachen miracles, and would eventually become a supporter of Therese Neumann. She also belonged to the *Liebesbund*. After the miracles of Aachen, she declared, "Schippach and Mirebeau are one." Described by one Catholic doctor as being on the "border of religious eccentricity," her involvement in Vachère's German visit caused Cardinal Schulte not only to condemn the bloody picture, but also to ban the *Liebesbund* branch based in Aachen. He gave members eight days to sever their association with the group or be denied communion. Weigand's followers in the Rhineland and *Ruhrgebiet* already sold copies of the Mirebeau picture in 1912 and visited Vachère in France after his excommunication. Referring to their involvement in 1920, one priest complained, "The *Liebesbund* has only spread mischief until now. Their danger is underestimated."[36] The connection between Aachen and Schippach reveals the broad webs of miracle enthusiasts that spread throughout the country after the First World War and the confusion they sowed among the laity for whom the pastoral leaders were responsible. By sending signals that contradicted the faith as defined by bishops and priests, these groups posed a threat to the power of clergy who were already overwhelmed by the instability unleashed by the First World War.

Barbara Weigand herself, who personally never showed up in Aachen, represents an interesting case in the post-war era. Like Vachère and Putt, her movement grew in the years before the First World War, peaked in the middle of the war, and revived for a few years after the conclusion of hostilities. Although not a stigmatist, Weigand received visions of heavenly personalities while experiencing psychological and physical discomfort. She shared these prophesies from heaven in seven books that she dictated to her two most devoted female followers. Reminiscent of heretics from the Middle Ages such as the Waldensians, Weigand also embraced pious forms of worship that caused physical suffering to seek penance for the sins of Europe's Christians. For example, she undertook a long pilgrimage of penance in 1900 in her bare feet while carrying a heavy cross on her shoulder. Like Putt's supporters, she blamed a materialistic church for secularism and sought a reform based on her traditionalist practices.

Although she possessed some male advocates, Weigand differentiated herself from many other mystics of the era through the noticeable presence of women in the leadership of her organization. She complained through her visions about the insignificant roles for women in church leadership and called in particular for the elevation of young girls to a higher status within Catholicism. While convergent with many of the trends in miracles of the era, Weigand more blatantly flouted church authority than most female religious figures and pursued a more direct emancipatory course for women. While Putt and the female followers of Vachère embraced a patriarchal vision of society even more conservative than mainstream Rhineland Catholics, Weigand radically tried to overturn male dominance of the faith.[37]

Like other seers of this era, Weigand focused on the theme of apocalypse and salvation throughout the war. She argued that the sinfulness of the populace as well as the Protestant or secular faith of Germany's political and military leadership caused the outbreak of war. Through her recounted visions, she also argued that widespread acceptance of her *Liebesbund* provided the only pathway to success in the war. She proclaimed that the construction of a large basilica in Schippach that would rival Lourdes as a pilgrimage destination was the only act that could bring God's mercy to Germany. After the German defeat and her own group's condemnation by the bishops, she cited failure by the German military, the Vatican, and the German hierarchy to heed her advice as the primary reason for the country's military defeat. Although intensely religious, Weigand's movement became increasingly political after the war through its condemnation of Protestantism, the Hohenzollern monarchy, the liberal parties, the social democrats, and the Bolshevik Revolution of 1917. Her final book of prophesies contained regular criticism of the clergy and proclaimed a world view shaped by severe religiosity, extreme material and physical sacrifice for the well-being of others, and a rejection of almost all political ideologies of her time. She mixed a reputation of humble service for others with brazen attacks on the powerful inspired by her heavenly visions. For example, she fasted for long periods in order to give the bread she did not eat to children who suffered from the economic and agrarian upheavals of the 1920s. Her simple living quarters contrasted with the 1.8 million Deutschemarks she raised to build her basilica.[38] While Weigand's imagined utopia of Christian penitence and pity proved unrealistic for much of mainstream Germany, it inspired a following of thousands in several regions of the country and contributed to Catholic interest in the miraculous after 1918. In sum, Weigand inspired impressive devotion by employing similar themes to those of Vachère and Putt, but lacking church sanction, she failed to penetrate the circles of power in Catholic Germany. These three seers inspired remarkable zeal but struggled to endure as public figures beyond the early 1920s. They embodied the longing for such devotional forms after the war, but the paradoxes of gendered expectations for male and female mystics, the ways they undermined the coherency of doctrine, and their subaltern threat to institutional power hampered their enduring influence. They challenged the power of the male-dominated Catholic patriarchy in Western Germany, but could only lay the groundwork for future movements instead of diminishing mainstream Catholicism themselves.

The Stigmata of Anna Maria Goebel

The Aachen blood miracles of 1920 constituted a symbolic reactivation of several networks of seers and holy women with roots outside of Germany and before the First World War. The rise of several new mystics claiming to experience stigmata, however, recalled the fame of Anna Katharina Emmerick from the early nineteenth century.[39] Although with a sometimes similar set of national advocates, the rise of stigmatized women attracted even greater numbers of Catholic congregants and ultimately eclipsed the importance of mysticism from the previous era with the explosive popularity of Therese Neumann. Prior to Neumann's celebrity, the stigmata of Anna Maria Goebel represented the most contested example of a Catholic miracle during the decade and provided numerous antecedents and parallels to the better-known Konnersreuth case. The narrative of Goebel's life and medical examination by the church intoned the themes of apocalypse and salvation attractive to many Catholics after the war. Her case also illustrated the friction between the ecstatic rebels and institutional centres of Catholic power, including the bishops and the Catholic Centre Party, who sensed subversive potential in their following. Finally, Goebel's message of physical suffering in the name of penance and hope for a better future both imbued her own battered body with agency and resonated with an increasing circle of like-minded Catholics.

Maria Anna Goebel of Bickendorf, born in an Eifel village of one thousand residents in 1886, lived a seemingly average existence until she turned fifteen. The death of her father in 1901 sparked a steep descent of her mental and physical health. Suffering for years from ulcers, rheumatic disorders, kidney failure, gallstones, a heart defect, and a rapid decline in her appetite, Goebel transformed from a hard-working asset to her rural family into a bedridden dependent in the household of her sister and brother-in-law. In the early 1920s she began bleeding profusely in a manner that flustered her doctors. By 1922, religious visions accompanied the blood and her symptoms miraculously disappeared on some holy days or when Goebel desired communion. One such vision implied a reason behind her suffering:

> On this day she saw the savior in a vision, with a cross on his shoulders, a frightfully bloody face, and a crown of thorns upon his head. He displayed for her a cross with golden, Latin letters that read: 'Your patience is purified through suffering and tested in love and faithfulness.' Underneath it said in blood: 'Control yourself! You will suffer and be despised through my will.' Her body was covered in blood the entire day so that her underclothes were soaked. Blood also flowed in streams from her eyes. In the afternoon, she only bled from her forehead in a crown of thorns, but by nightfall her entire body bled once more.[40]

Goebel interpreted her sickness and blood as a necessary ordeal to fulfil God's will. If she patiently endured as God's instrument, Goebel felt she would bravely demonstrate her Catholic faith to others and spark spiritual revival. This element of Goebel's experience converges with the role of suffering for many Catholics in Europe and the United States. Writing about American Catholics with disabilities during the 1920s, Robert Orsi says, "Pain had the character of a sacrament, offering the sufferer a uniquely immediate and intimate experience of Jesus' presence."[41]

Goebel's symptoms ultimately settled into a pattern similar to those of other stigmatics from the nineteenth and twentieth centuries. She bled from her hands, feet, chest, and forehead on Fridays and some religious holidays for several years and experienced regular religious visions. Frequently ill from several physical problems, she experienced sudden and short-lived cures on certain holy days and to attend communion. Goebel's appetite gradually diminished until she claimed to permanently fast and abstain from almost all food. Many of her visions and messages focused on blood and suffering. Perhaps a metaphor for a country overwhelmed with death from the First World War, the influenza epidemic, and political and economic uncertainty, the stern tone and violent imagery of the Goebel stigmata stoked the apocalyptic mood of the 1920s. Her call for patience with suffering to demonstrate faith in God's will offered a harsh but meaningful path to salvation in such perilous times. Her "child-like joy" and feminine endurance provided hope in the midst of despair for some Catholics. In fact, the transformation of the wayward became her primary mission. For example, on 23 April 1923, a voice told her, "You should especially suffer from now on for the conversion of sinners."[42]

These themes of stern punishment, hope through feminine faith and sacrifice, and reconversion of the immoral through God's miraculous presence on earth resonated widely. Goebel possessed great loyalty within the town. Her brother-in-law; a farmer; and local priest, Father A. Faber, provided steadfast masculine support. Female seers without powerful male advisors, such as Barbara Weigand, remained rare, and these men oversaw much of Goebel's relationship with the public. While Weigand pursued feminine emancipation, Goebel openly embraced the patriarchy and traditional gender dynamics of her family and parish if not her diocese. As the bishopric and press investigated Goebel's case, the pious village of Bickendorf generally spoke of Faber in "high regard" and testified to the honest and moral life of Goebel herself.[43] This internal legitimacy provided the basis for the change of the sleepy village into a pilgrimage site without the infrastructure to handle such crowds. A sceptical doctor recalled:

> On Good Friday of this year [1927] I had the possibility to see the stigmatized woman. This was primarily the suggestion of the mayor of

> Bickendorf, who notified me of the large crowds and asked me to visit the local 'saint.' The sight that I witnessed on Good Friday was not particularly edifying. Allowed inside to see the stigmatic in groups of ten people, hundreds jammed the area in front of her house. It occurred to me on the way to Bickendorf that the tremendous traffic and the hundreds of bikers and foot pilgrims on their way to the stigmatic's room was enormous for such a locality.[44]

With her brother-in-law at the foot of her bed, Goebel became a figure of widespread devotion through the middle years of the 1920s, stimulating enthusiasm for direct physical signs of God's will on earth. A symbol of Germany's devastation and simultaneously offering potential salvation for the future, Goebel's stigmata captivated a subset of rural pilgrims and Catholic journalists alike.

Goebel's critics were just as passionate as her pilgrims. Several Berlin newspapers suggested a fraud in Bickendorf, while others who believed in the authenticity of the miracles worried that they lacked religious meaning. Eduard Aigner, a well-known monist and doctor of neurology, obsessively tracked stigmata for its scientific purposes, believing that deep study of Goebel's body would benefit the scientific community. Parapsychologists covered the Bickendorf events with great interest, suggesting that Goebel's blood and visions had more to do with telepathy and the scientific importance of paranormal activity than they did with religion.[45]

However, several elites of the Catholic Church emerged as her fiercest critics. Concerned about Goebel's mental state and her family's willingness to display her wounds, the bishop of Trier, Franz Rudolf Bornewasser; several influential theologians of the Rhineland; and the Catholic Centre Party all sought to distance themselves from Goebel's following. One Catholic doctor suggested hysteria was possible and complained that Goebel's family turned a sick woman into a "show piece (*Schaustück*)." Another priest, displaying ignorance of the female reproductive system, suggested that Goebel smeared her own body with menstrual blood to fake the stigmata every Friday. Norbert Brühl, a Redemptorist based in Trier who later criticized Therese Neumann, and a group of Catholic doctors became powerful and combative opponents of Goebel's family from within the diocese of Trier.[46]

George Priller, Friedrich Ritter von Lama, and Robert Ernst, Goebel's three most active journalistic advocates, complained bitterly about the Centre Party's disruption of the Bickendorf events. Priller suggested that Centre Party figure Johannes Fuchs personally led a campaign against the stigmata. Priller groused about how the party for which Goebel's family had always voted assailed her in their own newspapers. Fuchs, a lawyer from Bickendorf who became *Oberpräsident der preußischen Rheinprovinz* (Highest executive of the Prussian Rhine province) from 1922 to 1933, apparently wished to avenge an old feud with Goebel's brother-in-law and shrank with embarrassment from the mysticism suddenly popular in his home town. Fuchs epitomized the simultaneous power and anxiety of the Centre Party's male elite. Influential enough to shape the bishop's reaction to Goebel, Fuchs's ruinous financial situation paralleled similar problems facing Centre Party infrastructure during the late 1920s. Such a powerful enemy doomed the movement surrounding the stigmata, as Goebel's advocates blamed Fuchs for the decision to remove Father Faber from his post in Bickendorf and for the lawsuit filed against Georg Priller for publicly criticizing the church's medical investigation. When Fuchs's investments vanished during the Great Depression and the Nazis pushed him out of office, Goebel's supporters viewed it as a punishment from God for a man who became too materialistic to genuinely represent the Catholic faith.[47] Threatened by the bid for spiritual power by Goebel's family, the powerful Catholic politicians, bishops, and theologians of Western Germany repudiated the movement in Bickendorf by removing the priest who gave it institutional legitimacy and by declaring Goebel a false prophet after their own medical investigation. Goebel's devotees in turn blamed an overly modernized church establishment for the downfall of a potential saint. They continued the damaging narrative that the church was infiltrated by the very modernism that caused secularization, making it an ineffective vessel for change.

The tension between Goebel and Fuchs symbolized the struggles of the once powerful Centre Party. Goebel's stigmata became one issue among many as Catholics debated how to best reconcile their religious identity with modernity and a post–First World War reality. The anxiety over Goebel's threat to traditional Catholic power brokers replicated the concerns over voters leaving the Catholic parties for movements to the left and the right. Finally, the bitter dispute over Goebel's sanctity fuelled the loss of faith in the Centre Party so that there was very little empathy when men like Fuchs lost power in 1933. Controversies over miracles contributed to the internal disputes plaguing the Centre Party as it declined and mustered little resistance to National Socialism at the end of the Weimar Republic. The inability of political Catholicism and confessional associations to address the severe angst after the war drove a cross section of Catholics towards unmediated mysticism.

The medical exam of Anna Maria Goebel would be a cautionary tale for Therese Neumann of Konnersreuth. The exam results short-circuited Goebel's popularity, while her closest supporters viewed it as a betrayal by both the church and the medical system. Despite reservations Goebel allegedly agreed to the exam out a deep sense of obedience to the church. Undermining the wishes of her bishop would contradict her outspoken notions of feminine obedience to God's will and undercut one of her appeals among Catholic pilgrims. Examined in a sealed hospital room from 21 April to 20 May 1927, Goebel claimed that doctors forced her to eat against her will and coercively bandaged her wounds. She and her supporters viewed such actions as a desecration of her sacred body and unfair in an investigation they felt should prove the authenticity of her bleeding and fasting. The doctors, however, accused Goebel of attempting to hide her urine and observed an unhealthy mental state. They concluded that she might be opening her wounds with a toothbrush and informed her that the miracles lacked supernatural explanations. They also portrayed her behaviour as hostile and unruly as they delivered their results. Opponents of the stigmata within the diocese of Trier and the Rhineland viewed Goebel as a hysterical and unhealthy woman victimized by a fraudulent brother-in-law.[48]

The case of Anna Maria Goebel demonstrates the pitfalls of claiming spiritual power through stigmata. Goebel, her family, and her advocates used her direct access to God in order to accumulate spiritual capital and lay claim to at least some of the church's "goods of salvation." They did so outside the mainstream power structures of Western Germany where men wielded tremendous authority. Goebel attempted a fragile balance in this bid for religious agency. In order to challenge the establishment without being cast away as a marginal cult figure, Goebel required powerful male Catholic patrons and a chance at eventual church recognition. Furthermore, she needed convergence with the gendered tropes of European stigmatics since the nineteenth century of patient suffering and steadfast obedience to God's will to preserve legitimacy with the mystical wing of the German Catholic public. In Western Germany, this visionary of Bickendorf drew the ire of the influential associations and Centre Party officials, who projected a more rationalized type of Catholicism focused on integrating Catholics into the German nation state and stabilizing political Catholicism after the Great War. This context made her enemies far more influential than her allies. Her movement also collapsed under the paradox of the medical exam in 1926. If Goebel refused the exam, she would appear as disobedient to church authority, and therefore her family felt they had little choice in the matter. However, the exam placed her in the hands of Catholic doctors and nurses who viewed the role of miracles differently and were unlikely to render a positive verdict. Stripped of her aura by an exam that exposed her miracles as worldly, the church could more convincingly paint her as mentally ill and her family as profiteering. Much like those involved in the Aachen "blood miracle," Goebel receded into anonymity to all but her most ardent followers until her death in 1939 despite her disruptive moment of spiritual power during the Weimar Republic.

The Trier Cures of 1933

While the pilgrimages to Kevelaer and Neviges represented institutionally supported piety and the phenomena of Aachen, Mirebeau, Schippach, and Bickendorf lacked any official sanction, the miracles at the Holy Tunic of Trier straddled the line between these two poles. The same diocese of Trier that repressed the Goebel miracles enthusiastically planned and promoted their most significant relic and its display for the first time since 1891. Approximately thirty thousand sick pilgrims praying for cures also gained special access through an institutionalized process that required recommendations from priests and doctors, and there was an even larger "sacred economy" distributing items that touched the relic to Catholics unable to complete the trip to Trier.[49] The Trier Pilgrimage Committee examined those who claimed cures, with further reports from doctors and priests needed to determine a miracle's legitimacy. The pilgrimage to Trier in 1933 possessed the same mixture of modern medicine and bureaucracy as the Lourdes shrine and it enjoyed the full support of the bishop of Trier. Furthermore, this worship of the seamless robe of Jesus also built upon the Christ-centred piety of the Cult of the Sacred Heart, popular since the late nineteenth century. The spectacle of Trier in 1933 emphasized Catholic faith in the possibility of miracles as long as it remained under the strict supervision of the bishops and clergy and within parameters defined by church history. It promoted a similar personal connection between Catholics and heavenly figures as Goebel and Weigand but possessed greater legitimacy due to official mediation that ensured consistency with the faith and the absence of fraudulence.

1.1. Therese Neumann ca. 1927. Bundesarchiv-Bildarchiv Bild 102–00244.

The tension between church-approved piety and grass-roots enthusiasm emerged most clearly when Therese Neumann of Konnersreuth prayed at the Holy Tunic on 18 August 1933. Encouraged to make the trip by a powerful admirer, Bishop Ludwig Sebastian of Speyer, Neumann and her entourage met resistance from Bishop Franz Rudolf Bornewasser of Trier. Wary of an "untoward incident" where Neumann might reach a state of ecstasy before throngs of pilgrims visiting the relic, Trier's bishop permitted her presence only after the stigmatic's priest assured him that no such episode would occur. Tensions he faced with National Socialist officials in the direct aftermath of the concordat between the Vatican and Germany probably heightened Bornewasser's caution. The party infringed on his authority during the pilgrimage by usurping security functions and demanding prominent places in some ceremonies.[50] Weakened by Nazism, Bornewasser likely feared the myriad ways in which Neumann's presence could further undermine him.

Despite these anxieties, Neumann's visit caused less controversy than expected. After verifying the authenticity of the relic from an "inner voice," Neumann became intensely emotional during her visit. She "burst into tears" upon seeing the blood stains on the garment and secretly snuck into the cathedral at odd times to "pour forth her soul in thanksgiving and adoration, petition and atonement." She also appeared "rapt above the earth" when she saw "the throngs from Cologne and other cities pass through the streets praying and singing."[51] Neumann's presence linked her own miracles to a broader revival in miraculous faith during the 1920s and 1930s as she joined the 2.1 million pilgrims visiting the sacred object.[52] Bornewasser's concern about her stay also illustrates the discomfort when faith in the miraculous tested the boundaries set by an institution determined to restrain such engagement with the supernatural. By curbing her emotional reactions to ecstasies and visions, Neumann effectively adhered to the line drawn by the bishop and this attracted neither his intervention nor his scorn.

Despite the trappings of church support, the cures of these anonymous pilgrims possessed a rebellious edge that the bishop's residence in Trier found just as distasteful as the notion of a Therese Neumann ecstasy in the middle of its pilgrimage. The bishopric accepted none of the eighty-three pilgrims who petitioned the church for recognition, rejecting most cases as examples of hysteria, fraudulence, short-term cures, or cures with natural causes. Hoping to avoid embarrassment and movements that might develop beyond their control, the bishop's office erred on the side of caution when dispensing official sanction to such events. These eighty-three pilgrims illustrate how everyday Catholics built on official teaching to create direct relationships with heavenly figures. In so doing, they crossed a line that created discomfort among church leaders hoping to restrain beliefs that would confuse the laity about the true teachings of the church. While most of these pilgrims were not as dangerous as Anna Maria Goebel, their stories demonstrate how the church could not shut off the spigot of supernatural belief once they encouraged emotional relationships with the divine.

The stories of individual sick pilgrims illuminate the types of religious sensibilities that motivated Catholic faith in heavenly intercession. Before their cures, a combination of religious faith and physical suffering sent the sick pilgrims on a sacrificial journey to Trier. In a simulation of past Catholic pilgrimages, these patients bore a cross of suffering during long journeys to the shrine. For example, Maria Hepting, a devotee of Therese Neumann of Konnersreuth, was perilously ill, causing both her doctor and priest to discourage the journey to Trier. Her priest refused to write a letter of support and said: "How can one be so foolish as to bring a person who is closer to death than to life and almost impossible to transport to Trier?" Rejecting the warning, Maria responded: "It is not as foolish as you say. If God distributed as much grace everywhere as he did at pilgrimage sites, then we would not have to offer such a sacrifice." Maria left, accompanied by a nun who acted as her nurse, without the letter. During the train ride, her heart failed her and she received two injections and a stimulant in Koblenz while changing trains. Upon arrival, her escort sought permission for Maria's access to the shrine. Frustrated by the bureaucracy of the pilgrimage leaders, she thought she would fail to acquire the necessary documents until a young boy directed her to the proper office. When she rewarded him with twenty pfennig, he bought a memento of the holy coat and gave it to her. After the miracle, the nun believed the boy was a "guardian angel" who guided her patient through her time of turmoil.[53] Maria and her escort believed God intervened both before and during her cure because of the great sacrifice she made in her journey. This narrative portrays a female pilgrim who believed in a direct relationship with the heavens in open defiance of her Catholic doctor and priest. In her eyes, a modernized approach to mysticism by the institutional church created unnecessary hurdles for a suffering patient seeking heavenly assistance. Hepting's faith in the holy tunic trumped the admonishment of her spiritual leader, whom she demonized in her account despite the fact that his concerns were probably only for her well-being.

Several cures did not last and the files document numerous regressions within a period of three years, yet they still sparked much hope among pilgrims and their communities. Despite these setbacks, many pilgrims remained psychologically uplifted. For example, Hepting died in June 1934 after a partial recovery from her life-threatening illness. During the nine months after her cure, however, she lived a vigorous life, travelling to Munich, Starnberg, Freising, and even Konnersreuth. Her priest and doctor asserted that the cure was still a blessing because of the happiness it provided her before death.[54] In another example, Elisabeth Lenenbach died from a recurrence of tuberculosis after her youngest son, who accompanied her to the relic in Trier and witnessed her cure, died in 1935. Her priest maintained, however, that the experience in Trier provided her with the "peacefulness" and "patience in her soul" to endure the illness and die happy.[55] Despite the recurrence of illness, many pilgrims had new life after their experiences in Trier.[56] Furthermore, the physical, emotional, and spiritual stories told by these sick pilgrims also paralleled the widely circulated accounts of nonconforming stigmatics of the 1920s, such as Goebel and Neumann, who also patiently suffered before experiencing partial or entire cures from heaven in moments of intense spiritual fervour.

The narratives of these cured Catholics provide data regarding gendered expectations and the miraculous as well. Although women made up the majority of sick pilgrims in Trier, the files about the relic's cures provide insights about how both male and female Catholics approached religion. Only eleven men claimed to have been healed, but many of them revived their religiosity as a result of the Trier experience. A parish priest wrote that Josef Zumbroich, a merchant in Eschweiler, was not "eager" when it came to church. After the cure, however, he noticed a "complete turnaround." His experiences in Trier attracted him to weekly mass and communion. Another male pilgrim, Heinrich Meyer, a pious accountant who converted from Protestantism to Catholicism, received praise about his religious credentials from his priest after the cure. Johann Kessler, an injured miner from Elversberg, was a former socialist who found religion after his accident. Before the pilgrimage, his priest wrote: "Kessler has been very pious for some time. He fasts strictly every Friday and attends communion often. He travels the relatively arduous path from the Herrnstraße to the church or cloister chapel without having to be encouraged."[57] These stories of the converted men actually mirror a common trope surrounding European mysticism. While spiritual communities expected women to remain patiently faithful to God despite hardship, they anticipated wayward men who would then renew themselves after experiencing miracles.[58]

Men balanced the outward expression of emotion and piety necessary for a miraculous cure with a rational spiritualism to assure their communities of their masculinity. In a representative example, the local priest described Oskar Greiner, a textile worker, as a "sober person with a healthy piety." This comment suggests that Greiner was not overly prone to emotion like a female pilgrim. Although little information exists on Paul Steinhäuser's religious practice before the cure, his priest portrayed him as the congregation's most active participant afterward. He said: "The attitude of Mr. Steinhäuser since his cure has been impeccable. He receives communion daily, participates yearly in Spiritual Exercises, and is active daily as a tireless lay helper for Catholic matters. He is about the entire day in service to the parish, the Catholic associations, and various brotherhoods. No work is too hard for him; no path too long. From now on, he sees his life mission, to work only for God the father and matters of our Church."[59] Steinhäuser's activities conformed to the models for masculinity encouraged by the program for Catholic Action and its encouragement of lay male activism. By expressing piety in the form of the strictly disciplined Spiritual Exercises, he affirmed his credentials as a rational male. Steinhäuser further compensated for his mysticism through active participation in associational life that engaged with the public sphere and masculine realms within Catholic communities.

Men also faced accusations of fabricating cures more often than women. Initially keeping his cure a secret, Kessler eventually had to fend off attacks from both the socialists and Catholics in town. Before his cure, he fought with the miners' union over his pension. His priest wrote, "There are nasty tongues that imply Kessler is a fake, who acted his illness all these years to receive a pension." Catholics doubted him because of his past as a socialist and a "bad man." Paul Steinhäuser also encountered doubters. One of his neighbours allegedly saw Steinhäuser walking around his apartment before the cure.[60] Like the Abbé Vachère, these men faced criticisms that differed from those directed towards their female counterparts. Fraudulence remained the most common charge levelled against pious men, whom were assumed to be less prone to mental illness.

Women faced their own challenges when claiming cures at the shrine in Trier. For over a century, female seers and conduits for the miraculous suffered from the stereotype of the hysterical woman. The reaction to the Trier miracles was no different. Catholic women felt comfortable with public proclamations of their cures and communities spared them mockery. Within mystic Catholic communities, supporters expected emotional piety from women. Seers and stigmatics lacked credibility unless they performed their ecstasy with sufficient expressiveness. Therefore, women cured at shrines also embraced and promoted their intimate moments of spiritual intensity more willingly than men and with greater acceptance among many Catholics. Many sceptical church and medical officials, however, viewed them as overly emotional and psychologically unbalanced, leading to the common rhetoric about hysteria. Embroiled in this gendered paradox, it was difficult for them to obtain formal recognition.

All medical questionnaires asked whether patients were impressionable, prone to fantasy, or hysterical. Doctors and priests often disregarded cures when they declared women psychologically unfit or emotionally fragile. Therese Isemann's doctor worried about her psychological state. He complained about her "clear hysterical reactions." Her priest later dismissed the cure, citing these reports as the justification. Father Neumann of Lauschied also removed his support from Anna Schappert's cure because he judged her too fragile. Despite the disappearance of her symptoms and her ability to do her housework, he recommended an abandonment of clerical investigation into her miracle. He wrote: "This person is hysterical."[61]

In her book about Lourdes, Ruth Harris examines "social cures in which the entire community experienced and enjoyed the grace of one lucky pilgrim." It is important to analyse in a similar way the extent to which German society accepted, rejected, and neglected the Trier miracles in 1933. Most cures failed to reach a wide audience. The bishopric never published information about the miracles and the press rarely reported them. The public usually learned of astounding recoveries through local communities, hospitals, and rumour. Religious officials, doctors, and town populations reacted to the cures with profound ambiguity. Reports of perceived miracles caused the church discomfort. It often approached miraculous recoveries with great concern for fraud and discouraged their appearance for fear of public embarrassment. Official recognition of the ability of the Trier garment to heal pilgrims, however, enabled special access to the robe for the sick. Therefore, the diocese of Trier simultaneously encouraged and discouraged the miraculous power of the relic.

Local pastors often greeted claims about Trier miracles with greater enthusiasm than the bishop and other bureaucratic officials from Trier.

These men served as crucial local patrons who granted the cures legitimacy and endorsed the faith of congregations in their revered heavenly figures. They viewed the events as symbols of Catholic resiliency during an age of great challenges and hoped they would spark greater devotion among their congregations. For example, Agnes Heggemann, who was critically ill and could not walk without a cane before the Trier pilgrimage, received the unwavering support of the priest in Wellingholzhausen. He explained the patience with which the twenty-year-old girl and her family accepted hardship, including the death of her father during the First World War and her life-threatening illness.

Some priests also opposed the proclamation of cures by their followers, hurting their chances for regional acceptance. The most common reason for a lack of clerical support was the accusation of hysteria, as discussed above. These clergy imposed discipline on what they viewed as excessively feminized piety, causing miracle advocates to accuse them of taking an overly modern and rational approach to religion. In the case of Anna Kurth of Waldorf, both doctor and pastor agreed that her illness was in part psychological. This fact cast doubt upon her cure's authenticity. The priest commented, "It is my impression that there is a certain desire for admiration and hysteria at work here."[62] Other pastors remained reluctant because of their opposition to "superstitious" piety that distracted their followers from church doctrine. They also remained embarrassed about how "backward" traditions might influence public perceptions of the church. Father Meisner, head of a parish in the Eifel, criticized the cure of Katharina Rodermund because he wanted to avoid a public spectacle.[63]

The medical profession approached the miraculous with surprising ambiguity. Many almost exclusively Catholic doctors avoided public discussion and withheld their services when they heard the purpose of the examination. They feared for their scientific credentials among colleagues and patients. Demonstrating a masculine rationalism and a modernist interpretation of faith, a handful of doctors openly mocked their patients' belief in religious intercession. This discouragement was especially prevalent in the cases of male pilgrims. For example, Oskar Greiner's Catholic doctor responded with scorn when asked for an examination prior to the Trier pilgrimage. He asked Oskar's father: "Do you actually still believe in that fraud?"[64]

Several files, however, indicate cautious wonder by some medical officials at the improvement by patients. Maria Hepting's doctor wrote that she experienced an "extremely astounding" but "authentic improvement" after her return from Trier. Mrs Franz Drügh, a fifty-year-old woman who suffered serious heart problems and only walked with great difficulty, also enjoyed medical support for her claims. Her doctor testified, "The sick patient is full of life's joys and ambitions once again." Furthermore, he concluded that "the change in her condition cannot be explained through natural means."[65] This division between Catholic doctors who became passionate supporters of miracles and those who angrily rejected them as an embarrassment of the faith replicated the debates surrounding Therese Neumann of Konnersreuth.

Like the clerics and doctors, local communities also vacillated between scepticism and belief. Each alleged miracle possessed both doubters and believers. The records contain some instances of public misgivings about cures. As discussed above, many communities criticized men and accused them of faking their illnesses. Some towns also hesitated when illnesses recurred or they deemed witnesses untrustworthy.[66] Many communities, however, experienced the cures along with the sick pilgrims. Maria Lotschütz of Landsweiler received a heroine's welcome upon her return. She ran into the sister of a church official on the train. Her uncle claimed, "She was so astounded that she could barely contain her happiness and she offered her heartfelt congratulations that Maria could walk again. She said she would notify her brother and he would be happy as a fellow *Landsweiler*." When Maria and her uncle arrived at the train station, a worker shouted: "What? Your niece can walk again!" By nightfall the entire town knew of the cure.[67]

Most towns likely experienced the cures as short-lived spectacles with avid supporters and scornful doubters. The most complete account of a cure's popular reception is the case of Katharina Rodermund, whose experience in Trier earned her a brief tenure as a local seer. When she first returned from Trier, she created a "town sensation." The local priest, who doubted the authenticity of her cure, refused to visit her in order to deflect the interest in the case. One woman approached him and said: "Herr Pastor, you must see her at least once and know how wonderful it all is." Katharina started attracting followers with religious visions and she was known around town as "the healed." Not everyone found her miracle so alluring. Her priest reported: "The population maintained and maintains a split attitude on the matter: one section, namely the gullible, is convinced by the miracle. They understand it as a special honor for the village that for the second time a congregation member was healed through the holy coat [in 1891 a similar case occurred, but the healed died already after three years].

The serious-minded villagers, especially the men, shrug their shoulders and remain silent." The priest also claimed the cure lost its appeal over time. In 1936, he declared, "Today the matter is totally forgotten."[68] This example reflects the deep fissure that mysticism created in all of Catholic Germany as such cures became a symbol of the type of spirituality a variety of Catholics wanted from their church.

Eighty-three pilgrims and their communities "lived" religious cures at the holy coat in Trier during 1933, a site where grass-roots piety awkwardly encountered official Catholicism. Numerous pilgrims and small-town Catholics, including many doctors and priests, welcomed the alleged miracles and rejoiced with the healed patients at the grace they believed God bestowed on them. The cures, however, also received criticism, doubt, and scorn from some doctors, a few pastors, and sometimes from large portions of the population. The cures demonstrate two divergent approaches to Catholicism as Germany experienced crisis. One group, led by the bishops of the northwest, wanted controlled veneration of saints and relics, but sought a tightly monitored and strictly scientific approach to theology and modern miracles. Another contingent sought current miracles as a sign of God's presence on earth in troubled times. Adapted forms of traditional piety contradicted northwestern efforts at a rationalized and modern Catholicism. These cures are evidence of how a revival of Catholic mysticism countered secularizing tendencies while also contributing to the fragmentation of institutional church authority in the modern era.

Conclusion

The supernatural occurrences of Aachen, Schippach, Mirebeau, Bickendorf, and Trier demonstrate the widespread existence of miraculous faith throughout Germany during the early twentieth century. Some episodes had roots in the pre–First World War era and reached their peak during and after the brutal conflict. Others constituted new phenomena more specific to the 1920s and 1930s. All the events reveal a linked series of Catholic miracles that transcended region. Although this chapter focuses on the Rhineland and the Eifel and the next chapter examines the *Oberpfalz*, numerous preternatural events emerged in other areas. For example, Ursula Hibbeln (1869–1940) became known as the "Visionary of the *Ruhrgebiet*" and Margarethe Schäffer (1878–1949) of Gerlachsheim became a noted seer in Baden. Like Barbara Weigand, both of these women rose to prominence prior to the war but received renewed interest in its aftermath. Kathrina Vogl (1871–1956) of Munich, on the other hand, recorded her heavenly voices and visions during the era of Therese Neumann from the 1920s until the 1950s. These examples of holy women indicate that both before and after Therese Neumann's rise to prominence, ample evidence exists of an audience of Catholic pilgrims eager to embrace such a spiritual figure.

The examples analysed here indicate the gendered paradigms through which miraculous movements were viewed and experienced. While the presence of male pilgrims at the holy shroud and as either seers or supporters of visions undermines any notion of miracles as feminized piety, they behaved in accordance with different expectations than women. Eager to either exhibit martial masculinity or to balance their emotional spirituality with evident rationality, they frequently defended themselves against charges of fraud. Women, on the other hand, embraced more public articulations of emotional sensibilities, which drew the charge of hysteria from their detractors. Gendered categories sometimes hampered the pursuit of agency and power when seers clashed with the institutions of the church. The patient obedience expected of women hindered their battle to overcome the entrenched power of the bishops. While Barbara Weigand faded perhaps due to her unwillingness to submit to higher authority, Anna Maria Goebel's movement deteriorated after she submitted to a Catholic medical exam that publicly discredited her experiences. It would be Therese Neumann's ability to simultaneously manipulate and transcend these same gendered paradoxes that made her a more enduring figure.

The evidence in this chapter also illustrates the complexity of miracles for church officials. Devotion towards women with direct access to the divine threatened their role as intermediary between the people and their God and destabilized the pastoral mission of clergy to defend their flock from heresy. It also offended those who supported political Catholicism and the Centre Party's attempts to integrate Catholics into the Reich and sometimes into political coalitions with liberals, nationalists, and social democrats. The voluminous maze of confessional associations in the Rhineland, *Ruhrgebiet*, and Eifel made the male elite of the Centre Party more of an obstacle than in other parts of Germany. Despite this palpable tension, miracle seekers also responded to the Vatican's emphasis on Marian devotion and the cult of the Sacred Heart as a way to attract believers in tumultuous and modern times. While encouraging intensive prayer to Jesus and Mary through officially sanctioned pilgrimage sites, relics, brotherhoods, and devotional associations, the church also curbed the autonomy of those who sought comfort from Jesus and the saints directly. The contradictory official stance of the hierarchy created communities of lay Catholics divided over the suitability of miracles as objects of devotion. This rift, which the popularity of Therese Neumann exposed, divided priests, theologians, religious orders, and even doctors. Ultimately advocates of miracles struggled with the church over the "goods of salvation" in the uncertain environment of the Weimar Republic. Faith in the miracles was meant by its advocates as a way to heal and restore a church battered by secularism. They unintentionally reduced the power of the formal church and its leadership. The rise of a post–First World War movement of more personalized mysticism empowered and showcased marginalized and devout German Catholics while simultaneously weakening the unity and power of German Catholic institutional influence. These trends would become even more apparent with the rise of Germany's most well-known and debated stigmatist of the twentieth century: Therese Neumann of the Bavarian town of Konnersreuth.

Chapter Two

The Rise of Therese Neumann of Konnersreuth during the Weimar Republic

Shortly after first experiencing stigmata in the spring of 1926, Therese Neumann of Konnersreuth, also known by the common regional nickname of Resl, became nothing short of a religious sensation. During the first two years after her miracles, thousands of visitors arrived at the doorstep of her simple rural home in the Bavarian *Oberpfalz* (Upper Palatinate). On average, two thousand visitors a week came during these years, although sometimes more than that came in a single day.[1] On one such occasion on Sunday, 30 May 1926, a throng of Germans, some of them from the nearby Sudetenland, swarmed around Neumann in the street as she made her way to church, prompting the local gendarme to intervene in order to ensure her safety. Many of the ethnic German pilgrims stopped in Konnersreuth on their way to a shrine in Münchenreuth and a hulking man emerged from among them to demand that Neumann show her wounds. She reluctantly stopped for thirty minutes to display her scarred hands. One woman shouted, "Please pray for me my girl for I am but a poor sinner in comparison to you."[2] This unsettling but dynamic scene foreshadowed a spiritual career that would span three-and-a-half decades and model an influential brand of modern spirituality.

No other twentieth-century Catholic figure received this sort of popular attention in Germany. The sick and spiritually troubled from the Bavarian countryside sought her counsel, while Germans travelled from all over to inquire about whether dead loved ones resided in purgatory or heaven. Protestants considering conversion made the difficult journey to Konnersreuth to see if this holy woman could inspire them, while wayward Catholics sometimes found their way back to the church after witnessing her blood-soaked body. Besides the estimated

500,000 pilgrims who travelled to Neumann's bedroom for a fifteen-minute glimpse of her weekly re-enactment of the crucifixion and stigmata during the Weimar years, she also appeared frequently in the press. The most important Catholic newspapers, church newsletters, and intellectual journals, including *Hochland* and *Stimmen der Zeit*, contained essays and features debating the authenticity of her experiences. The tabloid press, socialist newspapers, National Socialist propaganda, and publications devoted to parapsychology also committed space to either critiquing or marvelling at her deep trances.[3] Numerous German, European, and American bishops visited her in Konnersreuth as did several doctors, theologians, professors, psychologists, and priests. The Catholic aristocracy, papal representatives, leaders of Catholic political parties, and even Pope Pius XI made time to consider the case of Therese Neumann. She inspired intense debates among both elite Catholics and everyday churchgoers and the large number of worshippers who experienced her miracles either in person or through press stories. Her vast following and widespread notoriety paradoxically illustrated both an upswing in religious devotion and a decline in the power structures of the church.

Several thorough accounts of German Catholic history demonstrate religious decline during the years of the Weimar Republic. For example, Easter communion participation declined or stagnated in several heavily Catholic areas during the 1920s, including the populous archbishopric of Cologne where Catholics in its largest urban centre partook at a historically low rate of 41 per cent in 1924.[4] Furthermore, Catholic voluntary associations declined. These youth groups, professional associations, and devotional groups perpetuated ultramontane religious ideals since the unification of Germany in the 1870s when the country's Catholic minority rallied to defend the position of the church against Protestant nationalists and liberals during an era referred to as the *Kulturkampf* (culture war). However, the breakneck pace of urbanization in former Catholic strongholds, the upheaval of total war and inflation, and the rhetorical freedom of parliamentary democracy overwhelmed these religious organizations that had once seemed so innovative. The working class of cities like Cologne left their Catholic unions in droves and the middle class of the Black Forest abandoned their Catholic social groups. The combination of partial declines in communion participation, the decimation of urban male associational life, and the rise of cultural trends such as mixed marriages between Protestants and Catholics caused what some see as the start of a death spiral for German Catholicism.[5]

This understandable interest in the areas where religion waned motivates religious historians to overlook the Konnersreuth phenomenon for multiple reasons. First, the history of this popular but diffuse mystical movement breaks the mould of modernization and secularization theory.[6] With about three-quarters of its Catholics religiously active, the *Oberpfalz* and other rural Bavarian enclaves remained far more devout than most other regions in the country, but they lacked the dense networks of lay associations that characterized the northwestern areas. To an extent, the Konnersreuth Circle became somewhat amorphous and transregional as well because of the broad range of believers involved. Furthermore, Therese Neumann existed outside the formal power structure of the church, developing her own circle of worshippers with a singular infrastructure and hierarchy. Despite attempts by the beatification commission in Regensburg to restrict access to thousands of documents, voluminous material remains accessible to researchers. Diocesan archives outside Regensburg, such as in Munich and Cologne, contain rich holdings on Neumann's controversial influence in their regions, and the personal papers of Konnersreuth's critics, such as Georg Wunderle and Johann Baptist Westermayr, almost replicate much of the correspondence that would be in Regensburg files. This documentation exists on top of hundreds of memoirs, press articles, and published studies of those fascinated by Neumann. Such sources indicate a surprisingly large traditionalist movement that pressured the mainstream to return to more characteristically Catholic and mystical practices.

The meteoric ascent of this stigmatic from Konnersreuth illustrates a persistent variant of Catholic mysticism, one that fulfilled the needs of many believers at a uniquely turbulent moment in Central Europe. The waves of pilgrims, the innumerable press stories, the heated debates about Therese Neumann, and the widespread impact of her Friday Suffering reveal a Catholic subculture that sought a less mediated piety through which to process war, inflation, depression, and political crisis. In fact, there are signs of secular belief in miracles during the 1920s as well. Weimar Germany was open to divine intervention in hopeless everyday situations. Followers of Therese Neumann combined this more widespread thirst for the occult with the more specific tropes of Catholic ecstasies to create a modern religiosity that had less use for clerical mediation. Pilgrims experienced God directly through Neumann and without confession, communion, and other sacramental formalities. Engaging the bloody body of Neumann either in person, through the press, or through Konnersreuth relics frequently sparked a personal catharsis that marked the lives of many believers. While this enthusiastic reception of Neumann's miracles signified a growing mysticism that contradicts notions of an increasingly rationalized Weimar Germany, the Konnersreuth phenomenon simultaneously quickened the pace of the Catholic Church's regression. Neumann unintentionally created new and more personal forms of devotion that undercut the authority of clergy, bishops, lay leaders, and Sunday rituals. When pilgrims engaged their higher power through Neumann, they skipped over the authority of the church. This trend foreshadowed the individualization of faith and the rise of new age religions that would so dominate Germany after the 1960s. In sum, the Konnersreuth miracles shatter narratives about secularization, but they also weakened the church's already tenuous claim to widespread cultural authority in Germany.

The Rise of Therese Neumann

The biography of Therese Neumann remains elusive despite hundreds of books devoted to her life. Historians possess an interesting collection of stories from her anonymous existence prior to 1926, but most of it has been filtered through adherents eager to bolster her prospects for future beatification. Even her critics rely heavily on those with intimate access to the family, such as Konnersreuth advocate Fritz Gerlich. Nothing symbolizes the problem more than her birthdate. Although official records indicate her birth on 9 April 1898, Neumann's mother insisted that she arrived before midnight on 8 April. This dispute endured only because Good Friday fell on 8 April in 1898, thus enhancing the Konnersreuth mystique.[7] Nonetheless, Neumann's story offers a limited glimpse of how a rural girl "lived" her Catholicism in the early twentieth century. Furthermore, Resl's life after the stigmata indicates Neumann's spiritual meaning to the millions who travelled to her bedside or followed her endeavours in the press. By analysing Neumann's life and the first years of her celebrity, we grasp the significance of Bavarian Catholics' relationships with heavenly figures.

Therese Neumann was born as the eldest of her parents' eleven children, of whom ten survived childhood. Her parents conceived Therese out of wedlock, but married several months before her birth. Her father, Ferdinand, earned a living as a tailor and the family also owned a small piece of land for farming. According to the custom of the Upper Bavarian Palatinate that referred to people by their father's profession rather than their names, Neumann became known in the early part of her life as *Schneiderixresl*. Life in Konnersreuth seemed difficult for most

2.1. "Birthplace and Home of Therese Neumann." Bundesarchiv-Bildarchiv Bild 102-00241, *Der Gerade Weg*, 3 February 1930.

residents. Those with the best luck inherited land and infrastructure to run their own farms, but they laboured sixteen to seventeen hour days to reap what they could from the hard land of the region. Most families sent men to nearby glass and porcelain factories or quarries while women and children worked locally on their own land or as labourers for others. The overwhelmingly Catholic town had between nine hundred and one thousand residents and the closest train station was six kilometres away in the pilgrimage destination of Waldsassen, a situation that has remained unchanged to this day. The economic situation of the stretched Neumann family paralleled the difficulties of their fellow residents. Neumann grew up in a household legendary for its thriftiness. When the family's children received tips for delivering repaired clothing, they dutifully placed them in a jar next to their father's sewing machine for use when the family ran out of money. Therese marvelled when her own future employer's wife smeared her bread with butter since such luxuries were rarely available in her own house.[8]

Therese Neumann's religious practice prior to her fame is clouded by her hagiographers' desire that she be beatified. Despite an overemphasis on qualities that link her to Catholic mystics of the past, Neumann undoubtedly grew up with a deep sense of piety and clear relationships with heavenly personalities. One of Neumann's future critics, the Jesuit Johann Baptist Westermayr, admitted that she experienced a deep internal life of prayer and felt a strong relationship with God despite her low level of enthusiasm for formal rituals, such as reciting the rosary.[9] This religiosity stemmed from the practices of her region and family. The rural Upper Palatinate retained some of the highest levels of church attendance, Easter communion reception, and monthly communion participation in all of Germany. Neumann's father belonged first to the Bavarian Centre Party and later to the Bavarian People's Party and he participated in Christian farmers' associations. Her parents, who ruled the house with strict authority, instilled a stern sense of ritual in their children with family prayers at the start and end of each day and before all meals. Ferdinand Neumann, a rugged Catholic patriarch, also observed his children carefully during mass and punished those who misbehaved by making them recite the rosary while kneeling on a block of wood. This background made it Therese Neumann's dream to become a nun and a Catholic missionary to Africa. When her father's absence for service in the First World War postponed her pursuit of this goal, she sought comfort in Catholic publications about holy figures. According to both her critics and exponents, Neumann prayed particularly to St Francis de Sales and Therese of Lisieux, whose beatification and canonization would play a leading role in Neumann's own mystical career. Her reading list included *Rosenhain*, an illustrated publication dedicated to both figures; Francis de Sales's *Introduction to a Devout Life*; and Therese of Lisieux's autobiography. These details offer glimpses of how daily ritual, family acculturations, and print moulded approaches to Christianity. They also indicate the decreased importance of lay associations in rural areas, where parish life and ritual piety shaped church attendance and support for political Catholicism as much as the infrastructure of youth groups and women's organizations that dominated in the northwestern Rhineland, Westphalia, and Eifel regions.[10]

Other details about Neumann's childhood seem more directed at securing her legacy. For example, Gerlich suggested that when she received a puppet from the *Christkind*, she tore the doll apart and showed little interest in material things. Instead, she preferred living things, such as flowers, plants, and animals. This connection with nature persisted into adulthood and became part of the image perpetuated by her supporters, linking Neumann to St Francis of Assisi, the first stigmatic in the Catholic tradition. Neumann also allegedly disliked her father's fairy tales, preferring instead the "real" stories found in the lives of the saints. Several biographers also maintain that Neumann became intensely emotional about the passion of Christ from an early age. She burst into tears when she read or heard about the death of Christ and she used free time at school to meditate on the crucifixion. Her hagiographers also say she read her prayer books and catechism repeatedly, deriving immense pleasure from such activities.[11] Whether or not these stories are exaggerated, they mark Neumann as exceptional in relationship to others in her pious enclave, where Catholicism mixed messily with everyday compromises. Faith in religious norms usually existed side by side with quotidian sins against Catholic doctrine. Neumann's very common conception prior to marriage is one example of this ambiguity in lived religion from the most pious of Catholic families.

Throughout her teen years, Therese was a crucial economic asset to her family. A tireless labourer, she participated actively in the domestic work of the house and wielded great authority over her young siblings. At the age of fourteen, her father sent her to the household of Max Neumann (no relation), one of the landholders in town. Neumann performed hours of difficult outdoor labour during the war years, as she helped her family overcome the economic hardship brought on by her father's military service. Afterward she suggested that lessons from Therese of Lisieux's philosophy about everyday piety soothed the disappointment of not becoming a missionary.

On the morning of 10 March 1918, Therese Neumann's life changed dramatically. A massive fire started on a farm near her workplace. Neumann served a crucial role in a bucket brigade, handing water from a stool up to her employer as the entire household laboured to save his house and farm. Approximately two hours into the ordeal, Neumann dropped a pail of water and fell to the ground. Her back engulfed in pain, she could barely feel her legs. For the rest of the day, she could not find relief from her symptoms and she vomited most of what she ate. These ailments troubled her in the weeks after the fire, but she continued work as Max Neumann accused her of laziness and rumours circulated in town that she was shirking labour. She then experienced a hard fall down the stairs while working, knocking herself unconscious and becoming bedridden. For five years, she suffered constant physical pain, numerous accidents that caused further injury, and countless symptoms. Besides intense back pain that restricted her movements, she lost control of her bowels, went blind, lost large amounts of weight due to nausea, and experienced body spasms that left her unconscious. These problems worsened in part because a constant desire to return to work led to accidents where Neumann fell and experienced even more head trauma. Her future critic, Dr Josef Deutsch, found the nine accidents recounted in most of her biographies almost inexplicable. The inventory of maladies in these years amounts to an unpleasant list. She went deaf in one ear, became paralysed in one arm, suffered from gastric ulcers and boils, choked when eating from problems in the esophagus, and developed bed sores.[12]

A once active woman who contributed economically to her family and dreamt of religious adventure now became a bedridden dependent. She spent two months in the Waldsassen hospital where a series of doctors examined her with little success. She eventually received a pension for a diagnosis of hysteria. Although she became irritable in the early years of the illness, Neumann's hagiographers claim she found comfort in her Catholic faith. Building on Catholic tropes dominant in the devotional literature that Neumann read as a child, she embraced her sickness as God's will and attempted to endure her hardship with "feminine patience." This faith drew inspiration from Therese of Lisieux and modern stigmatics, such as the unofficial but widespread cult of Louise Lateau of Belgium. Neumann even claimed that her first miracle occurred in December of 1922 when she vicariously suffered a throat ailment for a theology student whose illness endangered his studies. Much like her contemporary, Anna Maria Goebel of Bickendorf, Neumann transformed her infirmed condition from a tragedy into a spiritual asset after years of medical problems.

Another turning point occurred with the beatification of Neumann's favourite Catholic figure, Therese of Lisieux, on 29 April 1923. On this day, Neumann regained her sight, which began a breathtaking series of miracles that improved her health. After a cure to a foot wound in 1924, Neumann's spine healed on the day of St Therese's canonization in 1925. When saying a novena in honour of the "Little Flower," Neumann saw a bright light and heard a voice that asked if she wanted relief. After responding several times that she desired only what God willed, the voice offered a cure with a stern warning that she would suffer much more in the future. The voice proclaimed, "It is only through suffering that you will be able to realize your vocation as a victim soul, and in this way help priests. Many more souls are saved by suffering than by the most brilliant sermons, as I have written."[13] From this time on, Therese Neumann adopted a mission sent from heaven. Her suffering would become a powerful spiritual asset, central to the survival of the church. By declaring her own pain as more important than the ministry of the church's clergy, this voice endowed Neumann with incredible agency and purpose. Later in the year, a relic from St Therese also miraculously healed Neumann from pneumonia and an appendicitis that threatened her life. These cures became a sensation in Konnersreuth and received the full support of Neumann's local priest, Father Joseph Naber.

During the Lenten season of 1926, Therese Neumann experienced stigmata for the first time. Bedridden once again with an abscess in her ear and severe headaches, Jesus appeared to Neumann suffering in the Garden of Gethsemane and she bled from her side. More visions of the passion continued on Thursdays and Fridays until Good Friday when she bled from her eyes, hands, and feet for the first time. She concealed her experiences until this point, but revealed them at the orders of Father Naber. Naber later wrote to Gerlich that Neumann "lay like the picture of a martyr, her eyes stuck together with blood, two streaks of blood flowing down her cheeks as if she were dying."[14] Neumann would experience her "Friday Suffering" continuously until her death in 1962. By the fall of 1926 when she bled from eight head wounds in imitation of the crown of thorns, a weekly pattern developed with the display of her stigmata. She became ecstatic around midnight on Thursday and suffered for thirteen hours until one o'clock on Friday. In this time she saw the passion of Jesus of Nazareth, broken into about fifty scenes from his prayer in the Garden of Gethsemane to his death on the cross. She viewed each event as if seeing it for the first time and would bleed for hours from her eyes, head, heart, side, feet, and hands. During the visions, she and Naber created what Paul Siwek called a "drama of life and movement" for visitors, where she orally shared what was happening and demonstrated intense emotion with arms outstretched and pantomimed movements replicating what she saw. Naber would narrate every scene for first-time visitors. After the conclusion of her visions, Neumann lapsed into an "infantile state" where she could barely communicate and provided only simple answers to questions as she readjusted. A state of exalted rest usually concluded the spectacle where she answered questions from visitors on behalf of Jesus himself.

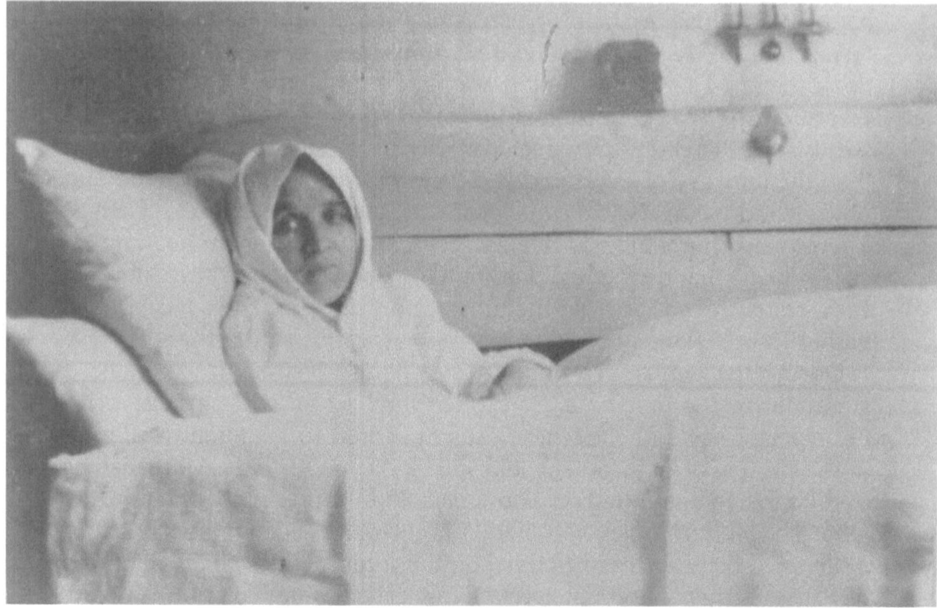

2.2. Therese Neumann in her bedroom. Provinzarchiv der deutschen Augustiner, Würzburg Nachlass Georg Wunderle.

Although sensational, the Friday Suffering became but one of numerous miracles performed by Therese Neumann. She experienced several other visions as years went by, including the birth of Christ, the visit of the Magi, the Annunciation, the Transfiguration, and scenes from the lives of several saints. In some of her visions, she heard and then repeated Aramaic words, something seemingly impossible for a peasant woman with only a rudimentary primary education. While in a state of exalted rest after visions, she dispensed advice on behalf of Jesus and sometimes possessed clairvoyance. She identified strangers before they introduced themselves and allegedly knew that Pope Pius XI had given her a special blessing in Rome long before the news reached her. She also distinguished authentic from fraudulent relics in this state. Furthermore, many Catholics who never met Therese Neumann asserted she appeared to them to solve medical or personal problems. Followers claimed that she received communion without swallowing and this process also sent her into a state of ecstasy. Therefore, she sat by herself behind the altar during mass so as not to distract other worshippers.

Finally, Neumann fasted for her entire life after receiving the stigmata, claiming to only subsist on communion hosts without losing weight. This final miracle, a characteristic claimed by several of the over three hundred alleged stigmatics that preceded her, became the most disputed issue among those who doubted Neumann's sanctity.[15]

These miraculous events understandably attracted attention from her neighbours as well as the press. Neumann became a noticeable figure to those in her Bavarian town. Siwek describes her presence: "Anyone visiting Konnersreuth from Sunday to Thursday may see Theresa walking through the village, wearing a simple black dress, a white kerchief over her hair, her hands covered in mittens. Her pace is slow and hesitant, for she must walk on tiptoe. These stigmata are no mere ornaments; they are meant to be a participation in the suffering of our Lord."[16] Her fellow townspeople all experienced what many believed to be a manifestation of God on earth through their daily encounters with her. The people of Konnersreuth also witnessed the appearance of thousands of pilgrims in their tiny town. Two events sparked a deluge of visitors. First, Father Naber published an account of Neumann's stigmata in a Waldsassen newspaper weeks before reporting to his bishop in Regensburg, Antonius von Henle. Although von Henle urged caution about broadcasting this news, it was too late.[17] The storm of interest in the case increased even more after the visit of Erwein Freiherr von Aretin, an editor with the *Münchener Neuste Nachtrichten* in late July of 1927. He published a positive account of Neumann's miracles in a supplement to the newspaper entitled *Die Einkehr*, which would publish more articles in the future praising Konnersreuth.[18] As the case became a subject for debate, derision, and curiosity in the tabloid, left-wing, and Catholic press organs, visitors poured into Konnersreuth for a glimpse of the Friday Suffering.

Pilgrims descended upon Konnersreuth in massive numbers from 1926 to 1928 despite major obstacles. The town possessed no infrastructure for tourism. It lacked adequate lodging, with only one pension owned by local businessman Hugo Schiml. Even when residents rented rooms in their homes, they could rarely accommodate demand. Konnersreuth did not have a train station, so pilgrims travelled by car, tour bus, bicycle, and even foot. Furthermore, the simple Neumann home could only hold a few visitors at a time, causing long lines outside the house on Fridays, waiting for a brief glimpse of the stigmata. Despite these logistical problems and the resistance of the bishop, Konnersreuth became a major pilgrimage destination. At its most popular, the town attracted several thousand visitors on Fridays. In the first months after Naber's newspaper article, 100 to 150 people visited the Neumann house daily and the town averaged about 1,000 visitors a week until 1928. While many of the statistics regarding visitation may not have been precise, the gendarme reports frequently confirmed them. Describing the diverse visitors on a busy Friday in Konnersreuth, Hans Natonek of the *Weser Zeitung* wrote, "Right next to each other at the coarse tables of the taverns sit a jumbled white-haired Dominican nun and elegant people from big cities."[19] One of the largest crowds for the Friday Suffering, 4,000 people, occurred shortly after Aretin's article on 12 August 1927. Local Bavarian pilgrims certainly constituted a large portion of the visitors, but Catholics and curiosity seekers arrived from the Sudetenland, the Rhineland, Westphalia, the Saarland, Berlin, northern Germany, Bohemia, Slovakia, Austria, and the United States. Located conveniently near the major spa towns of Marienbad and Carlsbad close to the border with Czechoslovakia, more affluent elites visited Konnersreuth than the towns of other Weimar-era miracle workers. In 1928, the diocese of Regensburg rejected such spectacles and banned all visitors who did not have special permission from church hierarchy while they investigated the case's authenticity. Ferdinand and Anna Neumann welcomed this respite for their daughter and their family's finances, as the crush of visitors was destroying the interior of their house. This ban limited pilgrims, although an impressive parade of bishops, theologians, psychologists, doctors, scientists, and journalists from all over the world still sought an audience in Konnersreuth. Around 200 elites came to town per week until 1933 in spite of attempts to reign in the enthusiasm.[20]

State reports suggest that voyeurism blended with piety in Konnersreuth, causing awkward juxtapositions and an occasionally tense environment. Tourists to the nearby spas in Czechoslovakia wandered over to Konnersreuth to explore the scene and journalists arrived to get a scoop on a lurid story. The widespread coverage of the miracles in newspapers of all political orientations and the unwieldly mixture of sacred and profane pilgrims revealed a desire for supernatural solutions in Weimar Germany that burst the boundaries of an exclusive Catholic piety. In the first month of Neumann's fame, mild unrest broke out among pilgrims who disagreed about the authenticity of the miracles. At one point fist fights occurred between those with different opinions.[21] Such disorder appeared in several larger cities and especially in Munich where the press obsessively debated Neumann's authenticity.[22]

Nonetheless, the local gendarme asserted that the majority left Konnersreuth stirred by what they witnessed in Neumann's room. Dr Wolfgang von Weisl described his experience visiting Neumann in a liberal newspaper:

> The previous visitors came slowly down the stairs in an altered state. The three men were shaking and the four women cried. Their faces looked so severe that they prepared the atmosphere for what we would meet at the top of the stairs. I convinced myself not to be influenced. I came to see and not to feel. I entered. I saw. I felt nevertheless uncontrollable empathy and then wonder. I would not have believed what happened here unless I saw it: a farm girl saw the passion of Jesus. And she watches with such strength, with such fervor, that blood runs in long streams from both eyes down her face, that blood reddens her shirt from a heart wound and her head scarf from head wounds. I watch and watch. Before me sits in the bed a picture of misery.[23]

The physical suffering and deep piety of Neumann merged with her miraculous visions to scare and inspire many pilgrims. Even those who came and went with no Catholic faith experienced at least vague spiritual agitation.

In certain cases, the fervour for contact with Neumann became overwhelming. During a visit by a large throng of pilgrims, one man broke from the group to hide in the house. When the others left and Neumann lay by herself in a trance and with eyes sealed shut from blood, he stole several objects from her room. He took cloth, blood from her wounds, and baked goods Neumann kept nearby for visiting children. The thief left a five-mark note under her pillow before absconding with his religious treasures. Other pilgrims cut pieces of wood from the stairs of the Neumann family home to take away as relics. The family had to install new steps because the originals had been "literally cut to pieces" by the crowds.

Therese Neumann and many of her public advocates, including Father Naber, promoted her miracles as capable of converting wayward Catholics and those of other faiths. When she became so sick that many feared she would perish in November of 1927, she saw a vision of St Theresa of Lisieux who told her she was not allowed to die because Neumann needed to demonstrate to a doubting world that God existed.[24] Such visions encapsulated the anxiety many Germans felt about the societal changes in the aftermath of the First World War. Neumann's inner circle believed that her suffering and visions came from God as a missionary tool for the Catholic faith. Neumann replaced her dream of converting Africans to Catholicism with using her miracles to combat the secularism of Europe. Many pilgrims, moved by their visits, heeded the call for deeper spirituality and travelled directly from the Neumann house across the street to the town's parish where visiting priests said several masses a day. Dr Kannamüller of Passau expressed astonishment with the heightened religiosity he witnessed in Konnersreuth: "Whoever enters the thickly filled Church in the early morning hours of a Friday starting at 5 o'clock where masses are read at several altars without interruption and whose internal devotion can be heard everywhere and whose formal flood of the Communion rail can be observed, must be deeply moved and say: Konnersreuth cannot be fraudulent! … For me this moral moment weighs heavily on the scales. Nobody can completely ignore it."[25] The deep religiosity shown by many pilgrims convinced its most ardent supporters of the miracles' importance. Unlike many German Catholics who sought integration into modern society, these traditionalist reformers fought for recognition because they believed such wonders possessed the potential to overturn what they perceived as over a century and a half of secularization and even the German Reformation. Friedrich Ritter von Lama, who edited a newspaper devoted to Konnersreuth and delivered lectures throughout the country on several Catholic miracles, shared numerous stories of secular liberals, Protestants, and Jews who undertook the difficult process of religious conversion as a result of contact with Therese Neumann. In one example that also reveals von Lama's anti-Semitic stereotypes, he described a Viennese university lecturer who read a "Jewish newspaper" while dressed in a "fine fur coat." He expressed doubt about Neumann's miracles but wanted to see the famous stigmatic while he was on vacation in Carlsbad. After fifteen minutes of seeing the Friday Suffering, the man appeared shaken. Von Lama wrote, "He had turned pale, and spoke stutteringly to Father Naber: 'Herr Pfarrer, thank Resl for me!,' and then to the stigmatist: 'Resl, I thank you, you have given me back my faith!' Weeping, he left the room, and went to the church."[26] While von Lama's intolerance for the Jewish faith and dislike for urban wealth is striking, such conversion stories enhanced Neumann's reputation as a stimulus for religious revival.

Some of Neumann's followers found that her ecstatic connection with God made the afterlife more concrete. Baden aristocrat Erich Fürst von Waldburg-Zeil became fascinated with Neumann's comments about people in purgatory while in a state of exalted rest. She explained the condition of his recently departed mother in purgatory, whose demise Neumann predicted, as well as his brother and father. He found it "comforting" to envision dead relatives together in purgatory and he found solace in the fact that they were close to earning their eternal salvation. He also believed these revelations about loved ones were a helpful reminder to the living to pray for them and to live moral lives in order to shorten one's own suffering after death.[27] Such personal information gained by those who witnessed Neumann's state of exalted rest became especially meaningful after Europe's experience with mass casualties during the First World War.

While numerous Catholics experienced moments with Neumann that enhanced their faith, others sought comfort in their daily lives through her supernatural abilities. Upon his first visit to Neumann Zeil expressed concern that his wife Monika had yet to bear him a child. Neumann replied, "Calm yourself. It will happen."[28] Parents of sick children brought them to Neumann for advice and prayer. Neumann usually counselled them when not in ecstasy about coping with God's will in moments of such hardship, but she sometimes prayed to vicariously suffer on their behalf. Several pilgrims credited Neumann with curing their children or themselves from illness. For example, von Lama described a chauffeur from Zweifalten whose broken foot needed amputation and saw "himself jobless and crippled for life." His wife both wrote and prayed to Therese Neumann, who visited her as a vision one night in her traditional "black gown and white head-dress." In the morning, the man felt no pain in the injured foot. As a result of such stories, any women unable to gain an audience with Neumann left notes for her at the high altar in Konnersreuth asking for her prayers regarding personal trouble in their marriages. Sometimes these same pilgrims returned to leave thank-you notes when they felt Neumann's prayers aided their problems.[29] Several worshippers wanted Neumann's attention in her state of exalted rest in hopes of finding out information about dead loved ones.[30] Many Germans sought non-conventional and sometimes occult avenues for comfort in frightening historic times, but Catholics felt most at home with Neumann forging a new and more personal spirituality from within the confines of their religious tradition.

Some Neumann enthusiasts also viewed her as a rural symbol of resistance against urbanization and the centralization of political power. In recording his impressions of Konnersreuth Antonie von Tänzl praised the town and its seer as a country oasis in a sea of modernity during the

1920s. He wrote, "It is a genuine Upper Palatinate nest where modern culture and advancement has not penetrated." He lauded Neumann's traditional country dress of a white head scarf (*Tüchel*) with a long black dress and gloves as well as her distinct local dialect. He claimed she spoke the same, whether conversing with a "*Fürst* or a farmer" and always dispensed friendly greetings as befitted local customs.[31] Enhancing such rhetoric, Leopold Witt, the local priest of a nearby village and early Konnersreuth publicist, articulated resentment against those enemies of Konnersreuth that "mocked" rural residents as a "dumb herd of sheep" for their religious piety and faith in Neumann.[32] Such accounts focused less on spiritual emotion and more upon Neumann's rural context, making her as much a nostalgic metaphor as religious figure. Although Neumann possessed national and international appeal, she found her most heartfelt early supporters in Bavaria where regionalism reigned supreme. The provincial nature of her affect struck a chord with all Europeans weary of materialism and rapid urbanization, but also with Bavarian Catholics who fiercely supported federalism and regional autonomy over centralization and political authority from Berlin.

Therese Neumann's persistence as a public figure relied on the early development of an elite circle of followers that championed her cause with economic resources and high social standing. The Konnersreuth Circle emerged quickly after the sensation caused by the stigmata. Neumann's family and her local priest, the aforementioned Father Joseph Naber, formed the first necessary layer of this circle. The steadfast faith of Ferdinand and Anna in her sanctity made their home open to religious figures and pilgrims hoping for contact with Neumann's sacred body. Naber exhibited not only belief in Neumann's miracles but an entrepreneurial spirit that spread word of her case to Catholic Germany. Sometimes ignoring the advice and orders of his bishop in Regensburg, Naber wrote newspaper articles and reached out to other clergy on a regional and national level in support of Neumann's holiness. However, the failure of Anna Maria Goebel's stigmata to mobilize a major movement illustrates that a supportive rural family and local priest could not prevent disgrace against a sceptical hierarchy if powerful forces from the laity articulated distaste for such a mystical interpretation of Catholicism. The emergence of trusted, unequivocal, and influential patrons became a necessary ingredient for Neumann's long-term prospects as a religious figure.

The Konnersreuth Circle commenced with the visit of Franz Xaver Wutz, a theologian and professor of oriental languages from the city of Eichstätt. Praised by some colleagues as a "universal genius" and a "fabulously original" personality, Wutz was a Bavarian Catholic elite.[33] After stopping by Konnersreuth in July of 1926 to check on the rumours about the stigmata, Neumann's miracles and charisma immediately fascinated him. Drawn to her specific descriptions of Jerusalem and the crucifixion scenes as well as her Aramaic phrases, he travelled over two hundred kilometres in his car every Friday to witness Neumann's weekly "suffering." Wutz received the complete trust of both Naber and the family and wielded power over their decisions regarding how to handle church authorities. He also protected and promoted Neumann as he used a wide circle of colleagues and influential friends to rally support for her cause within Catholic Bavaria. He became central to an Eichstätt wing of supporters including Capuchin Ingbert Naab, Abbess Maria Anna Benedicta von Spiegel, Professor Joseph Lechner, and Professor Franz Xaver Mayr. He also encouraged the first visit by the wealthy Waldburg-Zeil to Konnersreuth. Wutz's friendship with the editor of the *Münchener Neuste Nachrichten*, Erwein Freiherr von Aretin, encouraged the latter's visit and his conversion to the Konnersreuth cause. Beyond the impact of his 1927 newspaper article, Aretin was another powerful ally. A politically connected Catholic aristocrat with friends, family, and professional relations in Catholic Germany and Austria, Aretin would provide crucial support. Aretin's interest in Konnersreuth also encouraged the first visit of the circle's most famous member, journalist Fritz Gerlich. As the circle grew in stature and membership, Gerlich and Wutz emerged as its de facto leaders, commanding respect from prominent devotees with special access to the Neumann family, such as Berlin chaplain Helmut Fahsel and Monsignor Adalbert Vogl of the Altötting shrine in Bavaria.

The spiritual journey of Fritz Gerlich illustrates the intensity of the piety by members of this circle as well as the importance of Neumann's conversion mystique. As Aretin describes it, Gerlich was an "unpleasantly harsh and logical thinker" in the three years he knew him prior to 1927. As an historian, state archivist, and journalist, Aretin had usually only discussed politics with him. Gerlich responded with deep cynicism to Aretin's article about Konnersreuth and travelled to the town himself to investigate further. Aretin warned him, "Go there with the tranquil assumption that it is a fraud! But I warn you that you will not return the same as when you left." When Gerlich came home to Munich five days later, he went directly to Aretin's office and requested his company. They walked in the rain until the middle of the night discussing his trip. Aretin wrote that it was "staggering" to hear such a man discuss "our savior" all night and to watch Gerlich completely alter his outlook for the remainder of his life. He compared the conversion to that of Saint Paul. Gerlich became a constant presence at the Neumann household, visiting regularly and staying once for six weeks without interruption. He officially converted from Calvinism to Catholicism in a ceremony in Eichstätt in 1931. Gerlich immediately supported the miracles by publishing articles in the *Münchener Neuste Nachtrichten* in 1927, writing a two-volume book about Neumann, and founding his own political newspaper, *Der gerade Weg* (The Straight Path), that featured news about Neumann in the 1930s. Along with Wutz, Gerlich became the leading figure of the Konnersreuth Circle, using his narrative skills and social scientific authority to popularize and legitimize her religiosity.[34] His spiritual journey formed an engaging story, supporting the claim that Neumann's miracles possessed the power to reverse what Catholics perceived to be a decline in religious faith and morality.

While Gerlich's conversion story became the focal point of the Konnersreuth Circle, it remained far from singular among Neumann's devoted following. Johannes Maria Verweyen, a renowned philosophy professor in Bonn, returned to the faith of his childhood after carefully studying Neumann's miracles. Horrified by the First World War and attracted to monism and Freemasonry, Verweyen officially left the faith in 1921. However, he remained fascinated by many occult phenomena both religious and otherwise that contradicted his new world view before he published a careful analysis of Therese Neumann after multiple visits. Like von Lama and Gerlich, he interpreted the stigmata as an "alarm" and a "warning" for a life more focused on "God and Christ." Her wounds caused him to reconsider the "boundaries of enlightenment" and scientific explanations. Verweyen would eventually convert back to Catholicism in 1936 and described his decision to leave the church as the worst mistake of his life.[35] Verweyen's case indicates the modern role filled by Konnersreuth's brand of spirituality. A twentieth-century modernist whose faith was shaken by the war, Verweyen ultimately found his spiritual home in the unorthodox and dramatic miracles of Therese Neumann. He sought otherworldly and non-traditional solutions to seemingly insurmountable problems after the First World War as is clear from his dalliance with monism. However, he ultimately found his spiritual home with the Catholic mysticism uninhibited by clerical formality in Konnersreuth.

Such high-profile cases illustrate the dramatic role played by converts in bringing change to Catholic history. For example, converts from

Judaism performed a consequential part in shifting the church's intolerant teachings about Jews. Just as it took a "revolution" by new believers like John Oesterreicher to alter Catholic anti-Semitism, Gerlich and Verweyen challenged the church to reform in more conservative ways.[36] High-placed converts in the Konnersreuth movement played a central role in its rebelliousness.

While a small circle of elites enjoyed special access to Neumann, the outer layer of the Konnersreuth Circle included enthusiastic supporters and publicists who did not attain the same confidence of the family. Figures such as Georg Priller, Bruno Grabinski, Father Leopold Witt, and Friedrich Ritter von Lama published books and newspapers devoted exclusively to Neumann. For example, Priller's *Konnersreuther Sonntagsblatt* attracted a national following of ten thousand subscriptions by early 1928.[37] These men viewed her as confirming their desire for a more mystical faith, yet their sharp rhetoric and lack of discretion meant they possessed only limited contact to Neumann and her family. They nonetheless followed her case closely by reading accounts in several newspapers, hearing from other pilgrims, and keeping close to the rumour mill. They gathered such information and then released it to the public through their own writings and a series of public lectures. While such pursuits reaped profit for these individuals, they performed them mainly from a sense of faith and a desire to reshape doctrine to conform to their own spiritual outlook.[38]

As the most prominent and representative publicist of Konnersreuth, Friedrich von Lama wrote books and articles that indicate the spirituality influencing this sometimes unwanted campaign on Neumann's behalf. In his third book about Konnersreuth, von Lama warned openly of apocalypse in a "godless" age: "Therese Neumann's bloody tears are, it is my conviction, the expression of divine sorrow over the base ingratitude of the world, which owes its existence to God ... Therefore the bloody tears constitute another of the final warnings to mankind, which stands on the edge of the abyss." However, the longest section of the book emphasizes the conversions that occurred as a result of contact between visitors and Neumann's vicarious suffering.[39] Indeed, Neumann's German supporters understood her stigmata as a narrative of apocalypse and potential salvation. She suffered vicariously for the sins of an increasingly secular and violent world. War and depression served as punishment for these sins, but her miracles could convert apostates and non-believers, potentially saving the world from God's wrath. The Neumann family dealt with such support shrewdly. While

Neumann maintained correspondence with von Lama into the 1930s, she simultaneously kept her distance from him and his brazen attacks on the clergy. She wrote privately to Bishop Buchberger denouncing some of his writings on her behalf and restricted his admission to her household. However, she never contradicted his crusade for her holiness and maintained written correspondence, realizing how effectively he broadcast her message. Von Lama, as much as anyone else, represented the conservative heresy at the heart of the Konnersreuth movement that challenged the very foundations of clerical and hierarchical authority he believed had become overly rationalized.

Other aspects of Neumann's circle also pushed the boundaries of Catholic doctrine. Waldburg-Zeil asked Neumann in ecstasy about a property owned by his family. The nuns who occupied it believed it was cursed by demons. While in a state of exalted rest, Neumann responded that a horrible deed once occurred at the site. Rather than perform an exorcism, she said to leave the demons in the large property rather than cast them elsewhere where they could cause more trouble.[40] By offering advice about a haunted house, Neumann engaged with the miracle lust that became so culturally powerful during the perceived chaos of the Weimar Republic. Such advice connected her to the many other non-religious prophets and soothsayers of her era.

Therese Neumann inspired several secular miracle workers at the end of the Weimar Republic as well as an increased appetite for parapsychology, hypnosis, and telepathy. For example, one doctor famously claimed to have hypnotized a female patient into bleeding from her hands like Therese Neumann and Anna Maria Goebel. Another Protestant man outside of Hamburg claimed to experience miraculous phenomena after a car accident in 1928. Finally, a coal miner named Paul Diebel from lower Silesia stole some of Therese Neumann's headlines in the late 1920s as he also bled from his hands and caused a crucifix to appear in his blood. Diebel boasted control of his bleeding and imperviousness to pain. He claimed to manipulate his body through his mind during the First World War when escaping Russian captivity. He tried to commit suicide by cutting himself but suggested that his will to live stopped the blood. Diebel became a darling of the tabloid press and even appeared in a film and at the Berlin *Wintergarten* to perform. The key to his popularity was his renunciation of Therese Neumann. By suggesting that some humans were blessed with the ability to psychically regulate their blood flow, he refuted her sanctity and drew attention to his own act. Many came to believe that Diebel was a fraud.[41]

Nonetheless, his fifteen minutes of fame indicate the cultural reach of the Therese Neumann story but also the thirst for miracles either religious or secular in a fragile post–First World War Germany.

In fact, the rising field of parapsychology demonstrated this miracle lust that existed independently of Catholic mysticism. For decades advocates of the scientific study of paranormal events, such as telepathy, clairvoyance, and psychokinesis, created their own disputed subfield within the German scientific community, which reached a high point during the Weimar Republic. A series of public trials tested the occult skills of mediums like Claire Reichart of Munich who claimed to foresee the November Revolution of 1918/1919 and the Beer Hall Putsch; hypnotist Friedrich Gern whose wife solved crimes under his influence; and August Drost, another crime-solving telepath known as the "Sherlock Holmes of Bernburg."[42] Like the case of Therese Neumann, these court cases generated major debates among scientists and widespread press coverage. It is in the context of massive upheaval during the Weimar era that Neumann's miracles became so widely followed; she channelled this secular attraction to the paranormal into a Catholic tradition of mysticism.

Therese Neumann transformed in a matter of months from a sick and unknown young woman in rural Bavaria to an object of deep devotion and curiosity. Her stream of visitors and international attention endured due to the resonance of several themes emphasized by her family and followers. The tropes of apocalypse and salvation drew the attention of many Catholics in a tumultuous period marked by political and economic instability and deep concerns among Catholics about secular forces and a decline in Christian morality. Furthermore, the promise of mass conversion through the mystical presence of God in Neumann's body provided renewed hope in some that the tide could be turned against a Weimar culture that seemed at odds with the religious and rural values of many Konnersreuth followers. Neumann also became an enduring presence due to the elite status of many in her circle. By quickly securing the support of her parish priest, well-connected intellectuals like Gerlich and Wutz, and committed publicists like von Lama, Neumann enjoyed a celebrity with a further reach and a longer duration than Germany's other mystics who usually receded back into anonymity after an initial burst of interest. By mobilizing a team of conservative traditionalists unified by their distrust of an overly rational clerical establishment, Neumann developed a far-reaching network of powerful patrons and a mass following.

Conclusion

Therese Neumann's miracles, fame, supporters, and opponents reveal a tremendous amount about Catholicism during the Weimar Republic. First and foremost, her popularity shows the importance of mystical faith in an era of upheaval and anxiety. By attracting hundreds of thousands of visitors from all social classes and the attention of the Catholic press, theological studies, the medical community, tabloid newspapers, and even international observers, Therese Neumann became a religious phenomenon. In the aftermath of a destructive war and in the midst of economic and political turmoil, her grave warnings from the Saviour about the dangers of a secularizing world resonated with many Catholics of disparate backgrounds. In a cultural landscape that increasingly gravitated towards miraculous explanations, Neumann offered a home for those that sought the supernatural from within the Catholic faith. Furthermore, her message of hope through miraculous cures for herself and others, a direct connection with God, conversion of sinners, and her vicarious suffering for those in need eased the pain of Bavarian peasants, some elite clergy, and even certain urban dwellers from Munich to Cologne. Her prophesy while in a state of exalted rest helped pilgrims process a seemingly senseless world and the allure of the sensational stories from Konnersreuth at least offered engaging reading to German consumers. A tailor's home in Konnersreuth and the body of his exceptional daughter became sites where many European Catholics literally or metaphysically "lived" their religion, challenging the teleological assumptions of decline present in current histories of the period. Although support for political Catholicism, some confessional associations, and Easter Communion waned in certain regions of Germany during the Weimar Republic, the rise of the Konnersreuth Circle indicates an overlooked counterweight that supports Robert Orsi's "braided narrative" of secularization. In sum, Therese Neumann offered a chronicle of apocalypse and salvation that built upon the templates of several earlier twentieth-century seers and mobilized masses of Catholics behind a religious approach that emphasized the miraculous amidst the uncertainty of the late 1920s and 1930s.

Therese Neumann rallied Bavarians protective of their rural Catholic enclaves but her legacy was more than a regional exception. On the one hand, Anthropologist Ulrike Wiethaus persuasively argues, "'Backward' as it appeared to proponents of anti-regional national progress,

Neumann's cult provided agency, identity, and dignity for otherwise disenfranchised rural and small town populations left behind in the march towards 'progress,' urbanization, industrialization, and centralization, a process in regard to which they were given little choice, little participation, and little voice."[43] Due to this antimodern resistance, the base of her support undoubtedly rested in the piety of the Upper Palatinate as well as in Bavarian pilgrimage sites from Eichstätt to Altötting. Nonetheless, Konnersreuth Circle adherents and pilgrims hailed from all regions of Germany and several other European countries. Although a less powerful minority in their own areas, patrons and enthusiasts from the Rhineland, Westphalia, the Saarland, Baden, and the Emsland illustrated a wide-ranging appetite for Catholic mysticism that transcended local subcultures. The undercurrent of support for the stigmata in the more "rationalized" Rhineland and the existence of fierce critics of Konnersreuth within "traditional" Bavaria illustrates that the "braiding" of the Catholic narrative of secularization and the divisions within the Catholic milieus occurred on national, regional, and local levels.

Neumann surpassed the constraints that limited other visionaries, such as Barbara Weigand and Anna Maria Goebel, largely because of the men of high standing that she converted to her cause through her charisma and their unique vision for post–First World War Catholicism. With the support of influential theologians, journalists, and doctors who possessed political connections as well as financial and educational resources, she enjoyed protection from opponents that other mystics lacked. She endured and developed international standing because her movement shifted from a grass-roots experience to one that consisted of debates about the direction of German Catholicism by German elites. Furthermore, she benefited from becoming more mainstream than many other forms of Catholicism by tapping into widespread interest in miracles that departed the boundaries of the church. Her core of traditionalist reformers and unconventional converts provided a solid base on to which a mass movement was built.

Although the Konnersreuth case indicates an undercurrent of cathartic religious faith, it also disrupted the church enormously. Many of Neumann's pilgrims articulated a storm of emotion through their piety in ways that were separate from the formal rituals of weekly worship. Advocates defined their own brand of personal devotion as Neumann replaced the church as the primary focus of their prayers and they set their own rules with flexibility regarding official doctrine. Therese Neumann always professed loyalty to the religious leadership that gave her legitimacy, but she undercut its authority. She built on an eagerness for miracles in the zeitgeist of the Weimar Republic and encouraged a fragmentation of church authority and a personalization of Germans' relationship to God. This challenge to the clergy and bishops became most apparent in the very public debate about Neumann's authenticity, which ultimately contributed to the divisions that disarmed the strength of political Catholicism.

Chapter Three

Saving Souls and Making Enemies: The Struggle over Konnersreuth and the Downfall of Political Catholicism

In 1927 a clergyman revealed to prominent theologian Georg Wunderle that Catholics "argued in the streets" of Munich about the Therese Neumann stigmata as if it were a "political election."[1] Disputes at cafes and along boulevards simulating politics were quite poignant given the intensity, divisiveness, and political connections of the struggle over Konnersreuth in the concluding years of the Weimar Republic. Just as a political Catholic establishment that was a bedrock of German elections since the 1870s self-destructed in the death throes of the Weimar parliamentary system, an intense national debate over Neumann and her miracles drove a cultural wedge between German Catholic constituencies that wanted fundamentally different things from their faith in the uncertain environment of the late 1920s. By disrupting Catholic belief systems and power structures, Neumann's stigmata also disordered Catholic politics.

The debate about Konnersreuth represented a power struggle within the Catholic community over the identity and future of the church. On the one hand, the Konnersreuth Circle passionately defended the authenticity of Neumann's vast number of miracles. Viewing her manifestation of Jesus's suffering on earth as a sign to repent or be punished, they approached her cause with utopian zeal. Constructing a web of publications and lectures, they brought their unique brand of spirituality to millions of Germans in hopes of a wave of conversions. Although Neumann offered a beacon of hope to the downtrodden, several powerful men joined her circle and provided invaluable support in extending her renown and defending her legitimacy. Their opponents contained an equally influential group of Catholic doctors, theologians, and priests who preferred a brand of Catholicism more in line with mainstream doctrine and demanded absolute scientific proof for any proclaimed miracle. The German bishops also became divided between Konnersreuth sympathizers and enemies and Bishop Michael Buchberger of Regensburg found himself caught in the middle. In this way, Therese Neumann became a symbol in a greater discussion about the role of faith in a rapidly modernizing world. Her circle leveraged her popularity in an entrenched battle for the "goods of salvation" against well-heeled adversaries.

Stephen Schloesser's *Jazz Age Catholicism* offers particular inspiration when interpreting the case of Therese Neumann.[2] Schloesser examines French avant-garde artists and intellectuals, such as Jacques Maritain and Georges Rouault, drawn to Catholic mysticism after the First World War, rejecting the notion that modern means secular. Such work demonstrates that men without typical Catholic upbringings engaged a Catholic revival in unorthodox ways in order to cope with the grief and trauma caused by the Great War. The Konnersreuth Circle also spearheaded a unique reawakening that used mystical faith to process German disillusionment during the 1920s. Even when posing as anti-modern traditionalists, the Konnersreuth Circle formulated a unique approach to Catholicism set firmly in the crises of the 1920s. While using rituals and symbols from both the early modern era and the ultramontane period of the nineteenth century, they deployed Neumann's stigmata to grapple with the destructive possibilities and threats singular to the twentieth century. Neumann's blood, visions, and miracles brought a new sense of order to a profoundly disoriented world. The so-called rational beliefs of their antagonists also constituted yet another method of enduring the uncertainty of the 1920s and 1930s for Catholic elites. In the Bourdieusian struggle between the Konnersreuth Circle, its enemies, and the church hierarchy, each side employed spiritualties intimately suited to Germany in the 1920s.

The fight over Neumann's sanctity between a mostly Bavarian set of loyalists and detractors from the northwest illustrates the cultural underbelly of divisions within Catholic politics that would ultimately doom the two parties that represented church interests. The shocking collapse of the Centre Party and Bavarian People's Party (BVP) in 1933 destroyed what had been a steady political minority since the 1870s and paved the way towards Nazi dictatorship. This disastrous decline occurred in part due to the self-interest, authoritarian political leadership, and spiritual crises of Chancellors Heinrich Brüning and Franz von Papen, as well as Centre Party Chairman Ludwig Kaas, between 1930 and the Enabling Act of 1933 that cemented Hitler's dictatorial power.[3] Some social historians suggest that the church and its political party could no longer use past explanations to solve the modern problems of massive unemployment and political crisis. For example, the once powerful *Volksverein für das katholische Deutschland,* an intellectual and literary centre for the working-class wing of the Centre Party, rapidly deteriorated due to financial crisis, scandal, falling membership, and a rhetoric of "social ethics" that failed to connect with the Centre Party's right or left flanks.[4] Most significantly, political Catholicism struggled because of the combination of its socio-economic diversity and its crucial role as coalition maker in the Weimar political system. As minority parties that were always central to creating functioning democratic coalitions with the Social Democratic Party, the liberal parties, and the nationalist parties, the Centre Party and the BVP consistently played prominent roles in the most controversial legislation of the era. Representing all of Germany's Catholic minority, their voters varied from Rhineland professionals to *Ruhrgebiet* workers to Bavarian peasants to Westphalian aristocrats. The compromises made by the Catholic parties while working in coalition with political movements their leaders and voters found repulsive simultaneously pushed away the working class to the left and alienated their conservative voters. Political Catholicism faced the unsavory task of maintaining Catholic authenticity while pursuing the necessary compromises with social democrats and liberals that came in a deeply divided parliamentary democracy.[5]

The fight over Konnersreuth's miracles highlighted a cultural element to this lack of unity within political Catholicism. Neumann and her circle fenced with the left-wing press over charges of fraud, using the opposition to her miracles by socialists, liberals, and communists as a method to mobilize Catholic support on her behalf. Her supporters also depicted elements of the Catholic political establishment as more friendly to these largely secular opponents of mysticism than to their own religious voters. They captured the widespread Catholic suspicion that their own party and clergy had been infiltrated by the very anticlerical forces of modernity that threatened the secularization of faith.

Prominent members of the Centre Party in northwestern Germany opposed the brand of piety espoused by the Konnersreuth supporters and proposed an approach more likely to gain acceptance among non-Catholics and the German middle class. Konnersreuth supporters responded with aggressive accusations against the Catholic authenticity of such politicians. They sometimes combined their attacks on the socialist, Communist, and liberal press, which regularly mocked Neumann as a fraud, with assaults against what they perceived to be "modern" or "rational" Catholics who hindered Neumann's perceived potential to convert wayward Catholics, Protestants, and Jews en masse to the Roman Catholic Church. Despite much stronger ties between the BVP and the Neumann family, Konnersreuth enthusiasts sometimes accused even this more rightward-leaning variant of political Catholicism as being too willing to compromise with the left of the political spectrum. The exaggeration of left-wing threats to Therese Neumann's safety and the allegations against the Centre Party as representing these non-Catholic interests simultaneously eroded the unity of political Catholicism and made Centre Party cooperation with liberals and social democrats more challenging. Nonetheless, Konnersreuth also showcased qualities that made devout Catholics an occasional thorn in the side of the Third Reich after 1933. The ideas about a Christian brand of human rights and the advocacy for cooperation with non-Catholic parties, including the social democrats, by Fritz Gerlich in his Konnersreuth-inspired newspaper provided a blueprint for anti-Nazi activism and the pursuit of Christian Democracy after the war.

The Konnersreuth Circle's bombastic attack on opponents further burdened an already strained Catholic political establishment. Yet Gerlich's mystically inspired political ideas foreshadowed the post-war cooperation with non-Catholic political entities in a stable parliamentary system opposed to fascism and communism. The cultural power of the Konnersreuth Circle damaged an already weakened political Catholic establishment and Weimar democracy but its disruptive force also introduced a set of conservative traditionalists to the Christian Democratic ideas that would dominate the 1950s.

The Struggle for Konnersreuth

After establishing her stature as a public figure, Therese Neumann faced an intense battle with Catholics and non-Catholics alike over the legitimacy of her miracles and the sanctity of her spiritual message. Neumann and her family first needed the support of her own town as Konnersreuth ultimately became a place that revolved around her weekly stigmata and the visitors she attracted. The Konnersreuth Circle also waged a campaign to have Neumann officially recognized by the church, a battle that lasted decades without a firm resolution. The debate over how and when she should be medically examined became particularly contentious. The German Bishops, including Regensburg's Michael Buchberger and Munich's Michael Faulhaber, remained divided over the meaning of Neumann, leaving the controversy about her miracles inconclusive. The deliberations about her sanctity indicated not only disagreement about the meaning of Catholicism in an industrialized age of mass politics but also provided the cultural background that helps explain the downfall of political Catholicism.

Neumann enjoyed enormous popularity within Konnersreuth and its surrounding towns. One local devotee proclaimed that the seer received "great honor and admiration" from her fellow townspeople because she represented a sanctuary that was not to be "touched by unclean hands." She also lauded Neumann's ability to communicate with everyday people despite her celebrity, comparing her to a professor who "disguises his title."[6] Dr Emil Scheller, who vacillated between support and doubt about Neumann's miracles, confirmed this depiction of village support. He wrote, "The background of Therese Neumann is unimpeachable and reputable. Therefore it is not only her faithful priest who has held his post for seventeen years that vouches for her but, besides her parents, the entire village."[7] This local popularity spread to neighbouring towns such as Waldsassen and Kronach as well as nearby Sudeten villages like Eger.[8] The Neumann family cemented this support by providing special access to their daughter. After Bishop Buchberger formally limited the flow of pilgrims to town, locals could still visit Neumann without restriction or special permission from the diocese on Good Fridays.[9]

While faith and a reputation for strong moral fibre drove much regional support, economics played a role as well. While Konnersreuth never opened shops that marketed religious kitsch like Lourdes, local businesses benefited enormously from the stream of pilgrims into town. The only pension in town owned by Hugo Schiml constantly filled its fifteen beds and even built an extension in the early 1930s. Other townspeople took pilgrims into their quarters to manage the crowds. Although they generally charged what outsiders regarded as fair prices, some reports suggested a gradual inflation during the early years of Neumann's celebrity. Neumann's elite guests also benefited the townspeople who supported her. For example, Dr Josef Mittendorfer of Munich, who became Neumann's confidant and personal doctor, frequently treated locals free of charge. While Mittendorfer proved a source of frustration for some other medical professionals already practicing in the area, his pro bono work aided Konnersreuth residents. A combination of local piety, loyalty to an upstanding family, and economic upswing turned residents into powerful advocates for Therese Neumann. In fact, when members of the tabloid press tried to photograph Neumann against her wishes the mayor and several neighbours rushed to her defence.[10]

Although the village appeared unified behind the Konnersreuth miracles, tension also emerged as Neumann's fame caused a degree of discontent. Among faithful Catholics in Konnersreuth, many churchgoers complained that Father Naber ignored all of his other duties in order to exclusively tend to the needs of his prized seer. This tension became even more pronounced when the Neumann family renovated their house and Therese spent several weeks in residence with Father Naber at the parish rectory. Many troubled residents suggested that their movement gradually became less focused on everyday Catholics and favoured those with intellectual or financial resources. Rumours circulated that the family accepted gifts and improved their lifestyle as a result of the stigmata. The increased presence of Erich von Waldburg-Zeil drew particular notice as did the Neumann house improvements. The purchase of a commercial truck by Neumann's brother-in-law, Johann Härtl, also attracted negative attention. Despite the fact that the family enjoyed a steady socio-economic ascent, they never openly profited from the stigmata and turned down several opportunities to cash in on the phenomenon through films, plays, or tabloid stories. The economic concern of their neighbours, however, also coincided with a sharp downturn in the fortunes of others. Sixty to seventy workers in town lost their jobs at nearby factories in 1930 and many farmers found themselves in severe debt as the depression deepened. The juxtaposition of one family's good fortune with everyone else's misfortune caused dissonance. While Neumann's spirituality comforted some townspeople in challenging times, her fame troubled others as they suffered the consequences of the century's worst economic crisis. Furthermore, many blamed the family for purposely limiting the number of pilgrims to the village, even though orders from Bishop Buchberger also influenced this development. Fewer visitors put pressure on men like Hugo Schiml who expanded to accommodate the larger crowds of 1926 and 1927. Finally, the Neumann family and their circle developed a reputation as bullies who used Neumann's spiritual capital to attack those who did not believe in her miracles. For example, a local bricklayer sued Fritz Gerlich for writing that his son's mental illness resulted from his lack of faith in the miracles. The young man apparently said in a local tavern that he would not believe in the Neumann family's "fraud" until he became "crazy (*narrisch*)." Gerlich suggested that God punished him when mental illness actually afflicted the man.[11] This inability to tolerate the limited dissent towards Neumann's stigmata created tension with the population. Despite these examples of local frustration, Therese Neumann enjoyed more support than scorn in her village.

Neumann's neighbours illustrated the quotidian local disputes over her sanctity, but the national debate became a war among Catholic intellectuals over the nature of the church. Although the strongest strains of Catholic criticism emerged from Centre Party strongholds of the northwest, two Bavarian theologians also challenged both the Konnersreuth Circle and the Bavarian bishops whom they viewed as too flexible with the spiritual rebellion they sensed in the *Oberpfalz* (Upper Palatinate). Johann Baptist Westermayr, leader of a seminary just outside Munich, and Georg Wunderle, a Franciscan who became rector of the University of Wurzburg, emerged as influential voices against the Konnersreuth Circle from within Bavaria itself. Theological specialists in the history of Catholic mysticism, they used the examples of past stigmatics to contest Neumann's authenticity. Konnersreuth understandably concerned these men because the lurid stories embarrassed the church and they felt duty-bound to protect the faith. They also astutely understood the subversive potential of the miracles for hierarchical authority at a time when it was already under siege.

After initial captivation by Neumann's charisma, Johann Westermayr decided her stigmata was inauthentic. He suspected mischief from the constant interference in Neumann's visions by the men who surrounded her, such as Naber and Wutz. It troubled Westermayr that they asked leading and sometimes non-spiritual questions while she was in a state of exalted rest, turning her into an "oracle." While he never accused her of fraudulence, he felt the truth about her miracles could not be known until the bishop removed her from Naber and Wutz and placed her in a convent for careful observation.[12] Westermayr scrutinized Neumann in order to compare her with sanctioned mystics of the past. He and other theologians relied on a scholarly understanding of such phenomenon. By applying academic theology to the study of miracles, he opposed Naber's abandonment of pastoral norms.

While the Konnersreuth Circle angered Westermayr as a theologian, he saw it as a threat to the coherency of the faith. For example, he overhead Neumann advise a priest to break with the rules governing confidentiality during confession. While the breach of protocol upset him, the interference by Neumann's state of exalted rest with the church's usual lines of authority irritated him even more. Furthermore, Westermayr expressed frustration that Neumann instructed an abbess of a convent to undertake a massive construction project that had been rejected by her superior while in a state of ecstasy. Breaches of doctrine and disrespect for the chain of command within the church threatened its long-term existence. Westermayr wanted to protect the faith from potentially pagan practices and save Neumann from her own worst excesses.

Finally, Therese Neumann upended Westermayr's sense of hierarchy. He became agitated about Neumann's empathy for Sister Canisia of Freiburg, a deceased and disgraced mystic devoted to the Sacred Heart whose family asked the Konnersreuth seer about the fate of their daughter in the afterlife. Neumann's confirmation of this woman's place in heaven while in exalted rest robbed her spirituality of legitimacy in Westermayr's eyes since Sister Canisia had been excommunicated. He questioned how the church could sanction a stigmatic who sanctified its most bitter opponents. With many similarities to Barbara Weigand, Sister Canisia argued in favour of elevating the worship of the Sacred Heart. With two rebellious priests that consecrated her hosts, she dispensed communion herself and led her own Eucharist processions without the endorsement of her diocese. She also argued that women should be permitted to take Holy Orders just like men. Sister Canisia became pregnant by one of the priests in her circle during the First World War and proclaimed that the child would be the second coming of Christ. If the population did not show faith in the messianic nature of this pregnancy, she suggested France would win the war and occupy Germany. More than any other miracle worker of her generation, Sister Canisia used her spiritual gifts to pursue an openly feminist agenda. Neumann said that Canisia suffered from mental health problems, excusing her from her sins. Westermayr complained bitterly about the hardship caused by Canisia who apparently died cursing members of the clergy. Neumann angered men like Westermayr even further when she described past popes and bishops of Regensburg suffering in purgatory. She even allegedly told a clergyman that he would go to purgatory because of how "dumb" his attitudes about her stigmata were.[13] In Therese Neumann, Westermayr correctly saw the potential for another female visionary with a more powerful circle of friends that could shake the foundations of clerical authority on a level far greater than Sister Canisia was capable. Neumann used her visions to depict an egalitarian afterlife where church fathers could suffer while awaiting entrance into heaven for longer than an excommunicated feminist. One wonders whether Neumann consciously or subconsciously elevated a woman who undermined the male-dominated hierarchy to advocate increased spiritual leadership for women.

Much like Westermayr, Georg Wunderle started his investigation of Neumann with some sympathy for her cause and retained a degree of personal respect for her after becoming an opponent. Wunderle conceded that Neumann had integrity and concluded that her experiences were deeply pious but not miraculous. Wunderle wanted an extensive investigation and medical exam before any proclamations could be made on Neumann's behalf.[14] He also disagreed with Neumann's inaccurate description of some gospel scenes from her visions. Although accused of malice against the family because they banned him from their house after a few visits, Wunderle claimed that his "struggle was purely scientific." In a letter to Cardinal Eugenio Pacelli, Wunderle claimed his "viewpoint" represented that of the "educated Catholics of Germany."[15] Much like Westermayr, Wunderle opposed the Konnersreuth Circle in favour of a more intellectual Catholicism grounded in careful study of past seers endorsed by the church.

Georg Wunderle reserved his greatest outrage for the Konnersreuth Circle's perceived assault on ecclesiastical power. He believed the Neumann family's rural innocence was ruined by powerful men like Gerlich and Wutz who sought personal gain from the miracles. Wunderle viewed these men as a threat to the dignity of the bishops. He agreed with a fellow Konnersreuth adversary, Fritz Kern, who referred to Gerlich as a "half-baked Catholic." Wunderle felt Gerlich and Naber turned a pious and spiritually gifted woman into a "Christ oracle" with no credibility. He pressured the Bavarian bishops to take a firmer stance against the group and lobbied for Father Naber's removal from his post in Konnersreuth.[16] Wunderle protected the church's control of the "goods of salvation" from upstart theologians and converts.

A much larger group of doctors, professors, and clergy from northwestern Germany used medical science to more sternly challenge the stigmata. While explanations varied from fraudulence to hysteria to telepathy, a "united front" of Catholic intellectuals emerged that supported an influential network of middle-class associations and several strongholds of the Centre Party. Concerned about the reputation of the church among educated Germans as well as preserving their own power within the Catholic community, these men left questions about Neumann's state of exalted rest to the theologians and instead parsed her medical miracles.

This Catholic medical establishment relied on the evidence of Dr Otto Seidl from a hospital in nearby Waldsassen. Seidl treated Neumann's illness starting in 1920 and along with the Protestant Dr Ewald of Erlangen he oversaw Neumann during an official fourteen-day examination in her home with four nuns. Ordered by Bishop Buchberger of Regensburg and reluctantly permitted by the Neumann family, the exam scrutinized Neumann's weight, urine, stool, and stigmata wounds while the nuns allowed her no privacy to rule out the possibility of fraudulence. These fourteen days from 13 July to 28 July 1927 remained the only official exam ever permitted by the Neumann family. Seidl reported his findings in a public lecture to the Catholic Medical Association of the Netherlands on 4 November 1928. It speaks to the burning nature of the Konnersreuth question that 250 Catholic doctors from Germany and the Netherlands attended this event. While Seidl felt assured that Neumann received no nourishment during the two weeks, her weight and urine tests suggested she was not fasting. While her defenders used these results to confirm the miracle, Seidl still had doubts and suggested another exam. Much like his Bavarian counterparts, Westermayr and Wunderle, Seidl expressed sympathy for Neumann and her family. He described them as "simple, upright, religious, hardworking, and very austere people." However, he diagnosed Neumann with hysteria prior to her miracles. He concluded that her blindness and paralysis had roots in the trauma experienced during the fire. After the 1927 assessment, he concluded that Neumann could be easily manipulated by others and theorized that autosuggestion remained a distinct possibility. He felt Father Naber and the religious environment of her family caused subconscious changes in her psyche that produced the visions and bleeding. Despite his fondness for the family and the desire of the Konnersreuth Circle to use his exam as evidence in favour of Neumann's miracles, he doubted the religious nature of her experiences and instead thought they could be explained with the growing field of parapsychology.[17] Grounded in the belief that paranormal events have scientific explanations, parapsychology influenced German medicine from the late nineteenth century until the mid-twentieth century and led many doctors to discount stigmata and Marian apparitions as resulting from "natural" causes, such as telepathy and hypnosis.[18] The emphasis on ideas like parapsychology among doctors who presented their viewpoints as rational illustrates that these men were no more or less modern than the Konnersreuth Circle. Both advocates and critics of Konnersreuth converged with a broader German fascination in the supernatural during the Weimar years.

The material produced by Seidl and Ewald sparked one of the most aggressive attacks on Konnersreuth's legitimacy by Dr Josef Deutsch of *Dreifaltigkeits* hospital in Lippstadt. His first book on the matter in 1932 advanced a scientific reproach of the miracles with less of the personal praise for Neumann and her family. Genuinely perplexed by what he perceived as a threat to his faith, he based his analysis upon published accounts as well as thousands of pages of correspondence with proponents and opponents of the miracles.[19] Deutsch used his medical expertise to challenge the scientific claims made by Fritz Gerlich and Chaplain Helmut Fahsel of Berlin in favour of the stigmata. For example, he mocked Gerlich's method: "The diagnoses of Gerlich can best be described with the following 'recipe': One takes a set of possible but implausible theories; mixes them with one or the other impossibility; spices everything with blatant fantasy and some quotes and press clippings from those with preconceived opinions; and then the diagnosis is finished." Deutsch argued hysteria was the most likely cause of Neumann's miracles. He cited five doctors that examined Neumann prior to her fame as well as the disability pension she received for several years before 1926. Deutsch contended that her eleven accidents in less than a half-year indicated an unbalanced woman in the aftermath of trauma. He wanted all means necessary used to coerce an exam where a conclusive diagnosis could be reached and demanded discipline of priests like Fahsel who wrote in favour of Neumann before the matter reached resolution.[20] Fearless in his denunciation of clergymen who supported or enabled Neumann, Deutsch's writings were just as destabilizing of church hierarchy as those of Neumann's advocates.

A desire to defend the faith from embarrassment and define it as a genuinely modern belief system motivated Deutsch. Claiming to speak for a majority of Catholic doctors, he felt duty-bound to protect his religion from humiliation and demanded deeper measures by the bishops to protect their own reputations.[21] In a letter to Wunderle, he defended his book against critics with the following response: "As a Catholic doctor it is my duty to cause doubt." In another letter to Westermayr he suggested that it was his "task to protect Catholicism from disgrace." He went further to say that the religion represented in the publications of Gerlich and the Konnersreuth Circle represented a "metaphysical-sacramental positivism" that was "anything but Catholic." In the same letter he also accused the Konnersreuth Circle as being so "psychopathic" that its members could not be considered truly Catholic.[22] Rejecting a reductionist understanding of the miraculous, Deutsch sought reconciliation between Catholic customs and science. He argued that natural laws and the scientific order of God's world proved one of the greatest cornerstones of Christian faith and should not be discredited by false prophets. While Deutsch believed in the existence of religious miracles that happened in the past, he believed new miracles needed to pass rigorous tests of logic. Allegiance to fake miracles would unnecessarily erode the scientific order at the core of the human belief in God.[23] While the Konnersreuth Circle experienced salvation from disorderly times through the stigmata and other physical signs of God's presence, men like Deutsch responded to the same era by seeking comfort in the natural order of God's plan.

Although Deutsch aligned himself with other doctors and theologians demanding a rigorous clinical exam, he placed less faith in parapsychology than Seidl and others of his era. Deutsch also rejected a well-known study by Albert Lechler of a German girl, Elizabeth K., whom Lechler caused to bleed while hypnotized. Instead he relied on an explanation of feminine hysteria, a concept with roots in the nineteenth century.[24] Unlike Seidl, who depicted Neumann as pliable in the hands of powerful male supporters, Deutsch felt hysteria subtly caused her to exploit others. "Hysterical piety" led to unconscious trickery that fooled enthusiasts hunting for miracles. Deutsch compared Neumann to young women from his practice whom he blamed for wildly ripping open their wounds and bandages after surgery. He described hysterical women as "I-centered" beings who naturally subverted and feared their doctors.[25] Deutsch suggested that hysterical patients could never be trusted because of their predisposition to lie.[26] This gendered interpretation of feminine hysteria caused him to diagnose Neumann as a mentally ill manipulator of the church that had to be stopped for the sake of its image among educated Germans. His writing caused even more outlandish descriptions of hysteria by other critics. Some doubtful clergy carefully tracked the amount of blood from Neumann's eyes during the stigmata because they believed it replaced the blood she would have shed in a normal menstrual cycle. They linked the alleged cessation of menstrual bleeding by Neumann in 1919 to hysteria. Some observers went even further to suggest that her fragile mental state caused her to spread her own menstrual blood or that of her mother on her face and body for the Friday Suffering.[27] In hindsight this misogynist viewpoint is as incongruent with modernity as faith in stigmata. Much like his colleagues' promotion of parapsychology, Deutsch's attachment to a diagnosis of feminine hysteria for a patient he had never personally seen illustrates that even those who perceived themselves as rational Catholics departed from a truly empirical process when discussing miracles.

Deutsch's book sparked an alliance of largely northwestern Catholic practitioners that coordinated a counternarrative against the publications of the Konnersreuth Circle. Like Wunderle and Westermayr, some critics resided in Bavaria. However, most of them emerged from Centre Party strongholds in the Rhineland, Westphalia, the Eifel, and even Alsace. Deutsch, Dr H. Heermann of Essen, Dr Paul Martini of Bonn, and Dr Michael Witry of Metz led a circle of intellectuals that published anti-Konnersreuth books, essays, and articles in coordination with one another. These Catholics united behind their "medical authority" to thwart the activities of Gerlich, Wutz, and Fahsel and depict their approach to Catholicism as erroneous.[28]

This activism among Catholic doctors paralleled the distaste expressed by both clergy and lay leaders in the dioceses of Münster, Trier, Osnabruck, and Paderborn – all of whom rallied around the writings of Deutsch and strengthened the regional divide. For example, *Domprobst* Adolf Donders of Münster, a confidant of Bishop Clemens August von Galen, supported Deutsch and complained about the positive press Konnersreuth received in the influential Catholic periodical *Hochland*. Furthermore, another theologian and professor from Münster attacked Gerlich as a psychologically unbalanced convert after witnessing him interrupt one of Wunderle's lectures about Neumann to a closed audience in Erfurt. The outspoken Norbert Brühl passionately opposed Konnersreuth from Trier as did well-placed clergy in Osnabruck and Paderborn. Johann Westermayr received letters from several of these regions charging Neumann with fraud, brazen disobedience, and possession by the devil.[29] The leaders of lay associations in the northwest also supported Deutsch's writings. Caritas leaders in Paderborn complained about "terrorists" like Friedrich Ritter von Lama who used all means necessary to attack opponents of Konnersreuth, and the director of a Catholic press in Saarbrücken organized lectures in the diocese of Trier by Wunderle for several Catholic associations.[30] This elite regional support for men like Deutsch and Wunderle illustrated the concern about church authority and the synthesis of scientific rationalism and

Catholic faith in the heartland of the Centre Party. Ecclesiastical and lay authorities alike objected more frequently to Therese Neumann than Bavarian elites.

The Konnersreuth Circle responded to the onslaught of Catholic sceptics with rhetorical appeals of their own. Those with some distance from Neumann's immediate circle tended to be more aggressive in their attacks on a church establishment they felt abandoned God's call for repentance. Von Lama led this group of Catholic publicists and pilgrims, accusing the clergy of not representing the "true" church. Von Lama also directly challenged the Catholic integrity of doctors like Deutsch and Heermann, who he felt favoured the interests of the medical community over their Catholic faith. He also reproached them as a "clique of free masons" rather than genuine Catholics.[31] Von Lama questioned the Catholic faith of those opposed to Konnersreuth in brash and uncompromising terms. Neumann's visions sometimes stoked such anger with the clergy. Catholic convert and reformer John M. Oesterreicher remembered one of Neumann's visions of Calvary where "Prelates of the Church" appeared in "red capes" sneering and mocking the dying saviour.[32] Many in Konnersreuth interpreted such images as critiques of priests and bishops who doubted her authenticity and who were secular agents from within the priesthood.

Those closer to Neumann's inner circle calibrated their message more carefully, yet insinuated similar charges against their adversaries. Seeking to deflect accusations regarding obedience to authority, Gerlich and Wutz challenged their opponents without openly flaunting religious officials. The leaders of Konnersreuth used their own credentials as historians, theologians, and doctors to combat the intellectual authority of men like Deutsch. Furthermore, Gerlich published the ideas of Professors Johannes Bauer and Johannes Maria Verweyen in the pages of his newpaper, *Der gerade Weg* (The Straight Path). Gerlich used logical analysis and the credentials of sympathetic medical professionals to establish scientific and rational grounds for faith in Konnersreuth as well. For example, he used the writings of Dr Joseph Höhn, the director of a medical research institute in Essen, to rebut a Heermann article published in *Theologie und Glaube* (Theology and Faith), a periodical for clergy in the diocese of Paderborn.[33]

Gerlich used such analysis to challenge the scientific process of Konnersreuth critics. He accused Deutsch and Heermann of presenting their viewpoints as the "only" authority on the matter. Since the study of medical science required debates about competing hypotheses and opinions, he suggested this stance undermined Deutsch's own medical legitimacy. Often accused by their critics of stubbornly advancing only their own steadfast faith in Neumann's miracles, the Konnersreuth Circle reversed this charge against the doctors who discredited them. Gerlich also used an intercepted letter that attempted to formalize this so-called "united front" among doctors opposed to the Konnersreuth miracles. Once again, Gerlich questioned the objectivity of medical professionals who approached a topic they already agreed upon without including any dissenting voices. Gerlich insinuated that such practices indicated a hidden agenda that lurked beneath a "mask" of scientific study and interest in the greater good of Catholicism.

Unlike von Lama, Gerlich never openly accused doctors like Deutsch and Heermann of secret Freemasonry. Rather he implied it by presenting them as eroding the Catholic faith from within. Using a letter from a priest in Nurnberg, Gerlich compared the Konnersreuth Circle to the "meek," whom the Gospels ordained to carry the word of God, and their opponents to the "powerful," who presented obstacles to their mission. Furthermore, Gerlich likened the rise of National Socialism and communism in his own era to the prevalence of "paganism" in the Holy Roman Empire. Catholics who claimed that miracles were only needed during Jesus' lifetime – and not in the modern world – threatened the persistence of Catholic faith. In an age of violent anti-Christians, Gerlich understood Neumann's miracles as central to prove the existence of God in an increasingly godless world. Gerlich implicitly questioned the motives of Catholics who challenged modern miracles as pursuing an alternate agenda. He also highlighted the collaboration of Deutsch and Heermann with monist Eduard Aigner and Protestant Dr Ewald. He accused elite Catholics connected to external enemies of the church of a plot to undermine religious visionaries and by extension the entire Roman Catholic religion. Such attacks had similarities to charges against the Centre Party for its coalition work with social democrats and liberals.[34] Gerlich, like von Lama, viewed anti-Konnersreuth circles as threatening not only to their interpretation of Catholicism but also to the entire existence of the faith. Each side in this debate imagined their own interpretation of Catholicism as pure and any deviations caused them to question the authenticity of their intraconfessional opponents.

The struggle over Konnersreuth attracted a wide array of devotees for Therese Neumann. For example, when Neumann stopped for a break during a longer trip with Wutz and Naber in the Bavarian town of Seinsheim, a wealthy local businessman and BVP politician saw her and immediately kneeled on the sidewalk as she passed.[35] However, several prominent Catholic patrons materialized outside of Bavaria as well. In the heart of the generally hostile *Ruhrgebiet*, Caritas director Otto Schluesener of Recklinghausen emerged as a believer in Neumann. A congregant from a parish in Cologne also wrote to Wunderle in opposition to the stance on Neumann by the "largely educated clergy" in his diocese, whom he accused of a materialistic and rationalistic interpretation of Catholicism influenced by monism that undermined faith.[36] Furthermore, Neumann also found benefactors at the pilgrimage shrine of Altötting and in the bishop's residences at Speyer, Stuttgart, and Eichstätt. The mystic travelled to Speyer where Bishop Ludwig Sebastian conducted his own examination of her.[37]

The hotly contested battle over the Konnersreuth miracles entrapped Bishop Michael Buchberger, leader of Neumann's own diocese of Regensburg. His personal style tended towards reconciliation rather than conflict and Therese Neumann's rise to celebrity disrupted his entire reign. Buchberger succeeded Anton von Henle, who expressed severe reservations about Neumann but also oversaw a theologically divided bureaucracy in Regensburg. Brought in as an outsider to make peace among the high-ranking officials of the diocese, Buchberger arrived from Munich as a close protégé of the city's powerful cardinal and Archbishop Michael Faulhaber.[38] This desire to find safe middle ground in theological and political disputes made Buchberger the focal point of activists both for and against the Neumann miracles. Attacked by the Konnersreuth Circle as abandoning God's urgent presence in Neumann's stigmata and scorned by Konnersreuth opponents as too weak with rebellious congregants, Buchberger tolerated but never sanctioned the worship of his diocese's most famous Catholic.

Initially Buchberger showed more sympathy with Therese Neumann than the previous bishop.[39] When Johann Westermayr wrote to Buchberger about his increasingly sceptical attitude about Neumann, the bishop answered with a warning not to rush to judgment. Buchberger referenced the positive impressions by Neumann on several officials he sent from Regensburg and he expressed hope that Catholics would not join the "enemies of the Church" who mocked Neumann in the left-wing press.[40] Furthermore, the diocese of Regensburg purportedly aided the Neumann family financially in its lawsuits against secular groups that exploited Neumann's image without permission. For example, Buchberger helped the family litigate against a theatre group that put on a play about Neumann in Berlin.[41] Although such court cases opposed groups that used Neumann to negatively portray Bavarian Catholicism more broadly, Buchberger's financial assistance demonstrated at least some empathy with the mystic and her family.[42]

Michael Buchberger's attitude towards Konnersreuth soured starting with his own visit to Neumann on 22 March 1928. He travelled with his suffragan bishop as well as four university professors, including the Catholic medical researcher Paul Martini of Bonn. Buchberger hoped to assess Neumann's condition with professional assistance, convince the family of the urgency of a clinical exam, and halt the flow of pilgrims to Konnersreuth. Under the influence of Martini's negative assessment, Buchberger left Konnersreuth frustrated. The gruff reception by Neumann's father perturbed the bishop. Although impressed by the simplicity and austerity of the now famous Neumann home as well as the piety of Therese Neumann herself, she proved evasive with respect to Buchberger's wishes. Neumann argued that her family and her priest could not turn away pilgrims because the saviour wanted her miracles to convert sinners. Furthermore, she informed him that Jesus had no desire for her to undergo further medical tests since most doctors lacked the necessary religious devotion.[43] More critical than Buchberger, Martini theorized that either Neumann perpetrated a "pious fraud" or suffered from hysteria. He complained bitterly about the family's regular clearance of Neumann's room at scientifically important moments to open windows and improve air flow in the tiny house. Martini worried that Neumann found herself in over her head with no other option except continued profession of her own sanctity.[44] Although not as sceptical as Martini, Buchberger's correspondence gradually became more negative towards Konnersreuth after the visit. As an editor of a major encyclopedia of theology, Buchberger lost much reverence for the Konnersreuth Circle when it obstructed a scholarly assessment of the stigmata.

Buchberger's exchange with Bishop Augustinus Kilian of Limburg in 1930 summed up his developing position. As an admirer of Neumann, the aging Kilian scorned Buchberger's decision to drastically reduce the number of visitors to Konnersreuth by requiring pilgrims show a letter of permission from the bishop's office. Hoping to curb attention to Neumann until a final decision on her authenticity, Buchberger instituted this policy in 1928. Defending the "mindset" of the "entire Catholic population" Kilian contended that a bishop's office had "no right to forbid Catholics from visiting a household of good standing with moral goals in mind." In response Buchberger lashed out against Neumann's followers. First, he disliked the stream of pilgrims to Konnersreuth whose sensationalist interests embarrassed the church. He also discouraged the "miracle-seeking" clergy attracted to Neumann. Furthermore, Buchberger derided Neumann's role as "oracle" and "information bureau" when she informed people about the fate of dead loved ones, and he denounced the Konnersreuth Circle's subversive attitude regarding his power as their most serious infraction. He expressed frustration that Neumann travelled all over Germany without notifying him while he wrote permission forms for visitations. He complained that Ferdinand Neumann's demeanour towards church authorities was "correct in principle but dismissive in practice." Later in the letter, Buchberger sarcastically wrote, "The so-called Konnersreuth Circle knows everything and the Bishop is proficient in nothing. The Protestant Dr. Gerlich knows much more about the events in Konnersreuth than the bishop of the diocese."[45] Buchberger turned personally against the Neumann family because he recognized the danger they posed to his own power and the unity and coherency of the faith.

In addition to personal disillusionment, Buchberger endured tremendous pressure from Catholics in Germany and especially the Vatican to maintain a stricter stance regarding Konnersreuth. Buchberger received regular correspondence from anti-Konnersreuth figures, such as Deutsch, Wunderle, and Brühl, which no doubt burdened a leader averse to conflict. However, figures close to the Vatican played a particularly significant role in pushing Buchberger towards action. Augustino Gemelli, a Franciscan experimental psychologist and rector of the University of Milan, visited Konnersreuth in 1928 and issued a critical report to Buchberger. He doubted the authenticity of the miracles and questioned the demeanour of Naber, Wutz, and Neumann's family. Gemelli believed autosuggestion was the most likely cause of Neumann's symptoms but also considered fraud a possibility. Gemelli recommended a clinical exam as soon as possible where Neumann would have almost no contact with supporters, friends, or family members. Gemelli's report waded more deeply into the Konnersreuth struggle, praising the sobriety of Konnersreuth critics and condemning the blind faith and interference of Naber, Wutz, and Gerlich. In fact, the Konnersreuth Circle's threat to the church's top-down structure represented his gravest concern as he disparaged the many lay Catholics who consulted Neumann about theological matters suited only for the clergy. Gemelli appealed to Buchberger for swift action, requesting the removal of Father Naber from Konnersreuth.[46]

Augustino Gemelli signified more than just another medical observer of these miracles. Rather he represented a powerful Catholic intellectual with close ties to the Vatican, carrying even more weight than Professor Martini. In aiding Gemelli's Konnersreuth visit, Cardinal Michael Faulhaber indicated that Gemelli came at the behest of the Secretary of the Holy Office, Cardinal Merry del Val, and possibly even Pope Pius XI himself. The standpoint of the Vatican seemed ambiguous as Pius XI gave Therese Neumann an official papal blessing in the 1920s and is rumoured to have sent her a sacred relic on the eve of his death. There is also alleged evidence in the Vatican archives that Eugenio Pacelli, the future Pius XII, harboured hopes that Neumann's stigmata would prove genuine.[47] Nonetheless, several forces within the Vatican desired a clear medical verdict to avoid embarrassment. Therefore, Buchberger responded to this critical report concurring with Gemelli's assessment of Wunderle and assuring the professor that he denied Fritz Gerlich's book the church's official imprimatur.[48]

More pressure emerged after the visit of an official from the Apostolic Nunciature in Munich, Monsignor Dr Brunelli. Describing his first minutes witnessing Neumann in a state of ecstasy, Brunelli expressed understanding for those with faith in her miracles: "I confess that my first sight of her made a strong impression. Therese sat in bed, her arms outstretched and face full of blood. Her shirt was also tarnished with blood as was her headscarf." However, he quickly felt "indifferent" towards the spectacle and increasingly suspected fraud. He expressed disappointment that her blood seemed dried and did not appear to originate from her eyes. Furthermore, he accused Naber of tampering with her ecstasy and nervously evading Brunelli's questions and requests. For example, Naber refused to show him Neumann's head wounds and denied having photographs of Neumann that a teacher in town insisted he had seen. He characterized the Konnersreuth Circle as having "excuses, contradictions, insecurity, and possibly lies." Brunelli claimed to leave Konnersreuth "disappointed, doubtful, and unsatisfied." He expressed his greatest concern once again with the lack of respect shown to him as a member of the clergy. Neumann's parents made him linger at their door in cold weather for fifteen minutes and Naber forced him to wait for another half hour. Once inside the house, the Neumann family treated him curtly and he found Naber uncooperative. Brunelli recommended an immediate transfer of Naber away from Konnersreuth, adding another critical voice to Buchberger's pile of correspondence on the matter.[49]

Buchberger responded to such critical reports by taking a public stand in favour of a new assessment of Therese Neumann. Although an exam had been the subject of negotiations since his visit to Konnersreuth in 1928, Buchberger remained largely silent on the issue in public. However, he used the occasion of the Bavarian Bishops' Conference in 1932 to openly request that Neumann submit to an exam with the support of his fellow bishops. This statement caused a renewed wave of correspondence between Bishop Buchberger, Cardinal Michael Faulhaber of Munich, and Ferdinand Neumann about a temporary institutionalization. Many adherents suggested that Neumann remained open to it in 1932, but she obeyed her father when he snubbed the bishop's request. Critics maintain that Neumann could never have embraced the idea of an exam since she and Naber previously claimed that the voice of the saviour told her not to submit. If she relented in 1932, it would contradict her earlier prophesy and invalidate her spiritual capital.[50]

While Buchberger publicly leveraged the prestige of his office to force Neumann into a clinic, he privately offered numerous accommodating ways to assuage the fears of the family. For example, Buchberger and Faulhaber arranged for Neumann to see a Munich doctor who treated one of her ill siblings in previous years and whose Catholic credentials were above reproach. Faulhaber promised that Neumann should have no concern about any "doubting Thomases" in this exam. They also offered the possibility of a four-week exam in a convent where Neumann could be shielded from the public gaze. It seems unlikely that the family would have paid for any medical expenses as several Catholic doctors also offered their services pro bono. Furthermore, Faulhaber carefully explained that Buchberger asked for a service similar to that of the medical bureau at the pilgrimage site in Lourdes. Nonetheless, Neumann refused to grant consent and deeply embarrassed Buchberger. Besides rejecting Buchberger's public command, the Neumann family courted bishops from outside of Germany to contradict him. For example, the Konnersreuth Circle publicized the temporary opposition of Cardinal Karel Kaspar of Prague, a Konnersreuth ally, to a coerced medical test. Although Kaspar eventually reversed his public stance, Faulhaber and Buchberger regretted the incident. They both complained that Ferdinand Neumann and his "house friends," such as Gerlich and Wutz, made it impossible for Buchberger to fulfil the command of the twenty-fifth session of the Council of Trent that demanded a Catholic man obey his diocesan bishop. Buchberger gambled that a pious family would not dare such a public rebuke to their bishop, but he underestimated the power of Neumann's stigmata among her family and followers who privileged her direct spiritual connection with God over obedience to him.[51] Indeed the Konnersreuth Circle crafted a brand of Catholicism less dependent on official leaders and more reliant on unmediated and personal relationships with God.

Despite such bitterness over the failed attempt to resolve the Konnersreuth crisis and the public loss of face, Buchberger ultimately stayed the course of moderation. While he and Faulhaber worked to reign in as much of the debate from the public as possible, Buchberger chose not to ostracize the Konnersreuth Circle from the Catholic community. To the great frustration of critics, Buchberger rejected the suggestions by Brunelli and Gemelli to relocate Father Naber or excommunicate the Neumanns as punishment for their disobedience. This decision resulted in part from Buchberger's desire to avoid extreme confrontation and also from the pressure caused by the widespread devotion to Neumann. She had numerous enemies but also a broad national and international support system as well as grassroots backing within Buchberger's own diocese. The Bavarian bishops received correspondence that accused them of endorsing Konnersreuth but just as many letters scorning them for their lack of sustenance for the Neumann family.[52] Despite a rising distaste for the ways that the Konnersreuth Circle challenged him, Buchberger could not risk alienating an entire segment of fiercely pious Bavarian Catholics. Buchberger seemed more exhausted by the Konnersreuth struggle than mobilized for a fight. In the aftermath of the argument over a medical exam, the Konnersreuth Circle considered moving Therese Neumann to Eichstätt where Wutz lived and Neumann's sister worked as his housekeeper. This strategy would situate her close to several elite allies and under the protection of the more sympathetic Bishop Konrad von Preysing. When Buchberger corresponded with Preysing about the potential move he expressed enthusiasm to be rid of the controversy. It was only the embarrassment for church authority that caused Buchberger to oppose such a course of action.[53] He lacked the charisma and decisive action to challenge a now popular mystic in his diocese and permitted her an indefinite ambiguous status that allowed those who found her compelling to venerate the stigmata without threatening their relationship to the institutional church.

The curious relationship of Buchberger's mentor, Michael Faulhaber, to Therese Neumann also sheds light on Buchberger's caution. While publicly coy towards the Konnersreuth miracles, Faulhaber ultimately demonstrated genuine faith in the stigmata. Faulhaber's initial stance exhibited cautious optimism about the authenticity of Neumann's bloody spectacles and clairvoyance. In a public sermon on 9 November 1927, Faulhaber expressed wonder and dismay at the growing hostility in the public debate. He declared, "The public discussion of Konnersreuth will not find peace. In families, on street cars, on the way to work, and in breaks from work, the tongues of Munich residents discuss the matter to the point of exhaustion and the European press spreads the issue to even wider circles." While he reminded the audience that Jesus performed miracles and faith in them was central to Catholicism, he stressed that the Christian saviour also cautioned against false miracles. While taking a firm stance in favour of a prolonged university exam of Neumann and advising doubters that there was no compulsion to believe in such miracles even when they had official sanction, Faulhaber subtly revealed his sympathies. The cardinal marvelled at how Neumann converted the wayward and compared the "village child" to saints who turned sinners "back to Christ" through their miraculous works.[54] While maintaining a diplomatic tone, Faulhaber explicitly encouraged tolerance for Neumann's followers.

Faulhaber's personal involvement with Konnersreuth was significant. He visited Neumann and reportedly said mass in her room in 1928. He also invited Neumann, Gerlich, Wutz, and Naber to sleep in his residence during a trip they already planned to Munich. Von Lama revealed the nature of these visits in newspaper articles to the intense frustration of Faulhaber. Although clearly intrigued by Neumann's mysticism, he protected Buchberger through public silence.[55]

Such caution emerged once again with the publication of Gerlich's books about Neumann. While Faulhaber's correspondence indicates a friendly relationship with the man whose life he would try to save during the Third Reich, he maintained distance from Gerlich's book. He explained that only Buchberger could grant an imprimatur since the stigmata occurred in his diocese, but he encouraged Gerlich to only publish with such support from his protégé. Faulhaber also prevented lectures by men such as Johannes Mayerhofer, who promoted the Konnersreuth Circle in Munich, and he criticized the writings of von Lama.[56] Once again Faulhaber maintained private devotion to Neumann's miracles, but avoided formal links to the Konnersreuth Circle.

This search for middle ground despite his sympathies led to great misunderstandings about the powerful cardinal's attitude. While the Konnersreuth Circle claimed Faulhaber as one of their own, many observers mistook him for an opponent of the stigmata. For example, Johann Westermayr insisted that despite Faulhaber's restriction of his anti-Konnersreuth lectures, the cardinal saw the phenomenon from his critical point of view.[57] Furthermore, champions of Konnersreuth blamed Faulhaber's silence and public ambivalence for legitimating the positions of critics such as Josef Deutsch.[58] In fact, Faulhaber officially broke with Konnersreuth on the issues of a medical exam and clerical power. He became incensed at the Neumann family's refusal to submit before a request from their bishop even after his own personal intervention in the matter. He sarcastically wrote to Cardinal Kaspar of Prague: "It is impossible to understand how the Bavarian bishops could commit such barbarism as to want Therese subjected to the entire medical staff of a university." He articulated concern about the contradiction between Neumann's increasingly hectic travel schedule and the family's stated desire to shelter her at all costs. He also accused her followers of "fanatically" searching for new miracles.[59] Weary with the public debate, Faulhaber became almost as exasperated with Konnersreuth as Buchberger.

Despite such anger, Faulhaber possessed a persevering private bond to Therese Neumann that separated his viewpoint from that of the Regensburg bishop. Despite continued drama over a potential exam during the Third Reich, speculation swirled about Faulhaber's secret relationship to Neumann because some journalists said the stigmatic relieved the major health concerns plaguing Faulhaber during the war. Although Faulhaber once again sought public distance, he admitted that the visit to his residence had occurred and he thanked Neumann for her prayers.[60] While never a full member of the Konnersreuth Circle or even the most enthusiastic Catholic bishop in support of her cause, Faulhaber nonetheless cultivated a private spiritual connection to this religious figure. He therefore became a powerful protector whose affections likely bolstered Buchberger's hesitance to pursue the most severe discipline possible. From Bavarian peasants to Germany's most influential cardinal, the miracles of Therese Neumann shaped the experience of Catholics as they endured the tumult of the Weimar Republic and the start of the Third Reich, driving even a bastion of institutional power to a more personalized piety outside the confines of formal liturgy. The spectre of a powerful Bavarian cardinal privately supporting Neumann against the wishes of several Catholic professionals and intellectuals in the northwest also accentuated the regional and cultural divides between the leaders and voters of Weimar's Catholic political parties.

Religious Culture and the Downfall of Political Catholicism

One of the great tragedies of German history is how the Catholic political establishment, which resisted the *Kulturkampf* (culture war) of Otto von Bismarck and German liberals during the 1870s, withstood the revolutionary fervour of 1919, and led the Christian Democratic wave against communism during the 1950s, meekly facilitated the death of Weimar democracy and the rise of the Third Reich. The burdens of coalition governance in a parliamentary democracy, which they escaped prior to the First World War and shared with Protestants after the Second World War, proved a challenge that Catholic political elites could not overcome. Serving as a minority party crucial to making every governing coalition function, the Centre Party became increasingly partitioned from within. Party members and voters also grew weary of anticlerical coalition partners. Divisions and fragmentation best explain the collapse of political Catholicism, and the political connections within the debate over Therese Neumann provide social and cultural context to this downfall. While revealing some of the grass-roots causes for the segmentation of Catholic political relationships, the Konnersreuth Circle's most prominent and exceptional member, Fritz Gerlich, also demonstrated the basis upon which some elements of Catholic Germany would resist Nazi Germany and spark a broader and more successful Christian Democratic movement after the war. In sum, the Konnersreuth Circle and its opponents both inside and outside the Catholic community present a microcosm for the fall of political Catholicism and its rebirth as Christian Democracy.

The advent of Weimar democracy plunged political Catholicism from the fringes of the Wilhelmine power structure into the mainstream, but it also exposed numerous divisions within its party infrastructure and electorate. The Centre Party, which represented voters from everywhere outside of Bavaria and found most of its support in the northwest, suffered from divisions between its workers' movement, led by Adam Stegerwald and Joseph Joos, its centrist democrats, represented by Wilhelm Marx, and its right-wing nationalists, led by Ludwig Kaas and Franz von Papen. In fact, the Catholic community disagreed about the very legitimacy of democracy in Germany as characterized by the public 1922 debate between the antidemocratic Cardinal Faulhaber of Munich and the prorepublican Konrad Adenauer of Cologne at the annual Catholic Congress.[61] Although it featured in every coalition and produced several chancellors and one serious presidential candidate, the party lost male voters to the social democrats and the German nationalist parties. It maintained its share of the electorate by successfully courting Catholic women, newly enfranchised in 1919.[62]

These divisions became even deeper when Bavarian Catholics departed the Centre Party at the end of the First World War to form the BVP. Formed largely to defend Bavarian regional interests and promote federalism, the BVP also tended to be more conservative and patriarchal than the Centre Party and proved less likely to participate in coalitions at the national level. The party nonetheless governed the Bavarian state in coalition with right-wing parties throughout the Weimar Republic under the leadership of Heinrich Held and controlled a crucial Catholic constituency that sometimes became important in the Reichstag. Nowhere were the divisions among German Catholics more pronounced than when the BVP tipped the balance of the 1925 presidential election to the Protestant nationalist Paul von Hindenburg for president instead of the Centre Party's Wilhelm Marx – who relied on social democrats for support. The BVP also played a role in foiling the influential and controversial Centre Party chancellorship of Heinrich Brüning in 1930 despite his shift to the right of the political spectrum. One of the central points of contention between the right and left flanks of political Catholicism became whether to cooperate with liberals and especially social democrats in order to legislate. While the parliamentary system could barely function unless Catholic politicians took the responsibility of governing with other prorepublican forces seriously, the anticlerical views of many liberals and socialists made such alliances too distasteful for many Catholics. Those that worked with social democrats and liberals suffered from withering attacks by their co-religionists. Increasingly deep divisions between Catholics made united resistance to Hitler impossible by 1933, and the persistent culture wars by the church against Protestants, liberals, socialists, and Communists produced untenable dissonance for the long-term stability of democratic coalitions.[63]

The deep links between the Neumann family and the BVP, as well as the regional nature of the struggle over Konnersreuth's legitimacy, demonstrate the cultural underpinnings of divisions within political Catholicism. In a 1928 newspaper column, Fritz Kern wrote that Konnersreuth was a "mirror" for the culture of the era, comparing those "shouting miracle and fraud" to parliamentary politicians who could not come together.[64] Kern accurately noted that the debate over the nature of modern religion reinforced the larger conflict over how best to pursue Catholic politics. The regional tension in the Konnersreuth controversy formed a compelling undercurrent to the political divisions between the BVP and the Centre Party. The largely urban northwest, backed by a vast network of associations and youth groups, by and large opposed Neumann's stigmata and preferred a "rational" and "modern" Catholicism to a return to miracles coming from rural Bavaria. Despite a vocal minority of Rhineland and Saarland Catholics in support of seers and visionaries of the 1920s, the powerful male elites of the northwest came out against the Neumann family. It was this same set of power brokers that formed the backbone of the Centre Party. While the Centre Party grew largely hostile to Therese Neumann, the regional particularism of Neumann's dialect and dress as well as her traditional piety appealed to many voters in the BVP.

Unlike Anna Maria Goebel, Therese Neumann was not abandoned by the party for which her family had long voted. Ferdinand Neumann became involved in local BVP politics before his daughter's fame and many within the local party rallied to the family's cause. The Konnersreuth Circle also reflected these political loyalties. Although BVP membership was no requirement for membership in the network, it became the most common political affiliation of the group. Several members of the party showed sympathy for the Neumann family as well. The party's primary newspaper, *Bayerische Kurier*, provided relatively positive coverage and printed a column by Franz Xaver Wutz attacking Johann Westermayr. Heinrich Held and his son enjoyed a warm relationship with Fritz Gerlich and the mayor of Munich, Karl Scharnagl, visited Neumann and heeded her advice that his daughters should dress more modestly. The Neumann family's bold reprimand of Scharnagl's family illustrated their willingness to wield power against Catholic political elites, but Scharnagl's reverence demonstrates Neumann's allure to many within the party.[65] Although Neumann received criticism from Bavarian theologians as well as Bishop Buchberger, a public advocate of the BVP's more conservative wing, the regional party largely lined up behind her, endorsing an infusion of miraculous faith into the fabric of modern Catholicism.

The case of Therese Neumann joined several other issues that separated the Centre Party from its co-religionists in the south. A letter to the editors in the pages of the *Konnersreuther Zeitung* in 1927 demonstrates the linkages between Konnersreuth and larger debates about political Catholicism. A Rhineland Catholic questioned the religious authenticity of his local Centre Party that "cow traded" with anticlerical social democrats while simultaneously mocking Therese Neumann in their publications. Much like other supporters of Konnersreuth, he insinuated that the religious elites of his region rejected Neumann because they were not Catholic enough. He associated negotiations with social democrats to Konnersreuth opposition.[66] This rhetoric illustrated the difference in Catholic world views by those who supported and opposed religious miracles and it contributed to the deepening divide between the left and right of the Catholic community. The BVP's deeper reservations about compromising with socialists was attached to its support of Konnersreuth while the Centre Party's pursuit of coalition bargaining was tied to its advocacy of a more modern Catholicism less reliant on faith in miracles.

The letter cited above feared Centre Party criticism of Neumann with cause. The *Kölnische Volkszeitung,* a press organ that openly supported Centre Party interests, published anti-Konnersreuth columns. It became one of the primary tools for publicity by Dr Josef Deutsch in his campaign to discredit her miracles, but the newspaper also published the opinions of an anonymous Protestant who cast doubt on the miracles. In a column by the newspapers editors, Neumann was compared to a secular and an allegedly fraudulent "miracle man" and the authors complained that the church suffered from comparisons between the two. Johann Westermayr also noted that the newspaper would be friendly to his ideas when the *Bayerische Kurier* in his own region refused to publish them.[67] Just as the doctors, bishops, and clergy in the dioceses of Cologne, Paderborn, Osnabruck, and Trier advocated against the Konnersreuth Circle, their political representatives did the same. Fearing that mysticism inhibited Catholicism's mainstream appeal, they rejected Neumann for having narrowed their political options as they negotiated difficult compromises with the non-Catholic parts of the country.

A letter from Heinrich Brauns, a notable of the Rhineland Catholic political establishment and a frequent member of Weimar cabinets, to Bishop Buchberger best characterizes the opposition to the Konnersreuth Circle by the Centre Party. He complained about the section of the Catholic population and clergy, "especially in Bavaria," that used faith in Therese Neumann's miracles to fight culture wars against the non-Catholic parts of Germany. Much like other well-heeled northwestern elites, he expressed embarrassment at the "great masses" who visited Konnersreuth. However, Brauns also suggested that the Konnersreuth Circle did Centre Party representatives no favours as they tried to negotiate compromises between elements of his Catholic voting bloc and the social democrats. Brauns argued that the publicity given to Konnersreuth caused unnecessary revulsion by Catholic coalition partners. He also believed that the overreaction by Bavarian Catholics to every social democratic article criticizing Konnersreuth was equally unhelpful. Brauns worried that in "difficult cultural and political circles" the Konnersreuth Circle placed a "weapon in the hand" of church enemies.[68] The Centre Party ultimately opposed the Konnersreuth miracles because they contradicted its vision for modern Catholic politics and made the difficult work of compromise in a fragile parliamentary democracy all the more difficult.

Brauns's fears that the Konnersreuth miracles fed a culture war by liberals, social democrats, and communists against Catholics were not unfounded. The "left radical" press criticized Neumann so harshly that local authorities feared violent unrest in the Upper Palatinate.[69] Inventing stories about Neumann birthing illegitimate children, the Communist press also released a string of articles attacking both her and the church. One essay accused Konnersreuth of fraudulence and mocked Neumann's fasting by imagining her caught eating a Bavarian sausage. Caricatures suggested that the church failed to condemn the Konnersreuth events to make money from the miracles. Despite Bishop Buchberger's hatred for communism, he expressed frustration that he and other Bavarian bishops appeared in the press as co-conspirators with the despised Konnersreuth Circle. One article even suggested that the bishops threatened violence against any doctor that would contradict the miracles.[70] While less virulent than the communists, the social democratic press also engaged in anticlerical attacks during the Konnersreuth controversy. One caricature portrayed priests using the stigmata to trick peasants into thinking their meagre incomes were livable if one could endure suffering like Therese Neumann.[71] In the early flurry of publicity about Neumann's stigmata especially, elements of the left-wing press made the Konnersreuth spectacle central to their reporting. The gendarme in Konnersreuth sensed the tension as he himself was accused by Communists as being the "protector of the cultural scandal of the twentieth century." He worried briefly about violence erupting in the town if left-wing radicals came to confront the "unruly Catholic masses."[72] Such press assaults might have gone further but the church sued a Communist paper for accusing it of secretly arranging the entire Konnersreuth drama itself and won its libel case, limiting future press critiques.[73] These anticlerical criticisms used Konnersreuth as a tool to advocate for issues such as the separation of church and state and to embarrass Catholic political elites.

3.1. "With Saint Therese of Konnersreuth: Look people, Resl has not eaten for two years. If you become just as pious, then you will be used to fasting and be able to get by with your wages." Provinzarchiv der deutschen Augustiner, Würzburg Nachlass Wunderle, *Fränkische Tagespost*, 21 September 1927 (Social Democratic Newspaper from Nuremburg).

Advocates of Therese Neumann responded to left-wing attacks both by criticizing their own leaders and by overemphasizing the threat of communism to their movement and the safety of Germany. Bishop Kilian of Limburg used communist attacks to shame other members of the Catholic hierarchy who refused to endorse Neumann. He wrote: "How much does faithlessness sting! The communists encourage the state to use violence in the name of reason to eliminate Konnersreuth and they threaten to use violence themselves if necessary. And we Catholics remain silent."[74] Kilian insinuated that those who did not rush to the defence of Konnersreuth sided with the left wing in the church's culture war against liberals, socialists, and communists. In the context of a tenuous democratic experiment in which Catholics played a central role, such accusations of inauthenticity damaged the culture of compromise.

The Konnersreuth Circle itself engaged in such exaggerated rhetoric, fanning the fire of an already inflamed anti-Communism among Catholics and other Germans. For example, Father Naber asked the state to suppress Communist criticism of Neumann. He even accused communists of sending him letters threatening to "lynch" him and burn the Neumann house. Despite a lack of evidence, Naber spread vast concern about Neumann's vulnerability to a violent attack by communists or some other leftist foe, such as a Freemason or a liberal.[75] The overstatement of violence by communists converged with larger Catholic concerns about revolution after the First World War. In a sign of Konnersreuth's role in stoking a red scare, those who aggressively attacked communists in the Catholic press were courted as guests to Konnersreuth even after Buchberger banned such visitation.[76] Such public feuding with Communists and socialists formed the cultural underbelly of the political crisis at the heart of the Weimar Republic. The Konnersreuth controversy made Catholics even more hostile towards cooperation with non-Catholic parties and limited the options of their representatives in Berlin.

Bavarian Catholics facilitated the rise of Nazism despite their opposition to many of its racial theories because their intense fear of communism swayed them towards ideas that aligned with certain types of National Socialist thinking, a paradigm that functioned within the Konnersreuth Circle.[77] Most of the rhetoric from Neumann's supporters attacked their left-wing opponents with far more vigour than their opponents to the right. For example, when General Erich von Luddendorff, a racist nationalist, attacked Konnersreuth, Georg Priller accused him of using communist rhetoric. Even when refuting right-wing critics, communists were attacked. There was also sympathy with causes to the right of the BVP in Neumann's circle. Publicists Friedrich Ritter von Lama and Erwein Freiherr von Aretin both supported Bavarian monarchism and veered to the right of all politically Catholic parties in the Weimar Republic as enemies of the BVP. Neumann also received a visit from Adrej Hlinka, founder of the Slovak People's Party, as well as many Catholic aristocrats from Bavaria and Westphalia, including relatives of the overthrown Bavarian royal family. Links to the Bavarian monarchy were quite common in the BVP as well, but this rightward leaning element in Konnersreuth certainly undermined political

Catholicism, bolstered Catholic conservatives that opposed Centre Party republicanism, and contributed to the Nazi rise to power. At best these connections further contributed to the divisions between Catholics devoted to democracy and those who doubted its legitimacy. At worst, the presence of anti-republicans at the centre of the Konnersreuth Circle helped Bavaria shift from political Catholicism to the National Socialism after 1933.

The Konnersreuth Circle's greatest Weimar Republic enterprise indicates the ambiguous political legacy of the group. With the assistance of close Konnersreuth associates, including Father Ingbert Naab, Fürst Alois Erich von Waldburg-Zeil, Father Naber, and Neumann herself, Fritz Gerlich founded a mainstream political newspaper entitled *Der gerade Weg* (The Straight Path), which covered the major political events of the Weimar Republic's final years while fiercely opposing the totalitarian ideologies of revolutionary communism and National Socialism. The history of this newspaper indicates how Neumann and her family remained within the self-destructive conservative wing of the BVP in Weimar's final years while simultaneously inspiring progressive Catholic ideas.

Therese Neumann exercised tremendous authority in the founding of this newspaper, whose circulation hovered just below 100,000 copies during its short-lived but influential existence from 1931 to 1933. A prophecy by Neumann while in a state of exalted rest sparked Gerlich's interest in the newspaper and she also procured the funding for the project from Waldburg-Zeil. In fact Gerlich regularly sought answers from Neumann while in her so-called state of exalted rest regarding the everyday functioning of *Der gerade Weg*. She frequently resolved conflicts between Naab, Waldburg-Zeil, and Gerlich and served as peacekeeper through the newspaper's financial trouble and the private and public tumult caused by Gerlich's famously hot temper and sharp prose.[78] Furthermore, Neumann's miracles shaped Gerlich's political ideology. One biographer describes her influence upon his politics as "overwhelmingly catalytic." Previously a liberal, nationalist, and anti-socialist, he entered the arena of political Catholicism and became more open to the compromises needed in a parliamentary democracy.[79] The interaction of Gerlich's ideas and experiences previous to conversion to his newfound spirituality created a political viewpoint unique in the late Weimar period that would have been mainstream after 1945.

Gerlich's journalism disrupted the political Catholic establishment as he diverged from many of the tropes present in the Centre Party and the BVP. Always the contrarian, he did not officially join the BVP until after the Nazi rise to power as an act of political defiance against Hitler. Although Gerlich encouraged voting for the Centre Party or BVP as the best possible option, he purposely sought a wider audience with his newspaper, hoping to overcome the traditional political and confessional boundaries in Germany. He broke with the practices of regional Catholic newspapers and sought broad distribution outside of Bavaria and into the Protestant mainstream as well. Gerlich understood his project as one to "educate" and inform the German public about the twin perils of communism and fascism as he also sought fresh solutions to the political stagnation of the early 1930s. Frustrated by the conservative turn by the Centre Party and the BVP in the late Weimar years, Gerlich aggressively attacked Centre Party chancellor Heinrich Brüning, the local BVP, and other major power brokers. Serving as a gadfly, Gerlich also exasperated the political leadership of the very movement he supported.[80]

Der gerade Weg broke with the BVP chiefly because of its treatment of National Socialism. Most Catholic political newspapers and church periodicals opposed both Nazism and communism but usually singled out the left of the political spectrum for more criticism than the radical right. This habit aided Hitler's rise to power as it conditioned German Catholics to view him as the lesser of two evils and to develop affinity for the Third Reich's powerful anti-Communist message. While Gerlich made clear his disdain for Stalinism and the German Communist Party, his assault on Hitler and other famous Nazi politicians received the most emphasis. Portraying Nazi leaders as criminals, liars, and sexual deviants, he and Naab wrote numerous articles that both assailed the moral fibre of the NSDAP while also undermining the mystique that many attached to Hitler's cult of personality and his party's rapid ascent at the polls after 1929. He feared that a Hitler chancellorship would plunge the country into violent civil war between Nazis and Communists, ultimately resulting in a Soviet-style revolution. Although wrong with this prediction, Gerlich's singling out of Hitler as the greatest threat to Germany's well-being set the stage for his own martyrdom in 1934 as well as the resistance by the minority of Catholics who refused to integrate into the National Socialist regime.[81]

Even more exceptional than Gerlich's aggressive campaign against the increasingly popular National Socialists was his advocacy of Catholic cooperation with the social democrats. When collaboration with socialists became increasingly unpopular both with the Catholic electorate, the BVP, and the previously more open-minded Centre Party after the financial crisis of 1929, Gerlich saw the need for parliamentary compromise in order to save German democracy and ward off the far more damaging alternatives on the radical left and radical right. Gerlich reserved special ire in this regard for the BVP, whom he viewed as too obstructionist and too far to the right of the political spectrum. He seemed to have good relations with Bavarian state minister Heinrich Held and his son, but held other party leaders in low regard. The sort of democratic cooperation between Christians and socialists envisioned by Gerlich would not be seen again until the Grand Coalition of the Christian Democratic Union and the Social Democratic Party during the 1960s in Cold War West Germany, making his newspaper more congruent with post-war democracy than the Weimar Republic.[82]

Although the Konnersreuth Circle reshaped Gerlich's political viewpoint, Neumann, Naber, and Naab pulled Gerlich more towards the political mainstream rather than entirely supporting his groundbreaking approach to Catholic journalism. They all wrote to Gerlich many times encouraging a moderation of his tone regarding prominent Catholic figures. For example, Gerlich accused Georg Wohlmuth and members of the BVP press of promoting a "Positive Christianity" more in line with a wing of the NSDAP than the dogma of the Catholic Church. Naab counselled Gerlich that as a new convert he should refrain from publicly attacking church figures on the matters of catechism and doctrine. Therese Neumann herself contradicted Gerlich while in a state of exalted rest while his newspaper fiercely attacked the emergency decrees of Centre Party Chancellor Heinrich Brüning and his government. Many historians blame the fall of Weimar democracy in part on Brüning's decision to rule by decree as it undermined a more genuine democratic process.[83] Speaking for God, Neumann said that Germany was safest with President Paul von Hindenberg and Chancellor Brüning "at the ruder," which led her to counsel more restraint from Gerlich in his coverage of their governing strategies. This exchange shows Gerlich's singularity within the Konnersreuth Circle. In his disdain for the Brüning decrees, Gerlich actually fell in line with the Bavarian federalists in the BVP who feared too much centralized power in Prussia and Berlin. However, the support of Neumann for the conservative rule of Brüning against Gerlich's objections about anti-democratic behaviour further illustrates his role as the political visionary of the group.[84]

3.2. "Big cleaning in Mrs Germania's political kitchen," after the NSDAP lost ground in the Reichstag Elections of 6 November 1932. Bayerische Staatsbibliothek München, *Der Gerade Weg*, 6 November 1932.

3.3. "Max: 'Teacher, but the dot is not in the middle.' Teacher: 'That is correct, every child knows that the Center has moved always more to the right.'" Caricature in Fritz Gerlich's *Der Gerade Weg* about the rightward shift of the Centre Party during the early 1930s. Bayerische Staatsbibliothek München, *Der Gerade Weg*, 11 September 1932.

Despite his intransigence against the political class of the Centre Party and the BVP, Gerlich supported a uniquely Catholic ideology previously articulated by politicians such as Adam Stegerwald. He grounded his suggestions for domestic and foreign policy in notions of a Christian natural law as first articulated by Thomas Aquinas in the Middle Ages and translated into political action by European Catholics during the nineteenth century. Rejecting his past ideology of liberalism as well as communism, socialism, and capitalism as being too materialistic, Gerlich embraced the idea of human rights in the context of an individual's duties and obligations to both God and the community. He sought a Catholic middle way between free market capitalism and socialism with broad enough appeal to reach Christians of all denominations and with enough flexibility to facilitate compromise with other democrats. This faith in a Catholic natural law underpinned his opposition to communism and Nazism as well as his desire to seek a broader political tent that would include all Christians. While seeking a domestic "front" against Marxism and fascism and an economic policy situated between free market capitalism and state socialism, his foreign policy encouraged reconciliation with the French in order to create a more peaceful Europe and a check on the Prussian militarism of the past.[85] Not original in his ideas, Gerlich repeated some of the concepts made most famous by Stegerwald, a Bavarian Centre Party politician and interdenominational proponent. All of these notions were aligned with the Christian Democratic movement that Gerlich would not live to see and especially with the wing of the CSU led by future Neumann family ally Josef Müller. Although not the only Catholic figure with such ideas during the 1920s, Gerlich's lonely struggle inspired by his new faith in the miracles of Therese Neumann challenged the conservative drift of political Catholicism and even his own spiritual inspiration.

Conclusion

The Konnersreuth debate tore open the wounds of Catholics who interpreted their faith differently after the First World War. On the one hand, this movement's new Catholic ideal represented an explicit challenge to the primary power brokers of Catholic Germany. The Konnersreuth Circle confronted powerful bishops whom they felt inadequately fought the secularization of Europe and bore some responsibility for the disasters of the early twentieth century. They also attacked the lay elites who forged modern associations and political parties for sacrificing the purity of the church for the sake of conforming to sinful cultural norms. The Konnersreuth enthusiasts regarded their Catholic opponents as equally responsible for the crises of the 1920s as socialists, liberals, and Communists. Despite this hostility towards mainstream Catholicism, Neumann and her closest followers simultaneously saw the existential need for church legitimacy. She and her circle massaged their relationships with powerful men like Faulhaber and balanced their harassment of powerful Catholic figures with a healthy enough respect for church leaders to prevent radical measures. Neumann's ability to survive with neither endorsement nor condemnation facilitated her persistence as a major figure until her death and beyond.

The opponents of the Konnersreuth Circle represented a version of Catholicism more integrated into German political diversity than Neumann's disciples. A group of theologians and doctors staged a counteroffensive against Neumann's advocates, seeking a modernized, rationalized, and doctrinaire Catholicism that they reconciled with faith in science and modernity. While most of these men believed fervently in the miracles of the gospels and the potential for God's intervention on earth, they supported the primacy of science and theology. Asserting the model presented by the Lourdes shrine in France, the anti-Konnersreuth faction resurrected a compromise between faith and science. The anti-Konnersreuth group deemed a strong hierarchical church as central to the battles against secular forces during the 1920s. With good reason they considered Neumann's motley crew of converts, rural pilgrims, disillusioned aristocrats, and contrarian theologians as an insidious rebellion against the hegemony of bishops and a coherent system of beliefs.

Despite representing themselves as "modern" Catholics, it would be a mistake to take these historical actors at their word. Relying on diagnoses of feminine hysteria laced with misogynist sentiment as well as faith in telepathy, hypnosis, autosuggestion, and traditional Catholic theology, this largely male contingent was no more or less modern than the Konnersreuth Circle itself. Rather they shaped Catholicism in ways that made them feel most comfortable as they faced the trials of the 1920s. The Konnersreuth Circle and its foes innovated competing ways to spiritually grapple with a chaotic decade, causing a Bourdieusian skirmish for power that contributed to the division of Catholic unity. In fact the Konnersreuth Circle anticipated the path taken by many German Christians in the 1960s and 1970s in what Thomas Großbölting refers to as the "me generation." Modern Germans became less tied to mainstream institutional Christian churches and instead sought independent forms of spirituality with more direct access to some sort of higher power.[86] While such "new age" and ecumenical approaches would have been met with disdain by Therese Neumann, her movement's emphasis on access to God without mediation by clergy unintentionally contributed to Germany's more secular future.

The struggle over Konnersreuth revealed a church divided. Catholics cannibalized their own faith community, accusing one another of siding with anticlerical forces and delegitimizing the entire belief system in the process. A dynamic and evolving church transformed as its members contested religious meaning. On the one hand, it demonstrates the dynamism of religion in the early twentieth century. A blood feud over doctrine and the church's direction indicated a cluster of elites and everyday Catholics who cared deeply about their faith and their confessional identity. On the other hand, the debate over Neumann unmasked the profound fissures within the church as political Catholicism splintered on the eve of Nazism. Always regionally diverse, the fractures within German Catholicism became particularly combustible in the political, economic, and cultural environment of the 1920s. Although not a church in preordained decline, its internal debates made the faith an unlikely base for constraining the rise of National Socialism.

The Konnersreuth Circle caused disruption during the downfall of political Catholicism and the demise of democracy in the early 1930s. The participation of Neumann and much of her circle in the right wing of the BVP and conservative monarchism contributed to the segmentation of an increasingly diverse Catholic electorate. Furthermore, the hyperbolic anxiety at the prospect of Communist terror in Konnersreuth and the cultural war between the Konnersreuth press and the political newspapers of Communist, socialist, and liberal parties added a layer of stress to the crucial work of the Centre Party in Berlin already made untenable by a host of other issues. The internal Catholic battle between the rationalized northwestern homeland of the Centre Party and the mystical Bavarian heartland of the BVP illustrated the cultural basis for the wavering allegiance between these two factions whose cooperation was necessary for the health of many failed parliamentary majorities. The relationship of Fritz Gerlich to Konnersreuth also exposes how the seeds for Christian Democracy were planted just as political Catholicism combusted. The model of interdenominational politics and European rapprochement that Gerlich emulated anticipated a more successful democratic future even as Germany's first parliamentary experiment crumbled. The stigmata's disruptive force also created space for productive ideas that might not have otherwise received the emphasis necessary to be enacted after the war.

While the controversy about Konnersreuth revealed much about the fall of political Catholicism, it also highlighted the complexity of gender in a patriarchal church. Therese Neumann and her male followers revealed many important feminine and masculine tropes within their spiritual rebellion and their sexual politics intersected with numerous contemporary debates of the Weimar era.

Chapter Four

Between Feminine Agency and Moral Utopia: Gender and Sex in Konnersreuth

On 24 April 1932, Fritz Gerlich's newspaper, *Der gerade Weg: Deutsche Zeitung für Wahrheit und Recht* (The Straight Line: A German Newspaper for Truth and Justice), published the latest in a long line of articles attacking National Socialism for its immorality. In this particular instance, Gerlich highlighted the "homosexual element of the leadership" in the NSDAP and its "abandonment of all moral boundaries."[1] Gerlich's combined discussion of perceived moral decay and anti-Nazi politics illustrates yet another way in which the miracles of Konnersreuth departed the confines of German Catholic piety and encountered broader social and political issues. This passage indicates the Catholic political activism of the Konnersreuth Circle in the waning years of the Weimar Republic, but it also unveils the group's use of religious morality and normative sexual values to both reflect and shape the rhetoric surrounding gender throughout the 1920s and 1930s. The Konnersreuth Circle illustrated the ways a feminine seer could work within Catholic and rural patriarchy to achieve limited autonomy and showed how men could engage sentimental piety while remaining aligned with hegemonic models for masculinity.

Many histories of the Weimar Republic suggest a steep regression for women's emancipation during the 1920s despite the newly won right to vote and popular culture depicting sexually free "new women," but more recent work advances feminine agency, especially in the realm of national parliamentary legislation. On the one hand, women made little progress towards professional equality and remained entrenched in normative values about maternity, family, and the domestic sphere, a pattern with special poignancy within the Catholic Church.[2] Few women of this era challenged male control of religious institutions or positions about maternity, family planning, and popular culture.[3] On the other hand, left-wing sex reformers and changing views about birth control and abortion opened some avenues towards greater freedom for women during the Weimar era. Even conservative and sometimes Catholic women pursued social and political power despite their steadfast faith in biological determinism. For example, the Catholic Centre Party became so successful with female voters that conservative parties imitated their platform. Women constituted a powerful 60 per cent of the Catholic Centre Party's electorate during the late 1920s.[4] Within this impressive voting bloc, young female teachers and social workers undertook a "generational revolt" against the older values of confessional associations from within the Centre Party, such as the *Katholische Frauengemeinschaft Deutschlands* (KFD). In the early years of the Weimar Republic, the Centre Party actually tolerated some progressive ideas from women who resisted clerical authority and advocated pacifism and flexible rules on birth control. After the rise of future chancellor Heinrich Brüning in 1929, the Centre Party converged with the conservative position of the clergy on maternal values; most women supported this policy shift at the ballot box despite continued dissidence from the youth.[5]

Therese Neumann's story occurred in the context of this Catholic sphere during the late Weimar Republic. The powerful male elites that surrounded her and opposed her within a deeply patriarchal church and traditionally rural context illustrate the difficulty female seers had in finding paths to power and emancipation open to other European women. Neumann embraced traditional feminine roles in an exaggerated fashion to gain as much legitimacy as possible with the men she needed to protect her sanctity. Such observations seem to present Neumann as symbolic of the regression in women's rights after the First World War. However, this rural mystic manipulated the gender norms of her time to survive as a public and holy figure where other mystics faded and accumulated more spiritual capital than just about any other Catholic female of her era. When she spoke in trances, men of great education, economic means, and political power listened. She also leveraged her spiritual capital into a more public and rewarding life than would have been possible for a typical woman of the Bavarian countryside. Therese Neumann of Konnersreuth was neither a feminist advocate of emancipation nor a powerless pawn of traditional patriarchs. Rather Neumann illustrates both the subtlety necessary to utilize a rigid gender order for one's own benefit and the empowerment that came with being the focal point of a movement hoping to recast the social order. Furthermore, Neumann's male following also managed their masculinity as they formed the core of a circle focused on emotional piety in a country increasingly informed by martial formulations of manhood. Men such as Fritz Gerlich, Father Joseph Naber, and Ferdinand Neumann balanced the effeminate emotion needed for acceptance among pilgrims interested in miracles with rationalism to maintain contact with mainstream norms of masculinity. The Konnersreuth Circle was a bedrock of Catholic masculinity despite the stereotype of religious mysticism as a feminine realm in modern Germany.

Neumann and her closest advocates also entered a much broader political debate about sexuality that roiled the Weimar Republic in its final years. The "moral right," led in part by the Catholic Centre Party and Bavarian People's Party (BVP), used maternal appeals and open attacks on perceived sexual excess of the 1920s to rally their flagging and splintering base. Chastity and sexuality became primary themes in the debate about Konnersreuth as Neumann, her family, and her local priest transformed their village into a moral utopia where they used their fame and powerful contacts to bully neighbours into compliance with a rigid interpretation of Catholic ethics, rejecting those among the Catholic youth who favoured more flexibility on sexual principles. Specialists on the Weimar Republic debate whether a "moral backlash" that included Catholics delegitimized the parliamentary experiment and eased the Nazi rise to power on a law-and-order platform. Therese Neumann's rhetoric on sexual matters actually denied legitimacy to Nazism as well as the forces of republicanism, but the association of immorality with Weimar democracy undermined the struggling state at a fragile moment and the Konnersreuth Circle, at least unconsciously, contributed to this unfortunate disruption.[6] The importance of sexuality to the Konnersreuth events represents just one of many ways that these miracles became explicitly political. Catholic miracles intersected with gender and politics, demonstrating how these movements from outside the institutionalized power structures both reinforced and challenged Catholic values. While Neumann embraced an overstated version of Catholic domesticity, she also fashioned a flexible gendered identity that allowed the persistence of her miracles and an extension of her personal power. She and her circle advocated for the Catholic Church's war on immorality during the 1920s, but she also used her chastity as a tool with which to bludgeon the male elites threatened by her power.

Feminine Power and Masculine Mysticism

A gendered analysis of Therese Neumann proves an immense challenge due to the contradictory accounts of her behaviour. While some supporters emphasized her strict obedience to the will of God and her priest, Father Naber, others focused on her sharp tongue, charisma, and ability to reduce the self-importance of powerful men. One contingent of critics suggested Neumann was just a naive young woman stage-managed by the men around her, but many detractors decried how she actually controlled the men who should have been in control of her spirituality. Finding the truth amidst these conflicting portrayals is made more demanding by Neumann's current beatification process – which makes almost all of Neumann's voluminous personal correspondence unavailable for research. This unobtainable material includes her letters with women of the Konnersreuth Circle, such as the Abbess Maria Benedicta von Spiegel and Maria Monika Waldburg-Zeil. This unfortunate circumstance makes her consciousness as a feminine mystic difficult to capture.[7] Her actions and words are largely filtered through her male advocates and disbelievers. Despite these difficulties, Therese Neumann's agency emerges as she embraced an extreme version of Catholic patriarchy in order to fully capitalize on her spiritual gifts.

The Roman Catholic tradition required a stigmatic like Neumann to obediently submit to the will of God, her confessor, and the church. By accepting and promoting this trope, she and her supporters presented an image of feminine docility that went far beyond what was expected of most Catholic women. Friedrich von Lama argued that Neumann's grace emanated from her complete submission to the will of God. According to his account, Neumann received her three cures because she prayed without asking for them. He even went so far as to suggest that "self-will is the beginning of spiritual descent." Neumann represented the ideal seer because she asked for nothing in return for her suffering and opened herself entirely to the will of God.[8] Neumann's reported patient suffering with physical pain and strict obedience of superiors was needed to court legitimacy from church authorities and pilgrims who sought connections between her stigmata and those of the past.[9] Therefore, she publicly presented the image of an uneducated rural maiden who obeyed and endured pain for the well-being of others.

Neumann's mystic suppression of "self-will" and total obedience to God contributed to a seeming dependence on several male authority figures. For example, Father Joseph Naber, Ferdinand Neumann, and

Franz Xaver Wutz controlled access to Resl and handled relations with visitors. Male intellectuals, such as Gerlich and von Lama, presented the case for authenticity to the public. Several reports and letters by her critics actually absolved Neumann from any guilt in the alleged fraud of Konnersreuth. Georg Wunderle and Johann Westermayr both viewed Resl as a victim of Naber and Wutz. Wunderle complained that his former colleague, Wutz, exploited "poor Therese" and her "suggestible nature."[10] Westermayr also worried about the "influence of the men" whom he observed conducting long conversations with her before visions and ecstasy. In fact Westermayr stated on several occasions that Neumann possessed no "guilt" for the events in Konnersreuth since she had difficulty differentiating the good in her visions from the "necessary doubt" needed to assess their sanctity. Rather he agreed that Naber served as Neumann's "theatrical director" in the "drama" they performed for visitors with the Friday Suffering. Even Neumann's supporters viewed Naber's role as essential to guiding the "simple country girl" on the correct spiritual path.[11] The gendarme reports from Konnersreuth also suggest Naber's domination of Neumann. Criticizing Neumann's extended stay at the parish residence with Naber while workers completed a renovation of her parents' home, Westermayr wrote that she repeated Naber's orders as if "they came from Jesus" and that she was entirely under his influence.[12] While Therese Neumann excelled in a role traditionally gendered female by Catholic tradition, she limited her agency to the realm of apolitical and feminine mysticism. While women's religious associations increasingly contained more emancipatory rebellions from youth, the Konnersreuth Circle enforced Catholic patriarchy. Many admiring and disillusioned Catholics regarded Therese Neumann as both an ignorant woman with a feeble mind outside the narrow realm of mystical faith and as completely under the control of more capable men.

Neumann sometimes even presented herself as unintelligent, simple, and childlike, qualities that her male supporters encouraged. Her extraordinary bursts of emotion when discussing the death of Jesus seemed almost manufactured. For example, she wrote to a nun shortly after her stigmata expressing her desire to go to heaven where she could no longer "hurt the savior" with human sin. Neumann wrote, "Often I can't even pray anymore, just cry." Johannes Steiner described such devotion as "childlike-trusting resignation to our Savior and his divine will." He extended this analysis to her entire personality, characterizing Neumann as "honest and humble like a child." This emotional piety and infantilization of a grown woman seems an attempt to decrease the threat of her spiritual power to a male hierarchy that developed even in her own movement. A woman could only legitimately wield such mystical powers if her influence ended with her ecstasy. As a fully grown adult, Neumann sometimes referred to herself as a "dumb girl" and said, "I know that I'm stupid."[13] Posing as an unenlightened peasant child, Neumann defused potential tension with male sponsors.

This excessive gender conformity reached its peak with the debate over her medical exam. Neumann and her followers did as much as possible to depict her as submissive to both her father and the church. In all discussions about the exam, Neumann deferred to her father's authority. Her public stance projected obedience to both her parents and the ecclesiastical authorities. She expressed her own willingness to submit to Bishop Buchberger's wishes, but refused to disobey her father's request that no exam take place.[14] She and her supporters depicted the church's desire for a second exam as an "attack" on her father's "domestic rights (*Hausrecht*)."[15] Although her opponents viewed this stance as privileging her father's authority over that of the bishop, she insisted on her sincerity. In a letter to Wutz she articulated her position: "It's all the same with me; I'll go with anything. Even if they told me today that I was supposed to go right into a clinic, that's all right with me. I really have nothing to fear and our dear Savior takes care of everything so that it will be all right. But my father says he won't let me go; he says that once before he gave in, at home, and the Ordinary was satisfied, but these people think one thing today and something else tomorrow. And you know my father."[16] This quote articulates her desire to appease those who wanted a submissive feminine mystic. Forced to choose between the will of her father and that of her bishop, she chose to obey the fourth commandment to honour one's parents over the Council of Trent that affirmed ecclesiastical authority over the laity. However, one also glimpses the subtlety of Neumann's position in this quotation. She used her respect for patriarchal authority to criticize the position of the bishop as unfair and fickle. She also is said to have revealed in ecstasy that "the Saviour" had no desire for a second exam. This evidence indicates that Neumann hid behind an overstated obedience to masculine will in order to fight for her own spiritual legitimacy without threatening her fragile yet influential position.

Neumann transformed this exaggerated gender conformity into a base for immense power. Her respect for gender hierarchy aided

Neumann's enduring sanctity given the Catholic Church's desire for rigorous medical examinations of the miracles and stigmata. After submitting to one inconclusive official church test of her nutrition intake in the late 1920s, her family refused all future requests for three decades. The desire of her bishop in Regensburg as well as the Bavarian Bishops' Conference for conclusive evidence of the supernatural nature of her bleeding and cures placed Neumann in an awkward position. Neumann and her circle knew well the fate of past stigmatics after official examination. Naber cited the case of nineteenth-century seer Anna Katharina Emmerick. Her vicar general "forced her to undergo one clinical examination after another" and Naber despaired at the "psychic and physical" demands of such intrusions. Her family also profoundly distrusted medical science. Her father famously said, "They can put Resl in a glass house somewhere and observe her all they want, but they're not going to experiment on her." Neumann herself tried to flee a hospital in fear while receiving treatment for ailments prior to her stigmata, suggesting an early distrust of the medical establishment. Despite this desire to avoid another exam, she coveted institutional approval of her stigmata and projected total obedience towards male superiors. However, she evaded the conflict by privileging her father's authority over that of the church. He protested against his daughter becoming an indefinite curiosity for scientists and accused the exams of violating the chastity of his daughter. As this reasoning persisted into the 1950s when Therese was a woman in her fifties and sixties, she used an exaggerated respect for male patriarchy in order to avoid any potential loss of her religious authority.[17] Neumann's use of paternal authority fit into a Catholic intellectual tradition that favoured patriarchy. Catholic thought about the Christian natural law, based in the ideas of Thomas Aquinas, promoted the need for wives and daughters to submit to a man's authority to achieve a natural hierarchical order.[18] She selected an interpretation of Catholicism with legitimacy that ultimately rejected the ruling of the church hierarchy on her case.

Neumann's circle used three major reasons for refusing the exam on the basis of her father's authority. First, Neumann needed to respect the fourth commandment to honour one's mother and father, which her opponents rightfully suggested should not apply after her twenty-first birthday. However, Neumann claimed that she would not be able to return to her father's household if she disobeyed his wishes and believed it was too great a hardship to endure. By justifying her subversive behaviour through a disproportionate reverence for paternal patriarchy, Neumann undercut those who would depict her as a woman without boundaries or control. In this way she escaped the gendered traps set for previous mystics like Anna Maria Goebel. Her other reasons, however, became increasingly challenging to church authority. By claiming that the saviour told her not to submit to the exam, she asserted that her connection with the saviour trumped the teachings of the clergy. Furthermore, she and her family suggested that belief in her miracles was a matter of faith and not medical science. Those who chose not to believe could just leave her alone. In this way, Neumann leveraged her popularity, intuiting that the bishop of Regensburg could not discipline her without creating terrible divisiveness in his diocese and alienating powerful colleagues, such as Cardinal Michael Faulhaber of Munich and Bishop Konrad von Preysing of Eichstätt. In fact, this approach yielded positive results as even Neumann's most bitter critics blamed Wutz, Naber, Gerlich, and her father for her disobedience.[19] Neumann used her image of feminine artlessness to displace blame for her bold defiance of a hierarchy that controlled the fate of her spiritual legacy to her male followers. Therese Neumann defied church authority without disturbing her important reputation for obeying the will of God and respecting superiors. Therefore, Neumann's unbending respect for patriarchy should be viewed as a shrewd strategy for protecting her "goods of salvation" rather than just a sign of powerlessness in the midst of imposing Catholic men.

In accounts of her behaviour during the exam debates, Neumann displayed charisma, agency, and power. Neumann's critics like Paul Martini sensed that Neumann controlled the men around her and not the other way around. He believed that Father Naber was the gullible rural priest and Neumann his puppet master. Jesuit Paul Siwek also contradicted those who viewed Neumann as under Naber's control. He wrote, "In her ecstasies Theresa often foretells future events to Father Naber and tells him 'in the most exact manner' how he is to conduct himself. She tells him how he is to direct her, which visitors he should admit and which he should refuse and the like." Neumann stood strong against powerful male supporters and critics as well. For example, Franz Xaver Wutz reportedly told her that she was "a little stupid" for making an error about bible stories. She responded, "And I think you are even more stupid." Neumann's strong backbone frequently became apparent through the sharp tongue that made her controversial.

She famously told Paul Martini that Socrates was wise even though he did not know everything when the cleric criticized her for shortcomings in her knowledge of doctrine. Neumann also threw clergy out of her home whom she perceived to be non-believers, sinners, or lacking the proper respect for her family or her miracles. In another example, a critical visitor told Neumann she bled as a result of autosuggestion and psychosomatic illness. She replied, "Imagine you would be an Ox. Would you grow horns?"[20] While critics viewed such abrasive behaviour as negatively affecting her case for beatification or canonization, they clearly indicated a strong-willed woman who was not entirely boxed in by the male elites for and against her sanctity.

Besides her deft escape from the fate of other discredited feminine mystics of her era, Neumann displayed even more signs of self-empowerment within her patriarchal cultural context. She accumulated power within the community as not only a religious figure but also a healer and soothsayer with many clamouring for her assistance. For example, she visited the sick and comforted them with medicines received from pilgrims and with spiritual advice. Steiner reports that she "devoted herself to the sick with great love." She travelled with a horse and cart to provide care for people without access to a local doctor until after the Second World War. She frequently treated patients after they returned from doctor's visits and hospital stays in nearby Waldsassen. She also aided those with disabilities, inviting a local girl with paralysis into her home and giving a boy with mental illness one of her birds. In some cases clergy from the region sought her medical opinion when deciding whether to administer last rites. Her desire to adjudicate cases for salvation sometimes mixed with these medical activities. In one case she told a priest not to give a man his last rites and he died. Saving face, she later claimed in ecstasy that this occurred because the man lacked faith and therefore was punished by God through this denial of the final sacrament.[21] This role as unofficial health care provider gave Neumann status and bolstered her belief that her spirituality constituted her "vocation." Therese also became a community leader and mediator to whom local people came with their concerns. Her local priest took children to her bedside for religion classes. Neumann had a seat of honour behind the altar in her local parish and was granted free reign with decorating the altar and pews. For all of these reasons, Neumann transcended her somewhat constructed image as passive country girl in the hands of more sophisticated men.

4.1. Therese Neumann and Abbess Maria Benedicta von Spiegel. Staatsarchiv Amberg, Regierung der Oberpfalz, Kammer des Innern 13038.

While bound by the very respect for the patriarchy that empowered her, Neumann subtly supported other Catholic women with problems ignored by men of the church. For example, Monika Waldburg-Zeil, spouse of one of Neumann's wealthiest supporters, and Abbess Maria Anna Benedicta von Spiegel sought her counsel throughout the Third Reich as they balanced their spirituality and moral objections to Nazism with the desire to survive in the regime.[22] Many Catholic aristocratic women found deep comfort in Neumann as they suffered from the death or financial ruin of their husbands during the late Weimar years and the Third Reich. Elisabeth von Guttenberg's memoir highlights the uniquely feminine spiritual mentoring offered by Neumann to other women. She described Neumann's comforting guidance after the death of her husband:

> The day I reached Konnersreuth, Resl Neumann was out nursing a sick person in the village. Her mother took me to Resl's room and asked me to wait. This room had taken on the spiritual atmosphere of its owner. Sitting there on the small sofa, I felt myself embraced by the peace with which Resl herself radiates. After a time she returned. She already knew of the death of my husband. She sat down on the sofa beside me and took my hands in her own, which carried the marks of Christ's suffering. My anguished heart soon was eased in her peaceful, enlightened presence. I did not have to tell her all the things which were in my heart. Her shining eyes, under her white kerchief, looked out at me with great intensity of love which seemed to envelop me. Tears of sympathy ran down her face.[23]

Even while fulfilling roles traditionally gendered feminine, Neumann provided a sense of female community to elite women as they grappled with the tumult of modern Germany's greatest ruptures.

Neumann offered not only aristocrats her empowering communal support, but also everyday female pilgrims. In the early days of her celebrity, women flooded Konnersreuth to gain access to the new seer. They either asked Neumann personally for help when they could receive an audience or left notes for her at the high altar of the church in Konnersreuth. Women also wrote her hundreds of letters, to which Neumann frequently responded. In these interactions, Catholic women asked for either advice or comfort in dealing with drunk and abusive husbands, religiously wayward sons, or sick children. They brought their ailing or mentally ill children to her for blessings, counsel, and comfort.[24] While this personal assistance for her female following reinforced Catholic stereotypes that placed women on a moral pedestal in comparison to their sons, brothers, and husbands, she also provided a spiritual and psychological outlet for women who suffered from burdens caused by men.

In another example, Neumann's sister Ottilie became politically active and engaged within the confines of their rural Catholic upbringing due largely to opportunities offered by Neumann's celebrity and encouragement. Serving as a housekeeper for Wutz in Eichstätt, she escaped life in Konnersreuth and lived in a larger city. Neumann used her contacts to create a better life not just for Ottilie but for her entire family. Donations from pilgrims permitted a renovation of their house and she and her father enjoyed several trips in Wutz's car around Germany and to Switzerland. The Capuchins of Eichstätt made a house available to her for her frequent visits. The best professional opportunities that resulted from Neumann's celebrity went to her brothers, Hans and Ferdinand, whom Wutz placed at universities to study for their careers in dentistry and politics respectively. Nonetheless, her sister enjoyed many charitable activities as well, joined lay religious orders, and participated in local political meetings of the BVP in Konnersreuth and Eichstätt. Both women used their roles as spiritually revered women in a patriarchal system to improve their quality of life. Much like the nineteenth-century nuns who joined convents for female companionship and educational opportunities, the Neumann sisters enjoyed some of the vocational opportunities offered to women religious without the constrictions of convent life.[25]

Much evidence also exists that several orders of nuns in Germany actively sought Neumann's advice and leadership. For example, a seminar for prospective nuns at a convent near Trier made Neumann a regular theme and requested special permission to visit Konnersreuth despite the opposition to her case within their diocese.[26] In fact, part of Neumann's power rested in her ability to serve as a lay nun. She received even more public respect for her religiosity than most nuns and received many of the opportunities of those who took holy orders. Neumann referred to her visions, stigmata, and religious activities as her professional vocation – one that replaced her earlier desire to become a missionary in Africa. However, by never actually taking vows or submitting to the obedience of men as demanded by convent life, she also accrued more power and influence than women who officially served the church. With her traditional Bavarian headdress and dark garments as an unofficial uniform, Neumann healed the sick, administered last rites, and advised fellow women in spiritual distress. However, she also travelled through Europe, gained access to powerful men, and improved the professional prospects of herself and her family as a religious figure with no higher authority except the God whose will she articulated for the world.

Neumann's various states of ecstasy during her Friday Suffering also entailed flexible gender roles. In the aftermath of her visions she spoke in different tones of voice and dialects. After completing her visions of the passion of Christ while soaked in blood, Neumann always entered first into a state of "infancy" and then into her very famous state of exalted rest. In the first phase, she could barely communicate and focused on her own suffering. She also spoke her Bavarian dialect and remained extremely hesitant. Afterward, she changed dramatically. She spoke in "majestic" and much more masculine tones, switching to formal German and using terms and phrases never used in her everyday life. It was at this point that she answered questions posed by Naber on behalf of visitors, speaking for God.[27] She took on a masculine persona when at her most powerful and when passing judgments that mattered most to the lived experience of her visitors. This contrast between helpless woman and powerful man during her own ecstasy illuminated the limits on the power of female mystics. She could only speak with authority in the Catholic Church when a male God inhabited her body. However, this practice also demonstrated the careful course charted by this seer to attain as much power as possible within these patriarchal limits. She underwent similar shifts in her life outside of her stigmata. She alternated between bouts of pain and suffering that restricted her to the bedroom and spurts of energy where she went out and laboured in the fields with as much strength and efficiency as a man. This appropriation of male authority by the twentieth century's most noted stigmatic indicates the complexity of Neumann's relationship to power.

Perhaps the greatest evidence of Neumann's feminine power emerged through the threat she posed to male patriarchs. Theologian Paul Siwek articulated many of the common objections to Neumann, revealing how she subverted their expectations for the behaviour of a female mystic. Much like the Catholic doctors who accused Neumann of hysteria, Siwek argued that women at the centre of miracles needed careful scrutiny due to their frequent "emotional disturbances." He also accused Neumann of not understanding the necessary feminine humility both in and out of ecstasy. For example, Siwek argued that Neumann never asked God's forgiveness for her own sins and that she seemed selfishly consumed with the sins of others.[28] His writing conveys the anxiety of male leadership concerned with this stigmatic's challenge to the church's power structure.

The attacks on Neumann's uncomfortable feminine power frequently led to assaults on the masculinity of her primary spiritual advisor, Father Naber. Siwek suggested that Neumann lacked the firm male confessor necessary to challenge, guide, and sometimes humiliate a feminine mystic in an unveiled assault on Naber's manhood.[29] This example demonstrates the fragility not just of Neumann's attempt to wield power but also of her male followers as they charted public personas in favour of Catholic mysticism. While promoting Neumann's miracles, men like Naber and Gerlich needed to simultaneously embody the emotional piety of the Konnersreuth movement and assure the public of their masculinity in an era when Christianity could be easily associated with femininity.

Father Naber received regular praise for his embrace of emotional forms of piety, but struggled to project the masculine rationality many Germans sought. For example, Cardinal Kaspar of Prague praised Naber as a "model of piety, patience, sacrifice, and zeal for the honor of God." However, Siwek argued that he diverged from past confessors and spiritual guides for mystics. He wrote, "He ought to make clear to this simple country girl what St John of the Cross and other great doctors of the Church have to say about visions and similar charisms ... He ought to better maintain his feelings when confronted with the stigmata and not betray his veneration in her presence." Siwek echoed the criticism of many opponents who believed Naber needed to discipline Neumann. They believed he indulged her too often and encouraged a rebellious streak that made a mockery of church authority.[30] Konnersreuth's most outspoken opponent, Dr Josef Deutsch, used gendered imagery to exploit Naber's image as too permissive with his female apprentice. He argued that he took a "manly" interest in challenging the Konnersreuth narrative. Deutsch viewed his anti-Konnersreuth activism as providing patriarchal protection for the church against the "swindle" in Konnersreuth.[31] He insinuated that his intervention became necessary as unmanly clergy like Naber failed to perform their masculine duty as Neumann's leaders.

Although damaging in the fight over the Konnersreuth miracles, such attacks on Naber proved to be less than fatal. Neumann's proponents responded to such characterizations of Naber by emphasizing the importance of sensitivity in a rural cleric. His role as a member of the clergy made it less important to burnish his intellectual credentials and the positive image of a pious man of God dominated accounts by the circle's publicists. One Catholic visitor to Konnersreuth described Naber in the following manner: "A gentle restfulness is about him, his eyes are full of goodness, kindness, and mirror the simplicity of a noble soul. He is the right man in the right place." A Jewish doctor who converted to Catholicism after meeting Neumann described Naber in a similar manner: "He represents the highest type of country pastor; genuine childlike piety combined with earnest kindliness, and deep understanding of the human heart are his characteristics."[32] Konnersreuth pilgrims accepted Naber because of his willingness to embrace expressive spiritualties. His parish became a haven for men to articulate their hardships while finding hopefulness in Neumann's stigmata. One pilgrim described the following scene in the Konnersreuth church after witnessing the Friday Suffering for the first time: "In the aisle near the side door we saw the young man kneeling on the floor. His face buried in his hands, he knelt there, his whole body trembling, and sobbing with restraint. My friend and I knelt in a pew, our hearts almost breaking with joy. Three men in the quiet church of Konnersreuth, their eyes filled with tears."[33] The masculine model provided by Naber inhibited his appeal to the Catholic doctors, urban Centre Party politicians, and the sophisticated theologians already against the miracles. However, his brand of spiritual leadership opened a venue for German men to unexpectedly process their emotional interiors while on pilgrimage. He opened a space for men to perform emotional penance usually gendered feminine during a time dominated by martial masculinity, street fighting, and paramilitary organizations.

While Naber could persist as an exclusively spiritual Catholic man due to his priest's collar, the lay men of the Konnersreuth Circle pursued the fragile balance of showing the emotional side of mystical devotion while also assuring the public of rational masculinity. Nobody performed this balancing act more effectively than the male face of the Konnersreuth Circle during the late Weimar Republic: Fritz Gerlich. His conversion story became essential to the movement's popularity as it conformed precisely to the expectations of male behaviour regarding religion. Gerlich started as a secular male sinner and then found salvation from a pious woman. This sort of story possessed deep resonance with a public that expected unrealistic chastity and piety from women while almost encouraging male waywardness as long as repentance followed. Gerlich lived an entire life as a Calvinist, an alcoholic, a womanizer, a divorcee, and a secular liberal prior to Konnersreuth. He travelled to Konnersreuth as a doubter hoping to unmask Neumann as a fraud and expose an example of Catholic superstition. This background to his very sentimental conversion first to the Konnersreuth miracles and then to Catholicism made for compelling reading. The narrative of sin and salvation matched the rhetoric from Konnersreuth that Neumann came from God to convert Germans and save the country from future punishments for its sins. The fact that masculine sin preceded feminine conversion made Gerlich the poster child for the Konnersreuth Circle.

Once Gerlich joined the Konnersreuth Circle and quickly rose to the top of its power structure, he became vulnerable to attacks on his masculine rationality. His two-volume book about Therese Neumann served as the most public intellectual defence of these miracles. Therefore, opponents targeted Gerlich's intellectual credibility. While the most common assaults focused on his Calvinist background and unfamiliarity with doctrine, Deutsch undermined the very sagacity of his viewpoints. He portrayed Gerlich and Wutz as aggressive and angry in their public appearances and in the tone of their journalistic writing. Therefore, he presented Gerlich as a "pathological" person, incapable of reason on the matter of Konnersreuth.[34] While Gerlich struggled with accusations about his ability to speak for the Catholic faith, he successfully burnished the cerebral image of Konnersreuth. As a former state archivist and journalist, he brought impeccable professional credentials to his public advocacy. His books and newspaper columns about Neumann also used historical and social scientific reasoning to argue in favour of Neumann's sanctity. While unorthodox to theologians, this approach convinced many lay Catholics of Neumann's legitimacy. Furthermore, he recruited medical doctors, philologists, and other specialists to share empirical evidence and arguments supporting the cures and authenticity of Neumann's stigmata. While Gerlich's life conformed to the narrative of a movement preaching it could convert fallen men, his professional work illustrated a rational public persona that coexisted alongside the personal religious awakening that accompanied Konnersreuth's mysticism.

The story of Therese Neumann and her male advisors indicates the complexity of gender in Catholic Germany. This set of characters undoubtedly existed within a deeply patriarchal subculture that embraced hierarchy over gender equality. The rural location of Konnersreuth enhanced this accumulation of power for men at the expense of women.

Even in such an environment, Therese Neumann worked within the constraining gender norms of her religious habitus to become an immense power broker. Overcoming the institutional power of the clergy, northwestern associational life, and in some cases political Catholicism, she forged a new movement with herself as the most defining and influential figure. Although she relied upon a host of influential men to attain this power, she manipulated early twentieth-century understandings of patriarchy to nonetheless carve out a place for herself and her family that was far better than if had she never bled from her hands. Men like Gerlich and Naber also needed to reconcile their expressive religious devotion with acculturated expectations for male rationality. Gerlich particularly illustrated how modern men played an active role in shaping a spirituality usually associated with women in the modern age.

Policing Sexuality in the Moral Utopia of Konnersreuth

Sexuality became a central theme in the debate over Konnersreuth, shedding further light on the complex gendered dynamics within the Catholic community as well as the political importance of the miracles. The rhetoric surrounding sexual morality empowered Neumann as her chastity became a weapon with which to outmanoeuvre those wishing to discredit her as well as a platform for further power within her town. A life without sex became liberating for Neumann. Taking neither holy orders nor marital vows, she possessed less male oversight than many Catholic women. Neumann especially deployed chastity against sexual assault to protect her body in a patriarchal milieu. The use of Catholic sexual morals came at the price of emancipation for women more broadly. The rigid tone regarding sexuality set by Neumann shamed many young women in her sphere of power and damaged any attempt at reconciling physical desire with Catholic doctrine or recognizing the fragile sexual position that Neumann herself occupied in relation to male predators prior to her rise to fame. The Konnersreuth Circle contributed to the conservative turn in sexual politics by political Catholicism that some historians feel was partly responsible for the dissolution of Weimar democracy.

Like numerous young women of the 1920s, Therese Neumann survived sexual assault twice as she grew up in Konnersreuth, which shaped her standpoint on all carnal encounters. Such instances seemed tragically common in her town during the early twentieth century.

Anni Speigl, Neumann's close devotee, suggested that young domestic servants "barricaded" their doors at night for protection against male labourers. Neumann's sister asserted that rape and sexual harassment formed constant features in the Upper Palatinate: "Girls in towns have an easy life compared to a country girl in service. A girl seldom runs into danger in a town unless she looks for it herself. In the country, especially in service, a girl has to put up fierce resistance. Resl was no exception."[35] These passages indicate the ever-present danger of rape that forged the commitment to chastity by the Neumann women, but it also shows how that fear also turned into suspicion of urban women who dealt with their sexual identities differently than rural Catholics. Through Neumann's sister, one can already glimpse the way strict chastity both empowered rural Catholic women against male aggression and turned them against other women who adhered less strictly to Christian restrictions on female expression. Neumann and her sister coped with fears of male predators in part by blaming urban women for inviting sexual advances rather than taking the dangerous step of confronting male power brokers about their own sexual abuse.

The stories of the assaults against Neumann underline the power of the Catholic miraculous as well as her own will to preserve her chastity. The first attack occurred when a "farm hand" tried to make "violent love" to her in the loft of a barn where she worked. Neumann jumped down seven feet from the loft, barely escaping injury. Afterward she said she made the jump because she would "rather lose her life than her virginity." When another man aggressively sought her affection, she finally agreed to meet him later at night. When he arrived at their meeting place, she struck him repeatedly with a whip handle until he fled and never bothered her again.[36] While she credited luck and possible heavenly intercession with the first incident, her violent fight against the second perpetrator demonstrated feminine empowerment in the face of an epidemic of male sexual assault. These experiences also must have shaped both Neumann's spirituality and stance on sexual politics. Neumann responded to the problem of sexual assault in the countryside with an outspoken affirmation of unbending chastity. The narrative of Neumann's escape from these male assailants both set a precedent of Catholic female empowerment through a strict sense of sexual abstinence but also victimized women both Catholic and otherwise who challenged traditional morality during the 1920s.

Within Konnersreuth, Neumann, her family, and Father Naber constructed an unofficial theocracy in which they pressured residents of the town and pilgrims to conform with their lofty interpretations of Catholic righteousness. This moral authority emanated from Therese Neumann's own attire, which modelled the chastity she demanded from other women. Fritz Gerlich described her in the following way: "Therese Neumann's dresses are always black, high in the neck and reaching to the ankles; and the cape she wears is also black. On the street and at home she wears a black head cloth."[37] This mixture between the wardrobe of a Catholic nun and a traditional Bavarian peasant woman marked Neumann as abstinent. She also demanded purity from her family and followers. She explained to Johann Westermayr that she saved her sister Ottilie from the negative influence of young men, transitioning her sibling into her own caregiver. Once this transformation occurred, she procured Ottilie's spot as domestic servant to Professor Wutz in Eichstätt. Additionally Neumann would not allow Gerlich's conversion to Catholicism until he ended his second marriage and returned to his first wife.[38] Although she treated Gerlich far more gently than women who she viewed as violating her morality code, this example shows that Konnersreuth's men and women both received her scrutiny.

Neumann and Naber also policed their town for any questionable moral conduct. Neumann claimed to hear the lyrics of inappropriate songs by the town's girls even when she was not physically present to witness them and Naber reinforced her claim by preaching on the matter. In fact Naber regularly asked Neumann about the ethical behaviour of locals while she was in a state of ecstasy to publicly pass judgment on them. According to the local gendarme, many in town believed Neumann to be all-knowing and altered their behaviour to avoid her displeasure. In one sign of her influence, local women visited Neumann after marriage proposals to seek her blessing for the match before the wedding. She also campaigned against allowing dances in town, pressuring local establishments to stop the practice from 1929 onward. One local tavern owner refused to tell the gendarme whether he stopped holding profitable dances out of reverence or fear of Therese Neumann. Enemies of the Konnersreuth Circle accused her "cult" of terrorizing the local population.[39]

This policing of local morality led to a conflict with the notable Schiml family shortly after the Nazi rise to power. Owners of the primary pension in Konnersreuth, the Schimls took on great debt expanding their business through renovations and construction when the town received two hundred religious tourists a week. This stream of pilgrims declined after 1932 when the Bavarian bishops placed more severe restrictions on who could visit Konnersreuth. Hugo Schiml found himself in financial catastrophe. In order to make up some of the lost money, he hosted dancing during the carnival season of 1933. These events constituted a direct challenge to Therese Neumann since she suffered vicariously for all the sins committed during the Carnival season each year and she vocally condemned the tradition's excesses – which could only have exacerbated her conflict with Catholic notables in the Carnival-obsessed Rhineland. Naber preached against the event and refused communion to women who allowed their children to attend, even after they visited him in the confessional. Neumann instructed visitors to avoid the Schiml pension and stay elsewhere, starving the family of desperately needed business and wealthy patrons. With a sick wife and failing business, rumours through town suggested that the family patriarch considered suicide before reconciling with Therese Neumann by undertaking a fourteen-day pilgrimage.[40] This conflict illustrates both Neumann's local power but also the way she targeted women above men for upholding sexual morality. She ultimately forgave Schiml, but she and Naber publicly humiliated the town's mothers over the Carnival merriment enjoyed by their children. The decision to blame women for the perceived laxity in sexual behaviour during the Weimar Republic conformed with Catholic rhetoric dating back to the nineteenth century, but it also reveals a likely coping strategy for Neumann after her own sexual trauma. It was less painful to blame other women for making themselves vulnerable to male promiscuity than to explicitly challenge the power men expressed through sexual dominance of women and double standards regarding licentiousness.

The strict moral code enforced in town also extended to those wishing to visit Neumann during her Friday Suffering. Her father stood at the door and turned away any women who he deemed inappropriately dressed. Von Lama relates one story where a family from Braunschweig pleaded their way past Ferdinand Neumann despite his protests about the girls' dresses, which were quite modest by 1920s standards since they reached beneath the knees. However, the moment they entered her bedroom, Neumann said that there were children not properly dressed and that their mother was to blame. The family left Konnersreuth humiliated and in tears and the mother pledged the family to even less revealing attire.[41] This story was not exceptional as the focus on female dress in the Neumann house remained an obsession throughout the 1920s and 1930s. This public shaming imposed a narrow moral code on all women hoping for comfort from this mystical movement.

European and North American readers of Konnersreuth publicists, such as Friedrich Ritter von Lama, consumed narratives of redemption for fallen women. Von Lama, like other Neumann followers, filled his books, lectures, and newspaper articles with accounts of conversion since Neumann's purpose was to revive Catholicism in Germany and save the country from the abyss. While these stories included the spiritual reawakening of wayward men, Protestants, and Jews, they also focused on "fallen women" and mixed marriages. Neumann intervened in the lives of women who had previously been sexually active out of wedlock or who married Protestant men and counselled them towards a life of faith and conversion. In one passage of a book von Lama described a woman who engaged her parish priest in an affair and travelled to Konnersreuth without official permission from the diocese. After waiting outside the house in the snow for hours, her visit with Neumann triggered her conversion. Neumann even inspired a "vigil of prayer" on this woman's behalf in a nearby town. This story offers a deep sense of redemption for a woman facing spiritual trouble over her personal life. However, the event is also framed in such a way that the priest's indiscretions receive less emphasis in the story. This decision is even more shocking in light of the fact that this affair began when this woman was a twelve-year-old child.[42] The blame for transgressing sexual barriers erected by Catholic teaching fell to the female temptress even when the woman in question was exploited by her male clergyman since she was a minor. Even though Neumann chose not to criticize the abusive priest, this situation represents how she used chastity as a strategy against male predators within the church. The path to empowerment for this survivor of abuse in Konnersreuth was abstinence rather than a reckoning with the man who seduced a child. Neumann mediated this woman's path back to righteousness. This story subtly elevated Neumann's authority over that of this sinful clergyman and emphasized how her chastity arose in rejection of male sexual assault, but it marginalized those women protesting double standards regarding male sexual deviance in a more forthright manner. The unwillingness to openly challenge sexual abuse by male figures within the church would haunt Konnersreuth once again during the Third Reich.

Von Lama also used the context of Konnersreuth to mock the "new woman" of the 1920s. The Neumanns' home attracted pilgrims of all varieties in the early days of her stigmata, including those who came out of curiosity rather than religious conviction. Von Lama describes the arrival of a wealthy Italian woman who came to write newspaper articles about Neumann's stigmata. He criticized her male travelling companion, her expensive and fashionable clothes, as well as her perceived arrogance for the peasants of Konnersreuth. Von Lama wrote, "She was the only woman in the village who smoked cigarettes." He described with admiration how the village refused her requests for interviews and how Neumann's mother tried to inhibit her visit to the Friday Suffering before the woman and her boyfriend departed Konnersreuth for Paris.[43] The Konnersreuth Circle included such visitors in their accounts in order to contrast the strict morality of Neumann's movement and the austerity of the countryside with urban women who symbolized sexual emancipation and liberation during the Weimar years. While they offered redemption to women willing to conform to Neumann's views on sexuality, they heaped public scorn on those who rejected them.

Accusations of sexual immorality became a weapon in the struggle over Konnersreuth's legitimacy. For example, members of the Konnersreuth Circle used charges of misconduct against their opponents in the Catholic Church. Although absent from press accounts perhaps for legal purposes, the Neumann family accused powerful theologian and Neumann critic Georg Wunderle of touching Neumann's breasts inappropriately during an examination of her stigmata. Wunderle initially displayed some sympathy towards the stigmata in its earliest days before becoming an outspoken critic of the Konnersreuth Circle. The Neumann family used this story of embarrassing sexual temptation to explain his change of heart and to deny him future access to their home.[44] This story about Wunderle also contributed to one of Ferdinand Neumann's major objections to allowing his daughter into a clinic for observation. He suggested secular doctors would violate his daughter's sexual purity in the midst of intrusive medical exams. He referred specifically to the exam by Dr Ewald in 1927 and claimed he examined her to affirm her virginity without seeking permission or consent.[45] These concerns about Neumann's virginity being violated in a medical exam resonated with her followers and featured in the accommodations offered by Cardinal Faulhaber when negotiating for clinical testing in the early 1930s.[46] Neumann used her father's concerns about her virginity as one of several reasons to avoid an exam that might compromise her sanctity. Neumann's protectiveness against potential male predators must be grounded in her experience of sexual assault from her youth; moreover, she had good reasons to suspect priests and doctors of sexual harassment. However, she also used her chaste image to discredit opponents within the church and safeguard her status as a legitimate religious visionary.

Adversaries of the Konnersreuth Circle also tried unsuccessfully to discredit Therese Neumann through false charges of secretive sexual sin. Doctors like Josef Deutsch who claimed Neumann bled from hysteria insinuated that a woman without her mental faculties could lose control of her sexuality. Patients with hysteria were viewed as "sexual perverts." However, even most of Neumann's fiercest opponents rejected this view of her. Whatever the criticism, her credentials as a virgin seemed impeccable. Her communist opponents also used sex as a platform to embarrass the Konnersreuth Circle. Three communist newspapers published stories claiming Neumann mothered a child out of wedlock after an illicit relationship with a magician prior to her rise to fame as a stigmatic. Neumann's family won their court case against these editors, once again fending off an assault on her purported virtue and spiritual authority.[47] While these attempts to denigrate Neumann failed, they demonstrated the importance of sexuality to the debate about modern mysticism. Even her left-wing opponents understood that virginity represented one of Neumann's most treasured assets.

Therese Neumann's relationship to sex constituted a case of personal empowerment with political ramifications. Growing up in a vulnerable environment for women where rape, sexual assault, and sexual harassment shaped the experiences of her own youth, her endorsement of strict chastity out of wedlock represented her way of rejecting abuse by male patriarchs from within the context of pious Catholicism. Although her desire for a fierce defence of the female body against male lust through discipline, faith, modest dress, and even violence offered some women comfort and a path to redemption, it also perpetuated negative stereotypes about women and culturally supported a political direction that inhibited Weimar democracy. Neumann blamed women more than men for sexual misconduct, replicating the rhetoric of the church on such matters, and marginalized and humiliated women who even slightly transgressed her rigid system of sexual ethics. Either consciously or subconsciously, she likely chose to admonish fallen women rather than the male patriarchy for sexual vice because a more forthright condemnation of male sexual aggression would have been consequential and precarious. Neumann's actions and publicity also entered the public's consciousness at a fragile moment in the late Weimar Republic as Catholic women especially led a rightward political shift over issues such as sexual morality. While the early years of the Weimar Republic saw prominent Catholic politicians, such as Wilhelm Marx and Agnes Neuhaus, acknowledge their younger, female base by admitting the double standard present in legislation controlling prostitution, this compromise on religious morality experienced a backlash just as Therese Neumann became famous in 1927. The Catholic political parties and women's associations led a popular campaign against legislation providing more rights to prostitutes and against perceived sexual permissiveness from the moderate and left-wing parties of the republic, who were accused of "cultural Bolshevism."[48] The conservative shift on sexuality fractured the democratic coalition that Catholics held together between liberal and social democratic parties and Neumann's strict moral vision contributed to the downfall of cooperation between Catholics and other parties on this issue. This microhistory of one religious figure in small-town Bavaria shows how the vulnerability of women partially shaped the activism of Catholic women on matters of sexuality and reproduction.

Conclusion

The Konnersreuth story intersected not just with Catholic history but also interacted with some of the most pressing themes of the Weimar Republic in its waning years. The perception the new woman of the 1920s provoked both praise and scorn from a socially and politically divided country and Konnersreuth's presentation of gender existed within this larger debate. The place of women in a modernizing and urbanizing society also roiled Germany on the right and left of the political spectrum, making Therese Neumann's subtle consolidation of power all the more interesting. Broad debates about sexuality, prostitution, birth control, and abortion became prominent parts of political discourse after the First World War, contextualizing Konnersreuth's strict moral teaching. Finally, the struggle to maintain a democratic government in the face of fractious debates about cultural values, economic crisis, and the proliferation of competing political parties dominated the last years of the Weimar Republic and the downfall of political Catholicism played a prominent role in it. The case study of the Konnersreuth Circle illuminates some already known elements of the Weimar Republic's decline and uncovers their cultural roots through the practice of microhistory.

On the one hand, the sexual politics of Konnersreuth added to the moral backlash within Catholic and conservative parties that associated the republic with an unwanted shift in moral values. By promoting a rigid understanding of sexuality, Therese Neumann converged with the rightward shift of Germany's Catholics on the issue and assisted its implicit depiction of moral uncertainty that undercut the legitimacy of the parliamentary system. In addition to dividing an already segmented

Catholic political base over the issue of mysticism, the Konnersreuth Circle also contributed to the moral backlash against legislation like the anti-Venereal Disease Law of 1927 and the political rhetoric on birth control by Centre Party coalition partners. The moral politics regarding sexuality possessed political ramifications that undercut parliamentary rule on the eve of the National Socialist rise to power by presenting the republic as a government of disorderly immorality. Despite the fevered pitch to the anxiety about sexual morals in Konnersreuth, Neumann's advocates also attacked National Socialists over such issues. The opening vignette of this chapter illustrates how Gerlich used perceived sexual deviance among the SA as part of his plan to depict the National Socialist movement as morally bankrupt. The desire for moral utopia in Konnersreuth delegitimized both republicanism and fascism.

Therese Neumann and her followers confound as well as confirm past assumptions about gender, sex, and politics during the 1920s and 1930s. Neumann's ambiguous manipulation of power within a rural, patriarchal, and Catholic context contradicts any notion of religious women as anachronistic vestiges from the past. Although she promoted the hierarchy of the church and the countryside, Neumann used the cultural values of her upbringing to increase her influence over time. Her use of Catholic spirituality to cope with past sexual assault and mitigate future attacks also illustrates how even conservative world views empowered women. Even though she and her circle converged with the church's regressive view of gender, she nonetheless emerged as a formidable woman pursuing her own avenues to power despite the stereotype of modern religious women as antiquated.

Neumann's hard-fought feminine agency and her circle's prominence would face their greatest challenge after Adolf Hitler's appointment as chancellor. Attacked in this new political era by church, state, and hostile local actors, the Konnersreuth Circle faced a possible end to this stigmatist's great popularity. With less publicity, they undertook a careful quest for survival under a totalitarian state.

Chapter Five

Disruptive Potential: Catholic Miracles under the Third Reich

In the years between 1937 and 1940, four girls in the Catholic town of Heede saw the Virgin Mary over one hundred times. As they shared Mary's warnings about sinfulness and secularization, thousands of pilgrims streamed into their isolated region, motivated in part to protest the attempts by the National Socialist state to dissolve confessional groups, restrict religion to the private sphere, and remove clerical oversight from schools. At once an act of spirituality and religious protest, twenty thousand people overwhelmed Heede in one day at the height of the visions in 1937.[1] These events began a new phase of German Catholicism's era of modern miracles through the emphasis on Marian apparitions that would become ubiquitous during the post-war years, but they also illustrated the role of such unsanctioned mysticism during the Third Reich. As a form of piety, veneration of Therese Neumann's stigmata and the Virgin Mary articulated the mainstream Catholic desire to preserve the church's role in the midst of a National Socialist dictatorship interested in marginalizing the faith. As a subaltern cultural force, Marian pilgrims and Konnersreuth supporters understood this sacramental mission differently from their formal religious leaders, seeking public affirmation of otherworldly occurrences, God's comfort from personal hardship, and direct access to their higher power. Shutting down popular devotions to local seers proved elusive to regional bishops as well as the Gestapo. It entailed the alienation of an otherwise compliant population and the destruction of a movement without formal institutions and enthusiasm for martyrdom. Catholic mysticism possessed subversive potential that its mystics and pilgrims ultimately never entirely fulfilled.

Since many of her followers have shaped the existing narrative, the most common belief about Therese Neumann under Nazism is that she and her supporters formed a "nest of resistance." Rudolf Morsey, a well-regarded church historian, also supports such a depiction in his publication of Fritz Gerlich's correspondence.[2] Anthropologist Ulrike Wiethaus provides an alternative viewpoint, arguing that Therese Neumann represented the resistance of a rural culture against a modernizing and centralizing nation state. This thesis buttresses the more general claim by Thomas Breuer that rural Bavarian Catholic discord with Nazism constituted a protest against modernity rather than National Socialist ideology.[3] The Konnersreuth Circle contained too many layers of ambiguity to be exclusively labelled anti-Nazi or anti-modern. Therese Neumann's reputation as a bleeding oracle during the Third Reich overcame tremendous obstacles after the Nazi rise to power in 1933. After a tidal wave of press coverage, millions of visitors, and turbulent literary battles over her authenticity during the waning years of the Weimar Republic, Therese Neumann entered the Third Reich era with a strong infrastructure of support that survived a violent social and cultural coordination by the dictatorship. The NSDAP viewed Neumann with a mixture of fear, respect, and fascination, but ultimately remained concerned about her ability to disturb the social uniformity their state hoped to achieve. Therese Neumann of Konnersreuth possessed tremendous capacity to disrupt both church and state during the Third Reich, but she survived the era to become a hero of the early Federal Republic because of her failure to entirely fulfil this potential. Her persistently captivated followers formed a power base that concerned Catholic and Nazi authorities, but Neumann's unwillingness to transgress certain barriers prevented excommunication by the church or incarceration by the state.

Furthermore, Marian veneration followed a similar pattern. Although the Heede seers became the most popular and notorious figures involved in this movement, other evidence suggests a widespread upswing of worship of the Virgin Mary that provided the basis for the explosion of miracles at the conclusion of the war. If tens of thousands of people travelled to Heede during the early 1940s, millions of Germans participated in the miracle wave of the post-war period. The use of the Virgin Mary to subtly question the regime's religious policy, seek comfort from bomb damage, and channel dissonance from the losing war effort laid the groundwork for Mary's powerful symbolism at the start of the Cold War.

The stigmata in Konnersreuth and the rising faith in the Virgin Mary created a cultural undercurrent of the German Catholic community that interacted with the challenges the larger church faced under the Third Reich. After an initial modus vivendi between Catholicism and National Socialism through the concordat with the Vatican and the Centre Party's support for the Enabling Act of 1933, the relationship became more complex. While the vast majority of Catholics supported the regime's campaign of law and order and aggressive foreign policy, they bristled as the Third Reich limited the role of organized Christian churches. First, the new dictatorship murdered the most outspoken confessional critics of Nazism on the Night of the Long Knives. Then the regime limited the public spectacles of the Catholic faith, such as Corpus Christi processions, and undertook campaigns against confessional youth groups, voluntary associations, and the clerical role in schools.[4] All of this conformed to the larger NSDAP desire to have the party rather than the churches order the social lives and world views of German citizens. The regime even ran a series of anticlerical trials against priests and monks accused of sexual misconduct and corruption to embarrass the church.[5] While some bishops and many Catholic congregants expressed outrage at the state's church policies, dissent remained constrained enough so as not to threaten the overall functioning of the dictatorship. In fact many ecclesiastical leaders urged cooperation with the regime and caution in challenging invasive changes to religion. Many of the bishops and clergy actually appreciated the decline of powerful lay organizations as it concentrated more power within their own hands and they feared open opposition would only provoke more stringent anticlerical measures. They also avoided dissent given the nationalism among Catholic worshippers and their disinterest in aiding German Jews other than those who had converted.[6]

Researching Catholic mysticism in the 1930s and 1940s reshapes traditional views of the so-called "church struggles" described above in several major ways. First, many scholars view the National Socialist era as a period that contributed to the demise of the Catholic milieu. The combination of NSDAP restrictions against an active laity and the upheaval of a violent war that radically changed the demographics of the country made the Catholic subculture and institutional power of the early twentieth century obsolete.[7] However, the survival of the Konnersreuth Circle and the emergence of a powerful Marian revival offer an alternate narrative of religious development. While totalitarianism destroyed church institutions, Catholicism evolved into a more personalized and private faith that possessed dynamism but became increasingly free of formal church control. Second, the role of miraculous mentalities in German Catholics also illustrates the ambiguous nature of Catholic dissent against the regime. Seers and pilgrims challenged both Nazi authorities and their own bishops. There was not a binary relationship between Catholics and Nazis but triangular interplay between ecclesiastical leaders, party functionaries, and miracle enthusiasts. By turning miracle sites and pilgrimages into acts of dissent against anti-church policy, mystics irritated the Gestapo and disobeyed the calls by most bishops for caution. This dissidence contributed to the legitimacy for Christian Democracy after the war, but it represented only a minor challenge to the state. Supporters of unsanctioned miracles attacked church policy and sometimes became martyrs against the state, but they rarely used their spirituality to obstruct the vast human rights violations against Jews, communists, and others. The advocates of places like Konnersreuth and Heede also ultimately valued their own goods of salvation above all else. Hoping to survive the regime without dying or being excommunicated, they compromised with the state and sometimes even used its politically violent institutions to settle scores with their opponents.

Third, gendered appeals and sexuality continued as essential elements of struggle within the Catholic Church over miracles. Women like Therese Neumann became far more vulnerable and constrained in their exercise of power due to the dominance of eugenic thinking in the medical establishment of the Third Reich. Viewed by the regime as possible asocials, female seers faced the possibility of institutionalization, sterilization, or worse at the very moment that their male followers lost access to a free press that was necessary to advocate on their behalf. With many of the most outspoken members of the miracles movement imprisoned or killed, the cult of mystical masculinity now focused on the figure of Therese Neumann's father, Ferdinand Neumann, who compelled the Catholic public less than the murdered Fritz Gerlich. Despite such obstacles Therese Neumann actually used the upheaval of dictatorship to increase her own power and agency, which placed her in a uniquely influential position after the war. Finally, Therese Neumann and the seers of Heede continued a quest to remake the sexual order of Germany – in some cases against the objections of the Nazi state. However, this emphasis on chastity in Konnersreuth also made the movement vulnerable when its patriarchy became embroiled in scandals surrounding sexual abuse. In sum, the Third Reich combined with mystical movements to deepen the personalization of faith and weaken the power of bishops.

Konnersreuth and the Third Reich: Surviving Totalitarianism

The Konnersreuth Circle faced the greatest obstacles of Therese Neumann's lifetime during the Third Reich. First, the National Socialist state's reliance on political violence, censorship, and control of most social and professional organizations caused individual suffering and difficulties in maintaining a public profile. Numerous Neumann supporters were murdered, imprisoned, and harassed by a state suspicious of the circle's connections to the BVP and Fritz Gerlich. The gradual silencing of most Catholic press organs as well as all newspapers unaffiliated with the NSDSAP drastically reduced the reporting on the Neumann story. Furthermore, the Bavarian bishops converged with the feelings of most party officials that it was best if Neumann and her family faded from public view. After their decree of 1932, Bishop Buchberger welcomed the decline in coverage of his famous seer and requested that all parties cease open discussion of the matter unless the Neumanns agreed to a renewed clinical exam. Finally, the Neumanns and Father Naber struggled against forces within their own town and family that cast increasing doubts upon the legitimacy of her miracles. Despite these problems, Neumann survived the regime and yet another dispute with the bishops to renew her religious celebrity after the war. Such flexibility by Neumann and her following illustrates the durability of their movement.

The tragic outcome of Fritz Gerlich's struggle against Nazism badly damaged the Konnersreuth Circle in the first years of the regime. After having his newspaper ransacked, he endured imprisonment in Dachau during March of 1933 and died on the Night of the Long Knives as the NSDAP simultaneously eliminated Ernst Röhm, SA leaders, and other long-standing political opponents of the party on 30 June 1934. Martyred alongside the Berlin Catholic Action leader Erich Klausener, Gerlich became a symbol for many mystical Catholics who disagreed with elements of the new state but also a warning against taking too aggressive a stance. The NSDAP and the local gendarme reported unrest in Konnersreuth after Gerlich's death as Therese Neumann vented her anger at the town's market for all to hear. Neumann declared Gerlich to be a "martyr for his faith" after spotting him among the communion of saints in a vision on All Saints' Day. One Konnersreuth supporter spent time in the same Dachau Cell 46 where Gerlich had been and claimed that it was "filled with an atmosphere of sanctity" and "rare spirituality." Distress spread throughout Neumann's most intimate pilgrims as one female supporter was accused of spreading panic in the town and a former war veteran devoted to Neumann openly complained of unrest in Munich over Gerlich's fate.[8] Simultaneously outraged by the murder and inspired by Gerlich's powerful convictions, the Konnersreuth Circle grappled with his loss. The closure of his newspaper, which both promoted Neumann and articulated a fresh brand of Christian politics, meant that National Socialist censorship affected this group much earlier than other Catholic presses that would not be silenced in some cases until the late 1930s. The loss of his leadership and charisma created a gaping hole in this religious circle that would only grow with the untimely deaths of Ingbert Naab, Franz Xaver Wutz, Friedrich Ritter von Lama, and other dominant figures. Therese Neumann was left to negotiate the choppy waters of this violent dictatorship without some of her most dynamic and powerful patrons. She and her family also experienced multiple searches of their house by the local police in the first years of the Third Reich and likely saw the violence against their supporters as a grave warning.

While early harassment by the National Socialist state stifled the Konnersreuth debate in the press, the Bavarian bishops encouraged reticence on the matter from within the church. Angry about the open rebuke to his authority by the Neumann family and their circle, Bishop Buchberger of Regensburg implored Catholics to remain publicly mute on the debate until Therese Neumann submitted to the medical exam necessary for authorities to make a final decision on the legitimacy of her miracles. After the public statement by the Bavarian bishops of 1932 that articulated their desire for an exam, they requested that not only Konnersreuth supporters but also its critics take a vow of silence. As far as Buchberger was concerned, the less publicity that Konnersreuth received the better. While incapable of formally disciplining Neumann and her circle, he wanted to marginalize them. When combined with the shuttering of *Der Gerade Weg* in 1933 and the gradual restrictions of all press outlets by the Nazi regime, Therese Neumann faced the prospect of sliding out of the German and European limelight. This muzzling of the Konnersreuth debate affected the opposition to Neumann as well. For example, Neumann's greatest Catholic critic, Dr Josef Deutsch, remained in steady contact with Buchberger after 1932, sharing folders full of letters and documents he hoped would discredit Neumann. Yet he initially obeyed Buchberger's wish to keep such material away from the public's gaze. Furthermore, Dr Theodor Witry from Alsace also gathered much data that would expose the rabid and controversial Konnersreuth publicist von Lama as an "unctuous fraud" who allegedly believed himself "divine due to mental illness."[9] Buchberger successfully prevented such sentiments from reaching the press for a short time.

Neumann's primary public presence during the Third Reich shifted from the press to personal visits to sympathetic parishes throughout the country. She travelled through rural Westphalia and to towns like Bingen and spent considerable time in Eichstätt. She also visited several convents. In anticipation of her stopover, arrangements were made to elaborately decorate churches and draw large crowds.[10] While still a public figure, Neumann's reach receded with the contraction of available pilgrims and the closure of the open press.

The Bavarian bishops' decree and Nazi restrictions on the press led to several years of quiet regarding Konnersreuth, which loosened considerably from 1936 to 1938 with the publication of a book by Armenian-Catholic Archbishop Josef Teodorowicz of Lviv that argued in favour of Neumann's validity. At first sceptical of the Konnersreuth phenomenon, Teodorowicz finally drove from his annual stop at the baths of Marienbad to visit Neumann in 1931, eventually making a Konnersreuth visit part of his yearly ritual. Inspired by what he judged to be accurate prophesies about two people back in Lviv by Neumann, he became her most notable defender during the 1930s, alongside a string of other sympathetic bishops in Czechoslovakia, Austria, and the United States.

Teodorowicz published despite protests by German Catholic intellectuals because he believed the work of her German opponents prior to 1933, as well as international critics like French Jesuit Paul Siwek, created "a caricature of Konnersreuth."[11] Claiming to blend modern psychological methods with a precise sense of Catholic mystical tradition, the bishop refuted men like Josef Deutsch who depicted Neumann as hysterical. In the process, he explicitly attacked the field of parapsychology and other "pseudosciences" as examples of creeping materialism and atheism bent on the removal of spirituality from the European landscape.[12] Ultimately viewing science as a reflection of faith and not vice versa, Teodorowicz also questioned George Wunderle, Johann Westermayr, and Alois Mager for their misinterpretation of Catholic mystical traditions. For example, he suggested that such critics incorrectly used examples from the life of early modern saint Teresa of Avila to repudiate Neumann's authenticity.[13]

Teodorowicz reshaped several tropes common to the Konnersreuth debate during the Weimar years to fit the context of the 1930s. While stressing once again Neumann's heroic suffering, he focused more than previous writers on the stigmata as a method for personal and internal piety. He lauded Neumann's most significant trait as her desire to always be closer to God and suggested that her ecstasy imparted a similar interior relationship with Jesus for pilgrims. For example, she told him, "What then? Some praise me, and others call me a fraud. I pay no attention to the one or the other; because it does not lead to God."[14] The suggestion by Teodorowicz that this latter concern became Neumann's central message represented a new point of emphasis in an age of increasing authoritarianism. Mysticism ceased to be a public spectacle as it had been in the 1920s and now became a rallying point for private piety. A common reaction by many European Catholics who attempted to reconcile their faith with a sometimes hostile fascist opposition, this continued personalization of prayer also unintentionally contributed to the fragmentation of church authority. Teodorowicz used internal prayer and patient suffering as a model for how the Konnersreuth Circle and its followers might adapt and survive after the rise of the NSDAP, but he also frustrated German Catholic bishops who rightly feared the ways Konnersreuth disrupted their own influence and the significance of formal rituals, sacraments, and teaching.

Teodorowicz's challenge to the esoteric wing of science in Europe also took on new meaning during the Third Reich. Recent work by Eric Kurlander and others indicates the prevalence of a "supernatural imaginary" by the Nazi Party leadership, including interest and reverence for Ariosophy, "World Ice Theory," monism, and other mythological and occult practices. Featured most prominently in the writings and speeches of the neo-pagan propagandist and ideologue Alfred Rosenberg, these National Socialist "spiritualities" propagated by elites within the party articulated antagonism for organized Christianity.[15] The "new religions" of these Nazis were examples of how spirituality could devolve into a set of appropriative practices independent of Christianity, a pattern of great concern for the church. While Teodorowicz's passages that condemn modern materialism and rationalism might be interpreted as yet another example of Catholic leadership bemoaning post-Enlightenment secularism, his book also represented an attack on totalitarian forces of the 1930s, both fascist and communist, that posed a unique threat to Catholicism as rival new religions. Teodorowicz endowed the Konnersreuth Circle's battle with modern medicine and rationalist interpretations of science with a new edge that challenged the wing of the NSDAP enamoured with a mixture of pseudoscience and the occult. For example, he proclaimed, "Science which adores the material world as its ideal cannot be hit in a more vulnerable spot than when in a peasant maid the fundamental law of the preservation of life through nourishment is suspended in favor of a higher and spiritual food."[16] In such quotes Teodorowicz and other Konnersreuth followers not only converged with the same trend of supernaturalism that also consumed some elements of the party, but also openly protested National Socialism as a pagan materialist world view that rivalled their church as a source of spirituality. Nazi elites and Konnersreuth devotees sought personalized spiritualties with reduced involvement of organized religious institutions, while Neumann's followers disliked the complete rejection of the churches, neo-paganism, and reification of science by some of the high-ranking National Socialists enthralled by the occult.

Teodorowicz also altered the gendered depiction of Therese Neumann in the new environment of a politically violent dictatorship. Shorn of her most powerful male protectors, Neumann emerges in the account of Teodorowicz as the charismatic and gender-bending focal point of her circle. Gone were the dominant roles played by Wutz and Gerlich. Neumann appeared the master of her own spiritual domain. He wrote, "Therese Neumann's will governs her feeling and humors. She is in every way a strong type." The Polish-Armenian bishop ascribed to Neumann the masculine rationality built into the image of Gerlich prior to the Nazi regime. He described her "sober mentality," praised her "sphere of thought" as "masculine," and complimented her "masculine will." Teodorowicz suggested that Neumann always rejected "feminine handicraft" in favour of "oxen or horses that are to be driven and lead."[17] This new emphasis built on the gendered ambiguity inherent in a woman performing the passion of a male saviour. Wiethaus observes that women stigmatics undergo a "transgendering" when in ecstasy that carries over into their behaviour when not having visions. Neumann showed signs prior to the Third Reich of wanting to be a man and join the priesthood.[18] With only her father's patriarchy as the remaining check on her authority, Neumann's dominance of her own movement grew into spheres previously gendered male and supporters like Teodorowicz increasingly recognized her agency.

This depiction of Neumann's masculine elements was softened by attempts to reign in the threat she posed to the hegemony of male authority. The patriarchal dominance of her father, expressed through his curt treatment of visitors and stubbornness with the decrees of the church, was central in Third Reich publications by Neumann supporters. Teodorowicz also tempered his narrative of Neumann's agency in two ways. First, he depicted another side to Neumann's strong will. He described her as "weak" and "indifferent" to criticism when in her spiritual zone as she only cared about bringing herself and other Catholics "closer to God." He described her further as a "pliable tool in the hand of Christ." Presenting a double-sided Neumann with a powerful will when not in ecstasy and submissive while at her most spiritual, Teodorowicz defended her from accusations of mental illness while also protecting her from charges that she became too disruptive to the church or rural patriarchy. Second, he compared Neumann positively to the "new woman" of the 1920s. He claimed Neumann should not be viewed through the same lens as a movie star or sportswoman despite her starring role in the tabloid press during the Weimar era. Rather, Teodorowicz presented Neumann as the ideal for the "charitable" woman of religion, constraining her in this way to a traditionally feminine sphere.[19] While endowing Neumann with more agency and rationality than previous accounts, Teodorowicz bestowed Neumann with masculine power without stripping her of the femininity necessary for a prominent mystic.

This book prompted a published response by Josef Deutsch and a new public firestorm of attention on Konnersreuth. Unable to stay silent after the publicity of the Teodorowicz study, Deutsch broke his tacit agreement to keep the Konnersreuth issue closed to the public. Close to death, which the Konnersreuth Circle suggested came as punishment from God, Deutsch argued that Therese Neumann humiliated Catholic doctors and scientists and threatened the church with shame should she ever be revealed as a fraud. He declared his intention to "struggle for truth" until "his last breath."[20] Deutsch's book expanded the debate of the 1920s by mounting not only a critique of Therese Neumann and her circle for deviating from church authority, but also creating a defence of natural science within Catholicism. Deutsch claimed to be proud of his quest for "natural science" in "God's creation" in the spirit of Johannes Kepler. He expressed awe, wonder, and enhanced faith when viewing "God's order" for the world as expressed through science. In fact, Deutsch implicitly agreed with Teodorowicz in his rejection of the esoteric element to German intellectual culture present since the nineteenth century and prominent among some Nazi leaders. He once again attacked other critics of Konnersreuth, such as Eduard Aigner of the SS, who felt telepathy, hypnosis, or any other so-called "spiritualist" explanations for Neumann's stigmata departed from his diagnosis of hysteria. Deutsch's passion for battle against Konnersreuth emanated from his desire to protect Catholicism from kitsch, pseudo-science, and embarrassing standpoints that would make the church vulnerable to satire by the NSDAP. The regime's attraction to the occult and its desire to expose stereotypes about Catholic backwardness caused him to be especially fearful about what Neumann's popularity meant for the future of the church.

The Deutsch publication contributed to the pressure on the bishop's residence in Regensburg to pursue a clinical exam once again. Deutsch critiqued Buchberger and other authorities for not going further with his quest for a medical investigation.[21] He expressed tremendous anger that Neumann, Naber, and others had not been silenced and excommunicated ten years earlier and exhibited astonishment at the number of Catholic clergy and bishops in Europe who threatened the integrity of the church by expressing public or private support for Neumann's stigmata. Disparaging the judgment of the German bishops and defending his own credentials as a lay Catholic to intervene, Deutsch undercut church authority in a manner not all that different from the very men he detested most in Neumann's circle, such as Friedrich Ritter von Lama.[22] In a letter to his cousin, he said, "I am Catholic to the bone and as a Catholic I find the Konnersreuth comedy difficult and the abandonment of the clergy to be doubly bitter."[23] Deutsch went public with his attacks once more against the wishes of German bishops because he felt they abandoned their responsibility as stewards of orthodoxy. The renewal of the divide caused by Konnersreuth eroded Buchberger's authority even more deeply in the context of a totalitarian state already subverting his elevated status. The critics of Konnersreuth now destabilized Buchberger as much as the Konnersreuth Circle itself.

The pressure of renewed debate initiated fresh efforts by the church for an examination. These two books caused coercive pressure and negotiation between the church and the Neumann family. Urging Faulhaber to re-enter discussions about a potential exam with the Neumanns and implicitly referring to Deutsch and his supporters, Buchberger complained, "There are many genuinely Catholic men, priests, and doctors who do not believe in the alleged fasting."[24] Therese Neumann apparently agreed personally to an exam at this point but claimed her father's stubbornness prevented cooperation. Ferdinand Neumann's continued resistance to medical tests on his daughter thwarted the renewed attempt to resolve the controversy.[25]

In yet another sleight of hand, Neumann used her reverence for patriarchy to mask her rebellious rejection of an order from her bishop. Despite Teodorowicz's reinterpretation of Neumann as a masculine figure of strength, she retreated behind her father's authority in order to seem less disorderly once again. Such a manoeuvre protected her from excommunication and supported her image as obedient to the church. She tread a fine line between compliance and dissent in a letter to Buchberger on 21 November 1937. She claimed her father would disown her and cut off financial support should she submit to an exam against his wishes. Appealing to Buchberger for counsel, she asked, "What should I do after the exam? Where should I go then? I will no longer be allowed to go home as I know my parents too well. And who will support me since I no longer receive disability insurance? One needs clothes and above all a warm room since I am often cold. Please give me an answer and your advice."[26] By approaching the bishopric in this manner, she softened the reprimand that followed. Buchberger conceded that it was not Neumann the religious figure who denied his request, but her insistent father.

Ferdinand Neumann became even more integral to his daughter's defence than ever before. By reaffirming her decision to obey her father before her bishop, Therese escaped accountability for embarrassing Buchberger. Ferdinand was simultaneously displayed as the true problem of the bishopric as well as a father with understandable concerns. In the absence of Gerlich and eventually Wutz, he became the masculine face of the Konnersreuth movement. While critics attacked his rude disrespect for many different sorts of visitors, including church princes and doctors, advocates constructed him as the ideal rural patriarch nobly resisting the secular forces of modernity. Another book published from Lviv by a doctor named Peter Radlo, who claimed expertise in unmasking false stigmatics, defended Ferdinand against the withering analysis of Deutsch. Radlo praised him: "A good reputation is of the highest value for him. He acquired it through an upstanding life as a person, as a solider on the battlefield, as a father and educator of ten children, as a citizen of his village, and as a good Christian and practicing Catholic."[27] Radlo replaced the image of the rational man so carefully cultivated around Gerlich in the Weimar era with the idealized rural Christian and patriot. Ferdinand's stubbornness and brusque nature were to be understood in the context of his defence of a way of life particular to the Bavarian countryside. His agrarian ties, local colour, and First World War service made him less threatening than Gerlich in the Third Reich.

Ferdinand refused a new clinical exam on several grounds. First, he claimed that the bishopric broke their word when they promised no further exams would be needed after the fourteen-day observation in his home. His defenders pointed to this patriarchal sense of honour typical of the Upper Palatinate to make his obstinacy something to be admired rather than criticized. Second, Ferdinand expressed great distrust of the medical system and complained about intimidation by doctors and anonymous threatening letters. The National Socialist policies regarding sterilization of those with disabilities and Ferdinand's continued concern about his daughter's sexual purity during invasive exams were also considerations. Just as many prominent Catholic figures defended his decision as criticized it. Dr Rudolf Maria Hynek of Prague admired his "farmer's blood" that caused suspicion of outsiders and Bishop von Preysing of Eichstätt complimented his "hard head" on the matter.[28] By casting Ferdinand Neumann as the ideal rural patriarch nostalgically defending disappearing values, his dissent against the church lost its edge and provided Therese Neumann enough cover to avoid an exam that could have cost her spiritual legitimacy.

Advocates and opponents of Konnersreuth pressured Bishops Buchberger and Faulhaber as they considered the most recent failure to secure a clinical exam. For example, an anonymous letter to Faulhaber accused "priests" and "pulpits" of silence about Neumann's miracles and of joining the church's enemies for not supporting the stigmata. Besides the outspoken Deutsch, a phalanx of critics pleaded with Regensburg for either excommunication or denial of sacraments. Well-connected opponents from the Weimar era, including Norbert Brühl and Dr Paul Martini, lined up their high-ranking Vatican contacts against those of Neumann's elite supporters in the bishoprics of Prague, Innsbruck, Salzburg, and Lviv. Alois Mager attempted to sway then Secretary of State Eugenio Pacelli himself. Lurking beneath the surface of these efforts was also the widespread concern that the National Socialist state would step in to forcibly institutionalize Neumann independent of Catholic oversight.[29] Neumann's contentious status eroded church authority as her admirers and adversaries both felt aggrieved with a hierarchy that had forsaken them and threatened by a totalitarian state that sought to usurp their hegemony over such a spiritual matter.

The repeated refusal of the Neumann family ultimately led to a more strongly worded but curt statement by the Bavarian bishops on 10 December 1937. This new proclamation absolved the church of any responsibility for what transpired in Konnersreuth.[30] Frustrated with years of perceived disobedience, Buchberger created as much separation between his diocese and Konnersreuth as possible on the eve of the Second World War. A theology professor closely associated with Buchberger published an essay that argued Therese Neumann was in open conflict with the pope himself by privileging her father over her bishop.[31] Unable and perhaps unwilling to excommunicate the stigmata supporters due to their persistent popularity and still powerful connections, Buchberger dealt what seemed to be a serious setback to Neumann's desire for official church recognition. By publicly washing their hands of Konnersreuth, the bishops made the rebellious Neumann family even more vulnerable under the Third Reich without going so far as to actively repress her movement or its association with the church.

While the public feud within the church over Neumann went silent after the statement by the bishops, the controversy over her miracles smoldered within Konnersreuth and in the private correspondence. By the late 1930s and early 1940s the town of Konnersreuth became intensely divided. Some accounts suggest that Neumann and Naber continued their spiritual and cultural hegemony within the town. For example, a report by a student who visited Konnersreuth in the summer of 1938 indicated persistent faith in her mysticism by both locals and outsiders. This student interviewed numerous farmers from Konnersreuth, all of whom attested to her authenticity and good works. They recounted a woman whom Neumann healed from a deadly disease through vicarious suffering and a thirty-six-year-old man whom she also cured on his deathbed.[32] Another pilgrim to Konnersreuth during this time, who caught a rare glimpse of the Friday Suffering, wrote to Faulhaber not only attesting to the individual comfort he found from Neumann but also the tranquility, peacefulness, and spirituality of the family and the town.[33] Local business owner, Hugo Schiml, suggested that Neumann did not submit to an exam because she had a vision saying she would never return from the clinic, indicating his patronage for her against the German bishops.[34] This grass-roots support, built upon faith in supernatural intercession, created a powerful base that stood outside the usual institutions of church power.

Reports to the contrary also emerged, depicting a growing wing of hostility from within the region, town, and even the Neumann extended family. A Deutsch supporter visited Konnersreuth and described the town as being in "crisis." It was split between those who revered Neumann and those who felt she was fraudulent. He suggested that the closer one came to town the more the openly vocal opposition to Neumann grew. This division possessed political contours as the opposition to the stigmata centred on a married couple who both taught in the school and belonged to the NSDAP, while the Neumann loyalists were former Bavarian People's Party voters. Twenty-six residents of Konnersreuth joined the party in 1933 after the party and SA established a presence. They blamed Neumann and Naber for low enrolment of children in the Hitler Youth. Approximately 30 per cent of all eligible young people participated. The teacher who led the local faction of the NSDAP tried to counter Naber's influence by using time at school to prove Neumann's fasting a fraud.[35]

In one event highlighting Konnersreuth's disunity, Neumann found the moral high ground she seized in the Weimar Republic on the issue of chastity unexpectedly rocky. She used strict sexual morality to defend herself and other women from the constant threat of assault in rural Catholic enclaves during the 1920s, but she failed to stand up for such values when they contradicted her visions. A teacher in Konnersreuth who enjoyed warm relationships with the Neumann family was accused of sexually abusing at least six female students and he went to trial after facing similar accusations ten years earlier. His defence operated from the Neumann house and the Konnersreuth Circle paid his legal fees. After the teacher received a two-year prison sentence, Neumann let it be known in town that she prayed for him because the saviour assured her of his innocence in a vision prior to the trial. Konnersreuth sympathizers may have defended this teacher in light of the regime's widespread public morality trials used to embarrass the church. Sometimes clergy were falsely accused of violating their celibacy but in other cases the party used the toleration of abusive behaviour within the church to humiliate it. Whatever her reasoning, Neumann appears to have conformed to the patriarchal culture that protected male perpetrators of sexual assault in this deeply troubling case.

In his private correspondence, Trier Redemptorist Norbert Brühl used such an instance to assail the Neumann family's legitimacy, referring to the miracles as a "tragicomedy." He proclaimed, "Anyone can do as they please as long as they have faith in Resl." He depicted the family as cruelly wielding enormous power within town. In letters to Westermayr, Deutsch, and bishopric officials in Regensburg and Trier, he undercut the sexual politics of the Neumanns, arguing that Therese was born out of wedlock and that Ferdinand had a secret illegitimate child. He also insinuated that part of their devotion to the teacher's defence was to protect Neumann's father from being called to the stand. He asserted they wished to hide his role in the cover-up and that he had intimidated witnesses during the trial.[36]

The trial results that contradicted Neumann's visions contributed to her loss of credibility locally and in the eyes of a united circle of critics within the Catholic Church. The event did little to dent her national and international following. Even her harshest critics wanted the matter kept quiet. After the Third Reich used public show trials about sexual licentiousness and abuse to discredit the church during the 1930s, clergy wanted no public attention directed towards another sex scandal. As badly as some Catholics wanted Neumann discredited, they also feared the Nazi state using such stories to smear the entire faith. Finally, Neumann and Naber still wielded enormous power within one faction of the town, bullying many of their neighbours into silence on the matter.

Another local scandal posed an even deeper threat to Neumann's legitimacy when her seventeen-year-old niece claimed that her aunt hid food in her room and ate when nobody was around. The daughter of one of Therese's many sisters became embroiled in an ongoing dispute within Konnersreuth between a parochial vicar (*Benefiziat*) Heinrich Muth and Father Naber. It was Muth who contacted the state police regarding the sexual transgressions of the teacher protected by Therese Neumann. In a sign of Buchberger's growing impatience with Konnersreuth, Regensburg dispatched a series of three vicars to assist Naber in his parish who all somewhat sceptically examined the miracles while in town. Muth emerged as the most critical of the bunch and he participated in the local faction that opposed the Neumann family. Like his predecessors, Naber eventually used the pulpit to attack Muth and piled enough negative attention upon him that he eventually left town.

Muth claimed that Neumann's niece, Therese Härtl, told him she heard a clatter of dishes in her aunt's room. She snuck in and opened Neumann's storage space to find food, plates, and silverware. Among other suspicious activities, she allegedly walked in on Neumann in the kitchen before her aunt rapidly retreated. According to Muth, the Neumann family often left a place setting with food and then incorrectly blamed Therese Härtl for eating it. Muth took Härtl's statement and had it verified by three witnesses in town. Muth shared his evidence with representatives from the bishopric of Regensburg as well as Norbert Brühl in Trier. The Neumann family immediately moved

Härtl from Konnersreuth to Eichstätt, where she became a nun, and pressured Muth into leaving the town, even accusing him of sexual abuse against minors. Härtl later retracted her statement and Therese Neumann informed her bishop that she kept snacks and plates in her room for children that visited. Incensed both at his treatment in Konnersreuth as well as the seeming indifference of Regensburg to his findings, Muth felt Deutsch had not gone far enough in his criticism of Therese Neumann. He said that she was not hysterical but an outright fraud. Despite such stark opposition to the miracles, even Muth did not want the information to reach the public. He wanted a short statement from Regensburg declaring the miracles false and nothing more because he too feared major embarrassment for the church at the hands of the Third Reich. In fact, these details never made it into the public record in Neumann's lifetime and only emerged in anti-Konnersreuth essays by theologian Joseph Hanauer in the late twentieth century, pressuring officials in Regensburg to interrogate Härtl about the incident in vain during the 1980s. Regensburg never acted on Muth's charges as the bishopric believed not enough evidence existed to rule definitively. Even as Buchberger increasingly aligned himself with theologians sympathetic to Deutsch, he was unwilling to charge Neumann and her circle with fraud.[37] While the anti-Catholic sentiment within the regime made Neumann vulnerable, the fragile position of the church also protected her from what would have been her worst publicity. Furthermore, the ability of Naber to force Muth from town illustrated the persistence of Neumann's following. Despite local divisions, the Konnersreuth Circle won the power struggle given the continued reluctance of Buchberger to wage a full conflict against belief in the stigmata.

The battle over Konnersreuth raged on within the Catholic Church despite the altered conditions of the Third Reich. The 1930s and early 1940s marked Therese Neumann's most tenuous moments. The loss of valuable patrons to political violence, the measured public criticism by the Bavarian bishops, and divisive local scandals weakened her considerably. Nonetheless, Therese Neumann survived and in some ways strengthened her position. In the midst of such challenges, Neumann once again used reverence for patriarchy to protect herself from a medical establishment eager to disprove her supernatural power. Furthermore, when the chaste image of her circle came under pressure through local controversy, they lashed out against Muth in an attempt to once again seize the high moral ground by accusing him of sexual impropriety. Finally, the tragic loss of so many powerful men in the

Konnersreuth Circle made Neumann herself more powerful. Without Wutz or Gerlich, she transgressed more boundaries into the masculine sphere. While her father remained important and Naber too wielded authority, they would age in the post-war era when Therese herself increased her agency and spiritual authority. Neumann and her following survived the Third Reich even as the controversy surrounding her miracles weakened the already wavering authority of her bishops.

Konnersreuth's Ambiguity towards National Socialism

As Therese Neumann and her supporters managed their relationship with the Catholic Church, they also confronted an unfriendly National Socialist state starting in 1933. Most of the literature about Neumann suggests that she and her circle resisted Nazism unconditionally. Indeed much evidence confirms an antagonism between the Konnersreuth Circle and the Third Reich. When one untangles the myths and evaluates reality, however, the situation appears more complicated and layered. On the one hand, Neumann and her followers acted against the state at several points to uphold Konnersreuth's status as an independent spiritual stronghold and in favour of a politically Catholic alternative to National Socialism. On the other hand, they reigned in much of their anti-Nazi sentiment to facilitate Neumann's freedom and sometimes even used contacts in the NSDAP to resolve disputes.

The persecution of writers and journalists in favour of Neumann suggests anti-Nazism within the Konnersreuth Circle. Besides the martyrdom of Fritz Gerlich, von Lama died in prison, where he was either strangled or hanged in 1941 after years of harassment by the Gestapo. Johannes Maria Verweyen, a Catholic convert who wrote theological and psychological defences of Neumann, died of typhus in Sachsenhausen in 1943. Furthermore, Gerlich's closest collaborators on *Der gerade Weg*, Capuchin Father Ingbert Naab and Fürst Alois Erich von Waldburg-Zeil, endured death threats and house searches by the Gestapo. Eichstätt Professor Franz Xaver Wutz suffered imprisonment as did Erwein Freiherr von Aretin, Bruno Grabinski, and Johannes Maria Höcht. The Nazis briefly detained two of Neumann's brothers, Hans and Ferdinand, as well as her father for aiding Catholic dissidents escaping to Switzerland and admitting French POWs to their home.[38] Most impressively, Neumann's sister Ottilie hid a man of Jewish heritage who converted to Catholicism towards the end of the Second World War.[39] The most prominent writers of Neumann's circle experienced grave consequences for dissenting against the regime. Faith in Neumann's miracles did not lead directly to most of their travails, but it is more than a coincidence that so many of her associates became Gestapo targets for political opposition.

Within Konnersreuth, Neumann and her family remained loyal to the BVP both before and after its dissolution. In July of 1932, neighbours of the Neumanns tore down NSDAP campaign posters and attacked two SA members who displayed them. When the local gendarme arrived to discipline the assailants, Therese Neumann came outside to defend them. Shortly after the Nazis gained power Neumann reportedly refused to see pilgrims who frequented hotels or taverns owned by members of the NSDAP. For these reasons as well as the association with *Der gerade Weg*, local authorities searched the Neumann house on 26 June 1933 for BVP material. While they found nothing incriminating, the local gendarme accused Neumann and her father of verbal abuse.[40] The struggle with the state over the display of crosses in schools added to the tension. When a teacher sympathetic to the regime removed a large cross from a classroom wall, Father Naber preached against the action in the pulpit and Ferdinand Neumann led a procession of seventy-eight residents to the teacher's home to retrieve it despite orders by the local gendarme to clear the street.[41] The politics of the family and town, reinforced by Neumann's spiritual authority, caused skirmishes with the one-party state.

In addition to these incidents, many exaggerated accounts of Konnersreuth resistance circulated without documentary support. The rumours began during the Third Reich with claims that Resl of Konnersreuth predicted the outbreak of war as early as 1933 or the fall of the regime during the Second World War.[42] Another post-war rumour professed that when a man visited Neumann during her Friday Suffering with a picture of Adolf Hitler in his pocket, she took it screaming, "Smoke and Fire from Hell."[43] There is not sufficient evidence available to researchers to support these claims but they added to Neumann's post-war aura.

Numerous acts also suggest a willingness by Therese Neumann to cooperate with the Third Reich. She often defused rumours about disruptive behaviour herself. For example, when Catholic journalists from Vienna called her home to see if stories about her forced emigration to Switzerland or imprisonment were true, she and her father both reassured them that she remained safe in her bed. One of her advocates published an article in 1935 arguing that it was not only untrue but also libellous against the national pride of Germany for foreign journalists to falsely claim that the NSDAP sent Neumann to a concentration camp.[44] In 1938 she travelled to the local gendarme to deny several rumours, including some that she predicted war and planned to flee the country. She said, "None of these assertions are true. I do not have the gift of prophecy. I am also well aware that such statements could be punishable. For these reasons I would disregard such nonsensical talk."[45] Such actions indicate a clear unwillingness by Therese Neumann to put herself at risk of incarceration. She previously made numerous prophetic statements about church figures, opponents, and people's everyday lives prior to the Third Reich. She downplayed her clairvoyant power and disorderly potential out of a desire to survive in the Nazi state.

In an effort to endure the regime, the Konnersreuth Circle also used contacts within the NSDAP to protect Therese from potential persecution. The gendarme who searched her house in 1933 complained that Father Franz Xaver Wutz reached out to a member of the SA to conspire against him. Interestingly the gendarme, who admitted he had lost the confidence of the local population, received a transfer away from Konnersreuth. Furthermore, Wutz used contacts within the party to obtain his own release from prison. Wutz also apparently brought Neumann to Stuttgart to an SA Sturmführer there who was a close associate of the high-ranking Rudolf Hess.[46] A report from one of Neumann's most outspoken opponents, Father Norbert Brühl, asserted that in local quarrels over Neumann's authenticity Father Naber and the Neumann family also used contacts in the Gestapo to frighten sceptics from speaking out.[47] Bitter post-war Konnersreuth critic, Josef Hanauer, goes even further to say that Therese Neumann's youngest brother boasted of having a friend in the Gestapo and threatening that the Gestapo was "on call" for him, citing documents in the now-closed Regensburg files that he consulted during the 1970s and 1980s.[48] Neumann also developed a relationship with the *Landrat* (district administrator) in nearby Tirschenreuth. He was a NSDAP party member, who secretly informed her about upcoming house searches. She credited him with saving her from imprisonment in a concentration camp and from a coerced state exam by Reich Minister of Health Leonardo Conti.[49] Such evidence indicates the complex nature of life under Nazism. Even a group with numerous outspoken opponents based on past connections to the BVP and faith in Neumann's miracles sought out friends within the regime to protect themselves and settle personal disputes in their favour. The occult proved powerful enough to capture the regime's attention, but

Neumann recognized her limits in a politically violent environment where numerous friends had perished.

The Konnersreuth Circle also possessed a mixed record regarding Germany's Jewish population. It welcomed and even protected Jews who had converted to Catholicism. One of Neumann's closest friends included Bruno Rothschild, a man ostracized by his Jewish family for becoming a priest. Neumann also purportedly served as godmother to a convert from Judaism on a trip to visit the bishop of Speyer and helped Dr Benno Karpeles transform from what von Lama described as a "free-thinking" Jewish and socialist journalist to a devout Catholic and one of Austria's most public Konnersreuth devotees until his death in 1938. Nonetheless, traces of anti-Semitism typical of the Catholic Church prior to the 1960s exist in the records of the Konnersreuth Circle. For example, when Gerlich asked Neumann in late 1932 whether he should collaborate with the *Centralverein Deutscher Staatsbürger jüdischen Glaubens* (Central Association of German Citizens of Jewish Faith) in Munich, she answered, "Be Careful. I do not like it." Furthermore, the paper's financier, Fürst Erich von Waldburg-Zeil, complained bitterly about the probable and unwanted influence of "German Jewry" at the Dresdener Bank when he faced a troubling fiscal issue.[50] During the Weimar era, one of Neumann's most important supporters, Erwein von Aretin, also included anti-Semitic tropes in his political writing in support of Bavarian monarchism. For example, he blamed the Munich revolution of 1919 on "Jews from Galicia, Moscow and Petersburg" and associated a "Jewish essence" and "poison" with perceived foreign policy threats from Russia and the Balkans during the 1920s.[51] Finally, a document from the immediate aftermath of the war suggested a less than enlightened view on Europe's devastated Jewish population. Neumann critic Johann Baptist Westermayr received a letter from an in-law of Therese Neumann reporting a 1947 vision where she foresaw the rise of an anti-Christ in the 1950s who would be the son of a "Jewess." While it remains unclear whether Neumann actually had this vision, it illustrates the attitudes of some in her following. Many of the anti-Judaic themes of Jews as tormenters of Christ during the passion appeared in Neumann's Friday Suffering and other visions.[52] None of this evidence indicates an alignment between the Konnersreuth Circle and the Third Reich on racist anti-Semitism. Rather, these examples suggest anti-Judaism that was present in numerous parts of Catholic Germany.[53] This mentality prevented protest or discomfort with Nazi Jewish policy when it dealt with anyone other than Catholic converts and contributed to the silence about the Holocaust in the thousands of pages of material about the Konnersreuth miracles. Given the lack of documentation on the matter, one wonders what Therese Neumann's brother Hans, a former theology student conscripted for the war, witnessed on the eastern front and what he shared with his family.[54]

Neumann's vocal Catholic opponent, Josef Deutsch, also epitomized the ambiguous Catholic encounter with National Socialism. In many ways his correspondence illustrates the discontent felt by many on specifically Catholic issues. Like most church elites Deutsch remained silent about the fate of German Jews, but became agitated about the "pagan" wing of the Nazi party. Deutsch openly worried that supporters of Alfred Rosenberg would increasingly embarrass the church and felt increased urgency for a solution to Konnersreuth before the state used it to discredit the faith. He also followed the Nazi trials of Catholic priests and monks for sexual misconduct and fraud, expressing anger that in some cases the state uncovered "homosexual activity" that actually existed. He compared the church's toleration of priests who violated celibacy vows to its permissiveness with Konnersreuth, showing once again the power of sexuality in Catholic discourse at the time. Deutsch felt at least some of the clergy accused of sexual impropriety by the regime were guilty and he saw Neumann's convicted teacher as one of them. The desire to connect Konnersreuth to sexual abuse probably rested in the idea that feminine hysteria frequently resulted from either sexual trauma or deviancy. Deutsch also praised the Catholic doctors who lost their posts for refusing to cooperate with the regime's sterilization policies as much more noble than the Konnersreuth Circle members who said they sacrificed aspects of their lives for their faith under Nazism. While against Nazi show trials, Rosenberg's paganism, and coerced sterilization, he also formed something of an uneasy alliance with an SS doctor who also wanted Therese Neumann to submit to a clinical exam. While concerned about embarrassment, Deutsch used this SS figure to distribute his essay and even supported state intervention after the church stopped short of forcing Neumann into a clinic. Just like his enemies within the Catholic Church, Deutsch neither protested anti-Semitism nor avoided the tools of totalitarian coercion when settling his own personal disputes.[55]

The distinct piety of the Konnersreuth Circle only partially shaped the ambiguous relationship of its members to the National Socialist state. Examples of tragic martyrdom, open dissidence, and subtle dissent existed alongside cooperation for survival, collaboration in the name of power, and disinterest in some of the worst crimes of the regime on the Eastern Front, where one of Therese's brothers served in the Wehrmacht. Pre-Nazi attachments to the BVP and the political milieu of Konnersreuth drove the resistant acts as much as faith in Neumann's miracles. Although Neumann's stigmata clearly inspired Gerlich's most prominent efforts against Nazism, many of the state's other victims suffered as much for political attitudes that might have landed them in the cross hairs of the regime even without a link to Konnersreuth. Erwein von Aretin symbolized this tension. Imprisoned in Dachau primarily for articulating the interests of the Bavarian monarchy, he also claimed to be as well known for his advocacy of Konnersreuth as for his politics. He believed this association marked him as even more "reactionary" in the eyes of the regime and made him a more enticing target. Nonetheless, his political activism prior to the war and his loose association with conservatives that eventually tried to assassinate Hitler in 1944 played the most prominent role in his imprisonments and surveillance.[56] Efforts at cooperation, however, seemed motivated more by the desire of the Neumann family and their supporters to preserve Therese's safety and authenticity. Her body itself contained the sanctity worshipped by her followers and with it great cultural and religious capital for her region. Therefore, the acts of passivity and even collaboration seem intimately related to the Catholic mysticism of the circle. In sum, both the occult and political Catholicism generated Konnersreuth's many acts of disobedience, but faith in the supernatural character of Therese Neumann's physical presence and a fervent aspiration to preserve it produced the most prominent acts of cooperation with Nazism.

The National Socialist Response to Konnersreuth

The reaction of the NSDAP to Therese Neumann contained equal amounts of suspicion, antagonism, fascination, and even fear. The confluence of Neumann's Friday Suffering, grass-roots support in rural Bavaria, international following, and connections to the BVP opened Konnersreuth to surveillance by the party at a local and national level. Local officials disagreed about the extent of Neumann's threat to the state, while one member of the SS, Dr Eduard Aigner, took a special interest in her case. Disputed accounts of Konnersreuth's "liberation" by the United States military make the ultimate intentions of the party for Neumann difficult to assess, but the widespread faith in her sanctity within Germany and the international community curbed any desire to eliminate or imprison the Bavarian visionary.

Many high-ranking Nazis possessed negative attitudes towards the Catholic supernatural. The party viewed these popular religious traditions as threats to their desired totalitarian power over everyday life, competition for loyalty to National Socialist organizations and doctrine, and potential sources for dissidence. Party members, such as Heinrich Himmler, sought the widespread replacement of Catholic mysticism with an equally paranormal belief in the miracles of Nazi racism and the fated rule of Adolf Hitler.[57] Therefore, Third Reich officials largely viewed Konnersreuth negatively.

Many national and regional leaders within the party expressed reservations about Catholic miracles. Anticlerical leaders, such as Alfred Rosenberg and Gunter d'Alquen, used the press to cast doubt on the events of Konnersreuth. *Völkischer Beobachter* (People's Observer) already challenged Neumann's stigmata in 1927, although the rhetoric of these articles paled in comparison to the far more sarcastic communist press. Multiple speeches, reports, and other documents from the Propaganda Ministry and the Ministry for Church Matters suggested that Catholic folk religion "poisoned the soul of the people" and "endangered the National Socialist worldview."[58] This concern with Neumann's alleged supernatural abilities led to discomfort with her potential for dissent. The regional government viewed the "character" of the Konnersreuth area to be more uncooperative on issues such as the crucifix in schools, public processions, and the introduction of *Gemeindschaftschule* (comprehensive schools) due to Neumann's authority.[59]

Despite these numerous examples of antagonism with Konnersreuth, other evidence suggests a willingness by the party to ignore Neumann out of either indifference or deference. A document from the German Worker's Front argued that Therese Neumann had faded into the past. The document argued that "the small, farming region fell once again into the realm of the forgotten," an account that came after the bishops' statement of 1937 detaching themselves from her case.[60] Franciscan Georg Wunderle, an outspoken Neumann critic, interpreted the National Socialist stance as one of caution regarding the stigmatic. Unlike the German Worker's Front, he felt that her local celebrity worried the regime enough to leave her alone in order to preserve stability in the population. Finally, some popular literature on Konnersreuth suggests Adolf Hitler became obsessed with Therese Neumann, fearing her supernatural power, requesting updates on her activities, and demanding that she be left in peace.[61] This speculation lacks documentary support, but the rumours themselves indicate that at least some leaders of the party pursued caution in relations with Therese Neumann herself, if not the entire Konnersreuth Circle.

The Konnersreuth *Gendarmeriehauptwachtmeister*, A. Raml, a member of the NSDAP and a Catholic, became embroiled in an intense personal and political feud in Konnersreuth. Although Konnersreuth Circle member Franz Xaver Wutz used contacts to help Raml's son pursue a career within the church as a missionary, relations soured over the national election on 31 July 1932. After the Nazi rise to power, Raml searched the Neumann home, clashed with Neumann's father over international visitors, and wrote several reports depicting the Konnersreuth Circle's alignment with the BVP as problematic for the state. Raml viewed Neumann as troublesome not only for her linkage to the occult but because of her family's loyalty to political Catholicism. Her supernatural power became important mainly in her ability to ostracize Raml locally because so many residents respected and even feared her spiritual might, eventually forcing his transfer.[62]

Raml's superiors and his successor, however, viewed Neumann differently. They wrote less critical reports and suggested that Raml's unstable personality contributed to his problems as much as the Neumann family's attitude. Although concerned with the outlook of a few Konnersreuth pilgrims, they emphasized some of Therese Neumann's more passive actions. After visiting Neumann, one of them described her as "having her feet on the ground" and "much too clever to become involved in hopeless political conspiracies, such as atrocity reports or other unsavory things."[63] Despite such sentiments, the historical commission for Therese Neumann's beatification found a note in her prayer book about awaking one morning at 6:30 a.m. to two gendarmes searching her room in 1939.[64] This tension between treating Therese Neumann as both non-threatening and a potential traitor supports the notion of her as a disruptive force whose power possessed severe limitations. Her popularity, politics, and formidable contacts, all grounded in her unmediated access to heavenly figures, made her problematic to a dictatorial and controlling state. However, her desire to survive and her circle's wish to protect her sacred body led to a generally passive approach to the state. As long as she chose not to violate certain restrictions, state authorities tolerated her influence for the sake of public order.

The relationship of SS member and neurologist, Dr Eduard Aigner, to Therese Neumann indicates many of the complications in the Nazi approach to the Catholic supernatural. Aigner's concern with Catholic miracles pre-dated the First World War. As a leading member of the *Deutschen Monistenbund* (German Monist League), he published several essays attacking Germans who claimed cures at the Lourdes shrine from 1908 to 1910. As a monist promoting modern science and materialism in lectures famous throughout Europe, he opposed church dogma and the "medieval superstitions" of Catholicism.[65] Aigner developed what one could only call an obsession with Therese Neumann that lasted over a decade. Upon his first visit to Konnersreuth in 1927, he gained a personal audience with Neumann and also observed her Friday Suffering for hours. When he returned in 1928, Neumann's father did not allow his entrance after discovering his past attitude towards Lourdes. This ban from the Neumann home did not prevent Aigner from staying in town for two weeks and visiting three more times before 1944. His decision to live in Konnersreuth for weeks at a time without any hope of contact with Therese Neumann indicated the passion with which he followed a stigmata he believed to be real but in no way Catholic.[66] In fact, Aigner's persistent awe of such supernatural occurrences suggests he reflected a wing of the party consumed with the "spiritualities" that represented the mentalities of several NSDAP elite.

Aigner created much publicity in 1938 with the publication of two articles about Therese Neumann in *Das Schwarze Korps* and a book that summarized much of what he included in lectures delivered throughout the country. In a sometimes sober and objective description of the Konnersreuth miracles and the debate over their genuineness, Aigner argued that neither the bleeding nor the fasting of Neumann was falsified. However, he contended that they also possessed neither a Catholic nor a Christian message. Rather, Therese Neumann's physical condition represented a scientific phenomenon with materialist explanations. Aigner agitated for a comprehensive medical exam of Neumann so the German *Volk* and state could benefit from its potential scientific discoveries. Aigner suggested that in the name of "public hygiene" and "*Volksgesundheit*," the state should coerce the Neumann family into permitting an exam.[67] According to Fürst Erich von Waldburg-Zeil, he appealed personally to Heinrich Himmler for an intervention in the matter.[68]

Although Aigner coordinated his messages with one of Neumann's most vocal church critics, Dr Josef Deutsch, he found himself in conflict with most of her Catholic detractors. George Wunderle warned Regensburg of Aigner's attempt to make Therese Neumann a state matter when he believed her case to be strictly of concern to the church.[69] Aigner in fact attacked the bishops for not insisting enough on an exam: "The police have taken sharp action against the exhibition of birth defects and human abnormalities at festivals and fairs. With Therese Neumann there is always an exception: here the Roman priests have taken the role of booth owner and rake in their Therese money." In an era of forced sterilizations and even euthanasia of those deemed disabled, both the church and the Konnersreuth Circle feared the sort of institutionalization sought by Aigner. Leaning on rhetoric from the eugenics movement, Aigner genuinely believed such a step would yield beneficial scientific discovery and worried Neumann would die before doctors conducted comprehensive exams. He believed that Neumann's bloody tears likely resulted from autosuggestion and that it would be "physiologically" valuable to better understand the process.[70]

Simultaneously fascinated and disturbed by Catholic stigmata, Aigner represented the muddled Nazi viewpoint regarding religious miracles. He and many within the party passionately opposed what they viewed as old superstition within the church and promoted instead a modern rationalism mixed with social Darwinist pseudoscience. Nonetheless, Neumann's exceptional experiences resonated with a National Socialist desire to understand seemingly irrational phenomenon in the framework of ideas such as parapsychology and monism. When delving beneath the surface of Aigner's rationalism, one glimpses a place for the occult in the Nazi world view. The failure of the Third Reich to act on Aigner's suggestion also further illustrates Therese Neumann's tenuous position between potential threat and passive bystander. Unlike the seers of Heede, the Gestapo never actually forced a Konnersreuth exam. As long as Neumann contained her extraordinary visions and bleeding within the private and local sphere, the state allowed her personal freedom thanks to Wutz's contacts in the party. The conciliatory side of the Neumann household emerged once again in 1944 when Father Naber brought Aigner into the Neumann home for a personal audience after sixteen years of hostility.[71] Although the reasons behind this decision remain unclear, one might speculate that Neumann thought a home visit might whet Aigner's appetite enough to curb his activism for her hospitalization.

Conflicting accounts of Konnersreuth's final day under the Third Reich only deepen the uncertainty of Nazi attitudes towards Therese Neumann. On 20 April 1945 much of Konnersreuth burned and Neumann herself barely escaped her smoldering underground shelter. The cause of this destruction remains in dispute. One story claims that a reserve battalion with a company of POWs rested in Konnersreuth on the way from Thuringia to Bavaria, provoking an American attack and the damage to the town. Members of the Konnersreuth Circle, however, maintain that an SS attempt to murder Neumann before Konnersreuth's liberation by the Americans caused the battle. They contend that the SS aimed artillery fire at the Neumann house and then drew American fire on the town as well. If this SS unit actually attempted to murder Neumann, it would suggest that the state's caution regarding her well-being was only to keep rural Bavaria settled during the war. The opposing stories of the war's end indicate the limited gaze of the historian and the constraints to speaking authoritatively about matters concerning Therese Neumann.[72]

The Marian Revival of the Second World War

The era of the Third Reich and the Second World War marked a period of perilous survival for the Konnersreuth Circle, which would emerge strengthened during the occupation and early Federal Republic. It also marked the start of the most dynamic string of Marian apparitions in modern German history. While the dislocation of war tore apart lay institutions such as youth groups, voluntary associations, and local parish traditions, reverence for the Virgin Mary flourished both as a symbol of resistance to secularization either by fascism or communism and as a coping tool for the violence and upheaval of total war. The upswing in Marian devotion also stimulated more widespread belief in heavenly intercession.[73]

The German interest in apparitions of the Virgin Mary drew some inspiration from the proliferation of visions in neighbouring Belgium. Specifically the appearances of the Madonna in Banneux during 1933 fascinated Catholics in Cologne. Several pilgrimage offices opened in the city to lead tours to the Belgian town and a business grew that imported and sold holy water from the sacred but illicit site. One of the organizers of this Banneux movement attested that several cures resulted from the bottles of water in the Rhineland. Pilgrims claimed that profits from the holy water were saved to pay for first communion dresses for girls from families impoverished by the depression. When the bishop's office worked to stop these activities, one advocate for the Banneux visions claimed that hundreds of residents in Cologne sought comfort from the Banneux Madonna.[74]

From 1937 to 1940 the spirit of Banneux arrived more comprehensively when hundreds of thousands of Catholics travelled to the small town of Heede to pay homage to four young girls who related messages from the Virgin Mary in a ritual with especially strong roots in early modern Germany, which would be repeated with great regularity after the war. The apparitions in Heede received such strong popular support because they occurred at a time when the Emsland felt under siege by Nazi restrictions of Catholic life. Indeed, they demonstrate how the miraculous remained influential in the imagination of the Catholic population. Despite interference from the Gestapo and the detainment of the four girls, thousands of people travelled to Heede from the Emsland, Westphalia, the Rhineland, and other Catholic regions through the Second World War. Furthermore "folk piety" became a coping mechanism for "private and collective angst in everyday life and especially crisis situations."[75]

The case of Heede also illustrates that the initiative for miraculous piety came from below rather than from above. Church traditions created the context for these miracles. The Virgin Mother appeared frequently as she was described in religion classes or popular literature about Lourdes, and local clergy provided credibility with their support.[76] However, Maria Anna Zumholz maintains, "The folk piety regulated above all the personal relationship between God and the people, individuals as well as communities, while the church as an institution played a subordinate role in this context." Just as in Konnersreuth the apparition movement of Heede represented a subversion of clerical power by the pious who wished for a direct relationship with heaven as well as a subaltern challenge to some aspects of the totalitarian state.[77]

The Heede movement contained similar themes to the miracles of Konnersreuth, emphasizing suffering, sin, redemption, and punishment. On one hand, Catholics sought hope and salvation through the traditional powers of an apparition site: prophesies, secret messages, and cures. The early message of the four visionaries was that the Virgin Mother wanted more prayer to avoid catastrophe. Similar to Therese Neumann's central message, personal prayer empowered vulnerable Catholics and provided them a perceived measure of control over their unstable lives. However, as time passed, leading visionary Grete Ganseforth had more threatening revelations. For example, she received messages that girls wearing inappropriate clothing or those who failed to pray enough would be punished, turning Heede into something of a moral utopia as well.[78]

There were other sightings of the Virgin Mary during the Third Reich. A butcher's daughter from the Bavarian town of Wigratzbad, Antonie Rädler, opened another branch of the family business on Lake Constance. She clashed there with local authorities for her refusal to take down a picture of the Virgin Mary that she had in place of a Hitler photograph. A long-time devotee of Marian piety, Rädler claimed that Mary came to her in a vision when she suddenly recovered from Spanish influenza in 1919. She belonged to the Schönstatt movement, which promoted Marian prayer from the Rhineland since the First World War. Upon her return home, Antonie built a Lourdes grotto where a man was cured of cancer and another woman in town saw an apparition of Mary. Advocates for the new vision oversaw the construction of a chapel, completed in 1940, that attracted devotion from many believers during the war and the ire of the National Socialist state. Antonie Rädler went into hiding to avoid imprisonment in a concentration camp. Even though Heede was the only site that attracted mass visitation, Wigratzbad existed alongside eight other documented examples of apparitions during the Third Reich, demonstrating the growing popularity of the phenomenon.[79]

Beyond the dramatic events in Heede and Wigratzbad, everyday devotion to the Virgin Mary increased gradually from 1942 to 1945 as Catholics sought her protection from the worsening conditions. For example, Bishop von Galen's followers in the diocese of Münster revived pilgrimages to shrines in Kevelaer and Telgte during the summer of 1942.[80] After Kevelaer faded as a pilgrim destination during the war's early years, it gradually attracted more people. An official working for the railroad complained that Catholic worshippers interfered with trains intended for the war effort through their journeys to Kevelaer. The Catholic community confirmed his fears on 7 June 1942 when thousands descended on the small Rhineland town for the three hundredth anniversary of its Marian shrine. The crowd, which consisted mostly of young women, shouted encouragement to Bishop von Galen after he spoke of loyalty to the church and the current difficulties of religious practice. This demonstration also emphasized the role of Mary as a protector in war. Von Galen called her "comforter of the sorrowful." He announced: "We greet Mary, our hope, and want to tell her today that we place our hopes in her in these bitter times of war. We present our suffering to her to ask her to help us, our fatherland, our soldiers in the field, our beloved dead, and for the many who suffer from need."[81] One month later, over ten thousand young people, both male and female, travelled to the Marian shrine of Telgte. As a result of train restrictions, almost all the pilgrims travelled in small groups by bike or foot. Some even arrived in horse and buggy. The main theme of the celebration was thanksgiving to Mary for her protection during the bombing campaign of Münster, which began one year earlier. Von Galen pronounced: "A year ago today the great attacks on the father city of Münster began and Mary protected the city from great danger."[82] War weariness as much as the ongoing church struggles stimulated renewed interest in the Virgin Mary.

Veneration of Mary expanded as war fatigue grew, moving beyond events endorsed by bishops such as those in the diocese of Münster. During the final years of war, the Eifel's Marian shrine in Heimbach reawakened. In 1943, the anxiety from bombing raids caused thousands of pilgrims to venture to the shrine, which the regime closed to the public except on Sundays and holidays. Catholics often travelled by foot or bike in small groups and arrived to locked doors. They prayed outside the church, and even the Reich Main Security Office (RSHA) eventually suggested reopening the shrine to improve morale.[83] The devotion to the shrine intensified from 1944 to 1945. Many credited the Virgin with protecting the church from destruction. While allied bombs hit and damaged the building, it remained in better shape than most other church property. This occurrence increased the interest in the shrine. When news of the Allied forces landing reached Germany, pilgrims flocked to Heimbach in "extraordinary crowds" for one of its traditional observances. The following year, after the Allied forces arrived in the west, forty-four processions brought 5,805 pilgrims to Heimbach for the same weekend celebration.[84] The Heimbach enthusiasm began spontaneously from the spirituality of Catholics in the Eifel disobeying both clergy and the state and grew into large church-sponsored pilgrimages at the end of the war.

A May celebration for the Virgin Mary in Aachen blended elements of institutional church teaching and spontaneous piety that extended beyond clerical approval. The church tried to organize the event in ways similar to youth demonstrations of the early 1930s. They attracted approximately 270 young people as well as several women and elderly men. Participants displayed great enthusiasm for the event. A Nazi report commented: "The attitude of the young people before the celebration was scandalous. They acted in the Cathedral as if it were a beer hall and as the brightest light illuminated the Cathedral, the youth let out a loud 'Ahhh.'" An NSDAP sympathizer reported: "For these people the celebration was a 'release valve.' The last weeks weighed down the souls of the population like lead … For all of them it does not matter what will come. This war will not end and the victor will be just as defeated as the loser. In this spiritual environment, there is only one thing that moves people and maintains resonance: that is the call to give oneself to a higher power." Furthermore, Catholics at the celebration believed in supernatural intervention by both the Virgin Mary and the pope. Rumours circulated around the cathedral that prayer to the Virgin would cause the pope to become a peacemaker in the conflict. They believed he stood ready to unleash a "secret miracle" to rescue the Catholic population from Russian invasion. Some believed he would "convert" the communists if they honoured the Virgin Mary. The Nazis complained that Catholics no longer believed in a "victory through arms," but maintained faith in a "miracle" and a "victory through the Holy Mother."[85] The belief in intercession by the Virgin Mary paralleled the hopes many Germans and more mainstream Catholics like the anti-Konnersreuth Bishop Jäger of Paderborn placed in the development of "miracle weapons" as a way to win the war.[86] The Aachen service in honour of Mary served as a spiritual outlet for a tired population threatened by Russian invasion and bombing campaigns. A state of despair caused many to believe in supernatural aid and strengthened their faith in a higher power.

The late stages of the war sparked widespread belief in Catholic miracles without encouragement from the church. For example, many Catholics grew interested in the Marian apparitions from Fatima in 1917. Interpreting the visions of the children in light of their own needs, they believed the girls foresaw an end to the Second World War. From this viewpoint, the more purely the population lived and the more frequently it prayed, the sooner the war would end.[87] A woman from Krefeld claimed that a German bishop, in communication with the Blessed Mother, learned that the war would end only after Germany prayed to her. Mary also allegedly declared a special connection between the virgin and "brides who suffered."[88]

Another common phenomenon after 1942 became "chain letters" and "chain prayers." Such forms of devotion included various prayers, some to the Virgin Mary and others to God directly, that many Bavarians believed would be heard if repeated a certain number of times and passed on to as many people as possible. They had been common during the First World War as well. For example, devotees claimed that one circulating prayer was found at the tomb of Jesus in the sixteenth century and it would protect loved ones from death in war as well as from other dangers. People warned that those who showed faith in the prayer would receive mercy while all others would be punished. Cardinal Faulhaber warned congregants of his and neighbouring dioceses against such practices but they persisted nonetheless.[89] Although it is difficult to measure how widespread faith in chain prayers came to be, their existence and persistence confounded expectations by the hierarchy and highlight a revival of Catholic faith in supernatural intervention that exploded after the war's conclusion.

During the final war years, a wave of spirituality engulfed Catholics of Western Germany. Their suffering from the extended conflict and the hopeless conditions of total war intensified their faith in Catholic holy figures. Their bolstered religious faith, however, often remained free of clerical control. Although this faith built upon parish teachings, institutional encouragement of Fatima devotion since 1930, and comments by bishops, thousands of believers pushed this devotion beyond where their leaders expected. This wartime reawakening came from below and would spark a form of post-war devotion that the clergy could not harness for institutional purposes.

Conclusion

Miracles during the Third Reich shed light on numerous existing debates about Catholicism during this era. On the surface, the regime hastened the pace of secularization given the ways in which the Konnersreuth movement weakened. Robbed of the public sphere and a free press to spread fame, worship of Therese Neumann became more private and local. The church struggles over the public role of Catholicism in the Third Reich and the continued debate about Neumann's authenticity also forced an unwanted new discussion about a clinical exam of the stigmata and Neumann's fasting. Continued reluctance to cooperate despite immense pressure from Regensburg and the Vatican led to the most severe break in relations between the Neumann family and their bishop since the first signs of stigmata. Furthermore, local and family quarrels over Neumann's fasting and sex scandals threatened to unravel faith in the Neumann miracles. The context of dictatorship and war and pressure from church and state almost relegated the Konnersreuth events to the margins.

Nonetheless, the Second World War marked the start of a new and even more active age of German Catholic miracles that would persist until the death of Therese Neumann in the early 1960s. Through savvy manoeuvring Therese Neumann challenged her church and state without stepping so far over certain boundaries that she suffered excommunication, imprisonment, sterilization, or hospitalization. She avoided a potentially harmful exam while preserving integrity with a wide enough following for her cult to persist. As her male protectors died during the 1930s she also positioned herself as an even more powerful figure within her own circle. Therese Neumann of Konnersreuth emerged from the Second World War armed with anti-Nazi credentials, a message that appealed to a traumatized population, and an occupying force looking for religious sites of post-war reconciliation. While traditional church power bases suffered long-term damage, Catholic women positioned themselves for a period of newfound influence after the war. Furthermore, the endurance of Catholic mysticism contributed to the waning power of clergy and bishops as the struggle over legitimacy in Konnersreuth and Heede exposed church leadership to withering attacks by opponents and advocates of miracles and blurred the lines of strictly defined Catholic doctrines, rituals, and hierarchies.

The messages and themes of Konnersreuth, Heede, and shrines to the Virgin Mary also grew in strength as the war turned against the Germans. Looking at God and his saints as figures willing to intervene in everyday lives in the midst of turmoil and dissonance drew believers. As the paranormal elements of Nazism lost relevance, many Germans sought new outlets for faith in supernatural solutions to earthly problems. The message of sin, punishment, and potential apocalypse as well as faith in salvation and heavenly solutions to intractable earthly problems attracted the faith of millions. Such spiritual habits foresaw a German future where faith traditions fragmented and religion became more individual and diffuse.

Despite overcoming the secularizing impulses of Nazism, mystical movements shared the same ambiguity regarding National Socialist ideology as the mainstream churches. Despite vast possibilities to disrupt the Nazi dictatorship, they valued the enduring sanctity of their shrines and seers more than any other cause. Therefore Marian movements and the Konnersreuth Circle inspired their share of dissidence without taking any action that could have saved the legacy of Catholicism in relationship to the Holocaust or Nazi-era imperialism. However, enough dissent existed within mystical circles that it endowed them with renewed legitimacy after Hitler's downfall.

The veneration of the Virgin Mary that increased at the end of the war set the stage for the post-1945 period. In the uncertain environment of occupation and democratization, West Germany experienced its most fervent phase of Marian apparitions during the modern age. These new visions created another cohort of rebellious pilgrims who challenged the Catholic establishment at it tried to recover authority lost during the National Socialist years.

Chapter Six

Miraculous Times in West Germany: Marian Apparitions during the Early Federal Republic

In a culmination of the so-called "Marian Century" that began in 1858 with the Lourdes visions, European apparitions of the Virgin Mary proliferated at an unprecedented rate after the conclusion of the Second World War.[1] The deep apprehensions of a continent ravaged by war, overwhelmed by the spectre of nuclear weapons, overrun with refugees, and fearful of communist revolution created the context for widespread faith in miracles. Displaying an enchantment with mysticism and the supernatural, Western European congregations reported thirteen to fourteen apparitions a year to church officials between 1945 and 1954. These included numerous Madonna sightings in Italy, France, Belgium, and the Netherlands. Building on the momentum of Marian visions during the Third Reich, eleven instances occurred in German Catholic strongholds, such as Bavaria, the Palatinate, and the Rhineland.[2] This far-reaching movement emerged as a reaction, not only to the Cold War, but also to anxieties about Americanization, consumerism, and Catholic narratives about the Nazi past. Furthermore, this brief but intense wave of faith in the Virgin Mary reignited the power struggle within the German Catholic community between traditional male power brokers and vulnerable (and primarily powerless) churchgoers over access to spiritual influence that began with the debate about Therese Neumann during the Weimar Republic.

Popular apparitions in the villages of Heroldsbach (Bavaria), Fehrbach (Palatinate), Niederhabbach (Rhineland), and Rodalben (Palatinate) illustrate the persistence of German Catholic faith in supernatural intervention after 1945. While anthropologists correctly connect belief in apparitions to crisis, dictatorship, and war, the phenomenon stemmed from other causes as well.[3] Monica Black's research about popular healer Bruno Gröning and widespread accusations of witchcraft in the early 1950s illustrates an underbelly of insecurity in the Adenauer era despite its veneer of restored respectability.[4] Therefore, the Marian apparitions belong to this larger trend of faith in the occult that revealed the tenuous nature of the post-war democratic experiment. These visions provide the basis for a cultural history of the rise of Christian Democracy and the Federal Republic itself.

After the fall of Nazism and the division of the nation, Catholics found themselves in a unique situation in West Germany. No longer a minority due to the demographic changes of the early Cold War, they emerged as a political force within the ruling Christian Democratic Union / Christian Social Union (CDU/CSU). An interconfessional political project to unite former supporters of the Catholic Centre Party with conservative and liberal Protestants, the CDU placed Catholic elites from the Rhineland in positions of great influence while its sister party in Bavaria, the CSU, did the same for their prominent co-religionists of the south. In the early 1950s, German Christian Democracy promoted several central ideas as it laid the groundwork for political dominance that would last until the mid-1960s under the leadership of former Cologne mayor Konrad Adenauer. First, the Catholic wing of the party echoed Pope Pius XII's obsessive concern about atheistic communism and the potential for conflict in the East. In response, they revived notions of West Germany as a new Christian *Abendland* (Occident) defined by rigid social hierarchy, religious morality, and its opposition to materialist forces in modernity that fueled radical ideologies like Marxism and National Socialism.[5] Along with the German bishops and clergy with whom the party formed a close partnership in its earliest phase, this political movement also feared growing consumerism and Americanization because it threatened clerical control of moral values. These tendencies frequently led to the reassertion of patriarchy and normative gender roles for women.[6] Furthermore, the CDU/CSU aimed to integrate the millions of ethnic German expellees from Eastern Europe, which the party sometimes accomplished by marginalizing Polish and Jewish Displaced Persons (DPs). Finally, the church and the CDU/CSU alliance confronted the ambiguous Nazi past by inaccurately depicting religion as the exclusive bulwark against National Socialism.[7]

The apparitions in small villages throughout West Germany created dramas that awkwardly engaged issues central to the Christian Democratic agenda. While supporters of these visions sometimes re-enforced messages sent from above by church fathers and political leaders, they mostly complicated the narratives constructed by Catholic elites. On the one hand, appearances of the Virgin Mary contributed to the notion of a Christian *Abendland* facing the communist threat and supporting male patriarchy, conservative cultural values, and anti-materialism. On the other hand, supporters of the apparitions, who numbered in the hundreds of thousands, ultimately revolted against the authority of the church-state alliance of the early Adenauer years and contributed to the fragmentation of church influence and the secularization of the party.

The rise of apparition movements threatened bishops and urban-based clergy who, once again, almost universally condemned them as challenges to their monopoly on spiritual authority and dangerous to the coherence of doctrine at yet another moment of upheaval in German history. They opposed all eleven post-war Marian sightings largely because unrestrained mysticism undermined their attempts to regain prominence after losing much cultural relevance under the reign of National Socialism. These visions challenged the Catholic hierarchy due to their emergence in a fragile moment of reconstruction after the war, as well as their widespread popularity and interconnectedness to one another. The Marian movement developed an extensive network that transcended individual localities or milieus, connecting diverse apparition sites in the Rhineland, Bavaria, the Emsland, and the Palatinate, as well as rural pilgrimages from Westphalia, Switzerland, and the Netherlands and urban pockets of devotees from Cologne and Düsseldorf. The new political realities of West Germany made the struggle for power within an evolving Catholic habitus particularly interesting. Elite Catholic men of the CDU dominated Adenauer-era politics during the 1950s and clergy and middle-class associational leaders shaped local religious life, frequently supporting conservative cultural values and normative family structures. The attacks by male elites in the Catholic milieu on female seers and vulnerable men, such as concentration camp survivors and prisoners of war, suppressed a symbolic revolt by some of German Catholicism's most pious believers against a Catholic hierarchy that gained unprecedented power in the early Federal Republic.[8]

The dramatic appearance of Marian visions and the contentious battle over their meaning also highlighted what Till van Rahden has called the "inherently fragile nature of democracy," especially in West Germany of the 1950s.[9] Following anything but a straightforward path to liberal democracy, this Cold War frontier state staggered under the weight of millions of refugees, the violence of its recent past, and rapid demographic and economic change. The visions particularly served as contested sites where anxiety about ethnic German expellees, the Cold War, increasing consumerism, and the National Socialist past became palpable. The Virgin Mary became a symbol used by grass-roots pilgrims and Catholic elites alike to articulate their vision for a post-war Germany. In some cases, the most fanatical of believers in apparition sites became the "clumsiest" of democrats as they used notions of liberal democracy to combat the perceived overreach of their patriarchal opponents within the church and the Christian Democratic establishment.

Marian Miracles in Post-War Germany: Allegories of a Frail Democracy

As with the Heede visions in 1937, young girls in Heroldsbach and Fehrbach initiated mass interest in miracles at the end of the American occupation. The post-war seers initially used the traditional role as conduits for the Virgin Mary in order to enhance their own social roles. However, even within the context of this attack on clerical authority, these girls accepted and sometimes sought male leadership from their local priest and other notable men from the apparition movement, conforming to traditional patriarchy in exchange for legitimation. Rigid gender roles persisted when men institutionalized and validated devotion to the apparitions and a stifling masculinity in fact became the dominant force in many cases after the war. The extremely popular apparition locales in Heroldsbach and Fehrbach became battlegrounds where marginalized Catholic men fought with traditional religious leaders for influence upon the faith after the war. Competing notions of masculinity fuelled their conflict.

Although not the first apparition after the Second World War, the appearance of the Virgin Mary to several girls in the Bavarian town of Heroldsbach became the most famous and the most contested site of clashes between Marian worshippers and the clergy. By the time of the Blessed Virgin's tearful farewell to her four female visionaries in October 1952, an estimated 1.5 million pilgrims visited to witness its 3,000 apparitions. During this period the small town could attract up to 40,000 people in one day according to the figures of both journalists and local supporters of the visions. Heroldsbach's followers pursued a form of Catholicism based loosely on Vatican policy but free of strict doctrinal and clerical control. This disruptive brand of Catholicism included numerous spectacular claims that emulated aspects of the Lourdes and Fatima visions. For example, at the celebration of the Immaculate Conception on 8 December 1949, which attracted 10,000 visitors to the small town, spectators described a solar phenomenon similar to what accompanied the apparition at Fatima in 1917. Hundreds of people testified that the sun rotated quickly and changed colours from white to orange, rose, blue, and green. Furthermore, they claimed to see figures in the rapidly moving disc. In another example of Heroldsbach miracles, pilgrims claimed that a rosary floated in thin air at the apparition site. Sometimes, new holy figures appeared. At Christmas time, a nativity scene appeared, including shepherds, angels, and the three kings. Finally, the visionaries helped worshippers make contact with the Virgin. They guided the hands of believers to touch the Virgin Mary or the baby Jesus, whom she sometimes carried in her arms. The Christ Child offered information about missing sons stuck in POW camps or relatives who had died during the war. Pilgrims brought cards, wax candles, crosses, and other objects to the vision to be blessed. They left donations as a sacrifice to the Madonna, including cash and material goods, even in one of Germany's most difficult economic moments.[10]

Numerous spectacular reports support the notion that the Second World War and the Cold War stimulated interest in apparitions. For example, the young seers also carried out dialogues with the Virgin Mary, often articulating anxiety about Russians and communism. Emulating the anti-communist message of the Fatima apparitions, German Catholics found foreboding of catastrophic destruction in the visions.[11] During a Marian appearance in February 1950, Mary informed her seers what would happen in Germany if people disobeyed her wishes. She reportedly said: "The Russians will come and destroy you! Much blood will flow!" She went on to assert that if members of the diocesan commission investigating the apparitions prevented her will from being done, she would "punish" them.[12] In later visions Mary informed the children: "If you continue with your current activities, then perhaps I could prevent the catastrophe ... Pray and do penance for the conversion of Russia!" She also told the girls to "remain loyal" because the "Russians will come and bring starvation with them." Finally, several of the Heroldsbach seers saw visions of war and destruction in which soldiers dressed in greenish brown uniforms stormed the town with revolvers, killing priests, old men, women, and children. These soldiers also burned down the Heroldsbach Church. Summoning racial stereotypes, one girl saw "Americans with dark skin" and "Russian fighters with Mongolian features." When the girls asked Mary in May 1950 whether these visions would become reality, she answered: "Perhaps even worse if the people do not pray."[13] The proximity of Heroldsbach to the Czechoslovakian border during the communist consolidation of power in Eastern Europe undoubtedly contributed to these fears of Cold War apocalypse.[14] In this way the Heroldsbach faithful supplemented with potent cultural force the CDU/CSU's constructions of an imagined *Abendland* that used Christianity as a Western bulwark against communism from the East while simultaneously keeping the nuclear weapons and consumerism of the Americans at arm's-length.

An inner circle of male Heroldsbach supporters became "popular theologians," constructing a form of spiritually that brazenly rejected the authority of priests and bishops.[15] One of the site's most outspoken supporters, former theologian Johannes Baptist Walz, argued that the "carriers of heavenly teachings" need not come from the "hierarchical office holders of the church." Instead Walz suggested that "private revelations" mattered just as much if not more than official dogma. Therefore, inconsistences between the visions of seers and formal theology did not discredit them. In fact, when officials scrutinized the legitimacy of the visions, the girls claimed Mary told them any followers excommunicated by the bishopric of Bamberg could always receive the body and blood of Christ on the sacred hill where she appeared. The vision also asked pilgrims to recite the "Our Father" to atone for the sins of the bishop's office in Bamberg for unjustly rejecting it.[16]

Another popular theologian, Fritz Müller, relentlessly attacked the church and, in the process, called for a spirituality that provided much more autonomy to believers and their personal relationships with God.[17] For example, he circulated the following poem entitled, "Catholic Existentialism?"

> Man can exist,
> If he does not think,
> Never think of Heroldsbach,
> Otherwise you will be hanged ...
> Bamberg thinks for everyone,
> Rome willingly agrees
> Therefore quit your thinking,
> So that you will have peace.[18]

Many Heroldsbach pilgrims became so convinced of their special status that threats of excommunication failed to deter their stinging criticism of church leaders. In the process, they developed a critique of the

Catholic hierarchy that requested agency for members of the laity and challenged institutional legitimacy during the fragile post-war years, whereas bishops sought a restoration of power in alliance with the prominent Catholic politicians of the CDU/CSU.

While publications by Walz and Müller became central to understanding Heroldsbach and local priest Johann Gailer encouraged the seers, several other men rallied around their ideas forming organizations known both as the Lay Commission and the Pilgrimage Office of Heroldsbach. A mixture of former seminarians, such as Norbert Langhojer and Walter Dettmann, local farmers, such as Andreas Blum, and parents of seers, such as Josef Heilmann, from Heroldsbach and Nuremburg formed the core of the movement around the apparitions. While about a dozen men led the so-called *Heroldsbacher*, their unofficial organizations contained as many as fifteen thousand members. By collecting money, erecting altars and a chapel where the Madonna appeared, publishing periodicals, and organizing buses for pilgrims, they provided the infrastructure that created a mass movement of hundreds of thousands around the subversive theology proposed by Walz and Müller. The diocesan committee investigating the apparitions found it particularly troubling when these men actually used the visions to usurp ritual functions typically performed by clergy. For example, the Lay Commission sometimes organized penance where pilgrims admitted their sins to the Christ Child in the presence of the seers.[19] After their excommunication, some of the laity within this circle became increasingly more transgressive regarding Catholic norms, posing an even deeper threat to a church establishment hoping to impose discipline. In a power struggle over leadership of the group, Dettmann accused Langhojer of practicing "spiritism" and reports also emerged of unofficial exorcisms and accusations of witchcraft and devil worship within Heroldsbach in 1954.[20]

Dettmann's role in the Heroldsbach rebellion is particularly noteworthy given his past as a seminarian and war veteran on the eastern front. Dettmann was one of eleven thousand theology students, non-ordained religious brothers, and seminarians called to serve as soldiers in the army. Although forbidden to maintain the sacramental life of soldiers at the front, official chaplains were in such short supply that many of these men did so on a temporary basis. Perhaps Dettmann's disregard for the church's control over the sacraments resulted from the chaotic situation at the front where "priest-soldiers" blurred the typically rigid boundary between those who gave and received sacraments.[21]

Several scholars studying both the diocese of Bamberg and other regions of Germany argue that confessional associations and milieu structures remained weak in rural areas with a Catholic majority because of a lack of opposition, creating space for Heroldsbach's men to construct informal institutions for their outlawed visions.[22] Perhaps the Heroldsbach lay leadership became so powerful because long-standing cultural symbols mobilized the post-war population more than associations in an area lacking organizational infrastructure. The upheaval of the late 1940s and early 1950s made larger spiritual symbols more powerful than a regionally organized laity or traditional institutions and structures. Much like other parts of Bavaria, Heroldsbach experienced an influx of ethnic German expellees and DPs as well as other war-related demographic shifts. The expellees of Heroldsbach seemed divided on the issue of the apparitions. While one prominent member of the Lay Commission was an ethnic German, another refugee woman in town refused to allow pilgrims to walk across her orchard on their way to the visions.[23] However, the mere influx of Germans from Eastern Europe unsettled existing institutions, allowing the rise of a Heroldsbach power structure and prompting anxious reactions from the institutional church.

In opposition to this unmediated expression of Catholicism the diocese of Bamberg and the Vatican condemned their grass-roots movement.[24] Church leaders sensed the grave threat posed by religious radicals who sought a Catholic spirituality with less dependence on the clergy and a focus on extreme experiences unacceptable to many mainstream Catholics. Bishop Joseph Otto Kolb of Bamberg described Dettmann, the de facto Heroldsbach spiritual leader after Gailer's departure, as an "ill and dangerous priest" who used "scandal from church history and bible stories" to attract followers who had undergone difficult times.[25] The diocese of Bamberg banned all pilgrimages to Heroldsbach in March of 1950 and the Vatican declared the visions unauthentic in August of 1951. The commission from Bamberg investigating the events, led by Suffragan Bishop Landgraf, *Domkapitular* Franz Rathgeber, and diocesan secretary Paul Kupfer, removed Gailer from the parish and replaced him with Father Ernst Schmitt, a former infantry officer and opponent of the visions. The diocese also excommunicated over forty zealous adherents to the movement.[26] The bitterness of the conflict between pilgrims and institutional leaders became evident when a clerical representative from Bamberg arrived in late October 1950 to announce the church's prohibition of the "Heroldsbach cult."

Apparition supporters shouted: "Get out of here, hypocrite and Pharisee" and "You are the devil." The police protected him from the angry stone-throwing crowd.[27] The church brought charges against several of the Heroldsbach supporters for raising money to build a new chapel and to organize pilgrims. It also sued them for libel, physical assault against clergy opposed to the visions, and occupation of public space without permits. In the worst cases, Heroldsbach ringleaders received fines for hundreds of Deutschemarks and jail sentences of between fifteen days and four months.

Tensions flared shortly after Ernst Schmitt's arrival as the bishop's hand-picked priest to seize control of the town from the Lay Commission. Already unpopular among Marian devotees for removing statues from "the hill," as the apparition site was known, Schmitt also threatened to withhold sacraments from anyone in town perpetuating faith in the apparitions, which caused a retreat even by some of the young female seers. Upon his first visit to the apparition site, Schmitt met organized resistance. Supporters of the apparition within the town formed a "watch" to prevent Schmitt from taking down the altar and outdoor chapel at their sacred site. When he first climbed the hill, a group of young men told him to leave or they would throw him in the pond. As Schmitt returned to town, the father of one of the seers and the town butcher threatened him with his cane.[28] Such acts of militancy became common as men like Langhojer, Dettmann, and Heilmann declared their willingness to protect their sacred ground by force.

Father Schmitt and representatives of the bishop's residence in Bamberg aligned with prominent local CSU representatives, the local authorities, and town politicians to marginalize the radical upstarts of Heroldsbach. Schmitt gained the allegiance of two local teachers. One of them led pilgrimages to church-sanctioned Marian sites with schoolchildren and promised to "expel the influence of Gailer" from them. Schmitt also received a boost by the election of a mayor, Andreas Rösch, who also opposed the apparitions and showed support for the embattled priest by marching next to him in a disputed Corpus Christi procession where the route had to be altered in order to avoid homes friendly to the apparition. Prelate Georg Meixner, leader of the CSU caucus in the Bavarian Landtag, also took a leading role in opposing the apparitions. He used his daily newspaper, *Bamberger Volksblatt*, to belittle the visions, calling them the "fantasies of small children." He publicly supported Schmitt's leadership in the parish and sued Walter Dettmann for defamation. Meixner's vocal opposition stemmed in part from his close personal and professional relationship with Bamberg Bishop Joseph Otto Kolb, a friendship that also assisted Meixner's own political rise after the war.[29] One of the last of the clergy active in Catholic politics, Meixner's opposition mirrored the way another politically active cleric, Heinrich Brauns, opposed Therese Neumann during the Weimar years.

Church elites combatting the Heroldsbach Madonna received unwavering assistance from the state government led by the CSU. State attorneys who oversaw cases against Heroldsbach supporters found a colourful newspaper story about the apparitions compelling. This report suggested that the apparition movement received support only from people outside Heroldsbach and mainly "asocials." Subsumed under this category were an elderly expellee from Eastern Europe, a visionary whose brother was imprisoned due to a "wild marriage" typical of the post-war period, and another seer whose father suffered from alcoholism. This assumption by municipal authorities that believers in the visions constituted an unwanted element put the state in lockstep with church authorities in Bamberg intent on stamping out the nascent movement. In a political environment where elite power brokers sought discipline and conformity in the midst of apprehension and disorder, they saw Heroldsbach as a symbol of all they wanted to overcome. CSU elites imposed their anxieties about unsettling demographic shifts, the ubiquity of refugees and DPs, and a perceived morality crisis in post-war chaos on the unwanted Marian visions and miracles. Perhaps as a result of these sentiments, the legal cases of Heroldsbach supporters tended to fail in court, while the church officials who sued men like Dettmann, Langhojer, and Gailer usually won their cases. These circumstances led many apparition supporters to view church and state in a partnership together against them.[30]

The diocese of Bamberg and municipal authorities cooperated in demolishing the shrine on the apparition hill of Heroldsbach. In the spring of 1953, police accompanied workers paid by the church to remove the outdoor altar and religious objects of devotion at the site of the visions. The fourteen state police officers purposely scheduled the removal for a time when it would be difficult for pilgrims to interfere. Jakob Maisch, a vision supporter who slept in the wooden chapel in the forest to keep watch over the altar, rang the bells before police could remove him. This alerted about sixty people from town who came to protest. Maisch attempted to rally others from neighbouring villages without success due to lack of transportation. The devotees of Heroldsbach, including the eldest seer, gasped, screamed, and cried when the workers accidentally dropped the statue of Mary and it broke. Unfazed by these events, Dettmann offered the workers cigarettes and then led his flock into the wooden chapel singing hymns. The removal of church sanction from the Heroldsbach events caused the state to refrain from viewing them as religious in nature. Therefore, the Heroldsbach contingent no longer possessed the right to practice their faith in public or to collect money from pilgrims.[31] Christian Democracy and the bishopric collaborated to marginalize a movement that threatened their hold on power, their reputation among non-Catholics, and the orderly conduct of pastoral work.

The theatre of battle focused mainly on Heroldsbach itself, but it affected Catholics throughout Germany given the popularity of the apparitions. The Lay Commission and Pilgrimage Office attracted pilgrims and other activists from Bavaria, the Rhineland, Westphalia, the Netherlands, Austria, and Switzerland. Although the Heroldsbach movement grew in an area shaped by rural Bavaria's traditional veneration of the Virgin Mary, it also reached Catholics throughout West Germany and Western Europe.[32] For example, a large Heroldsbach circle congregated in Düsseldorf and met regularly, much to the chagrin of local church authorities. Many Heroldsbach pilgrims came from the Rhineland. The archdiocese of Cologne employed tactics of intimidation to discourage their enthusiasm. They contacted several bus companies and drivers and pressured them not to transport pilgrims, sometimes under threat of excommunication.[33] The targeting of bus drivers for punishment slowed but did not stop pilgrimages to Heroldsbach.

Heroldsbach supporters responded to these efforts by using the tenets of liberal democracy to oppose the perceived church-state alliance that thwarted them. In their periodicals, Langhojer, Dettmann, and others suggested that the campaign against Heroldsbach violated the Basic Law that served as the basis for the newly founded Federal Republic in West Germany. They argued that a church with a profoundly powerful reach inhibited the right to practice their faith and their right to human dignity. Comparing the situation to the Middle Ages, the Heroldsbach advocates claimed that the close cooperation between church and state would harm the newly founded democracy. Before the elections for the Bundestag in 1953, Dettmann argued that all Heroldsbach pilgrims should find parties other than the CDU/CSU to support because their opposition would be more likely to leave Marian worshippers in peace. He named no alternatives, but he probably meant the separatist

Bayernpartei (BP) and the Sudeten and Silesian *Bund der Heimatvertriebenen und Entrechteten* (BHE). This subversion against the CSU came at a uniquely fragile moment for the party because they were on the eve of a 1954 election when a coalition of all the other parties put them out of power in Bavarian state government for the only time in their history. Furthermore, Heroldsbach supporters accused the CSU of electoral manipulation in the election of Andreas Rösch as mayor, since ten elderly Catholics brought by nuns supporting the apparitions were declared ineligible to vote.[34] Although these circumstances seemed unlikely to have turned this particular contest, the rhetoric of electoral regulation made the Heroldsbach devotees unlikely supporters of a new civil society. Their rejection of a close relationship between Christian Democracy and the Catholic Church also contributed to the secularization of German politics in the unlikeliest of ways.

In order to cement their democratic critique of the church and the CDU/CSU, the Heroldsbach movement frequently invoked the National Socialist past. For example, Fritz Müller illustrated the role of Catholic memory about the Third Reich during this confrontation with hierarchal authority. A Rhineland Catholic who saw the Virgin Mary from a hospital bed during the First World War, Müller devoted much of his life to publicity for apparition sites. He also rhetorically bludgeoned the church with his anti-Nazi credentials for its failure to recognize Marian miracles. Referencing his five-year sentence in Sachsenhausen for spreading anti-NSDAP pamphlets and resisting forced sterilization, he wrote: "I once had the courage in the death cell of a concentration camp to tell the camp commandant that I would not become a traitor ... Now more than ever I have reason to avoid the treachery of silence, even when threatened with excommunication."[35] By comparing time in a concentration camp to the diocese of Bamberg's excommunication of Heroldsbach followers, he linked the heavy-handed reaction of the bishops to the brutality of the Gestapo. Such rhetoric usually neglected the checkered past of some of Heroldsbach's most important supporters, such as Johann Gailer and the retired theologian and ex-National Socialist supporter, Dr Johannes B. Walz.[36] Debates about the mixed record of Catholics during the National Socialist years often became a cover for a struggle over the place of the church in post-war society. In this case, Müller invoked his persecution to pursue a faith grounded in mystical revelation.[37]

Dettmann went even further in his comparison between Bamberg officials and the Nazi dictatorship. He likened the morality trials of the 1930s when the Nazi state charged many priests and monks with child abuse, sexual impropriety, and economic fraud in the courtroom and the press to the church's attempts to discredit his followers. He suggested that the Gestapo entrapped priests by planting half-naked women in their residences and then showing up to photograph them. He compared these methods to what he viewed as false allegations of fraud against men like Father Gailer, depicted as emptying the donation box for himself, and the young seers, who were described as taking jewellery and other material goods left on the statues by pilgrims. Reviving fascist imagery and commenting on his loyal Wehrmacht service, pro-*Heroldsbacher* periodicals referred to Schmitt as the "first officer of the church." By claiming Marian supporters were largely resistors and victims of the regime, people like Dettmann failed to represent the past with total accuracy. His own record indicated a lack of enthusiasm for the National Socialist state, but Dettmann was declared unfit for service in 1944 after already fighting in France and the Soviet Union. State authorities suspected he had connections to someone in the machinery of the dictatorship that allowed him to escape duty while the country was in a state of total war.[38] The Marian movement converged with the church's larger desire to depict Catholicism in opposition to Nazism, but it also complicated this effort by reproaching the institutional church for imitating authoritarianism after the war.

Besides highlighting a compelling battle with church authorities, the Heroldsbach visions also demonstrate the constructions of alternate masculine identities surrounding pious events frequently assumed to be the realm of a feminized faith. The men of Heroldsbach and other Marian shrines advanced an emotive form of manliness. Their sentimental piety and angry rebellion was a contrast to the desire for sobriety and rational solemnity articulated by their mainstream CDU/CSU counterparts. Many of the men involved in the apparitions related their piety to tumultuous experiences from the war, the Third Reich, or their personal lives that rendered them vulnerable. Many West German observers spoke of a crisis of masculinity after the war because hardship on the eastern front and captivity somehow reduced the sexual virility of German men. Many Catholics hoping for re-Christianization viewed wartime imprisonment as a conversion opportunity and hoped the churches would reintegrate former soldiers and re-establish their manhood in a religious context.[39] By tying their perceived victimization from the war to affective forms of piety in honour of the Virgin Mary, men associated with apparitions performed this redemptive masculinity more effectively than the church itself. For example, Fritz

Müller connected his brutal imprisonment in a concentration camp with his faith in Marian apparitions, illustrating a larger trend among male supporters of Heroldsbach and other visions. Numerous camp survivors and former POWs became prominent as activists and seers at sites of Catholic miracles, linking their personal suffering through war and dictatorship with their attachment to the Virgin Mary. On the one hand, this public embrace of male sentimentality in the context of spiritual mysticism diverged from the martial masculinity of the interwar period. During the 1920s and 1930s, Catholic Youth organizations converged with post–First World War gender norms and rejected feminized Marian piety in favour of street marches, uniforms, and militarized language.[40] On the other hand, these former camp inmates also posed a counterpoint to the conservatives and liberals favouring rhetoric about "sober" fathers, "reliable" husbands, and "protectors of their families" in a revival of "traditional" patriarchy.[41] Male devotees openly espoused forms of spirituality and affected manhood usually labelled effeminate by mainstream Catholics and non-Catholics throughout the twentieth century.

Other examples at Heroldsbach confirm this trend but also illustrate additional categories of this emotive masculinity. For example, Walter Dettmann also channelled a difficult past both into his piety and his bitter confrontations with the church. As both an orphan and a war veteran, Dettmann seemingly found comfort in the narrative of Heroldsbach, which like Fatima called for the conversion of sinners in order to protect the world from further violence, upheaval, and nuclear catastrophe. However, Dettmann also embraced a rugged and violent masculinity that the church advertised when opposing him, which still diverged from the respectability of the CDU patriarchs but revived the militancy from the 1920s and 1930s. He thrived on confrontation and frequently found himself in court for physical assault against members of the clergy. In one instance, he threw the hat off a priest from Switzerland who entered his wooden chapel with Schmitt. Two years later, wearing a sign that said "this is sacred ground to us," he punched Schmitt in the face when the latter appeared on the hill again. In another case, Dettmann declared that with "the rosary in one hand and the sword in the other we will fight on."[42] Dettmann set the violent tone that others imitated as the men of the movement frequently formed a column to oppose critics of the apparitions investigating their sacred hill. For example, Erich Heller and Walter Schreckenbach, backed by fifty supporters shouting insults, attempted to throw Schmitt out of the wooden chapel when he interrupted prayer.[43] This mixture of tender religiosity and aggressive machismo captured the multifaceted ways the men of Heroldsbach acted out their masculinity in contrast to their strait-laced CSU opponents who hoped their staid sense of patriarchy would calm the torrents of post-war Germany.

The dominance of adult men in Heroldsbach not only demonstrated a subaltern emotive Catholic masculinity, but it also represented the dominance of patriarchy in post-war Marian movements. While young female seers, such as Antonie Saam, Kuni Schleicher, Gretl Gügel, Hildegard Lang, Maria Heilmann, and Rosa Bradl, remained central to the movement and its prominent depiction in a *Der Spiegel* cover in 1949, they exercised very little agency. Even though the magazine featured the girls in its photographs, the story devoted as much attention to Antoine Saam's father, the church organist, as it did to her, for example.[44] Male leaders seized control of the apparitions as Norbert Langhojer became the official speaker in front of all gathered pilgrims. The girls would relate messages from Mary to him and he would then share the news over a loudspeaker, a trend imitated throughout Europe after the war. At times, the press rarely mentioned the girls, devoting more space to the colourful personalities and sometimes radical antics of men like Dettmann. Advocates for the apparitions argued vehemently that parental rights to determine the spirituality of their children were violated by church and state in the struggle over Heroldsbach, but they never suggested that the seers of the hill had rights themselves.

The Lay Commission increasingly intervened with how the girls performed before the gathered crowds and how they interacted with the image of Mary. Critics claimed to overhear Josef Heilmann coaching the girls when to kneel and how to behave when they appeared on the hill. Losing his temper with the girls, he reportedly insulted one of them as an "ox" when she failed to follow his directives. At one point, the girls performed a "procession of penance," walking up the hill on their knees. If such an abusive practice originated with men like Langhojer or Heilmann rather than the girls, it indicates a callous disregard for the well-being of children. While investigating Father Gailer for fraud, the state also claimed that the priest used pilgrim donations to pay the legal expenses of a man on trial and eventually convicted of sexually abusing minors.[45] This example indicates that the Heroldsbach circle engaged in some of the worst excesses of institutional Catholic patriarchy and did not create a culture that prioritized the needs of girls. The Heroldsbach apparitions reinforced patriarchy as the struggle over the authenticity of the apparitions and control of the town remained a battle between the renegade men who believed in the visions and the traditional male power brokers of German Catholicism. The unbending hegemony of this male leadership group meant that its legacy would not be a path to emancipation for its seers. Instead it served as one more example of Catholic men who sought control over young women.

Several anecdotes suggest that the girls suffered not just from the men in their movement but also from the Catholic establishment as well. The early days of the apparitions certainly rewarded them with attention and the ability to shape their own agenda. For example, Kuni Schleicher asked the Virgin Mary whether her father made it to heaven after fighting on the eastern front. Nonetheless the press and the church frequently targeted Schleicher and others with criticism that was particularly harmful to young children. Journalists, church figures, and local authorities, pursuing every means possible to discredit the girls and their religiosity, accused them of imagining the visions after viewing the American movie about Bernadette Soubirous of Lourdes. State officials and members of the press claimed that the girls laughed and pretended to bless other children at school, implying that the mockery of their own piety proved dishonesty. Some opponents of the visions defamed the reputations of these children. Attorneys investigating the legal status of Heroldsbach said that one girl "spread her legs" towards a classmate and said, "I piss on you in the name of the father, the son, and the holy ghost." The girls underwent interrogations by police and church officials, in which their memories of the visions were parsed for inconsistency, and the church threatened to deny sacraments to them just as it did the adults in town.[46] Rigidly controlled by the patriarchs of the Heroldsbach movement and brutally criticized by opponents, the girls from the hill gained very little from their role as seers.

Although highly controversial and bitterly opposed by Catholic elites in Franconia, the Heroldsbach cult endured and symbolized many ambiguities at the heart of the early Federal Republic. Led by a group of men who verbally and physically assaulted their opponents, bullied their young seers, allegedly stole money from pilgrims for their own personal gain, and even perpetuated racial stereotypes, the Heroldsbach movement seemed limited in scope. The insolent behaviour of these men did indeed turn a powerful group of churchmen and politicians against them as well as enough residents of their own town to elect a mayor opposed to the visions. Despite this troubled legacy, the visions and their advocates engaged the most pressing political and cultural themes of the day. Their obsession with Christian prayer and conversion of sinners as the best way to combat communism, repel a Russian invasion, and avoid a nuclear conflict converged awkwardly with the

Christian Democratic notion of the German *Abendland*. Their use of the National Socialist past in their attacks on the church stole the narrative of the bishops and the CDU/CSU about persecution and resistance and flipped it on its head. Most significantly, their use of the Basic Law to justify their protests contributed to a fledgling democratic discourse and to the ultimate secularization of the CDU/CSU. In an odd twist these ill-behaved religious zealots argued against the direct partnership of clergy and politicians, which foresaw how the Christian Democratic parties would rid themselves of "prelate priests" like Meixner and distance themselves from the agenda of the German bishops. The connection of Heroldsbach to such a vast array of pressing issues perhaps explains how its pilgrims persisted until they eventually made peace with the bishopric of Bamberg in the 1990s when the church granted approval for an official shrine and rescinded the past excommunications.[47]

A similar set of apparitions also occurred in the town of Fehrbach in Rhineland-Palatinate at the same time as those in Heroldsbach. A twelve-year-old orphan, Senta Roos, saw the Virgin Mary for the first time on 12 May 1949. She visited Heroldsbach and a network developed between the two towns. Fehrbach pilgrims reported "solar phenomena" and the Virgin of Fehrbach also ominously warned that "something terrible" would happen if pilgrims failed her.[48] The bishopric of Speyer, which under an earlier bishop had supported the stigmata of Therese Neumann, opposed the vision with the same vigour as the diocese of Bamberg did that of Heroldsbach, threatening its supporters with excommunication.[49] Finally, Fehrbach also mobilized a national and trans-European response with worshippers arriving from neighbouring towns, far-flung regions of West Germany, and bordering countries, such as the Netherlands and Switzerland.[50]

As in Heroldsbach, Fehrbach villagers used their direct access to heavenly figures as well as references to the Catholic-Nazi past to challenge the institutional church for greater control over spiritual capital. For example, when the bishop from Speyer demanded that Roos inform only church figures about new revelations, she responded that Mary deemed such action unacceptable.[51] Local male elites sometimes wrote to the bishop, expressing similar anxieties about the destabilizing nature of the Fehrbach visions. One local man called for a new parish priest because he felt embarrassed by Father Matheis's support for the apparition movement. He complained about the cleric's "regular" contact with "card readers" and "fortune tellers" who posed "as blessed figures." He thought a priest should refrain from such "nonsense,"

6.1. Senta Roos next to a former POW who announced her revelations in Fehrbach. Bistumsarchiv Speyer, BO NA 23/10, 1/49.

which he felt "bordered on paganism." He also stated that many in the parish believed "the priest should spend more time with his actual tasks."[52] Replicating tactics sometimes employed by Therese Neumann and showing more agency than the girls of Heroldsbach, Senta Roos provocatively privileged a spiritual authority that transcended priests and bishops. Despite threats of excommunication, large crowds gathered for the apparitions. Furthermore, one group of residents wrote to diocesan authorities suggesting that the "greatest sinners" sat in the bishop's office of Speyer. They felt that Catholic leaders had abandoned their followers in a time of need, much as they did in "Hitler's time" when they avoided public protest and left their "flock" to their own devices.[53] This sensitivity about the church struggles during the Third Reich likely received attention because of an especially harsh standoff between local Nazi officials and the Catholic population in the diocese.[54] Like Müller and Dettmann in the Heroldsbach case, believers in the Fehrbach apparitions used the church's selective memory about persecution under Nazism against German bishops by casting them as Nazi collaborators and Catholic congregants as victims.

6.2. Senta Roos and the former POW who spoke on her behalf. Bistumsarchiv Speyer, BO NA 23/10, 1/49.

This confrontation with the church, however, included ambiguities. In the first place, it replicated the patriarchal nature of the institution it attacked. As in Heroldsbach, men quickly restrained the seers' agency by acting as spiritual advisors and publicists. Although women between the ages of forty and sixty constituted the majority of Fehrbach supporters, they accepted leadership from a small number of men in the movement. The firm support of their local priest remained a crucial litmus test for the popularity of a pilgrimage. In fact, Fehrbach supporters likely used respect for male patriarchy as a legitimation strategy to either consciously or unconsciously moderate their radical challenge to the spiritual authority of German bishops. Furthermore, a male schoolteacher, war veteran, and POW announced the revelations of Senta Roos over a microphone rather than accept a young girl in an unrestrained leadership role. Although apparition movements challenged hierarchy, their provocations left patriarchy untouched. Furthermore, the ultimate goal of apparition supporters was official recognition of the Fehrbach Madonna by the church. When the Vatican recognized modern apparitions, such as in Fatima and Banneux (Belgium, 1933), they usually reacted suspiciously at first but altered their course several years later. Pilgrims to Heroldsbach and Fehrbach expected such a fate for their apparitions. Over two thousand people wrote to the bishop of Speyer in hope of such a result. Despite their confrontation with institutional authority, it was the blessing of church officials that these Marian pilgrims craved most.[55]

Fehrbach emphasized fears about consumerism, sexuality, and secularization more than war memory. The defenders of the apparitions stressed the originality of their Madonna's central message: "I am the mother of the conversion of sinners." The primary revelations delivered by the "simple and artless" seer encouraged the return of prodigal Catholics back to the faith. Senta Roos's poverty and seeming rejection of material goods received much more public exposure than the fact that she had lost her parents to bombs during the Second World War.[56] At times the Fehrbach faithful used the visions to attack the rising tide of popular culture in West Germany. A pilgrim to Fehrbach wrote to Joseph Frings complaining bitterly about the cardinal's opposition to the alleged apparitions, which he credited for reviving pilgrimages. He said, "The people walk to so many sporting events and juggleries of all sorts, but they forget the valuable trips for prayer and reflection completely." The pilgrim believed that the events of Heroldsbach and Fehrbach combated this problem.[57] Another Fehrbach supporter wrote in despair over clerical criticism of the apparitions. He spoke of one priest who proclaimed he would rather attend the *Oktoberfest* in Munich than travel to an apparition site, but noted that the man had neither visited the places nor witnessed the heartfelt piety of their pilgrims. The Ravensburg pilgrim also complained about the sensational portrayal of the apparitions in the illustrated press, which he felt misrepresented the pious atmosphere of both apparition towns. He wrote: "Both opponents and supporters of the apparition sites are required to tell the truth, including illustrated magazines and sensational gazettes."[58] The targeting of football matches and the tabloid press revealed Catholic anxiety about the growth of popular culture after the war.

Fears about consumerism were frequently articulated with rhetoric about gender and sexuality. Fehrbach pilgrims contrasted their austerity and religiosity with the growth of the market economy and its perceived connection with the sex industry in the Federal Republic. One woman wrote to the bishop's office: "When, for example, a bar opens with a regular strip tease in an all-Catholic town such as Fehrbach ... then the call to emergency by the Virgin Mother cannot be loud enough."[59] Pilgrims associated their anxiety about consumerism and commercial sexuality with their fear of secularization. One *Fehrbacher* wrote: "If our priests hold devotions to Mary, who is there? Two or three old hags. The masses would rather seek pleasure. But a poor orphan was sought by the mother of God to convert these sinners." Therefore, apparition worshippers celebrated "countless" stories of wayward Christians who found religion once again after sexual misconduct and lapsed religious practice thanks to contact with the Fehrbach Madonna.[60] Just as the Konnersreuth Circle rallied around Catholic chastity during the Weimar Republic, the followers of Senta Roos viewed strict morality as an empowering defence against not only changing sexual norms but also a rising spirit of consumerism that came to West Germany with American popular culture and Cold War military installations.

The spectre of a new popular culture and its secular influence stoked the fears of Fehrbach as much as the prospect of another Russian invasion frightened Heroldsbach activists. Perhaps this different reaction resulted from Fehrbach's proximity to towns modernized by American military bases during the 1950s. Previously agricultural Palatinate towns, such as Baumholder, experienced radical economic and social changes with the construction of American bases starting in 1950, sparking anxiety by Christian politicians, priests, and social workers about the moral climate of the region.[61] While the Cold War provided the context for Heroldsbach because of its location near Eastern Europe, the pilgrims to Fehrbach expressed a greater concern with the threat posed by Americanization and consumerism to moral values, religious traditions, and rural ways of life in the Palatinate.

The Decline of the Marian Movement

Existing scholarship about faith in heavenly intercession naturally accentuates the most popular movements, but analysis of those that attracted less attention reveals just as much about this era of Marian piety. For example, a series of less accepted apparitions also transpired in the town of Niederhabbach when a thirty-five year-old rural labourer who was a war veteran, a former POW, and a refugee from the east saw the Virgin Mary in "a glowing blue robe and a white veil" multiple times in the summer of 1952 following a visit to Heroldsbach. After he predicted a vision for early September, between five thousand and eight thousand people travelled to his small town where pilgrims insisted they saw the sun rotate and change colour before the seer's latest vision. The crowd included mostly middle-aged and older women, a few "unhappy looking men," Heroldsbach supporters, a row of sick people hoping for cures, and Hungarian "gypsies." Reporting on conversations in the crowd, a journalist stated: "The names of miracles came up: Fatima, Lourdes, Konnersreuth, Heroldsbach … above all Heroldsbach." Another newspaper claimed that "people of all ranks, rich and poor, young and old, stood under a spell at the entrance to the house." Fritz Müller arrived with cards proclaiming the authenticity of the Niederhabbach apparitions and another Heroldsbach supporter presented the seer's stepson with an oil painting of the Heroldsbach Madonna. The event seemed as chaotic as it was pious. The police lost control as pilgrims overwhelmed them in a desire to surround the house, resulting in at least one broken leg sustained when a woman was trampled by the crowd. The press proclaimed that "this part of the mountains resembled an army camp by Sunday."

The behaviour of spectators, however, demonstrated deepening scepticism regarding controversial apparitions. One report described an ambivalent crowd: "The curious expressed surprise, made predictions, offered arguments, and proclaimed their displeasure. Disparaging looks frequently existed next to fanatical faith. Derogatory hand gestures were next to praying hands." Another journalist wrote: "Many of the curious came who did not share the beliefs of those standing next to them. They stared at the people, baffled at the mass psychosis."[62] An article claimed: "Two good friends got into a fight because the one did not want to believe what the other claimed to see." One reporter recounted the mixed reaction to the "solar miracle":

> There – the sign! Somebody wanted to believe they saw something in the sun. Something with the sun. The sun! Everyone stared at the sun. It shined through a milky veil of clouds – and turned, rotated, continually around and around. And it makes pale coloured blots and dots in the sky. It is the sign!
>
> 'My God, the sign.'
>
> 'Ach, what? No sign– it is always that way if one looks at the sun too long.'
>
> 'No it is the sign– see also the house and the bushes; they have the same bright, green, and gold spots and dots.'

As more apparitions occurred, they received greater publicity in the growing tabloid press and increased disillusionment among the mainstream Catholic population.

The Niederhabbach visions failed to capture the popular imagination because they lacked many of the essential features present in Heroldsbach and Fehrbach. First, the seer did not possess the support of either a local priest or even a spiritual advisor who could provide more legitimacy to his visions. As an adult male rather than a young girl, he departed from the usual script for successful apparitions. Furthermore, he lacked the infrastructure and the interest in creating a popular movement. According to the report of a Catholic theologian investigating the events of September 1952, the seer experienced relief when the crowd dispersed from the front of his house and reacted with indifference to the alleged solar miracle. His experience as a soldier, POW, and eastern refugee in combination with narratives of German suffering during the 1950s created the potential for a strong following.[63] However, his lack of education, profane language, erratic behaviour, and unconvincing descriptions of visions failed to impress potential followers or church officials. The archdiocese banned worship at Niederhabbach and no movement comparable to Heede, Heroldsbach, or Fehrbach emerged.

Despite the quick demise of the Niederhabbach movement, it nonetheless indicated the persistence of the confrontation between apparition supporters and the clergy. Although the Niederhabbach seer neglected the usual themes of anti-communism, anti-Nazism, and anti-consumerism, he nonetheless used his visions to critique the rigidity of clerical oversight. When interviewed by Cologne officials about his apparitions, he said, "During the first visit, she said that many priests would berate me over the miracles. Today she said that many priests have indeed berated the apparitions."[64] That such a crowd gathered to see a mentally unstable visionary who was indifferent to his own popularity is in itself a powerful testament to the geographical reach and determination of Heroldsbach's supporters and the willingness of thousands of Catholic to defy church leaders on the issue of religious miracles.

Another series of Marian miracles occurred in the Palatinate town of Rodalben, but they sparked more protests against suspicious claims of supernatural visions than they did faith in the Virgin Mary. A twenty-six-year-old woman claimed that Mary healed her from debilitating cramps and appeared with other heavenly figures in multiple apparitions. Anneliese Wafzig's hallucinations attracted the devotion of about sixty regular pilgrims who formed a so-called "prayer community" as well as hundreds of other visitors. The Rodalben visions contained the same apocalyptic tone as those of Heroldsbach and Fehrbach. Mary and personalities from the communion of saints warned Anneliese about calamities if she failed in her role as conduit to win back lapsed Christians. However, the visions rarely mentioned communism, Russians, or a potential third world war. Rather they encouraged conversion of sinners, such as a man in the same hospital where Anneliese experienced her cure. The Blessed Mother instructed her to place a Catholic medallion under his pillow so he would repent his sins. Finally, the Wafzig family and their followers undermined church authority and articulated a reformed version of Catholic piety through the visions. For example, one of Anneliese Wafzig's spiritual advisors wrote, "Not a religion of violence and strict laws, but a religion of love and the heart can and will save people." These pious dissidents believed that a more flexible and less legalistic approach to doctrine would not only lend their beliefs legitimacy but convert others to Catholicism. These proposals for a new spirituality, however, possessed similarities to the new religions of the 1960s and 1970s and undercut Catholic dominance and the institutionalized religions of the past.

As a result of a network of lay associations stronger than in the rural towns of Heede, Heroldsbach, and Fehrbach, the five thousand Catholics from the industrial town of Rodalben supported their priest and the church hierarchy in opposition to these alleged miracles. While the church excommunicated the seer, her family, and several followers, Catholic youth groups and the Kolping Association spearheaded protests against the apparitions in the hope of preventing an embarrassing spectacle. In the early days of the Rodalben events, the parish priest complained that Wafzig's visions became the butt of jokes at the local factory. Relations with the town worsened when Wafzig supporters accused a group of Rodalben Catholic youth of violently attacking her. Although the local police discredited this attack as fantasy, these youth had in fact vandalized devotional material of the nearby Fehrbach apparitions as well.[65]

The tension culminated on 1 July 1952 when the Rodalben "prayer community" ventured to the cemetery in order to witness a predicted miracle by the Virgin Mary. Over one thousand spectators cursed, threw stones, and intimidated them with threats of further violence. The men

6.3. Angry Catholics oppose the Rodalben Prayer Circle on 1 July 1952. Bistumsarchiv Speyer, BO NA 23/10, 1/49.

leading this crowd yelled, "You may not pass. We are the Kolping Association. You are blasphemers, dogs, and false priests." The Marian devotees retreated indoors under the reluctant protection of the police. Once inside the residence, the tumult spilled on to the front lawn as hecklers threw stones at the windows, threatened to storm the house, and more ominously discharged a revolver. One pilgrim "had the feeling that if this mob succeeded in entering the house, they would tear us all to pieces." At the moment when the violence outside reached a climax, the pilgrims claimed a miracle occurred indoors. The visionary and her supporters professed that a vision of Jesus miraculously engraved, in blood, one of her garments with an image of a communion host and chalice.

The Rodalben phenomenon remains significant for several reasons. Much like the more popular spectacles in Fehrbach, these miracles

6.4. Members of the Rodalben Prayer Circle Venerate the "Blood Miracle" of 1952. Bistumsarchiv Speyer, BO NA 23/10, 2/51, Bonaventur Meyer, Bericht über Rodalben.

emphasized fears of secularization rather than anti-communism. Rodalben shared Fehrbach's close proximity to the new American military bases in the Palatinate. When Anneliese saw a vision of Jesus Christ in tears during the "blood miracle," it suggested anger with secularization and scepticism by other Catholics rather than the imminent threat of war.[66] Second, those excommunicated for worshipping apparitions explicitly linked their fate to religious victims of Nazi persecution during the tense church-state struggle in the Palatinate during the 1930s. The family of the Rodalben visionary claimed they resisted National Socialism. One of their supporters argued that they were the "only" family in town that remained loyal to Catholicism, and that they had opened their home to those forced into hiding by the regime. The family also insisted that the local pastor entrusted them with incriminating

6.5. The Altar to the "Blood Miracle" of 1952. Bistumsarchiv Speyer BO NA 23/10, 2/51, Bonaventur Meyer, Bericht über Rodalben.

documents that he wanted to hide from the Gestapo. Once again, those devoted to Marian apparitions drew parallels between the Nazi suppression of free speech and institutional efforts to discourage miracles not sponsored by the Vatican.

One of two monks who became spiritual advisors to Anneliese Wafzig used traumatic Second World War experiences to defend the Rodalben apparitions. Father Gebhard Heyder spent time in a concentration camp for an inflammatory sermon and compared this experience to the church's attempts to silence Rodalben supporters. His superior within the Carmelite order offered the following description: "It is as a consequence of his time in the KZ and his suffering within the KZ that he developed an exaggerated sense of justice and punctilious drive to fight all injustice in the world." A disproportionate number of the small circle of men attracted to Catholic mysticism had endured concentration camps, POW camps, or expulsion from Eastern Europe. Although his younger colleague and protégé, Father Wolfgang Kimmel, fought as an officer in the Second World War, it was Heyder's victimization that received more attention in complaints about the church because they compared Nazi oppression with ecclesiastical repression of apparition devotion.[67] This encouragement of religiosity previously deemed feminine by men hardened by imprisonment and war continued the alternate direction in post-war Catholic masculinity started by Heroldsbach supporters, such as Fritz Müller.[68]

Furthermore, the events in Rodalben highlighted the divisions created by the apparition movement during the early 1950s. Bishops and priests became the fiercest enemies of Heroldsbach and Fehrbach. However, Catholic youth groups and confessional associations led attacks in Rodalben, indicating fatigue among lay leaders with what they viewed as superstitious, dated, and embarrassing forms of piety by rural women.[69] The wave of apparitions created a gulf between the traditional power brokers of the Catholic milieu, including the clergy and confessional associations, and rural adherents to piety outside the control of the institutional church.

The gendered relationships within the Rodalben prayer circle followed a similar pattern to Marian communities in Heroldsbach and Fehrbach. Although Wafzig exercised spiritual power as a seer, she required male leadership for more widespread legitimacy. She began with a lay advisor named Fideli Ransberger, an estranged Heroldsbach activist and a war veteran. Like Dettmann, Ransberger was a former "soldier-priest" who may have been influenced in his revolt against church hierarchy by the front experience. After the church excommunicated the Wafzig family and accusations surfaced about an affair between Wafzig and Ransberger, he fled. If true, this sexual exploitation of Wafzig by Ransberger indicates once again the existence of the worst elements of Catholic patriarchy in some Marian circles. Two monks with Heroldsbach connections, Wolfgang Kimmel and Gebhard Heyder, succeeded Ransberger as leaders of the small but intensely pious group. A war veteran, Kimmel was the third "soldier-priest" actively involved in the Marian movements that aggressively challenged church authority over the authenticity of apparitions. Anneliese Wafzig ended her brief period as a local celebrity by retreating to the care of Heroldsbach's most prominent observer, Dr Johannes B. Walz.[70] Miraculous visions undoubtedly provided Wafzig a "respite from powerlessness," but constant male supervision limited their potential for emancipation. Within her own movement, men sought control over her spiritual gifts.[71]

The Rodalben movement remained unpopular for many reasons. The crucial support of the local clergy eluded the Wafzig family, and clerical hostility, apparently, inspired the opposition of others in the town. Diocesan leaders observed: "To the honor of the congregation in Rodalben one must conclude that local Catholics with very few exceptions have followed their leaders and local clergy with strict discipline." Adherents of the more popular apparition movement in the neighbouring town of Fehrbach also looked with more scorn than enthusiasm on the events in Rodalben. Fehrbach pilgrims resented the Rodalben circle as a rival and worried that the Wafzig family's unpopularity would detract from their own claims of authenticity.[72] Although influenced by Heroldsbach through Ransberger and Heyder, Rodalben pilgrims proved incapable of winning support from the local and national network of Catholics fascinated by acts of intervention by heavenly figures.

The momentum of the apparition movement declined because of threats of excommunication as well as fatigue with numerous reports of miracles. The institutional church also slowed the trend by reasserting its power and by harnessing Marian piety within the boundaries of doctrine and formal practice. Pope Pius XII declared 1954 a Marian Year and Cardinal Frings organized the *Peregrinatio Mariae* (Travelling Madonna) in the archdiocese of Cologne.[73] This event brought an officially recognized model of the Fatima statue to three hundred parishes throughout the Rhineland. The church ultimately reduced the influence of Germany's seers by reappropriating their messages within the context of officially sponsored doctrines. It was also highly symbolic that the powerful cardinal of Cologne, the geographic heart of the new Christian Democratic political establishment, used this event to reassert institutional dominance over the rebels associated with Marian apparitions. The statue attracted sixty thousand visitors a day for over a week in Cologne and remained popular in its sojourn through the archdiocese.[74]

Frings's decisions to organize this devotion to the Fatima Madonna resulted in part from a papal policy that hoped to harness the fervour of Marian apparitions all over Europe, but also because worship of the Virgin Mary remained inspirational among Catholics who did not seek affirmation in places like Heroldsbach and Fehrbach. Several devotees of the Virgin Mary wrote to Frings in hopes that such an event would honour the sanctioned Fatima miracles. After hearing about Fatima statues in other countries, one woman wrote, "Please tell me why so many countries have had the great luck to receive the Madonna from Fatima … Most Reverend Father, do you not believe that She, who alone is powerful like a well-prepared army, would prepare the end of the unholy works of Satan in our country?"[75] Another man who admired the number of events in France honouring the Virgin Mary wrote, "We German Catholics do not want to say that we stand behind in worship of Mary."[76] Finally, one hundred men from Euskirchen wrote a letter to the Cologne Church newspaper asking for help convincing the hierarchy to bring a Fatima statue to the diocese for the Marian Year.[77] This correspondence converged with the Heroldsbach contributions to the cultural construction of a West German *Abendland* during the Cold War, but relied upon sanctioned piety rather than banned visions.

The archdiocese received numerous reports praising the mission-style atmosphere that surrounded the travelling statue. One such report said, "The procession turned into a glorious manifestation of Catholic faith … The number of participants became so large that the welcome ceremony had to be moved from the church to the square and carried out with a microphone."[78] A Düsseldorf cleric claimed, "I found people who have not received the sacraments in years fighting an internal struggle about whether to return to the confessional. They often knelt for hours until they luckily found the courage to come inside and speak openly."[79] The awakening that arose under the leadership of spiritual rebels in small towns like Heroldsbach was now replicated in the heartland of the CDU in the Rhineland.

While Catholic congregations flocked to the statue, many among the clergy in a region where the mainstream establishment bristled at Therese

Neumann during the Weimar Republic and mobilized against Heroldsbach after the war remained distant even towards such sanctioned mysticism. A parish priest from Brühl complained: "One issue that casts shade on this event and worries me is the position of the majority of clergy. Those who are undecided and possess doubts always have an 'if' or a 'but.' A noticeable portion of them are hostile and speak of 'nonsense' and 'fetishism' ... The Holy Father expects that we priests do all we can in this Marian year to lead the people to the Mother of God, but many have had a destructive influence." Nonetheless, even sceptical clergy embraced the successful tour by the Fatima replica perhaps because no new miracles or cures surfaced.[80] The tour of the "Traveling Madonna" proved the popularity of Marian worship in the Rhineland, but also illustrated the wider acceptance of authorized forms of piety in regions with carefully organized religious associations.

While the *Peregrinatio Mariae* emulated aspects of the apparition movement, it also co-opted its symbols for the purposes of the Catholic elites now dominant in the Rhineland and the West German political establishment. The success of the Fatima events was celebrated not just as a Catholic event but as an element of a newfound interconfessional consensus central to Christian Democracy. Despite a few tensions between Lutheran and Catholic congregations over the processions, non-Catholics allowed the Fatima worship to proceed with very little criticism or interference. In a heavily Protestant neighbourhood, a parish reported, "In the streets of this area with only a minimal percentage of Catholics, those with other beliefs did not express their disapproval on any occasion."[81] A clergyman from Remscheid triumphantly wrote, "What was impossible fifty years ago has become reality!" He recalled the arrival of a convent of nuns fifty years ago when a "mob" gathered around and ripped the veils off of some of its members. The priest contrasted this event to the peacefulness with which the Protestant community received the Madonna and remarked that a few Protestants even attended the Fatima procession into town.[82] Catholic clergy strategically highlighted the tolerance of German Protestants in a new era of confessional understanding. As interfaith partners in the CDU/CSU, they no longer confronted one another during such public celebrations.

Although the church rejected the German apparition movement of the early 1950s, the Fatima celebration reflected its Cold War themes with warnings about a third world war and redirected them towards the CDU's foreign policy alignment with NATO.[83] First, the reports filed to the archdiocese suggested a communist resentment towards the Fatima statue. For example, a Jesuit heard a group of "young Communists" in Mülheim suggest a bombing of the Fatima procession.[84] On some occasions, the Fatima events simply suffered ridicule by the working class.[85] Therefore, sermons at these events emphasized the anti-communist interpretations of the Fatima apparitions. One preacher proclaimed: "It is high time that all those of goodwill realized that everything depends on obedience to the demands of Our Lady of Fatima in 1917 who promised: 'If you do what I say, then peace will come.' We do not wish death upon the Communists, but we pray without end that the hatred against God will finally cease!"[86] An announcement of the Fatima procession in Euskirchen stated, "We know of another promise to save the world without Christ that has brought more than a quarter of the world and almost a third of humanity under its rule in about thirty years. Since this time the people live in fear of new invasions and bloody wars. Who can save us? Only the message of our 'loving Lady of Fatima.'"[87] The clergy used the Fatima events to contrast Catholicism with communism. They co-opted a central message from Heroldsbach and partnered it with sanctioned events of Fatima.

The anti-communist message resonated with many Catholics who participated in the Fatima events in the archdiocese of Cologne. A monk involved with the *Peregrinatio Mariae* wrote, "Every Church where the Fatima Madonna visits becomes a pilgrimage site. The message about the great danger that threatens the existence of the Christian West moves the hearts of many people. The promise that the pure heart of Mary will triumph, that Russia will convert, and that peace will finally arrive fills everyone with new hope."[88] At a Marian celebration in Mülheim, a worker whose colleague mocked his Marian worship, proclaimed, "If you do not visit this statue, then soon you will be forced to worship another image."[89] A fear and hatred of communism motivated many Catholics to worship the Fatima Madonna and attracted them to her message, building cultural support for the CDU's notion of an *Abendland* as a bulwark against communism.

As in Heroldsbach and elsewhere, the threats of the Marian apparitions received attention. In preparation for the *Peregrinatio Mariae*, a clergyman wrote: "During the third apparition in Fatima, the Mother of God mentioned a coming catastrophe and also offered the means to protect against it. In the meantime, the Second World War broke out with all its horrors, emergencies, and consequences. A third world war would undoubtedly mean the annihilation of a large proportion of humanity."[90] A German monk offered the following interpretation of the Fatima messages: "If the masses live today without remorse or conscience, then they build new guilt that will fall upon humanity like an avalanche. It is very dangerous to live without Christ. It is highly dangerous to accumulate sin upon sin. If enough atonement is not expressed, then new catastrophes will arrive." In his sermon at the Fatima celebration in Cologne, Cardinal Frings said, "Germany must listen to this message of salvation. The people of Europe would like to forget the fact that there are sins and that if they go without atonement, there is punishment."[91] Similar to the messages of the apparitions in Heroldsbach, the church used popular fears about destructive war, atomic weapons, and Cold War rivalry to attract followers to the Marian revival. They warned that without a deeper commitment to Catholic traditions, more destruction in Europe would follow. By doing so within the confines of approved visions, church fathers like Frings harnessed the messages of the Heroldsbach rebels within the boundaries of the hierarchical church leadership, rendering them respectable.

In the midst of sincere and heartfelt expressions of Marian piety by hundreds of thousands of Catholics, clergymen also fretted about secular impulses in the capitalist West. Cardinal Frings complained, "The amazing economic rise of the Federal Republic has not seen a parallel renewal in religious and moral values."[92] Much like movements in support of miracles since the 1920s, the Catholic Church used the Virgin Mary to question consumerist values. However, Frings translated the anxieties with modern economics into the rhetoric against materialism as articulated by the new CDU. Christian Democracy depicted modern materialism as the core of what was fundamentally deviant about both communism and National Socialism. It proposed Christian unity as the greatest protection for West Germany against extremism. Rather than promote the potentially disruptive anti-consumerist messages of Heroldsbach and Fehrbach in a way that could threaten strategic alliances with Protestant Christian Democrats and the American foreign policy establishment, the celebration of the Fatima Madonna instead used an anti-materialist message that more exclusively targeted totalitarianism.

Finally, this event relegated women to even more secondary roles than the prayer circles in Heroldsbach, Fehrbach, and Rodalben. Imposing discipline on the subverted gender order, male associations and youth groups carried the Madonna during processions and male Jesuits rather than female seers distributed the message of Fatima. Women formed the majority of spectators, but remained on the margins of all

6.6. Male leaders carry the Fatima statue during the *Peregrinatio Mariae* in 1954. Historisches Archiv des Erzbistums Köln Seelsorgeamt Heinen 118 Peregrinatio Mariae. Photo courtesy of Theo Felton, Cologne.

rituals during the statue's visits. In sum, the hierarchy defused the confrontation with Marian supporters by reappropriating Marian messages about fearing communism, consumerism, and secularization and seizing control of the "goods of salvation" from the excommunicated rebels in Bavaria, the Rhineland, and the Palatinate.

Despite its tremendous success, the Fatima celebrations of 1954 failed to produce long-standing devotion to the Virgin Mary or church institutions. After the Fatima statue's tour of the archdiocese, it was sent to a church in the town of Alzen, which Cologne officials hoped would become a popular pilgrimage site. Officials from Alzen, however, already noted the lack of visitors in 1955.[93] Catholic leadership in many of the locations where the Madonna visited also complained about difficulty in translating the event's popularity from a short-lived success to continued religious celebration. In Leverkusen, where clergymen expressed surprise at the enthusiasm with which Catholics greeted the Madonna's arrival, few Catholics increased their levels of devotion after the Fatima procession. Attendance at workday and Sunday mass remained level and confession and communion rates barely changed. Despite several new faces in the confessional while the Fatima statue resided in Leverkusen parishes, few returned afterward.[94] The *Peregrinatio Mariae* reinterpreted Catholic mysticism in such a way that it more clearly supported the mainstream vision of Catholic elites from the Rhineland. It bottled the Marian enthusiasm of the 1950s and used it to articulate a message in favour of Christian Democratic pillars, such as pro-NATO alignment against the communism, interconfessional co-operation, and the creation of a Christian bulwark against communist politics and materialist culture. While successful politically, this brand of rationalized piety eventually helped dampen some of the grass-roots enthusiasm of the apparitions and religiosity that accompanied them. Although the Catholic bishops overcame their adversaries from rural towns across in the Federal Republic in the short-term, they could not overcome the damage caused by rebellions in places like Heroldsbach and Fehrbach. As the Fatima Madonna of 1954 lost relevance, the cults of Heroldsbach and Fehrbach persisted and the strong influence of the Catholic establishment proved equally short-lived as religious faith fragmented and became more diffuse.

Conclusion

This analysis of Catholic mysticism in the early years of the Federal Republic illustrates the existence of a short-lived revival of Marian worship caused by spontaneous action from below as well as calculated planning by the hierarchy that stretched from Bavaria to the Rhineland and beyond. With apparitions in multiple locations and followers from several regions and countries, post-war faith in Marian intercession transcended any one locality. During the aftermath of war and the onset of the Cold War, Catholics coped with their anxieties through devotion to the Virgin Mary. However, religious miracles also engaged the other important tropes within the Catholic community of the early Federal Republic: anxiety about new forms of popular culture and early debates about the Nazi past. In post-war West Germany, Catholic politicians, clergy, and lay leaders supported the democratic process and Western allies that empowered Christian Democracy but also waged a moral campaign against the materialism and popular culture that came with this Western integration.[95]

Furthermore, apparition supporters reshaped the Catholic narrative of victimhood by using the Third Reich as a weapon against the institutional authorities who excommunicated them. They altered the selective memory of Catholic persecution to suggest that while church authorities collaborated, ordinary congregants suffered alone from the anti-Catholic bias of the National Socialist regime. Despite using anti-Nazi rhetoric to defend their Marian worship, they ignored Nazi anti-Semitism and the collaboration of some of their leaders. In sum, the Marian movement mobilized hundreds of thousands of Catholics who operated on the fringes of the German Catholic milieu by engaging mainstream tropes about anti-communism, anti-consumerism, and anti-Nazism.

This movement, however, sparked division within the Catholic community as well. Rural women, former POWs, camp survivors, and provincial priests instigated a standoff with other clergy, bishops, CDU/CSU politicians, and lay associations who found the miracles embarrassing and perilous to their spiritual authority. While pilgrims circumvented clerical authority by seeking salvation through direct access to God rather than the church, bishops threatened some of their most devout followers with excommunication and male association members even violently attacked other Catholics in Rodalben. This rebellion ultimately failed, as was the case, according to Bourdieu, with most power struggles from within the "religious field." Collaborations between German bishops and the CDU/CSU proved to be fruitful. Ultimately religious leaders relied on tools provided by their elite status to combat Marian pilgrims: theological education and control over canon law. Roman Catholic leaders operated from a position of power because they possessed what their adversaries ultimately desired: official standing within the church and recognition by the hierarchy. German bishops successfully isolated their most outspoken opponents through excommunication, verbal abuse, and even violence. They also re-established control over the most popular elements of Marian worship with the *Peregrinatio Maria*.

The most compelling element of this surge in Catholic mysticism remains its quick rise and fall from 1940 to 1955. On the one hand, the apparition boom illustrates the "braided" narrative of secularization. While other parts of the Catholic community became secular, sought modern reforms, or encouraged a return to the Catholic milieu of the 1920s, thousands of rural Catholics reformulated the values of the Lourdes and Fatima apparitions to articulate anxiety with the early Federal Republic and the Cold War in a divided Catholic community.

For a decade, Marian pilgrims undertook dynamic forms of worship, while mainstream Catholics participated less frequently in Sunday services and confessional associational life. On the other hand, the popularity of faith in miracles declined rapidly after 1954. Enthusiasm for the church-sponsored Fatima statue waned and the seers of the 1950s privately continued their spiritual journey with much less fanfare and a subaltern following. Bourdieu argues that the preservation of power in the religious field depends on one's ability to meet the needs of religious consumers most efficiently.[96] Perhaps the church discipline of the early 1950s alienated some of their most enthusiastic consumers, causing disunity at a fragile moment of reconstruction and secularization. Furthermore, the German Catholic Church seemed more effective at winning power struggles with their most pious followers than competing with the emerging affluence and access to popular culture during the 1950s. As enthusiasm for miraculous visions faded with the growing economic and political stability of the Federal Republic, attendance in church pews and membership in religious associations also declined in the late 1950s and 1960s. The Marian wave of the 1950s did not fulfil its desire to save Germany from de-Christianization. Rather it contributed to a growing trend that increasingly made spirituality and religiosity independent of church institutions. By creating religious practices and mentalities that could exist without clergy, such miracles strengthened Catholic fervour in the short-term but weakened the authority of church officials in the long run. This trend towards unmediated worship combined with demographic and economic shifts made the structures of what historians call the Catholic milieu increasingly uninfluential. The sorts of individualized faith expressed by Marian pilgrims would become the hallmark of a contemporary spirituality that increasingly relied less on the declining authority of bishops and male lay associations and more on personalized faith experiences. Walter Dettmann's desire for a separation of church and state came to pass, but it created a Federal Republic that was the opposite of the religious utopia he envisioned.

While the Marian veneration of the early 1950s struggled to endure, the stigmata of Therese Neumann remained relevant beyond her death in the 1960s. Shrewd in her tactics, the stigmatist moderated her message after the war to adapt to West Germany's rapid modernization. She overcame the pressures of patriarchy to wield great power in her corner of Bavaria during the Federal Republic.

Chapter Seven

Therese Neumann between Catholic Traditionalism, Cold War, and Economic Miracle

On Good Friday in 1948, the town of Konnersreuth hosted seven thousand pilgrims, all of whom travelled to celebrate mass in the local church and witness the Friday Suffering of Therese Neumann. Over two thousand American GIs arrived from all over occupied West Germany via tour buses while Germans rode packed trains to nearby Waldsassen and then walked five miles to the Neumann family home. Soldiers bought prayer cards and other devotional materials when they were not assisting local police in managing the large crowd. American chaplains and doctors proclaimed their wonder at Therese Neumann's stigmata.[1]

This anecdote reveals much about the cultural importance of Neumann after the war. Her popularity revived after the fall of Nazism. Although the statistical data is imprecise, pilgrims on Good Friday ranged between two thousand to twenty thousand from 1947 to 1961 and as many as five hundred thousand American soldiers contributed a significant portion of the visitors.[2] Konnersreuth did not wither after the restrictions of the Nazi era and the modernization of post-war West Germany. Rather the movement around Neumann adapted, evolved, and persisted. The lines of Good Friday pilgrims also linked Neumann to the larger enthusiasm for religious miracles after the war. Her stigmata symbolized the tropes of sin, redemption, and salvation that propelled her reputation after the First World War and now drove the popularity of the Heroldsbach and Fehrbach apparitions. However, the large number of American troops in the example above also exemplified the new path forged by Therese Neumann. Her town became an important site of German-American reconciliation and Neumann herself became meaningful for post-war Germans in ways that went beyond her religious significance to Catholics.

The re-emergence of Therese Neumann as a major national and international religious figure illustrated the deep ambiguities that challenged Catholics in the early years of the Federal Republic. On the one hand, her stigmata became a rallying point for post-war anxieties, a return to lost conventions, and a renewed rejection of modernism. Unlike the leaders of Heroldsbach and Fehrbach, the Konnersreuth Circle also moved past the initial post-war stress that drove the interest in miracles. Neumann and her advocates adjusted to life in a new democracy, a consumer economy, and a modernizing Bavaria. Caught between local customs and modernity, Germany's most famous seer faced many moments of dissonance and tension. However, she modified her appeal and expanded her influence from the religious realm to culture, economics, and politics. The awkward embrace of the free market and liberal democracy by a woman who seemingly stood for antimodern traditionalism became a parable for Bavaria's transformation from a largely Catholic and conservative rural province to the economically progressive heart of West Germany.

The continued popularity of Konnersreuth for pilgrims, journalists, and Americans occurred simultaneously with the secularization of Catholic institutions observed by scholars examining youth groups, confessional associations, and communion statistics. While these secular trends had already started in the 1950s, Catholics flocked to Konnersreuth on Good Friday. Therese Neumann attracted German worshippers, Christian Social Union (CSU) politicians, and American Catholics to a transnational site that affirmed Catholic mysticism as a meaningful force in everyday life and a cultural weapon against the Warsaw Pact in the Cold War. Unlike the Heroldsbach rebels, she embraced both the clerical-conservative wing of the CSU and their intraparty rivals who favoured a healthier dose of liberal capitalism. However, the Konnersreuth Circle also unintentionally hastened the larger church's decline in West Germany. By creating a subset of Catholics who pledged loyalty to Neumann's visions above all else, the authority of the bishops and clergy receded when they hoped for a restoration of power after the war. Neumann's religious appeal also transcended Catholic subculture as her story became a part of the process by which Bavaria redefined itself as a modern *Bundesland* where local traditions and modern economics intermingled. By practicing religion in a way that encouraged an integrated Bavarian identity, Neumann assisted the secular turn of the CSU and fostered some of the consumerist trends that overwhelmed clerical authority by the time of her death.

From Rebellion to Post-War Mainstream

Although Therese Neumann became embedded as the most famous figure of the post-war miracle craze she also sought to transcend it. Once again she embodied the anxieties and search for redemption in the aftermath of a world war even more brutal than the first. Some of the rebellious Catholics who sought freedom from clerical control thought Neumann could be their ultimate champion. Mystical Catholics who created a national and international infrastructure in favour of Heroldsbach and other apparition sites also carefully followed events in Konnersreuth. Nonetheless, Neumann sought distance from all other miraculous movements of the 1940s and 1950s, seeking power through singular spiritual legitimacy. Neumann consolidated her image after the end of the war by maintaining themes consistent with some of the turbulent debates of the Weimar era while also becoming more conciliatory towards church authority and appearing less radical in her public persona.

The rumours that surrounded Therese Neumann after the war demonstrated how many who felt displaced viewed her miracles as symbolic of the disorder in their own lives. Some Germans believed that Neumann made prophecies while in ecstasy about the coming of a third world war that would include the use of nuclear weapons. Others suggested that upon her death, the apocalypse would commence with the arrival of satanic figures. In a more hopeful variation, Catholics across the country suggested her supposedly looming demise would bring peace in the Cold War and an end to the sorts of bloody conflict such as the one that Europe just endured. This interest in Neumann's alleged prophecies led to conjecture that the stigmatic from Konnersreuth had indeed died, meaning that the fulfilment of such predictions could become imminent.[3] This speculation indicates how her Friday Suffering simultaneously epitomized both the end of times and the hope for salvation for many Germans in the mid-to-late 1940s.

Neumann also shared many of the same supporters and pilgrims as the apparitions in Heroldsbach. For example, one of the most ardent Heroldsbach organizers in the Rhineland, Fritz Müller, also passionately publicized Neumann's stigmata. Members of the Heroldsbach inner circle made several attempts to visit Konnersreuth, seeking official approval from Catholicism's foremost visionary. Many pilgrims and publicists who saw the rising tide of miracles across Europe as increasing evidence of God's concern with communism and Western materialism struck many of the same themes in writing about Neumann as they did when supporting Heroldsbach. Indeed, Neumann's German supporters understood her stigmata as a narrative of apocalypse and potential salvation. She suffered vicariously for the sins of an increasingly secular and violent world. War and depression served as punishment for these sins, but her miracles could convert apostates and non-believers, potentially saving the world from God's wrath. Johannes Maria Höcht, editor of the *Konnersreuther Lesebogen* and a tireless advocate of numerous miracles not recognized by the church during the twentieth century, revived these tropes most fervently. Höcht viewed the world wars and the potential for future nuclear conflict during the Cold War as punishment for sinners and Therese Neumann and other Marian apparitions as the last hope for salvation before the end of days. This pessimistic viewpoint sometimes included a critique of the United States because of their newfound military influence over Europe.[4] For example, Höcht suggested the "atom bomb catastrophes of Hiroshima and Nagasaki" caused harm to "shrieking and defenseless victims" and he attacked the "world powers" for their "feverish" pursuit of destructive weapons.[5]

A Catholic theologian with a passion for mysticism and miracles, Höcht viewed Neumann's stigmata and the proliferating claims to see the Virgin Mary across Germany and other parts of Europe as part of the same pattern. He interpreted them as a call from God to restore the supernatural in an overly rational and materialistic modern world. In opposition to technology and modern weapons, he called for a return to faith as the only hope for a West German *Abendland* about which he frequently wrote. Complaining about a divided clergy and Catholics who felt discomfort with the physical and violent stigmata, he called on Germans to rally around miracles as signs of the final bulwark against "godlessness" from the East and "de-Christianization" from the West.[6] In his extensive coverage of both Neumann and the visions of Fehrbach, Heroldsbach, and Marienfried, Höcht synthesized the dual fears of communist invasion and American consumerism. Although unique in his focus on miracles, Höcht's antimaterialism matched the early ideology of the CDU/CSU. A representative of rural populations anxious in the midst of rapid socio-economic change, Neumann embodied Catholic discomfort with the American forms of popular culture that accompanied Western integration. Much like Christian politicians and many clergy, the Konnersreuth Circle was uncomfortable with the budding American alliance due to the expansion of consumerism that accompanied the partnership.[7]

Some of these themes resonated with other members of the Konnersreuth Circle. Her followers projected Neumann as a counterpoint to the increasing urbanization, material success, and perceived Americanization of the early Federal Republic. Images of rural simplicity posed a stark contrast with the changes stimulated by the economic miracle, construction of American bases, and emerging popular culture in large West German cities as well as much of the countryside. German writer Luise Rinser wrote: "A person such as Therese Neumann is proof that in the middle of our bustling world whose silly conventions overestimate the world of work, success, money, bourgeois respectability, and similar fleeting things, another world exists that offers a spiritual life rather than a life of materialism."[8] Neumann represented German Catholic angst at the changing values during West Germany's stunning recovery from the war.

The most consistent rhetoric by Neumann supporters that rejected the American-style consumerism of the 1950s focused on the family's refusal to profit from their celebrity. Hagiographer Albert Vogl wrote, "Any exploitation of Therese's experiences bringing any material advantage to anyone has remained utterly absent from the spirit of dedication to the mystery of the Passion as it was relived in Konnersreuth."[9] Cardinal Faulhaber of Munich praised the Neumann family for rejecting several lucrative offers to shoot a professional documentary about her life for popular consumption.[10] Konnersreuth preserved its rural identity and promoted it as part of its message as a foil to increasing commodification of everyday life in the Federal Republic.

Much like other miracle groups in the 1940s and 1950s, the Konnersreuth Circle also aggressively promoted its dissent during the Third Reich to gain increased respect in the Federal Republic. Her followers highlighted Neumann's vulnerability to National Socialist programs against the disabled as well as her links to two prominent Catholic resisters: Fritz Gerlich and Father Ingbert Naab. Höcht narrated stories of the heroic sacrifice by Konnersreuth devotees, such as the way Friedrich Ritter von Lama was hanged with a rosary still around his neck, and connected them to Neumann's anti-Nazi spirit.[11] The circle carefully cultivated an image of martyrdom after the war in order to situate Neumann as a central figure in the so-called Christian *Abendland*'s struggle against both Nazism and communism. Unlike devotees of Marian apparitions, however, Neumann never compared the institutional church negatively to her war record. Instead, she and her circle used her legacy to bolster the notion that Catholicism and National Socialism were incompatible.

Despite her personification of post-war trauma and apprehension, Neumann consciously separated herself from other Marian movements. She denied rumours linking her to prophetic statements about politics or world affairs, such as a purported vision of world peace in 1952. Repeating her position from the war years, Neumann consistently argued that she was not an oracle and had nothing to do with politics. She also put up signs on her house discouraging visitors from asking about missing relatives from the war, which distinguished her from the Heroldsbach seers. She expressed deep empathy for the sometimes suicidal pilgrims distraught with loneliness and she frequently counselled them. However, she offered no direct connection with the dead. Neumann aimed to convert, comfort, and bring pilgrims closer to God but avoided expectations that she could solve their personal problems with supernatural intercession.[12] Rejecting bigger crowds through such caution, Neumann courted mainstream respectability. This stance also contradicted behaviour by members of her inner circle both before and after the war. There is ample evidence that she answered questions about economics, politics, and everyday concerns for people local to Konnersreuth and her closest family members and advisors. While not stopping such practices altogether, she removed them from public view to gain more acceptance from church authorities and the West German press.

Therese Neumann also rejected the numerous Marian apparitions that attracted mass popularity after the war. She sought distance from press organs that linked her to Heroldsbach, such as Höcht's *Konnersreuther Lesebogen*. Complaints from her circle forced Höcht to specify that his journalism drew inspiration from the Konnersreuth spirit but possessed no direct access to the seer or her closest advisors.[13] Father Gailer of Heroldsbach arranged a meeting with Neumann through a Catholic aristocratic intermediary in 1950 and Neumann showed complete indifference to the rebellious priest's showdown with church authorities in the diocese of Bamberg. When asked in ecstasy about the authenticity of the Heroldsbach apparitions, Neumann declared them fraudulent. Afterward her circle released the news to the press, dealing a major blow to the West German Marian movement. After surviving for decades without excommunication, Neumann expressed little interest in joining the brash Heroldsbach group or the discredited seer of Rodalben. By maintaining her singularity, she also accumulated more spiritual capital. As the only major German seer of the twentieth century who avoided formal condemnation by the church, Neumann allowed pilgrims to partake in her particular brand of mysticism without fear of official censure. An article in the *Süddeutsche Zeitung* demonstrated the success of such an approach. After visiting Konnersreuth in the early 1950s, Werner Kraus claimed that the town possessed none of the "mass psychosis" associated with Heroldsbach and remained grounded in the "sobriety of everyday life" with little commercialism or sensationalism by town residents.[14] Neumann avoided the divisive struggles that engulfed her during the Weimar Republic by denouncing the tumult of Marian sites elsewhere in the Federal Republic.

Due to Neumann's careful manoeuvring, she maintained a vast following without attracting as much contentiousness from within German Catholicism as she did during the 1920s and 1930s. Her town became a pilgrimage site for thousands while also maintaining respectability in the eyes of many mainstream Catholics. The bishopric of Regensburg reached an awkward détente with Konnersreuth in 1952, releasing a statement proclaiming that nothing in Konnersreuth could be considered supernatural until the church offered a final judgment on the matter. Privately, Buchberger made his disdain for Konnersreuth clear. He informed Cardinal Muench that he continued to be "distant" from the miracles and claimed that many people went to see Neumann full of hope and left "disappointed."[15] However, the bishop no longer fought the family for a clinical exam or demanded pilgrims gain special permission from his office for visits. Unlike post-war bishops in Bamberg, Speyer, and Cologne, Buchberger and his successors allowed mystical pilgrims access to their most popular unsanctioned site without public disparagement. In fact, Neumann maintained a relationship with the bishop's office after the war, scheduling meetings whenever she was in Regensburg visiting relatives. The bishop purportedly praised the spiritual comfort many Catholics received from Therese Neumann towards the end of his time in office while travelling through Konnersreuth for confirmations.[16]

Therese Neumann occupied a liminal space for the remainder of her life. With her miracles neither confirmed nor condemned by the church, she escaped the scrutiny of an exam and enjoyed de facto legitimacy to receive pilgrims and maintain strong institutional relationships from the church. Her following became a subculture within the Catholic subculture of West Germany. Placing greater emphasis on mysticism and miracles than the mainstream church, the Konnersreuth Circle practiced a brand of Catholicism that went around the clergy to exalt a female religious figure who enjoyed great influence. Such devotional habits became more problematic after the war given the entire cohort of seminaries who died at the front. With less clerical oversight, pilgrims could gravitate more readily to the ideas of Konnersreuth. The acceptance of such non-conformity was an admission to the limits of the bishops' authority and only encouraged German Catholics to seek practices that sometimes diverged from the top-down dogmas of the hierarchy. Buchberger faced the tension of Neumann's continued popularity when prominent Americans visited him in hopes of seeing the stigmatic. Always sure to point out that she possessed no church sanction, he frequently sent passive signals that American visits would not be opposed by his office. When one army chaplain found Buchberger inscrutable on the issue of Neumann, he asked "Are you indifferent to our visiting Therese Neumann?" Buchberger's affirmative response to this question demonstrated his dilemma. He could not back away from his previous battle with the Neumann household, but her renewed popularity after the war made it impossible for him to openly criticize her.[17] His authority wavered as the Konnersreuth miracles persisted. The Konnersreuth Circle continued to undercut formal church power even while trying to regain the confidence of church authorities.

Neumann's significance also became quite multidimensional throughout the 1950s. While she retained deep pious value for a set of German Catholics, she also became a Bavarian cultural figure somewhat removed from religious experience. The first part of this transition occurred through the discouragement of religious spectacle in Konnersreuth. While Neumann performed her Friday Suffering every week during the Weimar years, her public viewings became restricted to Good Friday and sometimes other Fridays in Lent. While Konnersreuth became a Good Friday destination for both American and German pilgrims, Father Naber and Neumann's family started deterring even these visits. In 1951, over ten thousand people arrived in Konnersreuth and attended a service led by Father Naber. When they crossed the street, expecting to view Neumann's re-enactment of the passion, Naber opened the upstairs window and informed them that Neumann failed to bleed this year in honour of the twenty-fifth anniversary of her stigmata. Neumann also experienced no blood and saw no visitors in 1956 for her thirtieth anniversary and in 1959 for the thirty-third anniversary – the age of Jesus of Nazareth when he died. The Neumann family also publicly asked visitors to stay away on Good Friday due to Neumann's declining health. For example, she fell and suffered a collapsed lung in 1950 and the press frequently reported near death experiences due to heart ailments or side effects of her continued flights into ecstasy.[18] A desire for privacy and a declining seer rendered the religious energy of Konnersreuth in the 1920s an impossibility during the early Federal Republic.

This decline in religiosity did not remove Neumann entirely from public life. Rather she increasingly took on importance as a symbol of Bavarian identity. In a struggle between regional traditionalism and modern integration, conservatives sought new ways to be Bavarian. They frequently chose local sites that could express some aspect of generic Bavarian tradition to pair with other elements of the region's increasing modernization. Neumann and her town became symbolic of how rural values persisted alongside the economic miracle. While her family received international renown and at least some educational and professional opportunities due to her celebrity, they maintained a rustic pride in their previous way of life.

German publications about Neumann shifted from narrations of religious miracles to descriptions of her family's austere life. Novelist Luise Rinser authored a book that signalled the transition from religious literature about Neumann to more secular interpretations of her miracles. An atypical Neumann admirer, Rinser associated herself with left-wing causes and would eventually became an outspoken critic of her own church. On the one hand, her book about Neumann confirmed Rinser's own belief in the existence of miracles, making her a spokesperson for the widespread faith in the supernatural after the war. In this sense, the book devoted much space to the debate about Neumann's bleeding and fasting, taking the stance that something remarkable and possibly miraculous occurred in Konnersreuth. However, Rinser also accentuated the character of Neumann and her family. Neumann's artless personality, gruff father, and pragmatic brother proved as important to her narrative as the miracles. She also stressed Neumann's role as comforter of the sick in her region and praised how hard she worked in the fields when her health permitted. Her father's persistence with his work as a tailor despite his daughter's international acclaim also impressed her. When *Konnersreuther Lesebogen* published excerpts from her book, it included pictures of Neumann farming and horses pulling wagons through Konnersreuth, instead of images of Neumann's blood-soaked eyes. Such decisions indicate the way Rinser, a Bavarian herself, honoured Neumann for the contrast her rural values created in an age of modernization.[19] Although still a sacred figure for some, Neumann also retained popularity as a reminder of a Bavarian past that even those who favoured progressive reform did not want to lose.

Konnersreuth and German-American Fellowship

Despite the reservations by many in her circle about American nuclear power and consumerism, the town of Konnersreuth became a place for everyday German-American reconciliation from the moment Bavaria fell to the allies. The friendship between the stigmatic and the Americans progressed to the point that one American journalist claimed to know Germany through three sources: Munich's Hofbräuhaus, West German Chancellor Konrad Adenauer, and Therese Neumann.[20] Always an international star, Neumann attracted the attention of influential American church figures from the early days of her stigmata. These elites publicized her case in a series of books and press articles, laying the groundwork for the mass enthusiasm expressed by soldiers and chaplains brought to Europe by the Second World War and the Cold War. This institutional groundwork combined with Neumann's appeal as an anti-Nazi German and embodiment of Bavarian tradition to attract devotion from hundreds of thousands of soldiers and officers.

The post-war enthusiasm built upon the deep impression Neumann made on American bishops in the Weimar era. Although isolated, her town's proximity to spa towns like Marienbad in Czechoslovakia caused many international church fathers to travel a few extra miles in order to witness her stigmata first-hand. The most powerful among these supporters included Bishops Joseph Schrembs of Cleveland and John F. Noll of Fort Wayne. Neumann apparently informed Schrembs of problems in his diocese that only an insider in Cleveland could have known. The latter bishop became particularly enthusiastic upon returning to the United States. First, he endorsed the work of Albert Paul Schimberg, who oversaw the translation of three volumes of work by Friedrich Ritter von Lama into English during the 1920s and 1930s, and he published his own book about Neumann after the war. Noll also sought assistance from Neumann's mystical powers through letters to Cardinal Faulhaber in Munich. For example, in 1932 Noll requested that Neumann be asked in ecstasy about the fate of the eldest baby of Charles Lindbergh, the future isolationist and Nazi sympathizer. The kidnapping of the "Lindbergh baby" became a sensational press story in the United States and Noll believed Neumann could use her supernatural abilities to crack the case.[21]

Besides bishops, several clergymen and wealthy American Catholics visited Neumann prior to the Second World War. One theologian, Reverend F. Thomas, CMF, started a long-standing relationship with Konnersreuth after receiving ecstatic advice about his sick and dying father.[22] Another prominent lay woman and convert, Elizabeth Marable Brennan, came to Konnersreuth with her husband and a bishop from Serbia. A leader of the International Federation of Catholic Alumnae and an organizer in the construction of the National Shrine in Washington, DC, Brennan claimed that a white rosary gifted to her by Therese Neumann would miraculously have six red beads at various moments. Besides publishing her experiences, she often spoke about Neumann for church associations, sodalities, and Sacred Heart leagues in the United States.[23] Such transatlantic publicity caused other Americans to write to Cardinal Faulhaber about Neumann's authenticity. For example, the Father General of a monastery in Garrison, NY asked for more information about the stigmata, claiming that most of what he heard was positive. In fact, the Catholic press in the United States offered somewhat regular reports about the well-being of Neumann during the Third Reich years when it became more difficult to see her in person.[24]

The interest of elites and their publicity laid the groundwork for an outpouring of devotion for Therese Neumann after the war. The wave of soldiers who visited with special frequency during the occupation years – but also in Lent throughout the 1950s – began with circumstances at the end of the Third Reich. As described in chapter 5, the end of the war in Konnersreuth is a matter of some dispute. However, Konnersreuth's American enthusiasts promoted Neumann's version of the liberation story. After the war she claimed that a member of a nearby SS division came to her home while she was away and threatened her family with a revolver when asking about her whereabouts in April of 1944. The SS allegedly then promised an attack if they did not receive the seer into their custody. The shelling of the town that followed destroyed seventeen homes, including that of the Neumann family. The Konnersreuth Circle added many anecdotes to this story over time. Allegedly the American army marked the town of Konnersreuth on their maps as a safe haven upon which they would not fire and they only engaged this SS unit to stop its assault on the Konnersreuth villagers. In some narratives of this event, Neumann used mystical powers, informing American troops of all the hidden SS locations around the town. Another account suggested that Neumann saw a vision of her patron saint, Therese of Lisieux, during the attack. The mythos surrounding the war's end in Konnersreuth established a firm friendship between the Neumann family and the American military. She represented a popular anti-Nazi figure with whom Americans could consult as they redirected West Germans towards a Cold War alliance.

The American military offered immediate support to Neumann after the end of the war. A French prisoner of war previously aided by the Neumanns helped an American chaplain locate the seer in the chaotic and heavily damaged town after hostilities ceased. She enjoyed the protection of GIs at the door of her house until the threat of vigilante justice from Nazi sympathizers subsided, and occupation authorities allowed Neumann to violate curfew rules in order to comfort sick and grieving families throughout the *Oberpfalz*. Soldiers even gifted her a horse, which eventually became an iconic symbol of American friendship. The horse pulled a wagon while she provided aid to refugees, the sick, and the poor in her region.[25]

Neumann's most steadfast American admirer was Max Jordan, a journalist who had researched her case prior to the war. A well-known radio journalist with National Broadcasting Company (NBC), Jordan was a German-born American citizen who began covering European news in the 1930s while also penning articles for the Catholic press. Known by colleagues as "ubiquitous Max" and described as an "inveterate newshound," Jordan became famous for beating such luminaries as Edward Morrow and William Shirer to scoops in the years preceding the war.[26] Travelling with the military, he landed the first interview with Neumann in 1945 and publicized her description of anti-Nazi resistance and persecution at war's end. Jordan's advocacy of this narrative converged with his work as a proponent of the German Catholic Church's record under Nazism. He became an opponent of American academic Gordon Zahn's work in the 1960s that accused German Catholics of complicity and he generally associated the German population with acts of resistance under Nazism.[27] He also regularly reported Neumann's contact with heavenly figures for an American audience. He marvelled at the appearance of St Therese of Lisieux as the SS assaulted Konnersreuth and the bright light Neumann observed surrounding the new bishop in Eichstätt, Joseph Schröffer, during his installation in 1948.[28] In part due to his devotion to Neumann, Jordan became a Benedictine monk, joining Beuron Abbey in 1954.

Max Jordan engaged a network of prominent Americans that admired Neumann during the military's occupation of Bavaria and afterward. He corresponded with Cardinal Aloisius Muench, the most powerful American Catholic figure in Germany during the late 1940s and 1950s. Formerly a bishop in Fargo, North Dakota, Muench became both the Vatican's Apostolic Nuncio to Germany and the official liaison between the United States' Office of Military Government and the German Catholic Church.[29] With relatives on his mother's side in the town of Kemnath, where Therese Neumann's brother became politically active after the war, Muench knew the *Oberpfalz* well and visited Neumann prior to the Second World War, expressing sympathy with her cause in his correspondence. He and Jordan kept one another current on the latest developments from Konnersreuth as Jordan waged his public campaign on Neumann's behalf.[30] Jordan and Muench represented the types of American contacts that facilitated Neumann's revival after the war.

Jordan also occupied a central role in an American debate over Neumann's authenticity that bore great resemblance to the bitter struggles within German Catholicism during the 1920s and 1930s. Jordan contested the claims of Hilda C. Graef, a German woman who converted from Judaism to Catholicism and subsequently emigrated to the United States. Mentored by Michael Waldmann, a Regensburg theologian opposed to the Neumann miracles since their inception, Graef authored the most prominent post-war critique of the stigmata. Resurrecting arguments from previous debates, Graef suggested that Neumann's miracles were the result of material rather than supernatural causes. Doubtful of Neumann's character, she illustrated how her family benefited from the visions and questioned the extent of their spiritual impact.[31] Jordan defended Neumann on several counts. He described the poverty of her town, rejecting the charge that Neumann became a "drawing card," and he depicted her as more obedient to church authority than Graef maintained in her book. His strongest critique revolved around how little time Graef spent in Konnersreuth. Experiencing only a short visit with Neumann and Naber, Graef depended heavily on documents provided by Waldmann. Jordan argued that one could not grasp the full nature of Therese Neumann's meaning until encountering her personal integrity.[32] Neumann's charisma remained her most outstanding asset in wooing followers.

The debate between Graef and Jordan sparked a larger controversy among American theologians and clergy that continued the renewed litigation of the Neumann stigmata. While some supported Neumann's miracles, and her potential for mass conversion, others recalled the conflict between Buchberger and the Neumann family and highlighted her lack of official church sanction. In one instance, Reverend Francis

Lally of *The Pilot* in Boston angrily wrote, "There is a large post-war cult here in the United States in regard to Therese Neumann which has encouraged much uncritical writing and talking on the subject."[33] On the other hand, Neumann's defenders attacked her critics as "radical rationalists" and the "tools of communists." One clergyman wrote a dissertation on Therese Neumann in her defence while another intoned Jordan's defence of her character. He wrote, "Hilda Graf has merely written a book. Therese Neumann has lived a life. Between these two accomplishments, I have no difficulty choosing."[34] The evidence of such fierce and public debate indicates the extent to which American clergy became invested in the events at Konnersreuth.

The fame of Neumann among prominent Catholics caused the major rise in the popularity of Konnersreuth after the war. Neumann's American critics argued that, were it not for her popularity with American GIs, she would have faded into obscurity. John Ross Duggan, a lay advocate for the types of liturgical reform ultimately pursued during the Second Vatican Council, wrote that the Regensburg decree of 1937 "drained" the Konnersreuth "cult" of momentum. It was exclusively the American military that made the town a pilgrimage destination again in the view of Duggan and other like-minded reformers with little interest in the forms of mysticism on display in this Bavarian town.[35] While this claim overlooked continued German devotion, the American presence in Konnersreuth became substantial. The Friday Suffering emerged as a destination for thousands of troops. For example, two thousand American soldiers joined a crowd of five thousand Germans on Good Friday in 1949, arriving on tour buses from Munich, Nuremburg, Wurzburg, and Frankfurt. By 1951, the crowd grew to ten thousand and in some years the Americans outnumbered the Germans.[36]

For many American pilgrims, Konnersreuth represented a profound religious experience. For example, the first chaplain to meet Neumann after Konnersreuth fell into American hands became an enthusiastic supporter. In images circulated by the National Catholic News Service, George Gallivan's publicized visit with her brought Neumann immediately to the attention of other chaplains serving throughout American-occupied Germany. Impressed by her widespread support in town, Gallivan professed his faith in the authenticity of her decades-long fast as well as her stigmata. He praised the book by Schimberg that spread news of her miracles in the United States, and formed relationships with Neumann allies, such as Jordan and Aretin, after the war. Upon returning to the United States, Gallivan, born in Boston to a family of ten, lectured in American parishes about his time with Therese Neumann; other chaplains and devout soldiers followed this example.[37] Gallivan's initial contact with Neumann symbolized the larger role played by chaplains in the American military in urging pilgrims to visit her. In accounts by soldiers convinced of Neumann's authenticity, they frequently credit a chaplain with notifying them of her existence or a commanding officer with granting them leave at the suggestion of a unit's priest. For example, Reverend Donald Murphy led Catholics from his unit to see Neumann and he celebrated mass for them in the church across the street as early as the summer of 1944. He also witnessed other chaplains speaking with Naber in Latin to bridge the communication gap for soldiers who spoke virtually no German. For years, several chaplains at bases across West Germany organized buses for large groups of soldiers to see Konnersreuth on Good Friday.[38] The religious conviction of these clergymen made Konnersreuth a major pilgrimage destination for hundreds of thousands of soldiers.

Albert Vogl, a relative of several priests who oversaw the Marian shrine in Altötting and an officer in the United States Army after his emigration, also visited Neumann shortly after the war. Enamoured with her personality, miracles, and charity, the stigmatist's miraculous cures and assistance to those in need impressed him most. In fact she helped him emotionally process the execution of his uncle by National Socialists. She also inspired Vogl to aid a nearby Benedictine Abbot at Schweiklberg, Reverend Willibald Mangref, whose monastery needed renovation after the SS had seized it for use during the war.[39] Like Gallivan, Vogl viewed American enthusiasm for Neumann in a strictly religious light and became a public advocate for her cause within the Catholic Church.

Many other soldiers who visited Neumann articulated deep religious conviction in her miracles and published in favour of her beatification. William Rodgers of Baltimore credited her Friday Suffering with causing him to pray daily to Neumann and St Therese of Lisieux. Thomas Christman Hobbs of New Mexico proclaimed that his visits with her "left an impression of God's might." Gerald Robertson of Florida said, "To me, her devout life was telling the world that Jesus Christ was real." Other men credited her with cures of their own war wounds and of relatives back home who touched her signed prayer cards.[40] Such stories indicate a group of American Catholics who embraced the mysticism of the Konnersreuth experience as a transformative moment in their spiritual lives.

Although Neumann existed exclusively as a religious figure to some Americans, others experienced her in more secular ways. Downplaying the religious element of American visits, Hilda Graef claimed that soldier visits resulted in almost no conversions even by Naber's own reporting. Rather these men received autographs as souvenirs from a sightseeing experience. While Graf does not account for the soldiers who approached Konnersreuth with reverence, her assessment illustrates that Konnersreuth pilgrimages sometimes became a religious tourist attraction with secular elements. *Stars and Stripes* described a mixed scene at Good Friday in 1947 where some soldiers showed more interest in purchasing prayer cards and devotional material than in Catholic spirituality. Even those who found Konnersreuth personally moving reported that many soldiers with them came out of curiosity and even scorn.[41]

Neumann's popularity with some Americans resulted less from her religious mysticism than her cultural significance. Her anti-Nazi credentials caused many Americans to seek her out as a symbol of cooperation after the war. For genuine advocates like Max Jordan, Neumann's narrative of opposition to Nazism supplemented his larger campaign to protect the entire church from charges of collaboration with the Third Reich. For many soldiers, legends of her dislike of Hitler possessed a more secular feel. Stories about Neumann answering the door with blood pouring from her eyes when the Gestapo came to search her house and about her predictions of Hitler's downfall held currency in the collective memory of soldiers even after she publicly denied the incidents.[42] These rumours usually lacked any reference to the religious meaning of the stigmata. Neumann's distance from National Socialism in both fact and fiction elevated Konnersreuth as a cultural symbol of which its religiosity was only one part.

Neumann also appealed to Americans because she fit their Cold War narrative. Besides an anti-Nazi past, she also performed the role of Catholic cold warrior. She served the impoverished and the ethnic German refugees in her area both out of Christian charity and as an act of cooperation with Americans and their efforts to halt communism. Neumann performed such services to expellees when local priests disparaged them for disrupting all-Catholic enclaves as many Protestant Silesian and Sudeten Germans settled in the most Catholic parts of Bavaria.[43] Instead Neumann sided with ecclesiastical figures who viewed the new arrivals as targets for political radicalism and argued for integration. Neumann's empathy with the largely Protestant newcomers therefore converged with American concerns about the spread of radical ideologies as the Cold War deepened. She used donations from Americans to support the integration of the migrants and evacuees. Neumann also inspired followers, such the Baroness Elisabeth von Guttenberg, to devote their lives and parts of their fortunes to caring for Germans made vulnerable in the aftermath of the Second World War. After discovering that one of her family's most valued properties suffered from post-war looting, Guttenberg transformed the location into a centre to care for elderly refugees after seeking Neumann's counsel.[44] This care for the poor and the populations displaced by war converged with Cold War aims. First, Neumann and her circle combined anti-communist rhetoric with this service to others. As early as 1945, Neumann told the Polish chaplain-in-chief that the Soviets were as brutal as the Nazis and needed to leave Poland after the war.[45] Second, she and her sister Ottilie extended their charitable endeavours to sending care packages to Catholics in East Germany, an effort they sometimes coordinated with American donors. Furthermore, this social activism led many to view Neumann as a critical part of the *Abendland* that protected West Germany from communists in the East and bound the new state to the NATO alliance. One American Catholic wrote that Konrad Adenauer, Pope Pius XII, and Therese Neumann were the Europeans he most associated with the *Abendland* concept that stood at the centre of the Cold War alliance during the 1950s. The cooperation between Bavarian Catholics and American soldiers performed at Konnersreuth reinforced such notions. One soldier recalled, "We were required to carry our carbines with us at all times during those days of occupation. Yet the churchgoers (in Konnersreuth) did not seem to mind rifle toting GIs. We were all one in Christ."[46] The symbolism of American arms in church at a Bavarian border town possessed immense power. Neumann cemented such sentiments when she signed prayer cards and addressed letters to Americans with sayings like "One in Peace."[47]

While these charitable activities and the *Abendland* concept were both religious in nature, their utility contained little connection to Neumann's mysticism. She represented more than a holy woman who converted sinners. She also symbolically fortified the West German-American alliance after the war. This cultural significance was most prominent when the American military provided a helicopter to place a two hundred-pound gold cross on top of the church in Konnersreuth.

Neumann used her religious prominence to raise money for the cross and exploited her connections with the American military to have the sacred item added to her reconstructed church. She appealed directly to one of her devotees, Lieutenant General Francis Farrell, and the fastening of the cross became a major event before fifteen hundred spectators in the small town. Covered prominently in press, this act became a local articulation of the mutual aid between the Federal Republic and its foremost NATO ally.[48]

Americans also appreciated Neumann's rustic sense of Bavarian identity. Albert Vogl wrote, "It was amusing to see her riding to a neighboring village in her cart, drawn by a horse which had been given to her by American soldiers."[49] The classic Bavarian countryside and Neumann's traditional mannerisms added to her allure. American modernity met Bavarian traditionalism in a friendly alignment to protect Western Europe from communism. Neumann's exaggerated sense of a Bavarian rural lifestyle enhanced her appeal to Americans. The imagined juxtaposition between Old World Bavaria and New World America represented the partnership needed to fend off communism.

The arrival of American Paul Neuland as new deputy state commissioner for Bavaria in 1952 demonstrated the secular role of Therese Neumann after the war. One of his first acts included a visit to Neumann; he left impressed by her personality and popularity. He followed this private encounter by performing a flyover above Konnersreuth to greet the stigmatic. Followed enthusiastically by the press, Neuland immediately used a new relationship with Neumann to establish legitimacy with Catholics in Bavaria.[50] To him, she represented German-American cooperation. While religiously significant, she also had meaning beyond those who found her particular brand of religiosity and mysticism compelling. She possessed cultural currency that bridged gaps between what remained of the American military after the occupation and a strategic area on the Cold War frontier.

While the American military admired Therese Neumann, she returned their affection despite moments of tension. She frequently posted a sign that read, "No visitors, not even Americans." In hopes of avoiding attention, she sometimes quarrelled with GIs who photographed her without permission. Nonetheless, she said she "rejoiced" at the American entry into her town and complimented the conduct of the American GIs. Elisabeth Guttenberg said, "Teresa is very fond of the American people and told me several times how much she likes the American Catholics." Neumann even said she was willing to overlook the fashions she associated with American women, claiming to accept dresses that were more revealing than she would like because of her appreciation for the Americans she came to know.[51]

The American attraction to Konnersreuth catapulted the town back into the limelight after the war. While a circle of German mystics continued their devotion to Neumann, the keen American interest in the stigmata drove Neumann's second act as a post-war religious celebrity. While many American Catholics visited Konnersreuth out of deep religious devotion that added to her appeal to American bishops in the 1920s, Neumann also became a rural and Catholic symbol of the *Abendland* and a cultural mediator between Bavarians and Americans after the war.

Therese Neumann and the CSU between Clerical-Conservatism and Liberal-Conservatism

Therese Neumann typified the ambiguities inherent in the politics and economics of Bavaria during the 1950s. The Christian Social Union (CSU) formed the region's sister party to the CDU after the war. Unlike the BVP during the Weimar Republic, this political party eventually became hegemonic in Bavaria from the 1960s onward. Throughout the final decade and a half of Therese Neumann's life, however, the party remained locked in a battle for its own identity and against other regional parties, such as the separatist *Bayernpartei* (BP) and the Sudeten and Silesian *Bund der Heimatvertreibenen und Entrechteten* (BHE). A clerical-conservative wing, which included many former BVP leaders, sought a mostly Catholic basis for the CSU. This approach included an aversion to modern consumerism, resistance to the free market, and suspicion of non-Catholics despite the interdenominational concept behind the Christian Democratic project. Another wing of the CSU, which would ultimately triumph under the leadership of Franz-Josef Strauss, promoted a more economically liberal interpretation of Christian Democracy. The ideas of the modernizers within the CSU emerged as West Germany began the rapid economic ascent that came with funding from the Marshall Plan, the common currency of the West, and the Social Market Economy that propelled the state to become one of the most productive markets in the world. As the CSU suffered from the disunity of this internal debate, it struggled to overcome the social-democratic, monarchist, and expellee parties that challenged it for power within the province. The Konnersreuth Circle, a bastion of CSU support, found itself in the middle of this political discord. Neumann's younger brother, Ferdinand (Ferdl) Neumann, embarked on a political career within the CSU. With a brother active in the party and several devotees in high-ranking positions, Neumann became divided between the clerical-conservative and liberal direction of the CSU. While her movement became most associated with the former, her divided loyalties demonstrated her ability to adapt and evolve as Germany entered a phase of unprecedented growth.

With an aging father and a patriarchal leadership void left by the deaths of larger-than-life personalities like Gerlich and Wutz, Ferdl Neumann became the de facto patriarch of the Konnersreuth Circle as he sought both political and economic fortune after the war. Konnersreuth admirer Luise Rinser described him as a pragmatist while Therese Neumann critic Josef Hanauer portrayed him as a corrupt opportunist. Born in 1911, Ferdl initially trained to be a tailor like his father. His older sister's fame after 1926 changed his prospects. Professor Wutz used his contacts to help him study for the seminary. He completed his Abitur in Bingen in 1937 and started a curriculum in theology in Eichstätt from 1937 to 1940, which he never finished because the National Socialist regime imprisoned him multiple times and forced him out of the university. Avoiding war service, he oversaw factories at the end of the war and afterwards invested in industries, such as the *Allunit-Werken* in Zwiesel. Ferdl became active in the CSU from its very inception. In 1946 he rose to the leadership of the CSU in Kemnath, becoming a representative in the Bavarian *Landtag* and eventually the *Landrat* in Kemnath from 1949 to 1954. His activism in favour of Christian Democracy aligned the Konnersreuth Circle with the vision articulated by Gerlich at the very end of the Weimar Republic.

As a local politician, Ferdl Neumann's career began awkwardly but quickly became focused on solving regional problems. In early 1946 he became ensnared in the election of a mayor in the Bavarian town of Oerlenbach, where he halted voting over incorrect ballots at the instruction of Engelbert Hoffmann, a CSU politician designated by the American military to run the town. A drunken police officer arrested and imprisoned him until Hoffmann had him released and the election proceeded.[52] Nonetheless, his activities engaged many of the most pressing issues of the day. For example, Ferdl led a campaign to build a new school in Kemnath, using his sister's contacts with the American military and Cardinal Muench to gain the financial assistance and permits needed to start work. He also founded a chapter of the CDU/

CSU youth group, *Junge Union* (JU), in Kemnath in 1949, citing the need to counsel youth who suffered turmoil from exposure to National Socialism and the disruption of war. He hoped that the group would not only generate faithfulness to the CSU but also turn young people back to Christianity and encourage loyalty to the new democratic order. He expressed commitment to the Christian Democratic project, calling for social reform grounded in a "revolutionary Christianity" to overcome the National Socialism of the past and the communist challenge of the early Cold War.[53]

Ferdl Neumann also served as a resource for Bavarians of the Upper Palatinate seeking assistance with difficult post-war situations. For example, one former colleague who studied with Neumann hoped the newly empowered CSU politician could help him find a job. Another acquaintance asked him to consult his sister while in her state of exalted rest regarding his future career.[54] However, it was most common for Germans struggling with the de-Nazification process to seek Ferdl as a resource. In one ugly episode, he travelled to Munich with a woman from Kemnath named Anny Schuller to help free her son-in-law from Dachau. Held by the occupation as a Nazi collaborator, she claimed he only joined the party to end the harassment of the rest of his family due to their loyalties to political Catholicism. Schuller expressed particular anger because the family business was now run by two Polish-Jewish Displaced Persons (DPs). The fight over this textile and wool enterprise illustrated the anti-Semitism and xenophobia present in this moment of demographic upheaval. Anny Schuler claimed her family had no advocates other than Ferdl and Cardinal Muench, who possessed family ties in Kemnath, because Sudeten Germans ran the local government at the behest of the Americans. She worried for the "pure Christian and Bavarian tradition" of the city because of the "foreign elements that did not fit in" and therefore actively supported Ferdl to become the *Landrat* of Kemnath. An American Catholic chaplain even suggested that the military official charged with adjudicating the case must be Jewish himself if he was favouring the DPs over a local German Catholic family. Such incidents revealed how Ferdl and other CSU politicians operated within a context where their constituents marginalized Jewish survivors and ethnic German expellees after the war. Ferdl, who successfully restored the Schuller family business, showed little sympathy with Europe's Jews in the aftermath of the Nazi genocide. While he did not necessarily spread the views of his voters, he apparently did not prioritize remorse for German anti-Semitism in the CSU's democratization project.[55]

Ferdl Neumann's political career benefited from his relationship with two of the CSU's founding elites, Josef Müller and Alois Hundhammer. Both men visited Therese Neumann and believed in her miracles.[56] They mentored and assisted Ferdl's political career due in part to this association with the Konnersreuth miracles. Unfortunately for the Neumann family, Müller and Hundhammer commenced a deeply personal and bitter fight with one another over the leadership and direction of the newly founded CSU during the occupation. Hundhammer, a traditionalist and so-called clerical-conservative, formerly belonged to the BVP and viewed Bavarian autonomy within the new West German state and loyalty to the deeply Catholic rural areas of the province as his highest priorities. Alternatively Müller advocated a liberal-conservative position that more openly supported the notion of an interconfessional party with a broader reach, a relatively strong central state in West Germany, and a place within the growing Christian Democratic movement in other parts of the allied zones of occupation. Even though Müller had formerly belonged to the BVP, his activities as a member of the military opposition during the Second World War and his imprisonment in the Flossenbürg concentration camp created a bond with other Protestant elites, such as Dietrich Bonhoeffer, that underpinned his commitment to Christian unity.

The forces backing Hundhammer proved powerful enough to derail Müller's attempt to become leader of the CSU. Proponents of Hundhammer even described Müller as "left of the SPD." The power struggle became so bitter at one point that the *Süddeutsche Zeitung* published attacks on Müller as a National Socialist sympathizer despite the fact that he served heroically as a secret courier to the Vatican on behalf of the military opposition to Hitler. This press smear that viewed Müller's final actions for the BVP during the Nazi seizure of power out of context even led to a de-Nazification process against him that prevented his rise to become Minister President of Bavaria.[57] Hans Ehard, a compromise candidate who leaned slightly to the right in this power struggle, led the divided party in its early years when the clerical-conservatives possessed a slight but not decisive advantage until a disastrous election in 1954 when the CSU lost power in Bavaria for the only time in its history. By the late 1950s and early 1960s the party successfully reconciled tradition and modernity in a way that ultimately empowered the liberal-conservative wing of the CSU. For Josef Müller this victory came after his retirement from politics and towards the end of Hundhammer's career.[58] This post-war battle reignited some of tension from the fight over Konnersreuth in the 1920s when a pro-modernity element of

German Catholicism confronted other Bavarians with more traditional understandings of religious identity and regionalism. This time the Neumann family remained flexible enough to endear itself, however awkwardly, to both sides in this divide.

The legacy of the Konnersreuth Circle's most prominent advocate, Fritz Gerlich, became contested in this leadership struggle in the CSU. During the occupation, the party founded its first newspaper. Müller oversaw the new publication and used the name *Der Gerade Weg* (The Straight Path) in honour of Gerlich and his martyrdom at the hands of National Socialism in 1934. An advertisement for subscriptions praised the "fight for truth and justice" by the new newspaper's namesake and pledged itself to uphold the legacy. Hundhammer's supporters objected to the use of the title as some claimed Müller would not publish articles that genuinely conformed to Gerlich's ideas. Among those initially opposed to the use of the name was Erich von Waldburg Zeil, Gerlich's former financier and collaborator and ardent Konnersreuth supporter. Despite Müller's alignment with Gerlich's forward-thinking ideas about interconfessionalism and foreign policy, Zeil argued that he created a newspaper too disconnected with local issues and aimed at an intellectual audience rather than a typical Bavarian farmer or worker.

Ferdl Neumann waded into the dispute as mediator as a close confidant of Müller, who enjoyed good relationships throughout the Upper Palatinate despite his progressive outlook. Although Müller continued as editor of the newspaper with his desired title from December 1948 until April 1949, the paper could not overcome this controversy or terrible financial trouble. It was refounded as the *Bayernkurier* in 1950 under different leadership. In this instance, Ferdl favoured his relationship with Müller over Hundhammer even if he provided only short-term assistance.[59] Although Konnersreuth seemed on the surface to be more in tune with the traditionalism of the clerical-conservatives, Müller's interest in economic modernism likely appealed to Neumann as he pursued investments in industry after the war and his commitment to breaking confessional barriers actually fulfilled Gerlich's legacy.

The tension between these CSU elites made an impact on Konnersreuth once again when Therese Neumann appeared at a 1947 rally of Alois Hundhammer in Waldsassen. Some accounts claimed she publicly supported Hundhammer while others maintained that she simply attended the rally to hear his speech. As the press moved to formally link the stigmatic to Hundhammer, Ferdl found himself in an unenviable position. Standing by his sister's seeming support of Hundhammer jeopardized his relationship with Müller and made her role as religious mystic too overtly political. Backing away from the appearance at the rally risked backlash from a powerful friend of the family in Hundhammer. Ferdl cautiously chose distance from Hundhammer as his sister told the press that she took no political stands and only attended the rally as a private citizen who wanted to hear the speech. Ferdl received an unhappy note from Hundhammer who blamed Müller supporters for how the story made it to the press.[60] From this point forward, Therese Neumann consistently denied that she possessed political importance and claimed her meaning rested exclusively in the religious realm. This incident indicated the fragile balancing act the Neumanns undertook in order to preserve relationships with both power brokers. It also demonstrated the overpowering sense of patriarchy that persisted after the war. In order to maintain her revival, Neumann left politics to her brother while her avenue to power rested in the feminine sphere of private spirituality.

Although much evidence suggests Ferdl favoured Müller over Hundhammer in the late 1940s, he remained close to Hundhammer. This became particularly true after Müller lost his bid to lead the party. Hundhammer displayed loyalty to the family on several occasions. For example, when Therese fell, suffering a major injury in 1950, Ferdl and Hundhammer rushed to her bedside from a joint appearance at the five hundredth anniversary of the Church of the Assumption in Kemnath, which Ferdl helped reconstruct. Hundhammer also attended Therese Neumann's funeral in 1962 as a state minister for forestry and environment. This persistent connection with Neumann caused public ridicule by his political enemies just one month after Neumann's death. On the downside of his career as an opponent of the increasingly powerful Franz Josef Strauss, Hundhammer suffered from mockery in the liberal *Simplicismuss* during a state election. In a caricature on the cover in October of 1962, the satirical magazine labelled Hundhammer as "Loisl from Konnersreuth" in imitation of Neumann's nickname and depicted him in a cartoon with blood on his face. He sued the editor but lost since Neumann had indeed attended his rallies. The enemies of the CSU saw similarities between the traditionalist politics of Hundhammer and the mysticism of Konnersreuth.[61] Ferdl's continued friendship with Hundhammer illustrated the way in which Konnersreuth remained a bastion of rural Catholicism for those who wished to see it that way despite signs of post-war evolution within its following.

Ferdl Neumann's career ended in a financial scandal that typified a more market-oriented Konnersreuth Circle despite the blow it dealt the group's mainstream respectability. He faced public disgrace after participating in a scheme to smuggle wine from South Tirol (Italy) into West Germany via Austria at the end of the occupation. After engaging in this black market activity in the late 1940s, the press targeted Ferdl over the matter during court proceedings held during the mid-1950s. Labelled the first "major financial scandal" in the history of the CSU, a wine dealer named August Eutermoser of Rosenheim worked with elites in the CSU and the Catholic Church to illegally import thousands of litres of wine from Italy in the guise of charitable donations to religious institutions.[62] Eutermoser made hundreds of thousands of Deutschemarks, the CSU enhanced its poorly funded coffers, and abbeys and monasteries received much needed cash after the war. Josef Plonnar, a friend and colleague of Ferdl, became the CSU figure most intimately linked to the operation. Ferdl provided access to a monastery in Eichstätt and used his family's contacts within the American military to obtain a licence from the American Catholic adherent of the stigmata, Morris S. Verner, who ran the import-export agency for the occupation. Therese Neumann became implicated because she allegedly assented to it when queried in a state of exalted rest. Plonnar himself consulted her while in ecstasy and Eutermoser seemed connected to her mystical circle as well. Augsburg judge, Dr Hans Gaugenrieder, declared, "I ought to close the entire road from Rosenheim to Konnersreuth." In fact, many of those charged possessed deep ties to Konnersreuth. Erwein Freiherr von Aretin's son, Freiherr Anton von Aretin, received punishment as did Dr Ludwig Weitmann, who claimed he participated only to help Ferdl, a friend of twenty-five years, save his business. The mysticism and bonds of friendship created in the Konnersreuth Circle plunged the CSU into a public scandal just as the party lost power in the state during the early 1950s.

These influential men of the Konnersreuth Circle broke numerous laws. They moved restricted goods during the end of the occupation, fraudulently labelled bottles of Italian wine as Spanish, forged documents, evaded taxes, and perjured themselves. The defendants in the trial served no time and only paid hundreds of Deutschemarks in fines each. However, the political careers of Ferdl Neumann and several other figures close to the Konnersreuth Circle ended by the mid-1950s as a result of these crimes.[63] Neumann and her circle suffered the consequences of an entrepreneurial spirit that shaped them after the war.

Three motives seem plausible for the Neumann family's involvement. First, the factory of which Ferdl was a partial owner teetered on financial collapse by the end of the occupation and he used the wine money to offset his losses. Therese and Ferdl also seemed genuinely committed to rebuilding institutions of the Catholic Church that had been sympathetic to their cause since the 1920s. Orders of monks and nuns who formed a bedrock of support for the Konnersreuth Circle received resources from the wine smuggling. Konnersreuth critic Josef Hanauer also argues that the Neumann family wanted funds for a guest house in Tirol that could serve as a place of refuge for the Konnersreuth Circle should unrest in Eastern Europe ever expose their border region to Soviet influence.[64]

While the image of the Neumanns and their village as free of consumerism contributed greatly to Therese Neumann's mystique and traditionalist appeal, the Eutermoser-Plonnar scandal showed that Therese and Ferdl embraced the spirit of the economic miracle before it even took hold. Their entrepreneurial pursuit of post-war prosperity linked them to the liberal-conservative wing of the CSU as much as their image of austerity tied them to the clerical-conservatives. They evolved on economic issues in ways that paralleled the entire CDU/CSU. While antimaterialist sentiments and Christian social teaching dominated the earliest days of German Christian Democracy, party figures associated with Finance Minister Ludwig Erhard depicted consumerism as a civic duty to oppose communism and indulged in the thriving economy by the late 1950s.[65]

Ample evidence exists that Neumann and her circle grasped and exploited the modernization of Germany's economy despite their harsh critiques of consumerism. Neumann's family cultivated and benefited from a religious niche. They astutely realized that their most important asset remained Therese's sanctity in the eyes of many Catholics around the world. Commenting on the family's refusal to profit from celebrity, Konnersreuth critic Hilda Graef insightfully wrote, "It seems probable that, confronted with the choice between their daughter's reputation for sanctity and the offer of Mammon, they would quite naturally choose the former."[66] This quote indicates that Neumann became more concerned with what Pierre Bourdieu calls the "goods of salvation" rather than pure economic gain. In a religious battle for church recognition, she and her family capitalized on their pious image more generally to increase their political, economic, and social standing. This arrangement meant seeking gain through Ferdl's political career until the dishonour of the wine scandal shone a light on activities meant to be kept away from public scrutiny. Rather than crassly cashing in on a film or the sale of tacky religious kitsch, they sought increased prosperity only behind the scenes. Therese Neumann transferred her spiritual capital as an austere visionary with supernatural linkages into tangible material gains for herself and her family.

Neumann's grandest economic projects included the creation of two facilities for religious orders near her village. She gained nothing materially from them, but they provided fulfilment and a more secure legacy within the church. In the first project, she facilitated the purchase of a castle in Fockenfeld that had been a monastery prior to the reformation. It became a Catholic gymnasium and monastery run by the Capuchins of Eichstätt for those who came to the priesthood as a late vocation in 1955. Filled with the religious symbolism of reclaiming medieval Catholic property and converting latecomers to the priesthood, this achievement required great guile by the Konnersreuth Circle. Neumann first learned of the property's availability because a confidant, Dr Josef Mittendorfer of Munich, alerted her that one of his wealthy patients planned the sale after souring on life as a farmer. After extended negotiations Neumann herself travelled to the American military leadership charged with war reparations in Frankfurt. She persuaded the authorities to compensate one of her aristocratic supporters, Erich von Waldburg-Zeil, over a million dollars for damaged forestry on his estate by the French occupation. Once Waldburg-Zeil received the funds from the American military, he bought and donated the castle. According to some accounts, money that supported the Fockenfeld purchase came from the profits made through the wine smuggled from Italy. The monastery possessed great religious significance, but it also shows how far Neumann had come as a result of her spiritual powers. Prior to her injuries, Neumann worked as a labourer on the property of Fockenfeld as a youth.[67] Now she had engineered its purchase for the church and as a part of her lasting legacy. Most of all, such a building project demonstrated her capitalist spirit after the war as she used her broad base of support and elite connections to raise money for church projects that benefited her rural region and her own aura.

Neumann also exploited her contacts with German and American Catholics, CSU politicians, and clergy to raise the money for the Carmelite convent that opened just after her death. This convent consolidated a partnership between Neumann and Rudolf Graber, Buchberger's successor as bishop of Regensburg. Neumann learned of his desire for a new facility. Despite her frail condition and advancing age, she immediately travelled to Lake Constance to spend a week convincing a wealthy devotee for financial support. When the so-called "Convent of Adoration" finished construction after the stigmatic's death at the cost of 1.5 million Deutschemarks, the bishop compared the new structure to the Sacré-Coeur in Paris. In his mind a place of worship and redemption fit Neumann's legacy. His support for Neumann after her death maintained the momentum necessary for her beatification process to commence decades later under one of his successors.[68] Both of the projects highlight the religious entrepreneurship of Therese Neumann and her circle. These were only the most prominent examples of Neumann's resolve when it came to post-war construction. She also leveraged her following and religious status to raise money for church bells, a new cross on the church, reconstruction of the Konnersreuth cemetery, an extension of the Neumann house for Father Naber's retirement, and a town garden. One of her closest friends, Anni Spiegl, said, "Every time you met Resl, she had new building plans." At times, these projects involved pressuring fellow residents in town to donate parts of their property.[69] By harnessing the potential of spiritual goods that had value to a vast but narrow segment of Catholics in Germany and the United States, the supporters of Konnersreuth mastered the consumer culture more effectively than some of their mainstream Catholic counterparts and adjusted well to the new environment of the post-war era. They also fused this capitalist spirit with Neumann's sanctity and desire for recognition from the church authorities.

The ambiguities of Therese Neumann's tense but fruitful relationship with the post-war order are nowhere more evident than in her approach to gender roles. Neumann's mystic suppression of "self-will" and total obedience to God contributed to continued dependence on male authority figures. For example, Ferdl took his father's place as Neumann's keeper and filled the void left by deceased and aging patriarchs from the Weimar and Third Reich eras. New male intellectuals, such as Höcht, replaced Gerlich and von Lama by presenting the case for authenticity to the public. Therese Neumann voluntarily limited her agency to the realm of apolitical and feminine mysticism, telling the press she possessed no political role and downplaying her influence with the American occupation and fledgling CSU. In sum, the Konnersreuth Circle emphasized the values of deference and gender hierarchy to a greater extreme than most clergy could have realistically expected. While women's religious associations increasingly contained more avenues for women's spiritual independence after the war, the Konnersreuth Circle enforced Catholic patriarchy to a greater extent than the church itself. Ferdl also adopted new masculine traits associated with the CDU/CSU after 1945. He embodied the trope of the "male producer" that Christian democratic rhetoric increasingly emphasized as the West German economy expanded while restricting his sister to the private sphere.[70]

Neumann, however, transformed this exaggerated gender conformity into an even broader power base after the war. With many male power brokers gone, Neumann became an activist in her own right. She no longer relied on men like Gerlich and Wutz to fight on her behalf. Instead, she cultivated her own powerful set of contacts from the moment the Americans arrived in Konnersreuth. She undertook a correspondence that included about 150,000 post-war letters and handled all important negotiations on her own. Naber and her father faded from the forefront, and Ferdl became involved in his own career. The stigmatic of Konnersreuth became her own advocate in the final two decades of her life. Neumann also performed only some but not all post-war feminine roles. On the one hand, she became the typical "*Trümmerfrau* (rubble woman)." Post-war commentators lionized women who helped rebuild Germany after the destruction of the war, opening a brief window in the late 1940s where women adopted masculine functions without resistance.[71] However, she never transitioned into the roles of housewife and consumer that the Christian establishment encouraged for most West German women after stability returned. She retained some access to the masculine power structure by pursuing construction projects and communal leadership.

In the spirit of their *Trümmerfrau* personas, Neumann and her sister Ottilie also enjoyed dynamic religious lives through the well-educated and wealthy Catholic men who surrounded them. Therese became a community leader and mediator to whom local people came with their concerns. Naber took children to her bedside for religion classes. She visited the sick and comforted them with medicines received from pilgrims and with spiritual advice. Prior to the arrival of Konnersreuth's first doctor in 1947, she was often the first caregiver that the town's sick visited. This role became particularly pronounced during the occupation after the damage done to the town in the spring of 1944 and as many displaced people from the east arrived in Bavaria. Many American soldiers recall Neumann asking for supplies to help locals with their ailments. Neumann also took over many aspects of the church's management. She oversaw most elements of building maintenance after 1945. While she always provided flowers for the altar, her role increased significantly after the war and as Naber aged.[72] Adoring pilgrims brought her gifts. Much of this revenue went towards charities, such as missions and organizations that cared for ethnic German refugees as well as her building projects. Nonetheless, access to financial resources gave her power to remake the post-war order according to her values. She also travelled throughout Europe with theologians and clergy as much as her health permitted and the Capuchins of Eichstätt made the house that previously belonged to Wutz available to her for her frequent visits. These perks enhanced her lifestyle immensely as she pursued her vocational passions. Her sister enjoyed many service-oriented activities as well, joined lay religious orders, and participated in local political life. Ottilie became the head of the Third Order of St Francis and assisted Therese with most charitable endeavours, even bringing beer and cigarettes to workers as she helped them on the job with renovations of the Neumann house and the local church. Both women used their roles as spiritually revered figures in a patriarchal system to improve their quality of life. Much like the nineteenth-century nuns who joined convents for female companionship and educational opportunities, the Neumann sisters enjoyed some of the public-sphere opportunities offered to religious women without the restrictions of taking vows.[73] These sisters lived in a rural Bavaria with deep attachments to patriarchy. Rather than challenge the power of these men, they sought their confidence and worked within traditional gender norms to carve out pockets of power that came from Neumann's spiritual gifts. As single women they offered an alternate Christian femininity to the ideal of homemakers who consumed goods produced by men.

Despite the persistence of her strategy to seek power by conforming to normative expectations for gender, Neumann disengaged from the politics of sexuality that dominated her circle during the end of the Weimar Republic. She no longer dismissed women who violated her strict expectations for modesty. She even expressed moral leniency for the fashions of American popular culture, which would have been unheard of during the 1920s in Konnersreuth. She also forged an unlikely alliance with Luise Rinser, who veered very far to the left in Catholic circles. Rinser remained Catholic and expressed much sympathy with Neumann's miracles, but she followed a very different path to emancipation. Married three times, Rinser challenged Vatican II for not offering enough support for women, and she would even one day publicly promote women's right to abortion. While these political positions were anathema to the CSU politicians who inhabited Neumann's circle, Rinser's left-wing leanings did not prevent her from forging a deep enough personal bond with the Konnersreuth seer to write a largely positive book. Neumann became more adaptable and flexible after the war even in regards to gender, permitting her continued relevance into the 1960s and beyond. Neither woman fit the feminine ideal proposed by the CDU/CSU establishment, which produced a sense of mutual admiration.

Conclusion

The positions of Therese Neumann and her Konnersreuth Circle indicate that the supernatural phenomenon of rural Bavaria possessed tensions typical of the CDU/CSU order of the early 1950s. The discomfort with modern consumerism coupled with the aggressive courtship of American military support mirrored the tensions of a Catholic elite who supported fierce NATO loyalty but opposed some aspects of a partially Americanized popular culture. Neumann's seemingly regressive stance on gender and her circle's construction of anti-Nazi mythology matched mainstream developments within the CDU/CSU and the institutional church. Nonetheless, the Konnersreuth Circle also overcame some of these tensions to create a lasting legacy and a vibrant international community of faithful believers that remains active to the present. Neumann and her supporters balanced their anti-consumerist image with a subtle marketing campaign that capitalized on the sensationalism of religious miracles without losing the overall perception of sanctity. Neumann's subtle manipulation of church gender norms also allowed a woman with a seemingly exaggerated sense of patriarchy to become one of the more powerful and popular Catholics in her corner of Germany.

The adaptability of the Konnersreuth Circle helped it survive even as the Catholic Church adjusted to the altered post-war landscape of Western Europe. The Second Vatican Council would seem to have been antithetical to the Konnersreuth project. Its commitment to modernizing the church and its shift away from Marian piety under Pope John XXIII challenged the values upon which Therese Neumann built her base of power. Her circle fought so long against the "rational" element in German Catholicism and opposed many of the trends among Rhineland power brokers prior to Nazism. Anni Spiegl suggested increasing distance between Konnersreuth supporters and the institutional church after Neumann's death. She said that theology shifted further and further from the bible in the 1960s, making mystical miracles more of a focal point for her than the dogmas of ecclesiastical authorities.

This distaste for Catholic reform drove those devoted to miracles even further away from the church. However, shortly before Neumann's death, she forged a friendship with one of the most powerful cardinals involved with Vatican II: Jesuit Augustin Bea. Although a church conservative in many ways, he was a powerful advocate of ecumenicism and the first president of the Secretariat for Christian Unity. Bea combined a zealousness for theological orthodoxy with a willingness to change. He became one of the driving forces behind *Nostra aetate,* which condemned religious anti-Semitism in 1963. He seemed an unlikely ally, but his ambiguous approach to Christian-Jewish relations that supported change yet also remained wedded to many theological traditions mirrored the multifaceted way that Neumann engaged with modernity.[74] He met Neumann as she raised funds for the Convent of Adoration in 1960 and supported her cause, asking that she pray for the council. As one of the prominent guests at a ceremony for the convent's opening after Neumann's death, he joined six other bishops in attendance. Neumann's compelling charisma and mystical message had its base in traditional rural Bavaria, but it also demonstrated a malleability that ensured her legacy's survival even as the institutions of the church changed and lost popular support in Europe after her death.

Conclusion

When I visited Konnersreuth in the summer of 2013, I stayed at the hotel still run by the Schiml family across from Therese Neumann's former home. In the dining area, there was a basket filled with hand-knitted white gloves for sale to raise money for the campaign in support of the stigmatic's beatification. This simple detail embodies the ambiguity of her legacy. On the one hand, it signifies the zealousness of her continued support that residents of Konnersreuth work so hard to secure official church recognition. On the other hand, the lonely basket of gloves seems so small in comparison to the vast neglect of Christian ritual throughout most of the country. This contradiction between tireless religiosity alongside the continued decline of sacramental piety necessitates a braided narrative of German Catholic history. It appropriately balances the trend away from formal religion in the twentieth century but acknowledges the numerous meaningful exceptions that contradict the mainstream perception of secularity. The history of Konnersreuth provides a unique opportunity to illuminate how the margins of a faith community interacted with the mainstream in impactful ways.

The uprising staged by traditionalist conservatives through increased faith in miracles that lasted from the end of the First World War until the death of Therese Neumann meaningfully alters how we view the role of Catholicism in German history. The participation of pilgrims at both sanctioned and unsanctioned sites, the widespread coverage in the press, the linkages of visionaries to the Catholic political establishment, and the ferocity with which millions of devotees fought for legitimacy from ecclesiastical authorities identifies Marian apparitions and examples of stigmata as cultural occurrences with widespread resonance. The revival in miraculous thinking was inspired partially

8.1. The grave of Therese Neumann. Photo courtesy of the author.

by the focus on the cult of the Sacred Heart and the elevation of Marian veneration by the Vatican. It was also caused by the tumult experienced by Germans from the conclusion of the First World War to the start of the Cold War. The devotees of Schippach, Konnersreuth, Heede, Heroldsbach, and Fehrbach demonstrate the importance of spiritualties at the margins of institutional religion. These religious miracles were accompanied by many other examples of belief in the occult and the paranormal that were less tethered to Catholic practices. Magical cures, secular miracles, superstitious belief, and examinations of telepathy became commonplace during this era. While formal religion did not always fulfil the spiritual needs of Germans, Catholics and non-Catholics alike sought connection to otherworldly phenomenon. Catholic experiences existed side by side with miraculous events with little or no connection to organized faith. The miracle movement itself was a braid of the spiritually mystical and the atheistic paranormal.

The seers of twentieth-century Germany and their rebellious followers differed from those of the nineteenth century and the early modern era. Although they built upon the templates of the past and revered mystics of all eras, such as Francis of Assisi, John of the Cross, Teresa of Avila, Anna Katharina Emmerick, Louise Lateau, and Bernadette Soubirous, these women operated in a uniquely modern context. Miracles and cults surrounding them proliferated at a rate never seen before or again in German history. News about miracles moved rapidly through the press and pilgrims travelled to unsanctioned pilgrimage sites en masse via train and tour bus. The spiritual approaches advocated by Barbara Weigand, Anna Maria Goebel, Therese Neumann, and other seers were propagated by circles of believers eager to earn salvation or profit from the sensational cures and visions. Tabloid and mainstream publications broadcast the latest developments of these miracles beyond the Catholic minority of Germany. While visionaries of the past had always been a matter of concern for local priests, regional ecclesiastical authorities, and theologians, these twentieth-century religious figures attracted support and media attention of unprecedented proportions. The miracles also occurred at a time of immense social, political, and economic change, which caused the battle over their legitimacy to become particularly intense. Drawing on other Catholic elites as well as millions of pilgrims, they spread their piety to a wider audience, caused deeper controversy, and challenged sceptical bishops to a greater degree than in the past. A passionate revolt by rural purists against mainstream church leadership, this upsurge in veneration of miracles disrupted Catholic Church structures and politics during the most tumultuous era of modern German history.

The circles of Catholics enchanted by stigmata and apparitions displayed impressive adaptability over time. The Konnersreuth Circle softened its rebellion after the trauma of the Third Reich. Zealous insurgents who helped fracture the Catholic minority's cultural and political unity during the Weimar Republic, the group retreated to the private sphere during the 1930s as many of its leaders died at the hands of National Socialist political violence. After the war, Neumann and her family sought alliances with American military authorities, bishops, and prominent political leaders despite some continued alterity in their following. This greater willingness to conform made Neumann's current beatification process possible. The Heroldsbach supporters, however, transformed without retreating entirely from their status as outsiders. While they made peace with the bishopric in the 1990s, the site of the apparitions became home to the most reactionary elements of European Catholicism. Playing host to right-wing populists, these provocateurs continued their challenge against mainstream German politics and culture by taking up the themes of more contemporary culture wars. While Konnersreuth has become a place of quiet religious tourism, Heroldsbach participates in the growing insurgency against the European Union.

It is a function of the miracles' singular modernity that they captivated influential members of the political Catholic establishment and the anticlericals among socialists and liberals. Therese Neumann's stigmata functions as a cultural history from below of the Catholic political narrative. She shaped the mindset of several influential Bavarian politicians and journalists. Her miracles created debates that epitomized the deep disunity between Catholic political figures and heightened tension between Catholics and social democrats. The standoff between her largely Bavarian supporters and the intellectuals and doctors mostly from the northwest underscored the division between the BVP and the Centre Party and the difficulties of forming parliamentary coalitions. The Heroldsbach Lay Commission also siphoned political loyalties away from the CSU in its troubled early years. Miraculous cults disrupted political elites who sought stability and integration for Catholics into a pluralistic German nation. By creating a space outside the typical Catholic institutions, miracles like Neumann's stigmata made room for productive new ideas as well. Therefore, the Konnersreuth Circle formed an important subculture within the emerging Christian Democratic consensus. By providing entry into Catholic politics for an independent thinker like Fritz Gerlich, groundwork for interconfessional cooperation was laid in Bavaria. After the war, Neumann's own brother joined with several other prominent Konnersreuth followers to fulfil Gerlich's ideas. While visionaries upended Catholic power structures, they also contributed to the more inclusive Christian Democratic concept.

Events like the stigmata in Konnersreuth, the Aachen blood miracles, and the appearance of the Madonna in Heroldsbach also granted new forums for the performance of Catholic gender identities. The overwhelming patriarchy of the miracle movement refutes notions of piety becoming a feminine realm in the modern world. Devout men surrounded the women and girls at the centre of most Catholic miracles. Given the widespread nature of tropes that cast Catholic mysticism as effeminate, these men used rural symbols, educational credentials, and militancy to balance the emotion they displayed when worshipping women in ecstasy. With the exception of Barbara Weigand and Sister Canisia of Freiburg, the women in this book did not articulate any sort of open emancipationist agenda. Instead they either became tragic victims of a subculture that tolerated sexual abuse and spread negative stereotypes about hysterical women or learned to work within the existing patriarchy to achieve as much autonomy as possible. The latter proved a difficult feat, but the case of Therese Neumann sheds interesting light on how religious figures negotiated the fraught power dynamics of a movement that relied so heavily on conservative traditionalism. Her experience also provides a rare glimpse into the world view of a devout Catholic woman. Balancing a desire to fulfil the role of obedient and humble seer with a willful assertiveness, Neumann embraced normative gender roles in an exaggerated way and gained immense power in the process. She used a fierce sense of chastity to fend off the threat of sexual abuse in the Bavarian countryside. She expressed obedience to her old-fashioned father as a way to escape discipline from the church. Neumann exercised influence upon powerful men, created a better life for her family, and enjoyed a spiritual vocation without giving up her independence to the institutional church. Rather than take the risks involved with challenging the patriarchy, she embedded herself within it and used it to her advantage. While some of her experiences were singular, aspects of the way she appropriated male gender roles can be seen in other seers and rural women of her era.

While the popularity of these religious miracles as well as their profound influence on gender and politics call into question the extent of Catholic secularization, other signs in the history of these visionaries conform with the notion of a twentieth century religious decline. The miracles were embraced by only a minority of Germans. The anticlerical mockery of them demonstrates the wide swathes of the population disdainful of such religiosity. Fierce opposition also existed within the Catholic Church. Bishops, theologians, and Centre Party politicians vehemently opposed such illicit articulations of piety and sought a more controlled faith, indicating the miracles' limited reach even among observant churchgoers. Catholic miracles could not penetrate German society as deeply as their advocates would have liked and remained the province of dissenters against church orthodoxy.

The miracles also unintentionally contributed to the secularization of ecclesiastical power. Church leadership correctly understood how these cures, visions, and bloody displays threatened the coherency of the faith and opened Catholics to embarrassment. One of the fundamental duties of regional bishops and priests was to enforce the boundaries of doctrine to prevent Catholicism from falling into heterodoxy. Firebrands such as Weigand, Friedrich Ritter von Lama, and the Heroldsbach Lay Commission were the latest in a long line of conservative heretics to challenge the church by calling for a return to past practices. Throughout the nineteenth century, German bishops successfully kept even the most popular seers in check despite the turmoil that resulted at a famous site like Marpingen during the *Kulturkampf*. However, from the First World War to the start of the Federal Republic, the sheer volume of new miracles tested their ability to enforce order. While successful in some cases, the bishops failed to contain the cults surrounding Konnersreuth, Heede, and Heroldsbach. The existence of spiritual movements that possessed Catholic roots and no church sanction existed alongside more pagan beliefs in the supernatural, which made them all the more subversive. Bishops also confronted this most recent heresy in an era of overwhelming challenges for pastoral care. The rise of urbanization, the anticlerical politics of Nazism, the violent demographic upheaval of the war, and the consumerism of the 1950s already made the preservation of a stable sacramental life next to impossible for clergy and bishops. The popularity of miracles grew out of these difficult historical circumstances and combined with them to fragment the Christian consciousness of most Germans.

This failure of ecclesiastical authorities to contain the miracle craze decreased influence by the church as German religious sensibilities became increasingly diffuse. Seers like Therese Neumann ironically contributed to the very secularization process they hoped to combat. They fractured a German Catholic community that already suffered from disunity and undermined the hegemony of institutional leaders already beleaguered by modern ideologies and unsettling economic trends. They also encouraged a type of personalized devotion that would become the norm, except many Germans would remove themselves entirely from the church's orbit in order to seek their individual connections with a higher power.

Besides its contribution to the splintering of Catholic mentalities, supporters of miracles participated in other elements of de-Christianization. Therese Neumann shaped the religious world views that informed Catholic politicians, but she also witnessed the secularization of Christian

Democracy. The CDU/CSU became a right-of-centre party by the time of her death with less emphasis on its Christian roots. The wing of the CSU that wished to fuse wistfulness for Bavarian custom with a modern economy triumphed over the clerical-conservatives. As a result, Neumann's own image became more secular by the late 1950s. She represented the lost "old Bavaria" for those that wanted local folklore with which to soften the transition of the modernizing state. Rather than a missionary to convert pilgrims, she became a focal point of nostalgia as Bavaria entered the tumultuous 1960s.

Neumann's model of femininity was influential for Catholics primarily of her generation, but not for those born in the middle of the century. The path of Neumann admirer Luise Rinser described in the last chapter became much more common than that of the stigmatic she studied. Catholic women became disillusioned with the church's teaching about reproductive rights, divorce, and clerical celibacy during the 1960s and afterward. Although voting in large numbers for the CDU/CSU, they sought emancipation from the strict morality and tropes about normative family life that had been hegemonic in Catholic regions for decades. Rather than conforming to the patriarchy, the majority of German Catholic women openly challenged it and in many cases exited the church when they felt their voice was not heard during the 1970s and 1980s. Religious crisis did not result in a complete secularization of West German Catholicism. Rather the church consolidated into a smaller, more unified, and more reactionary force that wielded immense influence on specific issues, such as abortion. Although less important in the lives of West Germans and less controlling of everyday experience, German bishops wielded greater authority in the latter stages of the Bonn Republic than during the 1960s by narrowing the scope of their ambition.[1]

This linkage between reproductive justice and Catholic influence is also apparent at the Heroldsbach pilgrimage site. The town, whose chapel is now sanctioned by the church even though its miracles are still not officially recognized, adapted its themes by becoming central to the antiabortion movement in Europe. The piety of the site focused on anti–European Union messages several years before the recent financial troubles, the refugee crisis, and the upswing of right-wing populism. Pilgrims articulated anger that there was no reference to Christianity in the EU constitution treaty of 2004 and Popes John Paul II and Benedict XVI both encouraged the town to become a centrepiece of European re-Christianization. EU abortion laws remain its primary target.

Pilgrimage organizers host an annual novena to the "mother of life for Europe" and encourage "spiritual adoptions" where visitors recite a prayer for an anonymous unborn child for nine months. Fueled by an antichoice group, Europrolife, Heroldsbach rituals depict a bleak picture of a secularizing Europe where a liberal EU represses Catholicism in particular. Abortion is linked to a low birth rate among white Europeans and causes pilgrims to imagine the end of a racially homogenous Europe through abortion and birth control. Throughout the 2000s, Europrolife and Heroldsbach attracted a right-wing nationalist element to some events.[2] The reincarnation of Heroldsbach as an anti-EU site of dissidence illustrates not only the persistence of its dark message from the 1950s but also the ability of adapted religiosity to shape the political narrative of Germany. Although not as controversial in their rhetoric, Konnersreuth supporters also joined the anti-abortion struggle of the twenty-first century by aligning themselves in the campaign for Therese Neumann's beatification with stark cultural conservatives such as Cardinals Joachim Meisner and Gerhard Müller.[3]

These findings represent just one way Catholicism remained an instrumental element in German society despite the downward trend in formal measures of religion, such as church marriages, Easter communion rates, and baptismal statistics. New religions received widespread coverage in the German media during the 1970s, leading some commentators to discuss a "return of religion." Many of these new practices and the journalists who covered them retained elements of their Catholic background even while breaking with church dogma. Their practitioners privatized their faith and mixed aspects of Catholicism with world religions they appropriated. Surveys today indicate that in the territories that used to belong to West Germany, 60 per cent of Catholics officially belong to the church and another study concluded that 70 per cent of all Germans describe themselves as "religious" and 18 per cent identify as "very religious." Besides wielding political power, Catholicism still exercises some control over the mindsets of German citizens even if it does not manifest as a unified set of beliefs as in the past. A significant minority of West Germans of all religious heritages find spirituality outside the churches appealing. In a recent survey 24 per cent identify as spiritual, 34 per cent find Christian objects such as crucifixes, crosses, and rosaries "helpful," and 23 per cent find new age materials including amulets, stones, or crystals useful. In East Germany, heavily secularized during decades of communist rule, the quantitative studies indicate a much deeper level of de-Christianization. Some academics view this data as confirmation of a godless society. However, the existence of personalized spirituality should not be dismissed from the narrative. The western territories with a heavier Catholic influence contain a diffuse, varied, and persistent religiosity.[4]

The tension between the survival of religious spirituality and the waning of formal rituals forms the focal point of this study. The perseverance of miracles into present-day Germany illustrates that the "alternative modernity" of Konnersreuth still exists. Therese Neumann's hometown attracts pilgrims worldwide. Her former home is now a museum to her legacy. Tour buses bring Catholics curious about her stigmata to town and the local parish hosts special services for those that pray to the woman they believe should be a saint. In 2005, Regensburg Bishop Gerhard Ludwig Müller opened the beatification process of Therese Neumann in response to tens of thousands of letters in favour of her candidacy and in response to a renewed openness to such miracles from the papacy of Pope John Paul II. After over a decade, the process is ongoing as the commission in Regensburg collects and studies thousands of documents related to her case. Residents of Konnersreuth still speak of Neumann with reverence.[5]

The continued veneration of Therese Neumann is not exceptional. Marian sites throughout Germany also endured without church sanction for decades. Heroldsbach built the infrastructure necessary to host thousands of pilgrims each year under the guidance of former Lay Commission leader Norbert Langhojer. Ecclesiastical authorities reached compromises with illicit shrines to the Virgin Mary in Marpingen, Heede, and Heroldsbach. Decades of "steady growth" in pilgrimage activity caused bishops in the 1990s to embrace these towns as "places of pilgrimage and prayer" without endorsing the alleged miracles that occurred. In a peace offering to avid Marian worshippers, they chose to focus on the present-day devotion in chapels built on former apparition grounds rather than relitigate the scientific authenticity of the miracles.[6] In fact, pilgrimages to Marian shrines have increased throughout Germany in recent years. The upswing caused theologian Bernhard Scheinder to comment, "Pilgrimage is in."[7] While some of these devotees visit the early modern shrines in Kevelaer or Altötting, many also venerate the Virgin Mary in Heroldsbach and Heede. The miracles from mid-century still serve as popular sites for spirituality.

Besides continued reverence for apparitions of the past, new miracles have occurred in the last three decades. People claimed to have visions of the Virgin Mary in larger cities like Düsseldorf and Leverkusen as well as small towns like Pocking during the early 1980s. Pilgrims alleged that the Madonna returned to Marpingen in 1999 and sixty pilgrims said they saw a statue of the Virgin Mary cry in Heroldsbach in 2007. In the most sensational case, the "Düren seer" Manuela Strack claimed to see the mother of God in the town of Sievernich from 2002 to 2005. These visions attracted press attention and sometimes visits from thousands of pilgrims. Even as Catholic churches struggled with small congregations each Sunday, such acts of piety received devotion over the last three decades. Pilgrims who visit Sievernich on the first Monday of every month occupy a church that no longer even serves as an independent parish due to the lack of congregants. These fundamentalist outsiders to the town also must negotiate compromises over ritual and devotion with local clergy given their strong preference for pre–Vatican II rites and practices.[8]

The most prominent figure in the most recent pilgrimage boom was not a seer or priest but an irreverent and famous comedian: Hape Kerkeling. Kerkeling's memoir, *I'm Off Then* (*Ich bin dann mal weg*), about his trek over the Pyrenees to the Spanish shrine of St James, became an international bestseller. It sold millions of copies in Germany alone and a movie was made based on the book. Seeking an opportunity for self-reflection after suffering several physical maladies, such as gallbladder surgery and partial deafness, Kerkeling spontaneously started his journey to France to hike twelve to eighteen miles a day for over a month until he reached the Spanish site of veneration. His humourous yet deeply contemplative description of this trip captured the German imagination. Besides reading the book, many Germans followed Kerkeling's lead and took the same pilgrimage. The popularity of the *Jakobsweg* increased by over 20 per cent after the book's appearance.

Like Therese Neumann, Kerkeling embarked on a physically demanding spiritual journey after suffering health crises that spellbound millions of readers and motivated thousands to undertake pilgrimage. The similarities end there. Kerkeling describes being raised in a Catholic family that was not so observant. Nonetheless, he always found religion fascinating and went willingly to confession and first communion. Yet his spiritual interests became diverse and he found multiple religions interesting. He considered converting to become a Lutheran minister, a sign of the ecumenical turn of German Christians after the 1960s. At the start of his pilgrimage, he considered his central question, "Is there a God? Or a Yahweh, Shiva, Ganesha, Brahma, Zeus, Ram, Vishnu, Wotan, Buddha, Allah, Krishna, Jehovah, etc.?"[9] He anchored his quest for meaning in a Catholic form of veneration due in part to his upbringing but he embraced a spirituality that mixed multiple world religions. Buddhism influenced the book just as much as Christianity. This wide-ranging approach to religiosity has its roots in the splintering of religious practices throughout the 1970s, 1980s, and 1990s. Kerkeling's fusion of Catholicism with other Christian denominations as well as Eastern belief systems demonstrates how religion persists despite the secularization of individual institutions.

I'm Off Then also integrates secularity. The book deals heavily with spirituality but it is also a funny story about travel that includes several colourful characters that Kerkeling met while hiking. While some journalists and religious figures understood the popularity of Kerkeling's book as a sign that Germans sought a vaguely defined higher power after the ideological struggles of the two world wars and the Cold War, others viewed the memoir as simple entertainment despite the religious content. Kerkeling himself argued that the book worked on "three levels": as a comedy, an adventure story, and a "spiritual journey." A Spanish woman who worked on the pilgrimage trail made a similar observation about the thousands of pilgrims each year that imitated Kerkeling. She said they conformed to three stereotypes: "those who sought adventure, those who sought religious awakening, and those that sought an orgy."[10] The way that the religious and the profane exist side by side in this memoir and its reception personifies the state of religion in Germany and much of Western Europe during the early twenty-first century. The purely secular and deeply religious intertwine with one another. Religion has not disappeared, but reappears in new forms.

The history of Therese Neumann and other visionaries helped create the world of Hape Kerkeling despite his differences from them and the wide range of non-Catholic influences that shaped the comedian. By inspiring religious passion in millions of followers, these seers encouraged the desire by Germans to seek salvation in dramatic physical manifestations of God's presence and through deep inner reflection and prayer. Despite their devotion to the Catholic Church, these mystics and their followers often encouraged such spirituality outside the boundaries of dogma and sanctioned church rituals. By challenging institutional authority, they assisted the rise of personalized devotion that came more and more to exist outside of religious orthodoxy despite their intentions to reform the church based upon a traditionalist agenda. The miracles of the mid-twentieth century contributed much to the fragmentation of religion that resulted in one man's Christian, Buddhist, and secular hike that enchanted contemporary Germans.

Notes

Introduction

1 Anni Spiegl, "Preface," in *The Life and Death of Therese Neumann of Konnersreuth* (Eichstätt: Carmelites of Regensburg, 2002); Max Rößler, *Therese Neumann von Konnersreuth* (Würzburg: Verlag Johann Wilhelm Naumann, 1989), 9–11; Die Stigmata der Therese Neumann von Konnersreuth, 1926–1953, Staatsarchiv Amberg (StaAm), Regierung der Oberpfalz, Kammer des Innern 13038; "Die Stigmatisierte von Konnersreuth," *Süddeutsche Zeitung*, 8 February 2011, accessed 4 June 2014, www.sueddeutsche.de.

2 Anna Maria Zumholz, "Die Resistenz des katholischen Milieus: Seherinnen und Stigmatisierte in der ersten Hälfte des 20. Jahrhunderts," in *Wunderbare Erscheinungen: Frauen und katholische Frömmigkeit im 19. und 20. Jahrhundert*, ed. Irmtraud Götz von Olenhusen (Paderborn: Ferdinand Schöningh, 1995), 221–51.

3 Paula M. Kane, *Sister Thorn and Catholic Mysticism in Modern America* (Chapel Hill: University of North Carolina Press, 2013).

4 For a review of debates about secularization see Detlef Pollack, *"Säkularisierung – ein moderner Mythos?" Studien zum religiösen Wandel in Deutschland* (Tübingen: Mohr Siebeck Verlag, 2003). For another depiction of uneven religious development during the nineteenth century, see Jonathan Sperber, *Popular Catholicism in Nineteenth-Century Germany* (Princeton, NJ: Princeton University Press, 1984).

5 Thomas Großbölting, *Der verlorene Himmel. Glaube in Deutschland seit 1945* (Göttingen: Vandenhoek & Ruprecht, 2013), 201–50; Olaf Blaschke and Frank-Michael Kuhlemann, eds., *Religion im Kaiserreich: Milieus-Mentalitäten-Krisen* (Gütersloh: Chr. Kaiser, 1996).

6 For a review of this older historiography, see Hugh McCleod, *Secularization in Western Europe, 1848-1914* (New York: Palgrave, 2000), 1–30. For an example of the neglect of Catholic history in German historical narratives, see Hans-Ulrich Wehler, *The German Empire, 1871–1918* (Oxford and New York: Berg, 1985). See also Margaret Lavinia Anderson, "Piety and Politics: Recent work on German Catholicism," *The Journal of Modern History* 63 (1991): 681–716; Oded Heilbronner, "From Ghetto to Ghetto: The Place of German Catholic Society in Recent Historiography," *The Journal of Modern History* 72 (2000): 60–85; Helmut Walser Smith, ed., *Protestants, Catholics, and Jews in Germany, 1800–1914* (Oxford and New York: Berghan, 2001); Michael E. O'Sullivan, "From Catholic Milieu to Lived Religion: The Social and Cultural History of Modern German Catholicism," *History Compass* 7, no. 3 (2009): 837–61. For the first use of the term, see M. Rainer Lepsius, "Partiensystem und Sozialstruktur. Zum Problem der Demokratisierung der deutschen Gesellschaft," in *Wirtschaft, Geschichte und Wirtschaftsgeschichte*, ed. Wilhelm Abel (Stuttgart: G. Fischer, 1966), 371–93.

7 Urs Altermatt, *Katholizismus und Moderne. Zur Sozial- und Mentalitätsgeschichte der Schweizer Katholiken im 19. und 20. Jahrhundert* (Zurich: Benziger, 1989).

8 Arbeitskreis für kirchliche Zeitgeschichte (AKKZG), Münster, "Katholiken zwischen Tradition und Moderne. Das katholische Milieu als Forschungsaufgabe," *Westfälische Forschungen* 43 (1993): 599.

9 Mark E. Ruff, *The Wayward Flock: Catholic Youth in Postwar West Germany, 1945–1965* (Chapel Hill: University of North Carolina Press, 2005), 1–2.

10 Christoph Kösters, *Katholische Verbände und moderne Gesellschaft: Organizationsgeschichte und Vereinskultur im Bistum Münster, 1918–1945* (Paderborn: F. Schöningh, 1996); Wilhelm Damberg, *Abschied von Milieu? Katholizismus im Bistum Münster und in den Niederlanden 1945–1980*, (Paderborn: F. Schöningh, 1997); Gerhard Paul and Klaus-Michael Mallmann, *Milieus und Widerstand: Eine Verhaltensgeschichte der Gesellschaft im Nationalsozialismus, Widerstand und Verweigerung im Saarland, 1935–1945*, (Bonn: Dietz, 1995); Joachim Kuropka, ed., *Grenzen des katholischen Milieus- Stabilität und Gefährdung katholischer Milieus in der Endphase der Weimarer Republik und der NS-Zeit* (Münster: Aschendorff, 2013); Andreas Henkelmann, *Caritasgeschichte zwischen katholischem Milieu und Wohlfahrtsstaat. Das Seraphische Liebeswerk (1889–1971)* (Paderborn: F. Schöningh, 2008); Benjamin Ziemann, *Encounters with Modernity: The Catholic Church in West Germany, 1945–1975*, trans. Andrew Evans (New York and Oxford: Berghahn, 2014), 1–20.

11 Wilfried Loth, ed., *Deutscher Katholizismus im Umbruch zur Moderne*, (Stuttgart: W. Kohlhammer, 1991), 9–15, 268–70; Jonathan Sperber, *The Kaiser's Voters: Electors and Elections in Imperial Germany* (Cambridge: Cambridge University Press, 1997); Helmut Walser Smith and Chris Clark, "The Fate of Nathan," in *Protestants, Catholics, and Jews in Germany, 1800-1914*, ed. H. W. Smith (Oxford and New York: Berg, 2001), 8–12; Jeffrey Zalar, "'Knowledge is Power': The Borromausverein and Catholic Reading Habits in Imperial Germany," *Catholic Historical Review* 86, no. 1 (January 2000): 20–46.

12 Christian Schmidtmann, *Katholische Studierende 1945–1973: Ein Beitrag zur Kultur- und Sozialgeschichte der Bundesrepublik Deutschland* (Paderborn: F. Schöningh, 2005); Thomas Großbölting and Klaus Große Kracht, "Religion in der Bundesrepublik Deutschland. Eine Einleitung," *Zeithistorische Forschungen/Studies in Contemporary History* 7, no. 3 (2010), www.zeithistosche-forschungen.de; Nicolai Hannig, *Die Religion der Öffentlichkeit. Kirche, Religion und Medien in der Bundesrepublik 1945–1980* (Göttingen: Wallstein Verlag, 2010); Klaus Große Kracht, *Die Stunde der Laien? Katholische Aktion in Deutschland im europäischen Kontext 1920–1960* (Paderborn: F. Schöningh, 2016).

13 Robert A. Orsi, *The Madonna of 115th Street: Faith and Community in Italian Harlem, 1880–1950*, 2nd ed. (New Haven, CT and London: Yale University Press, 2002), xiii-xiv.

14 Robert A. Orsi, *Between Heaven and Earth: The Religious Worlds People Make and the Scholars Who Study Them* (Princeton, NJ and Oxford: Princeton University Press, 2005), 9–10; see also Daniele Hervieu-Leger, "'What Scripture Tells Me': Spontaneity and Regulation Within the Charismatic Renewal," in *Lived Religion in America: Toward a History of Practice*, ed. David D. Hall (Princeton, NJ: Princeton University Press, 1997), 27.

15 Gerd Schallenberg, *Visionäre Erlebnisse: Visionen und Auditionen in der Gegenwart. Eine psychodynamische und psychopathologische Untersuchung* (Augsburg: Pattloch, 1990), 118–27.

16 Peter L. Berger, "Further Thoughts on Religion and Modernity," *Society* 49 (2012): 313–16.

17 Thomas Großbölting, "Religion, Individuum und Gesellschaft. Ein Versuch zur Erklärung des religiösen Wandels in den 1960er Jahren," *Schweizerische Zeitschrift für Religions- und Kulturgeschichte* 107 (2013): 389–406.

18 Rudolf Morsey, *Der Untergang des politischer Katholizismus* (Stuttgart und Zurich: Belser, 1977); Rudolf Morsey, *Die Deutsche Zentrumspartei, 1917–1923* (Düsseldorf: Droste, 1966).

19 Maria Mitchell, *The Origins of Christian Democracy: Politics and Confession in Modern Germany* (Ann Arbor: University of Michigan Press, 2012); Noel Cary, *The Path to Christian Democracy: German Catholics and the Party System from Windthorst to Adenauer* (Cambridge, MA: Harvard University Press, 1996).

20 Terry Rey, "Marketing the Goods of Salvation: Bourdieu on Religion," *Religion* 34 (2004): 331–43; Bradford Verter, "Spiritual Capital: Theorizing Religion with Bourdieu against Bourdieu," *Sociological Theory* 21, no. 2 (2003): 150–74; William F. Hanks, "Pierre Bourdieu and the Practices of Language," *Annual Review of Anthropology* 34 (2005): 67–83.

21 Chris Maunder, *Our Lady of Nations: Apparitions of Mary in Twentieth-Century Europe* (Oxford: Oxford University Press, 2016), 57.

22 Irmtraud Götz von Olenhusen, "Die Feminisierung von Religion und Kirche im 19. und 20. Jahrhundert: Forschungsstand und Forschungsperspektiven (Einleitung)," in *Frauen unter dem Patriarchat der Kirchen: Katholikinnen und Protestantinnen im 19. und 20. Jahrhundert*, ed. Irmtraud Götz von Olenhusen (Stuttgart: W. Kohlhammer, 1995), 8–21; Barbara Welter, "The Feminization of American Religion: 1800–1860," in *Clio's Consciousness Raised: New Perspectives on the History of Women*, ed. Mary S. Hartman and Lois Banner (New York: Harper & Row, 1974), 137–57.

23 Norbert Busch, "Die Feminisierung der Frömmigkeit," in *Wunderbare Erscheinungen: Frauen und katholicshe Frömmigkeit im 19. und 20. Jahrhundert*, ed. Irmtraud Götz von Olenhusen (Paderborn: F. Schönigh, 1995), 203–19; Michael B. Gross, *The War against Catholicism: Liberalism and the Anti-Catholic Imagination in Ninteenth-Century Germany* (Ann Arbor: University of Michigan Press, 2004).

24 Relinde Meiwes, *"Arbeiterinnen des Hernn": Katholicshe Frauenkongregationen im 19. Jahrhundert* (Frankfurt: Campus, 2000).

25 David Blackbourn, *Marpingen: Apparitions of the Virgin Mary in Nineteenth-Century Germany* (New York: Knopf, 1994), 7–15, 30–1, 140–1, 261–3; Maunder, *Our Lady of Nations*, 109–21.

26 Patrick Pasture, "Beyond the Feminization Thesis: Gendering the History of Christianity in the Nineteenth and the Twentieth Centuries," in *Gender and Christianity in Modern Europe: Beyond the Feminization Thesis*, ed. Patrick Pasture, Jan Art, and Thomas Buerman (Leuven: Leuven University Press, 2012), 7–26; Thomas Buerman and Tine van Ossealar, "Feminization Thesis: A Survey of International Historiography and a Probing of Belgian Grounds," *Revue d'histoire ecclésiastique* 103 (2008): 497–544; Ann Taylor Allen, "Religion and Gender in Modern German

History: A Historiographical Perspective," in *Gendering Modern German History: Rewriting Historiography*, ed. Karen Hagemann and Jean H. Quataert (New York: Berghan Books, 2007), 190–207; Bernard Schneider, "Feminisierung der Religion im 19. Jahrhundert. Perspektiven einer These im 19. Jahrhundert," *Trierer Theologische Zeitschrift* 111, no. 2 (2002): 123–47.

27 Robert Ernst, *Die Seherin aus dem Ruhrgebiet* (Stein am Rhein: Christiana-Verlag, 1988).

28 Blackbourn, *Marpingen*; Ruth Harris, *Lourdes: Body and Spirit in the Secular Age* (New York: Penguin, 1999); see also Raymond Jonas, *The Tragic Death of Claire Ferchaud and the Great War* (Berkeley: University of California Press, 2005); Suzanne Kaufmann, *Consuming Visions: Mass Culture and the Lourdes Shrine* (Ithaca, NY: Cornell University Press, 2005); Joseph P. Laycock, *The Seer of Bayside: Veronica Lueken and the Struggle to Define Catholicism* (Oxford and New York: Oxford University Press, 2014).

29 Monique Scheer, *Rosenkranz und Kriegsvisionen: Marienerscheinungskulte im 20. Jahrhundert* (Tübingen: Tübinger Vereinigung für Volkskunde, 2006); Maria Anna Zumholz, *Volksfrömmigkeit und katholisches Milieu. Marienerscheinungen in Heede 1937–1940 im Spannungsfeld von Volksfrömmigkeit, nationalsozialistischem Regime und kirchlicher Hierarchie,* (Cloppenburg: Verlag Runge, 2004).

30 Thanks to the generosity of Maria Anna Zumholz, I gained access to archival copies of the now closed files from the bishopric of Regensburg related to Neumann's stigmata.

31 Konrad H. Jarausch and Michael Geyer, *Shattered Past: Reconstructing German Histories* (Princeton, NJ and Oxford: Princeton University Press, 2003), 17.

1. Bloody Images and Miraculous Cures

1 "Frau Margareta Lippert, Anwesend Pfarrer Müller zu Camberg, November 3, 1933," Bistumsarchiv Trier (BAT) Abt. 90, Nr. 130: Heilungen und Gnadenweise, Unerledigte Fälle, Nr. 1–19, No. 8, Frau Margareta Lippert, Eschborn bei Camberg.

2 Blackbourn, *Marpingen*, 334–59.

3 Patrick J. Houlihan, *Catholicism and the Great War: Religion and Everyday Life in Germany and Austria-Hungary, 1914–1922* (Cambridge: Cambridge University Press, 2015), 118; Benjamin Ziemann, *War Experiences in Rural Germany, 1914–1923* trans. Alex Skinner (Oxford and New York: Berg, 2006).

4 William L. Patch, Jr., *Heinrich Brüning and the Dissolution of the Weimar Republic* (Cambridge: Cambridge University Press, 1998), 1–38; Gotthard

Klein, *Der Volksverein für das Katholische Deutschland, 1890–1933: Geschichte, Bedeutung, Untergang* (Paderborn: F. Schoningh, 1996); Dirk H. Muller, *Arbeiter-Katholizismus-Staat: Der Volksverein für das katholische Deutschland und die katholischen Arbeiterorganisationen in der Weimarer Republik* (Bonn: Dietz, 1996); Raymond Sun, *Before the Enemy is Within Our Walls: Catholic Workers in Cologne, 1885–1912: A Social, Cultural, and Political History* (Boston: Humanities Press, Inc., 1999); Julia Sneeringer, *Winning Women's Votes: Propaganda and Politics in Weimar Germany* (Chapel Hill and London: University of North Carolina Press, 2002).

5 Robert A. Orsi, *Between Heaven and Earth*, 2.

6 Scheer, 79–91.

7 Johannes-Dieter Steinert, *Kevelaer: Eine niederrheinische Region zwischen Kaiserreich und Dritten Reich* (Kevelaer: Butzo & Bercker, 1988).

8 "Kevelaer als Wallfahrtsort über eine halbe Million Pilger," September 1932, Klosterarchiv Neviges (KaN) 28.

9 Pilgerstatistik, 1913–29, KaN 500; Gerhard Haun, *Die Wallfahrt nach Neviges* (Wuppertal: Frohn, 1981), 52–4.

10 "Eine seltenes Jubiläum: 250 Jahre Hardenberg-Prozession: Der feierliche Empfang am Gnadenorte," 30 June 1932, KaN 28.

11 "Bußprozession im Wuppertal: Eine Anregung- 3. Zuschrift von J.U." April 1933, KaN 28.

12 "1300 Pilger bei der Gnadenmutter in Neviges," *Dorstener Volkszeitung*, 25 August 1932, KaN 28.

13 Raymond C. Sun, "Catholic-Marxist Competition in the Working-Class Parishes of Cologne during the Weimar Republic," *Catholic Historical Review* 83, no. 1 (1997), 20–43.

14 "Der Wallfahrtsort-Hardenberg-Neviges," 1926, KaN 28: Wallfahrtschronik, 1919–40.

15 "*Kath. Kirchenzeitung der Pfarre St. Ursula, Köln,*" 11 July 1926; "Pilgerfahrt der Zwölfhundert: Machtvolle Kundgebung der hl. Familie in Neviges," 12 July 1932; "Bußprozession in Wuppertal: Eine Anregung," 1932, all in KaN 28.

16 Haun, 57–60.

17 Raymond C. Sun, "'Hammer Blows:' Work, the Workplace, and the Culture of Masculinity Among Catholic Workers in the Weimar Republic," *Central European History* 37, no. 2 (2004): 245–71; Doris Kaufmann, *Katholisches Milieu in Münster 1928–1933* (Dusseldorf: Schwan, 1984), 77–97; Michael E. O'Sullivan, "A Feminized Church? German Catholic Women and Domestic Piety, 1918–1945," in *Gender and Christianity in Modern Europe: Beyond the Feminization Thesis*, ed. Jan Art, Patrick Pasture, and Thomas Buerman

(Leuven: University of Leuven Press / Cornell University Press, 2012), 190–211.

18 Philip Soergel, *Wondrous in His Saints: Counter-Reformation Propaganda in Bavaria* (Berkeley and Los Angeles: University of California Press, 1993); Marc Forster, *The Counter-Reformation in the Villages: Religion and Reform in the Bishopric of Speyer, 1560–1720* (Ithaca: Cornell University Press, 1992); Bridget Heal, *The Cult of the Virgin Mary in Early Modern Germany: Protestant and Catholic Piety, 1500–1648* (Cambridge: Cambridge University Press, 2007).

19 Houlihan, 117–52.

20 Mirebeau: Paroles de Notre Seigneur aus dem Bericht von AM Vachère (France), Staatsbibliothek München (StaabiM), Nachlass Friedrich Ritter von Lama Ana 445.

21 Henri Birven, *Abbé Vachère: Ein Thaumaturg unserer Zeit* (Brandeburg: J. Wiesike, 1928), 7–13.

22 Bishop of Hildesheim to *Generalvikariat* Cologne, 26 February 1924, Historisches Archiv des Erzbistums Köln (AEK), Gen I 31.6,1: Wunderbare Erscheinungen.

23 Victor Krebs to Cardinal Schulte, 1 July 1921, AEK Gen. I. 31.6,1.

24 Everard Feilding, *Sittings with Eusapia Palladino and Other Studies* (Hyde Park, NY: University Books, 1963), 299–314.

25 Busch, "Die Feminisierung der Frömmigkeit."

26 Jonas, *The Tragic Tale of Claire Ferchaud.*

27 Claudia Schlager, *Kult und Krieg: Herz Jesu-Sacré Coeur- Christus Rex im deutsch-französischen Vergleich 1914–1925* (Tübingen: Tübingen Verein für Volkskunde, 2011), 290–306.

28 Birven, 35 and 101.

29 Mirebeau: Paroles de Notre Seigneur aus dem Bericht von AM Vachere (France), StaabiM, NL Von Lama, Ana 445.

30 Feilding, 308.

31 Birven, 7.

32 "Die Wundergeschichte," Bischöfliches Zentralarchiv Regensburg (BZR), Ordinariatsarchiv(OAR) Bestand Therese Neumann (THN) 146, 112–14.

33 Tine van Osselaer, "Sensitive but Sane: Male Visionaries and their Emotional Display in Interwar Belgium," *Low Countries Historical Review* 127, no. 1 (2012): 127–49.

34 "Öffentliche Erklärung von E. Schoomeesters," 1910; Fritz Effertz to the *Erzbischöfliche Generalvikariat* Cologne, 15 January 1910; Letter to Cardinal Hartmann, Essen, 31 October 1916; "Eine Gottbegnadete," by Oberlehrer Kleinebrecht, Buer, *Essener Kirchenblatt für die katholische*

St. Johannes-Pfarrgemeinde, 28 March 1915; "Der Krieg als Förderer der Sekterei," *Essener Kirchenblatt*, 29 October 1916, all in AEK Gen. I 31.6,1: Wunderbare Erscheinungen, 1852–1935.

35 Schlager, 290–306.

36 "Vachère und Konnersreuth," "Einige Notizen aus Aachen über Vachères blutschwitzende Herz-Jesu-Bilder," and "Die Wundergeschichte," BZR OAR, THN 146/ 112–114.

37 Schlager, 290–306.

38 Barbara Weigand Gesellschaft, e.V., *Offenbarungen an Barbara Weigand*, Band 7, Juni 1908–September 1923, Nr. 899–1155 (Schippach: Barabara Weigand Gesellschaft, 2002), 160, 401–4, 432, 488–90.

39 Zumholz, "Die Resistenz des katholischen Milieus," 221–51.

40 Georg Priller, *Anna Maria Goebel, die Stigmatisierte von Bickendorf (Eifel)* (Tirschenreuth: E. Kohl, 1928), 45–6.

41 Robert Orsi, *Between Heaven and Earth*, 22.

42 Priller, 62.

43 Priller, 75, 93.

44 "Befundbericht ü.d. Stigmatisisierte M.Göbel von Medizialr. Dr Appelmann/Bittburg, BZR OAR THN 146/120–123.

45 "Bericht über die Ereignisse eines dreiwöchentlichen Aufenthaltes in Konnersreuth im Mai 1944 von Dr. E. Aigner, Freiburg," Provinzarchiv der deutschen Augustiner, Würzburg (PdAW) Nachlass Georg Wunderle.

46 "Befundbericht ü.d. Stigmatisisierte M.Göbel von Medizialr. Dr Appelmann/Bittburg, BZR OAR THN 146/120–123.

47 Priller, 16–17, 92; A. Faber to Von Lama, 25 April 1934, StaatbiM, NL Von Lama, Ana 445.

48 "Maria Göbel von Bickendorf war vom 21 April 1926 bis zum 20. Mai 1926 im Mutterhause der Borromärinnen zur Untersuchung ihrer Stigmata u. übernatürlichen Zustände," BZR OAR THN, 146/120–123; Priller, 15–17.

49 Skye Doney, "The Sacred Economy: Devotional Objects as Sacred Presence for German Catholics in Aachen and Trier, 1832–1937," *International Journal of Religious Tourism and Pilgrimage* 1, no. 1 (2014): 62–71.

50 Skye Doney, "Brown and Black Boundaries: Nazism and German Catholicism in the Summer of 1933," *Catholic Historical Review* (forthcoming).

51 Friedrich Ritter von Lama, *Therese of Konnersreuth: A New Chronicle* (Milwaukee, WI: Bruce Publishing, 1935), 34–8.

52 "Amtliche Pilgerzahlen," BAT Abt. 90, Nr. 161: Pilger der einzelnen Diözesen und Länder (Statistikbuch) and Nr. 173: Nachlaß Griepenkerl (Krankenwallfahrten).

53 BAT Abt. 90, Nr. 129, Nr. 10.
54 Ibid.
55 Ibid., Nr. 18.
56 Richard D. E. Burton, *Holy Tears, Holy Blood: Women, Catholicism, and the Culture of Suffering in France, 1840–1970* (Ithaca, NY: Cornell University Press, 2004).
57 BAT Abt. 90, Nr. 129, Nr. 34; Abt. 90, Nr. 130, Nr. 7; Abt. 90, Nr. 130, Nr. 7; Abt. 90, Nr. 129, Nr. 7.
58 Van Osselaer, "Sensitive but Sane," 127–49.
59 BAT Abt. 90, Nr. 131, Nr. 15; Abt. 90, Nr. 129, Nr. 34.
60 BAT Abt. 90, Nr. 130, Nr. 7; Abt. 90, Nr. 130, Nr. 15.
61 BAT Abt. 90, Nr. 129, Nr. 5; Abt. 90, Nr. 129, Nr. 15; Abt. 90, Nr. 130, Nr. 12.
62 BAT Abt. 90, Nr. 129, Nr. 16.
63 BAT Abt. 90, Nr. 129, Nr. 26.
64 BAT Abt. 90, Nr. 129, Nr. 7.
65 BAT Abt. 90, Nr. 131, Nr. 6.
66 BAT Abt. 90, Nr. 129, Nr. 2.
67 BAT Abt. 90, Nr. 131, Nr. 15.
68 BAT Abt. 90, Nr. 129, Nr. 26.

2. The Rise of Therese Neumann

1 *Die Seherin von Konnersreuth: Berichte über Therese Neumann, Separatabdruck aus dem Tagblatt Die Neue Zeitung,* (Vienna, 1927), 35.
2 Gendarmeriestation Konnersreuth an das Bezirksamt in Tirschenreuth, 3 May 1926, StaAm Bezirksamt Tirschenreuth (BT) 4169.
3 "Über Therese Neumann aus Konnersreuth. III. Ärztlich-medizinischer Bericht nach einem Vortrag, gehalten in Amsterdam am 4. November 1928 im kath. Ärzteverein Hollands, BZR OAR THN104/2; Gendarmerie Station Konnersreuth an das Bezirksamt Tirschenreuth, 14 April 1926, ThN 119/6; "Die katholischen Ärtzte Hollands und die Probleme von Konnersreuth," *Augsburger Postzeitung,* 16 November 1928, ThN 136/137.
4 Wilhelm Damberg, *Moderne und Milieu: Gescichte des Bistums Münster 1802–1998* (Münster: Dialog Verlag, 1998), 207–12; *Kirchliches Handbuch für das katholische Deutschland: Nebst Mitteilungen der amtlichen Zentralstelle für kirchliche Statistik,* vols. 5, 10, and 13 (Freiburg im Breisgau, 1916, 1922, 1926).
5 Oded Heilbronner, *Catholicism, Political Culture, and the Countryside: A Social History of the Nazi Party in the Countryside,* (Ann Arbor: University of Michigan Press, 1998); Sun, "Catholic-Marxist Competition," 20–43.

6 Siegfried Weichlein, *Sozialmilieus und politische Kultur in der Weimarer Republik, Lebenswelt, Vereinskultur, Politik in Hessen,* (Göttingen: Vandenhoeck & Rupprecht, 1996); Oded Heilbronner, *Catholicism, Political Culture, and the Countryside;* Thomas Breuer, *Verordneter Wandel? Der Widerstreit zwischen nationalsozialistischen Herrschaftsanspruch und traditionaler Lebenswelt im Erzbistum Bamberg,* (Mainz: Mattias Grünewald Verlag, 1992).

7 Paul Siwek, *The Riddle of Konnersreuth: A Psychological and Religious Study* translated by Ignatius McCormick (Milwaukee, WI: Bruce Publishing, 1953), 5.

8 Siwek, 5–9; Fritz Gerlich, *Die Stigmatisierte Therese Neumann von Konnersreuth, Erster Teil, Die Lebensgeschichte der Therese Neumann* (Munich: Kösel & Pustet, 1929), 6–7; Johannes Steiner, *Therese Neumann: A Portrait Based on Authentic Accounts, Journals, and Documents* (New York: Alba House, 1967), 19–20; Rößler, 16–18.

9 Bericht Westermayr u. seinen 2ten Besuch in Konnersreuth, 18 October 1928; Bericht über den 3ten Besuch in Konnersreuth, 22 January 1929, both in StaabiM Ana 338, Nachlass Westermayr, Akten Westermayr Konnersreuth I.

10 Klaus Unterberger, "Schwarz und kirchentreu, arm und eingeschüchtert?- Katholicshes Milieu und Nationalsozialismus in der Oberpfalz," in *Grenzen des katholisches Milieus: Stabilität und Gefährdung katholischer Milieus in der Endphase der Weimarer Republik und der NS-Zeit,* ed. Joachim Kuropka (Münster: Aschendorff Verlag, 2013), 323–57; Tobias Dietrich, *Konfession im Dorf. Westeuropäische Erfahrungen im 19. Jahrhundert* (Cologne: Böhlau, 2004).

11 Siwek, 4–10; Gerlich, 7–14.

12 Josef Deutsch, *Ärztliche Kritik an Konnersreuth! Wunder oder Hysterie?* (Lippstadt: C. Jos. Laumanns, 1938), 7–12.

13 Steiner, 23.

14 Joseph Naber, *Tagebücher und Aufzeichnungen über Therese Neumann* (Munich and Zurich: Verlag Schnell & Steiner, 1987), 27.

15 Siwek, 39–219; Steiner, 20–51; Gerlich, 16–99; Naber, 27–43.

16 Siwek, 25.

17 Naber, 7–19.

18 Erwein Freiherr von Aretin, "Die Erscheinungen von Konnersreuth," *Die Einkehr: Unterhaltungs-Beilage der Münchener Neuste Nachtrichten,* 3 August 1927; Fritz Gerlich, "Erlebnisse in Konnersreuth," *Die Einkehr: Unterhaltungs-Beilage der Münchener Neuste Nachtrichten,* 6 November 1927.

19 Schlammlinger, Stationskommandant, Gendarmeriestation Konnersreuth an das Besirksamt Tirschenreuth, 14 April 1926, StaAm, BT 4169; A.M. Salzmann, ed., *Therese Neumann: die Stigmatisierte von Konnersreuth, persönliche Eindrücke und Berichten von Augenzeugen* (Dessau: Martin Salzmann Verlag, 1929), 34.
20 Gendameriestation Konnersreuth an das Bezirksamt Tirschenreuth, 14 April 1926, 19 May 1926, 3 June 1926, 1 July 1026, 8 August 1926, 23 October 1926, 9 April 1927, 30 July 1927, 12 August 1927, 3 October 1927, 5 November 1927, all in StaAM BT 4169.
21 Gendarmereistation to Tirschenreuth, 19 May 1926, StaAm BT 4169.
22 Landessekretariat der Diözesanpriestervereine Bayerns an Wunderle, 8 September 1927, PdAW NL Georg Wunderle, Wunderle Briefe.
23 Salzmann, 31–2.
24 Gendarmeriestation to Tirschenreuth, 5 Novemeber 1927, StaAm BT 4169.
25 Salzmann, 70.
26 Von Lama, *Therese of Konnersreuth*, 101–2.
27 "Erinnerungen," 122–4, Fürstlich Waldburg-Zeil'sches Gesamtarchiv, Nachlass Fürst Erich von Waldburg-Zeil.
28 Ibid., 117.
29 Von Lama, *Therese of Konnersreuth*, 129; Gendameriestation to Tirschenreuth, 16 September 1927, StaAm BT 4169; Salzmann, 70.
30 Michael Buchberger to Augustinus Kilian, 5 February 1930, BZR OAR THN, Nr. 97, 15–18.
31 "Eindrücke in Konnersreuth," Antonie von Tänzl in der *Kath. Kirchenzeitung*, December 1926, StaAm BT 4169.
32 Leopold Witt, "Waren Sie auch schon in Konnersreuth?" *Grenzzeitung*, Waldsassen, 26 April 1926, StaAm BT 4169.
33 "Erinnerungen," 116, Fürstlich Waldburg-Zeil'sches Gesamtarchiv, Nachlass Fürst Erich von Waldburg-Zeil.
34 Erwein Freiherr von Aretin, *Die Sühneseele von Konnersreuth*, ed. Karl Otmar Freiherr von Aretin (Munich: Verlag Siegfried Hacker, 1956), 6–7; Gerlich, 1–4.
35 Johannes Maria Verweyen, *Das Geheimnis von Konnersreuth: Ein Augenzeuge berichtet und deutet die rätselhaften Vorgänge* (Stuttgart: Süddeutsches Verlagshaus, 1932), 59–62.
36 John Connelly, *From Enemy to Brother: The Revolution in Catholic Teaching on the Jews, 1933–1965* (Cambridge, MA: Harvard University Press, 2012), 5–7.
37 Verlag des *Konnersreuther-Sonntagsblatt* an Herr. J. Briegans, Waldsassen, 11 February 1928; Das Bischöfliche Ordinariat Regensburg an das hochw.

Erzbischöfliche Ordinariat Köln, both in AEK, Gen I 31.9: Therese Neumann in Konnersreuth.

38 Leopold Witt to Faulhaber, 13 September 1927; Friedrich von Lama to Faulhaber, 29 January 1928, both in Erzbischöfliches Archiv München (EAM), Nachlass Kardinal Michael Faulhaber 5945/2 Therese Neumann.

39 Von Lama, *Therese of Konnersreuth: A New Chronicle*, 3–8, 143–232.

40 "Erinnerungen," 124–5, Fürstlich Waldburg-Zeil'sches Gesamtarchiv, Nachlass Fürst Erich von Waldburg-Zeil.

41 Hilda C. Graef, *The Case of Therese Neumann* (Westminster, MD: The Newman Press, 1951); Josef Schmidt/Paul Diebel, "Sin Dolor," *Frankfurter Zeitung*, 11 October 1927; "Das Wunder von Konnersreuth ist erledigt!" *8-Uhr Abendblatt*, 30 July 1927, both in PdAW, NL Georg Wunderle.

42 Heather Wolffram, *Stepchildren of Science: Psychical Research and Parapsychology in Germany, c. 1870–1939* (New York and Amsterdam: Editions Rodopi, 2009), 233–62.

43 Ulrike Wiethaus, "Bloody Bodies: Gender, Religion, and the State in Nazi Germany," *Studies in Spirituality* 12 (2002): 193.

3. Saving Souls and Making Enemies

1 Landessekretariat der Diözesanpriestervereine Bayerns an Wunderle, 8 September 1927, PdAW, NL Wunderle, Wunderle Briefe.

2 Stephen Schloesser, *Jazz Age Catholicism: Mystic Modernism in Postwar Paris, 1919–1933* (Toronto: University of Toronto Press, 2005).

3 Klaus Scholder, *The Churches and the Third Reich*, 2 vols. (Frankfurt am Main: SCM Press, 1977); Patch, Jr, *Heinrich Brüning*; Larry E. Jones, "Catholic Conservatives in the Weimar Republic: The Politics of the Rheinish-Westphalian Aristocracy, 1918–1933," *German History* 18 (2000): 60–85; Larry E. Jones, "Franz von Papen, the German Center Party, and the Failure of Catholic Conservatism in the Weimar Republic," *Central European History* 38, no. 2 (June 2005): 191–217.

4 Klein, *Der Volksverein für das katholische Deutschland*; Heilbronner, *Catholicism, Political Culture, and the Countryside*; Douglas J. Cramer, "'To Avoid a New Kulturkampf': The Catholic Workers' Associations and National Socialism in Weimar-era Bavaria," *Journal of Church and State* 41, no. 4 (Autumn 1999): 739–60.

5 Ellen Lovell Evans, *The German Center Party, 1870–1933: A Study in Political Catholicism* (Carbondale and Edwardsville: Southern Illinois University Press, 1981); Derek Hastings, *Catholicism and the Roots of Nazism: Religious Identity and National Socialism* (Oxford and New York: Oxford University

Press, 2010); Martin R. Menke, "Misunderstood Civic Duty: The Center Party and the Enabling Act," *Journal of Church and State* 51, no. 2 (Spring 2009): 236–64.

6 "Eindrücke in Konnersreuth," Antonie von Tänzl, *Kath. Kirchenzeitung*, December 1926, StaAM BT 4169.

7 Dr Emil Scheller, "Bericht über die Stigmatisierte in Konnersreuth," Munich, 16 February 1927, EAM, NL Faulhaber, Therese Neumann 5945/2.

8 Gendarmeriestation to Tirschenreuth, 23 October 1926, StaAm BT 4169.

9 Gendarmeriestation to Tirschenreuth, 1 April 1929, StaAm BT 4169.

10 Gendarmeriestation to Tirschenreuth, 12 February 1927; 6 June 1929; 17 August 1929; 25 August 1929, all in StaAm BT 4169.

11 Gendarmeriestation to Tirschenreuth, 24 March 1928; 1 April 1929; 28 May 1929; 28 November 1929; 28 December 1929; 11 February 1930; 26 February 1930, all in StaAm BT 4169; Wunderle Briefe, Pfarrer Hof an Wunderle, Mitterteich, 11 February 1927, PdAW NL Wunderle; NL Westermayr, Dr J. Westermayr, Konnersreuth Korrespondenz, Westermayr an Regentie des Bischofl. Klerikalseminars Regensburg, 21 September 1929, StaabiM Ana 338.

12 Bericht Westermayr u. seinen 2ten Besuch in Konnersreuth, 18 October 1928; Bericht über den 3ten Besuch in Konnersreuth, 22 January 1929, both in StaabiM Ana 338, NL Westermayr, Akten Westermayr Konnersreuth I: Briefwechsel mit Bischof Buchberger und Erzbischof Teodorowicz.

13 Westermayr an Standiger, 24 August 1930, StaabiM Ana 338, NL Westermayr, Dr J. Westermayr Konnersreuth Korrespondenz; "Erinnerungen," 122, Fürstlich Waldburg-Zeil'sches Gesamtarchiv, Nachlass Fürst Erich von Waldburg-Zeil.

14 Wunderle to Buchberger, 1930, PdAW NL Wunderle, Wunderle Briefe; Georg Wunderle, *Die Stigmatisierte von Konnersreuth: Tatsachen, Eindrücke, Erwägungen* (Eichstätt: Schriftenreihe des Klerusblattes, 1927), 2–5.

15 Wunderle to Buchberger, 1930; Wunderle to Aretin, 24 July 1930; Wunderle to Pacelli, 18 December 1936, all in PdAW Nachlass Wunderle, Wunderle Briefe.

16 Wunderle to *Schönere Zukunft*, 3 March 1932; Wunderle to Deutsch, 26 October 1932; Wunderle to Dr Fritz Kern, 29 August 1929; "Konnersreuth 1928," by Fritz Kern, all in PdAW Nachlass Wunderle, Wunderle Briefe.

17 "Über Therese Neumann aus Konnersreuth. III. Ärztlich-medizinischer Bericht nach einem Vortrag, gehalten in Amsterdam am 4. November 1928 im kath. Ärzteverein Hollands, BZR OA THN, 104/2; Gendarmerie Station Konnersreuth an das Bezirksamt Tirschenreuth, 14 April 1926, ThN 119/6; "Die katholischen Ärtzte Hollands und die Probleme von Konnersreuth," *Augsburger Postzeitung*, 16 November 1928, ThN 136/137.

18 Wolffram, *Stepchildren of Science*.

19 A rare book dealer recently sold over three hundred letters between Josef Deutsch and Norbert Brühl to an anonymous institution with ties to the church in Regensburg. "Material im Fall Resl verkauft," *Mittelbayerische Zeitung*, 24 January 2014, accessed on 20 March 2014, www.mittelbayerische.de.

20 Deutsch, *Konnersreuth in Ärztlicher Beleuchtung*, 3–8, 14–15, 31, 35–8, 59–60.

21 Ibid., 71.

22 Deutsch to Wunderle, 24 April 1932, PdAW NL Wunderle, Josef Deutsch Correspondence; Dr Deutsch to Westermayr, 26 August 1932, StaabiM, NL Westermayr, Dr J. Westermayr, Konnersreuth Korrespondenz.

23 Deutsch, *Konnersreuth in Ärztlicher Beleuchtung*, 60–3.

24 Deutsch to Wunderle, October 1934, PdAW Nachlass Wunderle, Josef Deutsch Briefe.

25 Deutsch to Wunderle, 24 April 1932, PdAW Nachlass Wunderle, Josef Deutsch Briefe.

26 Deutsch to Westermayr, 20 September 1932, Staabi Munich Ana 338, Nachlass Westermayr, Dr J. Westermayr, Konnersreuther Korrespondenz.

27 Siwek, 112–13.

28 Dr Magerei to Westermayr, 27 April 1932, StaabiM Ana 338, NL Westermayr, "Konnersreuther Korrespondenz"; H. Heermann, *Um Konnersreuth* (Paderborn: Bonifacius Druckerei, 1932); Michael Theodor Witry, *Die Resl: Medizinisches aus Konnersreuth* (Saarbrücken: Saarbrücker Druckerei, 1934).

29 Norbert Brühl an .d Schriftleitung d. kath. Kirchenwoche, Stuttgart, 18 April 1939; *Domdekan* Beckschäfer to Westermayr, 1936; *Domprobst* Donders to George Westermayr, 19 June 1936; Pater Heuefelf to Deutsch, 15 February 1937; NL Wunderle, "Therese Neumann," Professor Strählin to Pater Agnostino Gemelli, OFM, 30 June 1930, all in StaabiM, Ana 338, NL Westermayr, Akten Westermayr, Konnersreuth 3.

30 "Therese Neumann," *Schriftleitung* Caritas to George Wunderle, 4 June 1932; Joseph Hall to Wunderle, 5 December 1927, both in PdAW Nachlass Wunderle.

31 Brief von Lamas zur Äusserung der bayr. Bischofskonferenz 1932, StaabiM Ana 338, NL Westermayr, Akten Westermayr, Briefwechsel mit Vätern d. Gesellschaft Jesu.

32 Connelly, 156.

33 Fritz Gerlich, "Die Nahrungslosigkeit im Fall Konnersreuth: Ein Gutachten von Dir. Dr. med. Höhn, Essen," *Der gerade Weg* (GW) 4, no. 55, 28 December 1932.

34 Fritz Gerlich, "Kampf um Konnersreuth: Ein Freidenker Versuch, die Konnersreuther Gegner zu organisieren,"*GW* 4, no. 51, 14 December 1932; Fritz Gerlich, "Kampf um Konnersreuth: die 'Einzelkämpfer' gegen Therese Neumann,"*GW* 4, no. 52,18 December 1932; Fritz Gerlich, "Kampf um Konnersreuth: Der Fall Deutsch," *GW* 4 no. 53 21 December 1932.

35 Pfarramt Markt-Seinsheim an Wunderle, 24 June 1929, PdAW Nachlass Wunderle, "Therese Neumann."

36 Anonymous letter to Georg Wunderle, 24 October 1927, AEK, Gen. I 31.9: Therese Neumann in Konnersreuth.

37 Von Lama, *Therese of Konnersreuth: A New Chronicle*, 24–38; "Dr Joseph Deutsch," Joseph Deutsch an Wunderle, October 1934, PdAW Nachlass Wunderle.

38 Klaus Unterberger, "Schwarz und kirchentreu, arm und eingeschüchtert?" 323–57.

39 Henle an Naber, 1 May 1926, BZR OA THN 102.

40 Buchberger an Westermayr, 25 March 1929, StaabiM Ana 338, NL Westermayr, "Akten Westermayr Konnersreuth I: Briefwechsel mit Bischof Buchberger und Erzbischof Teodorowicz."

41 Staatsministerium des Innern an der Filmöberprufstelle Berlin, 11 January 1928, Bayerisches Hauptstaatsarchiv München (BHSAM), MA 104527.

42 "Bericht über Theresia Neumann in Konnersreuth (1928)," BZR OA THN 149/21–25; Deutsch, *Ärztliche Kritik*, 13–29.

43 "Beobachtungen und Eindrücke in Konnersreuth am 22. & 23. März 1928," BZR OA ThN, 84/14–18.

44 "Beobachtungen bei Therese Neumann in Konnersreuth," PdAW NL Wunderle, "Untersuchung."

45 Buchberger to Kilian, 5 February 1930, BZR OA THN 97/15–18; Buchberger to Bishop Pelt (Metz), 7 January 1937, OA THN 97.

46 Augustino Gemelli Bericht, 26 May 1928, BZR OA THN Nr. 106/ 12–19.

47 Michael Hesemann, "Der spätere Papst Pius XII über Therese Neumann," *Kathnews Rom und Weltweit*, 13 January 2011, accessed 27 May 2014, www.kathnews.de; "Testament to Teresa Neumann," *The Catholic Herald*, 3 May 1940.

48 Buchberger to Gemelli, 19 July 1930, BZR OA THN 106; Faulhaber to Gemelli, 25 February 1928, EAM NL Faulhaber 5945/1 Therese Neumann von Konnersreuth.

49 Brunelli Bericht, 17 January 1931, BZR OA THN 99/14–16.

50 Feldman, 37; Luise Rinser, *Die Wahrheit über Konnersreuth. Ein Bericht*, (Frankfurt a.M: Fischer, 1953), 18; Hilda C. Graef, *The Case of Therese Neumann* (Westminster, MD: The Newman Press, 1951), 64–5.

51 Faulhaber to Ferdinand Neumann, 9 December 1932; Faulhaber to Michael Buchberger, 9 December 1932; Buchberger to Faulhaber, 24 November 1932, all in EAM, NL Faulhaber 5945/3; Faulhaber to Bishof Kaspar, 17 November 1932; Faulhaber to Kaspar, 20 February 1933, both in NL Faulhaber 5946/1.

52 Faulhaber to Braun, 21 December 1932, EAM, NL Faulhaber 5945/3.

53 Buchberger to von Preysing, 19 January 1933, BZR OA THN 111/23–24.

54 "Sieben Grundsätze über Konnersreuth: Predigt des Herrn Kardinals im Dom zu München am 6. November 1927," *Augsburger Postzeitung*, 9 November 1927, 4, BHSAM, Bayerische gesandschaft Päpstlicher Stuhl 1919.

55 Faulhaber to Naber, 3 November 1931, EAM NL Faulhaber 5945/1 Therese Neumann; Faulhaber to von Lama, 1 September 1928, NL Faulhaber 5945/2; Dr Himdringer to *Neues Wiener Journal*, 17 January 1929; Von Lama to Faulhaber, 2 February 1929; Elinor Niemann to Faulhaber, 16 March 1930, all in NL Faulhaber, 5945/3.

56 Faulhaber to Gerlich, 17 September 1929; Gerlich to Faulhaber, 19 November 1929; Faulhaber to Mayerhofer, 20 July 1933, all in EAM NL Faulhaber 5945/1; Faulhaber to von Lama, 28 January 1928, NL Faulhaber 5945/2.

57 Westermayr to Sanitatesrat Dr Bergmann, 21 April 1929, StaabiM Ana 338, NL Westermayr, Dr J. Westermayr, Konnersreuth Korrespondenz.

58 Faulhaber to Braun, 21 December 1932, EAM NL Faulhaber 5945/3; Ludwig Dietz to Faulhaber, 3 December 1939, EAM NL Faulhaber 5946/1.

59 Faulhaber to Kaspar, 20 February 1933 and 17 November 1932, EAM NL Faulhaber 5946/1.

60 Grabinski to Brühl, 23 August 1940, StaabMi, Ana 338, NL Westermayr, Akten Westermayr Konnersreuth (1940); Faulhaber to Westermayr, 13 September 1941, EAM NL Faulhaber 5946/2.

61 Robert Krieg, *Catholic Theologians in Nazi Germany* (New York: Bloomsbury, 2004), 25–7.

62 Julia Sneeringer, *Winning Women's Votes: Propaganda and Politics in Weimar Germany*, (Chapel Hill: University of North Carolina Press, 2002), 159–60, 184–5.

63 Falk Wiesemann, *Die Vorgeschichte der nationalsozialistische Machtübernahme in Bayern 1932/1933* (Berlin: Dunker und Humbolt, 1975); Joachim Sailer, *Eugen Bolz und die Krise des politicshen Katholizismus in der Weimarer Republik* (Tübingen: Bibliotheca Academica Verlag, 1994); Klaus Schönhoven, *Die Bayerische Volkspartei 1924–1932* Kommission für Geschichte des Parlamentarismus und der politische Parteien (Düsseldorf: Droste Verlag,

1972); Larry E. Jones, *Hitler versus Hindenburg: The 1932 Presidential Elections and the End of the Weimar Republic* (Cambridge: Cambridge University, Press, 2015), 24, 36; Noel Cary, "The Making of the Reich President, 1925: German Conservatism and the Nomination of Paul von Hindenburg," *Central European History* 23, no. 2/3 (June/September 1990): 179–204.

64 "Konnersreuth 1928," PdAW, Nachlass Georg Wunderle, Untersuchung.

65 Gendameriestation Konnersreuth an das Bezirksamt Tirschenreuth, 1 April 1929, StaAm, BT 4169; Rudolf Morsey, ed., *Fritz Gerlich- ein Publizist gegen Hitler. Briefe und Akten 1930–1934* (Paderborn: Ferdinand Schöningh, 2010), 29; Dr Johann Baptist Westermayr, Westermayr an Schriftleitung *Bayerische Kurier*, 9 March 1932, StaabiM, Ana338 NL Westermayr.

66 "Aus dem Leserkreis," *Konnersreuther Zeitung*, 25 November 1927, StaAm BT 4169.

67 "Dr Josef Deutsch," Deutsch to Wunderle, 2 February 1932; "Weitere Fälle," "Unpolitische. Das 'Gegenstück von Konnersreuth' als Schwindel entlarvt," *Kölnische Volkszeitung*, 10 April 1928; "Deutsch," "Die Stimme des Lesers," *Kölnische Volkszeitung* Nr. 587, 12 December 1931, 4, all in PdaW, NL Wunderle; Buchberger to Westermayr, 31 January 1930, StaabiM Ana 338 NL Westermayr, Akten Westermayr Konnersreuth 1: Briefwechsel mit Bischof Buchberger und Erzbischof Teodorowicz; Herbert Thurston: Therese Neumann, BZR OAR THN Nr 118.

68 Brauns to Buchberger, 22 October 1927, BZR OA THN Nr. 119.

69 Regierung der Oberpfalz und von Regensburg, Kammer des Innern an das Bischöfliche Ordinariat Regensburg, 19 September 1927, BZR OA THN Nr. 119/18.

70 "Konnersreuther Zeitungen," "Marxistische Konnersreuth Hetze," *Bayerische Volkszeitung*, Nr. 218, 23 September 1927; "Angriffe gegen Therese Neumann," "Der Volksbetrug in Konnersreuth," *Thüringer Volksblatt* 19 September 1927, all in PdaW NL Wunderle; "Im Blitzlicht. Es dämmert um Therese," *Westfälische Landeszeitung Rotes Echo*, 16 July 1927, BZR OA THN Nr. 112.

71 "Angriffe gegen Therese Neumann," "Bei der Heilige Therese von Konnersreuth," *Der Freistaat: Sozialdemokratisches Organ für Bamberg und für das westliche Oberfranken*, vol. 9, no. 217, 21 September 1927, PdaW Nachlass Wunderle.

72 Gendameriestation to Tirschenreuth, 25 September 1927, StaAm BT 4169.

73 Siwek, 50–1.

74 Kilian to Buchberger, 1 February 1930, BZR OA THN Nr. 97/10–11.

75 Gendameriestation to Tirschenreuth, 24 September 1927, StaAm, BT 4169.

76 Gendameriestation to Tirschenreuth, 19 November 1927, StaAm, BT 4169.
77 Cremer, "To Avoid a New Kulturkampf," 739–59.
78 Morsey, ed., *Fritz Gerlich*, 7–41, 51–60, 230–2.
79 Michael Schäfer, *Fritz Gerlich 1883–1934. Publizistik als Auseinandersetzung mit den 'Politischen Religionen' des 20. Jahrhunderts* (PhD diss., University of Munich, 1998), 6.
80 Schäfer, 21–4; Morsey, *Fritz Gerlich* 27–33.
81 Ingbert Naab, *Ist Hitler ein Christ?* (Munich: Verlag Zeichenring, 1931); Morsey, *Fritz Gerlich,* 183–4; Schäfer, 24–5; "Hat Hitler Mongolenblut?" *GW* 29, 17 July 1932.
82 "Wie hat der Katholik zu wählen?" *GW* 31 July 1932; "Deutsche! Eure Menschenrechte in Gefahr!" 24 12 June 1932.
83 Jones, *Hitler Versus Hindenburg*, 55–86.
84 Morsey, 148, 157, 161, 165, 170, 172.
85 Morsey, 85; Schafer, 18–30.
86 Großbolting, "Religion, Individium und Gesellschaft," 389–406.

4. Gender and Sex in Konnersreuth

1 "Kreuger Bankrott-Hitler Bankrott," *GW*, 24 April 1932.
2 Claudia Koonz, *Mothers in the Fatherland: Women, the Family, and Nazi Politics* (New York: St Martin's Press, 1988); Renate Bridenthal and Claudia Koonz, "Beyond Kinder, Küche, Kirche: Weimar Women in Politics and Work," in *When Biology Became Destiny: Women in Weimar and Nazi Germany*, ed. Renate Bridenthal, Atina Grossmann, and Marion Kaplan (New York: Monthly Review Press, 1984), 21–49.
3 Ursula Baumann, "Religion, Emancipation, and Politics in the Confessional Women's Movement in Germany, 1900–1933," in *Borderlines: Genders and Identities in War and Peace, 1870–1930*, ed. Billie Melman, (New York and London: Routledge, 1998), 285–306; Ursula Baumann, "Religion und Emanzipation: Konfessionelle Frauenbewegung in Deutschland 1900–1933," in *Frauen unter dem Patriarchat der Kirchen*, ed. von Olenhusen, 89–119.
4 Sneeringer, *Winning Women's Votes;* Doris Kaufmann, *Katholisches Milieu in Münster 1928–1933* (Düsseldorf: Schwann, 1984), 77.
5 Birgit Sack, *Zwischen religiöser Bindung und moderner Gesellschaft: katholicshe Frauenbewegung und politicshe Kultur in der Weimarer Republik (1918/ 19–1933)* (Münster: Waxmann, 1998); 152–65, 250–73, 401.
6 Laurie Marhoefer, *Sex and the Weimar Republic: German Homosexual Emancipation and the Rise of the Nazis* (Toronto: University of Toronto Press,

2015); Julia Roos, *Weimar through the Lens of Gender: Prostitution Reform, Woman's Emancipation, and German Democracy, 1919–1933* (Ann Arbor: University of Michigan Press, 2010).

7 Toni Siegert, personal interview, 22 June 2013.

8 Steiner, *Therese Neumann*, 68; Friedrich Ritter von Lama, *Therese Neumann: A Stigmatist of Our Day*, (New York and Milwaukee, WI: Bruce, 1929), 23, 46–7, 56–7, 66.

9 Paula Kane, " 'She Offered Herself Up': The Victim Soul and Victim Spirituality in Catholicism," *Church History* 71, no. 1 (March 2002): 80–119.

10 Wunderle to Fritz Kern, 29 August 1929 and Wunderle to Buchberger, 1930, both in PdAW, NL Wunderle, Wunderle Briefe; "Konnersreuth 1928" by Fritz Kern, PdAW, NL Wunderle, "Untersuchung."

11 Akten Westermayr Konnersreuth I, "Bericht über den 3ten besuch in Ko.," 22 January 1929; Westermayr to Härtl, 24 August 1930; Theordorowicz to Westermayr, 10 January 1933; Akten Westermayr Briefwechsel mit Vätern d. Gesellschaft Jesu, Pater Bleistein to Westermayr, 25 April 1928, Dr J. Westermayr, Konnersreuth Korrespondenz, "Blätter zur Frage Konnersreuth: Wunder oder Betrug?" Dr Deutsch, 1938, all in StaabiM, NL Westermayr Ana 338.

12 Gendameriestation Konnersreuth to Bezirksamt Tirschenreuth, 17 December 1927, StaAm BT 4169.

13 Steiner, *Therese Neumann*, 125, 139–44.

14 Feldmann, 32–5.

15 EAM NL Faulhaber 5945/3, Faulhaber to Herrn. Lic. Brauenlich, 21 December 1932.

16 Steiner, *Therese Neumann*, 74–6.

17 Feldmann, 35–9; Spiegl, 43; Siwek, 12; Steiner, *Therese Neumann*, 72–80.

18 Maria Mitchell, *The Origins of Christian Democracy*, 111–12.

19 Brief von Lamas zur Äusserung der bayr. Bischofskonferenz 1932; "Dr Johann Baptist Westermayr," *Münchener Fremdenblatt* to Westermayr, 8 March 1932, both in StaabiM, Ana 338, NL Westermayr, Akten Westermayr Briefwechsel mit Vätern d. Gesellschaft Jesu.

20 "Dr Josef Deutsch," Deutsch to Vetter Bernard, 13 November 1936, PdAW, NL Wunderle; "Untersuchung," Paul Martini, Beobachtungen bei Therese Neumann in Konnersreuth, 22./23. März 1928; Siwek, 57.

21 Steiner, *Therese Neumann*, 88; Josef Teodorowicz, *Mystical Phenomena in the Life of Theresa Neumann* (London and St Louis, MO: Herder, 1945), 400–1; Friedrich Ritter von Lama, *Further Chronicles of Therese Neumann*, (New York and Milwaukee, WI: Bruce, 1931), 12.

22 Toni Siegert, personal interview, 22 June 2013.

23 Baroness Elisabeth von Guttenberg, *Holding the Stirrup: A Bavarian Noblewoman's Adventurous Tale of Great Lords, Lofty Castles, the Decline of the Aristocracy, and the Plot to Assassinate Hitler* (Post Falls, ID: Lepanto Press, 1953), 165.
24 Gendarmeriestation Konnersreuth to Bezirksamt Tirschenreuth, 16 September 1927, StaAm, BT 4169.
25 Meiwes, *Arbeiterinnen des Herrn.*
26 Westermayr to bischöfliche Ordinariat Regensburg, 26 November 1936, StaabiM, Ana 338, NL Westermayr, Akten Westermayr Konnersreuth I: Briefwechsel mit Bischof Buchberger und Erzbischof Teodorowicz; Frau Maria Grisar to Faulhaber, 21 July 1930, EAM NL Faulhaber 5945/3.
27 Siwek, 32.
28 Ibid., 144, 163–5.
29 Ibid., 165.
30 Ibid., 65.
31 Pater Heuelf (Osnabruck), 15 February 1937, StaabiM, Ana 338, Nachlass Westermayr, Akten Westermayr, Konnersreuth 3.
32 Von Lama, *Therese of Konnersreuth*, 153, 207.
33 Ibid., 165.
34 Deutsch to Wunderle, 8 January 1933, StaabiM, Ana 338, Nachlass Wunderle, Dr Josef Deutsch Briefe.
35 Spiegl, 30.
36 Bericht an Bischof Buchberger, 22 January 1929, StaabiM, Ana 338, NL Westermayr, Akten Westermayr, Konnersreuth 1; Siwek, 8.
37 Von Lama, *Further Chronicles of Therese Neumann*, 13; Schlammlinger, Gend. Station Konnersreuth to Bezirksamt Tirschenreuth, Konnersreuth, 19 May 1926, StAm, BT 4169.
38 Bericht an Bischof Buchberger, 22 January 1929, StaabiM, Ana 338, Nachlass Westermayr, Akten Westermayr, Konnersreuth 1; Von Lama, *Therese of Konnersreuth*, 182.
39 Gendarmeriestation Konnersreuth to Bezirksamt Tirschenreuth, 24 September 1927, 1 April 1929, 11 February 1930, StaAm, BT 4169.
40 Gendarmeriestation Konnersreuth an den Herrn Vorstand des Bezirksamtes Tirschenreuth, 1 July 1933, StaAm, BT 4169.
41 Von Lama, *Therese of Konnersreuth*, 159.
42 Ibid., 144–52.
43 Ibid., 167–70.
44 Toni Siegert, personal interview, 22 June 2013.
45 Steiner, 79.

46 Ludwig Dietz to Buchberger, 18 December 1937 and Nr. 110/49–52, Michael Faulhaber to Ferdinand Neumann, 9 December 1932, all in BZR OA THN, Nr 98/2.
47 Siwek, 39.
48 Roos, *Weimar through the Lens of Gender*, 35–42, 184–92.

5. Catholic Miracles under the Third Reich

1 Zumholz, *Volksfrömmigkeit*.
2 Morsey, ed., *Fritz Gerlich*, 7–41; Feldmann, 82–94.
3 Ulrike Wiethaus, "Bloody Bodies: Gender, Religion, and the State in Nazi Germany," *Studies in Spirituality* 12 (2002): 189–202; Thomas Breuer, *Verordneter Wandel? Der Widerstreit zwischen nationalsozialistischem Herrschaftsanspruch und traditionaler Lebenswelt im Erzbistum Bamberg* (Mainz: Mattias-Grünewald-Verlag, 1992).
4 Michael E. O'Sullivan, "An Eroding Milieu? Catholic Youth, Church Authority, and Popular Behavior in Northwest Germany during the Third Reich, 1933–1938," *Catholic Historical Review* 90, no. 2 (April 2004): 236–59.
5 Hans Günter Hockerts, *Die Sittlichkeitsprozesse gegen die katholische Ordensangehörige und Priester 1936/1937. Eine Studie zur nationalsozialistischen Herrschaftstechnik und zum Kirchenkampf* (Mainz: F. Schöningh, 1971).
6 Kevin Spicer, *Hitler's Priests: Catholic Clergy and National Socialism* (Dekalb, IL: Northern Illinois University Press, 2008); Beth-Ann Griech Polelle, *Bishop von Galen: German Catholicism and National Socialism* (New Haven, CT: Yale University Press, 2002); Lauren Faulkner Rossi, *Wehrmacht Priests: Catholicism and the Nazi War of Annihilation* (Cambridge, MA: Harvard University Press, 2015).
7 Paul and Mallmann, *Milieus und Widerstand*.
8 "Lagebericht der Regierung (Juli 1934), Regensburg, 8. August 1934," in *Die Kirchliche Lage in Bayern nach den Regierungspräsidentenberichten 1933–1943 IV, Regierungsbezirk Niederbayern und Oberpfalz*, IV, ed. Walter Ziegler (Mainz: Mattias-Grünewald-Verlag, 1973), 31; Gendarmeriestation Konnersreuth an die politische Polizei, 25 July 1934, StaAm BT 4169; Von Guttenberg, 129–31.
9 Dr Witry, Metz to Westermayr, 4 November 1934, StaabiM Ana 338, NL Westermayr, Akten Westermayr Briefwechsel mit Vätern d. Gesellschaft Jesu; Deutsch to Wunderle, 15 November 1943, PdAW NL Wunderle, Dr Joseph Deutsch.

10 "Randbemerkungen zu Radlo"; "1940," Brühl to Westermayr, 1940, StaabiM NL Westermayr.
11 Teodorowicz, 108.
12 Teodorowicz and Westermayr, 10 January 1933, StaabiM NL Westermayr, Akten Westermayr 5: Briefwechsel mit Bischöfen.
13 Teodorowicz, 67.
14 Teodorowicz, 58.
15 Eric Kurlander, "Hitler's Monsters: The Occult Roots of Nazism and the Emergence of the Nazi 'Supernatural Imaginary,'" *German History* 30, no. 4 (2012): 528–49; Monica Black and Eric Kurlander, eds., *Revisiting the "Nazi Occult": Histories, Realities, and Legacies* (Rochester, NY: Camden House, 2015).
16 Teodorowicz, 503.
17 Ibid., 4–9.
18 Ulrike Wiethaus, *German Mysticism and the Politics of Culture* (New York: Peter Lang, 2014), 33.
19 Teodorowicz, 39, 97.
20 Deutsch, *Ärztliche Kritik am Konnersreuth*, 105–6.
21 Deutsch, *Ärztliche Kritik am Konnersreuth*, 3–5; Dr Karl Schmeing (Berlin) to Norbert Brühl, 7 April 1943, StaabiM NL Westermayr.
22 Deutsch to Wunderle 12 July 1937, PdAW NL Wunderle, "Josef Deutsch."
23 Deutsch to Vetter Bernard, 13 November 1936, PdAW NL Wunderle, Dr Josef Deutsch.
24 Michael Buchberger to Michael Faulhaber, 20 December 1936, BZR OA THN, Nr 112, 22–24.
25 Faulhaber to Gertrud von Zegschwitz, 11 October 1937, EAM NL Faulhaber 5946/2; Peter Radlo, *Trug oder Wahrheit. Neues über Konnersreuth* (Karlsruhe: Badenia, 1938), 123–6.
26 Radlo, 125–6.
27 Ibid., 160.
28 Ibid., 160–3, 173.
29 An die Herren Bischöfe, 1 January 1938, EAM NL Faulhaber 5946/2; "Dr Josef Deutsch," Deutsch to Vetter Bernard, 13 November 1936, PdAW NL Wunderle.
30 Radlo, 174.
31 "Randbermerkungen zu Radlo," StaabiM NL Westermayr.
32 "Aus dem Tagebuch eines Studierenden. Aufzeichnungen über Konnersreuth während eines sechswöchigen Aufenthaltes," July/August 1938, PdAW, NL Georg Wunderle.

33 "Ein wiederholter Besuch in Konnersreuth," 11 June 1937, EAM NL Faulhaber 5956/2, F. Nöpl.
34 "Randbemerkungen zu Radlo," StaabiM NL Westermayr.
35 "Auszug aus einem Brief v. Dr Karl Schmeing an Brühl," 7 April 1943, StaabiM NL Westermayr, Zerwürfnisse; Wiethaus, *German Mysticism*, 43; Feldmann, 88.
36 "Auszug aus einem Brief v. Dr Karl Schmeing an Brühl," 7 April 1943; Heinrich Muth to Brühl, 1 July 1943, all in StaabiM NL Westermayr, Zerwürfnisse; Monatsbericht der Regierung (März 1943) in *Die Kirchliche Lage in Bayern nach den Regierungspräsidentenberichten*, 318.
37 "Auszug aus einem Brief v. Dr Karl Schmeing an Brühl," 7 April 1943; Heinrich Muth to Brühl, 1 July 1943, all in StaabiM NL Westermayr, Zerwürfnisse; Josef Hanauer, *Der Schwindel von Konnersreuth: Ein Skandal ohne Ende?* (Regensburg: Eigenverl. der verf., 1989); Georg Denzler, "Achtung: Spontane Ekstasen," *FAZ* 8 April 1998, www.faz-archive.de.
38 Zumholz, *Volksfrömmigkeit*, 433–6.
39 Spiegl, 23.
40 Gendarmeriestation Konnersreuth an den Herrn Vorstand Bezirkamtes Tirschenreuth, 1 July 1933, StaAm BT4169.
41 "Monatsbericht der Regierung (Februar 1937), *Die kirchliche Lage in Bayern*, 117; Feldmann, 88.
42 Gendarmeriestation Konnersreuth an der Vorstand des Bezirksamts Tirschenreuth, 1 August 1938, StaAm BT 4169.
43 Ibid., 54.
44 Gendarmeriestation Konnersreuth an das Bezirksamt Tirschenreuth, 24 April 1935 and "Konnersreuth in trüben Lichte," *Konnersreuther Sonntagsblatt*, 17 March 1935, both in StaAm BT 4169.
45 Gendarmeriestation Konnersreuth an der Vorstand des Bezirksamts, 4 August 1938, StaAm BT 4169.
46 Gendarmeriestation Konnersreuth an den Herrn Vorstand des Bezirksamtes Tirschenreuth, 1 July 1933, StaAm BT 4169; Zumholz, *Volksfrömmigkeit*, 435; Wiethaus, *German Mysticism*, 157.
47 Heinrich Muth an Norbert Brühl, 27 August 1943, StaabiM, NL Westermayr, Zerwürfnisse in Konnersreuth Jahr 1943.
48 Josef Hanauer, *"Konnersreuth" eine ewige Lüge* (Regensburg: Eigenverlag, 2002).
49 "Der 'Konnersreuther Resl' als Zeugin," *Mittelbayerische Zeitung*, Ausgabe 112, 4 December 1948.
50 Morsey, *Fritz Gerlich*, 212, 232; von Lama, 201–5.

51 Erwein Freiherr von Aretin, *Das Bayerische Problem* (Munich: J. Lindauerische Universitätsbuchhandlung, 1924), 14, 26–7.
52 "Therese Neumann über die nächste Zukunft," 1947, StaabiM, Nachlass Westermayr; Steiner, 262–4.
53 Saul Friedländer, *The Years of Extermination: Nazi Germany and the Jews, 1939–1945* (New York: Harper, 2006), 58.
54 For a full account of such Catholics and the Holocaust, see Faulkner Rossi, *Wehrmacht Priests*.
55 PdAW NL Wunderle, "Josef Deutsch"; "Erinnerungen," 126–8, Fürstlich Waldburg-Zeil'sches Gesamtarchiv, Nachlass Fürst Erich von Waldburg-Zeil.
56 Erwein von Aretin, *Krone und Ketten: Erinnerungen eines bayerisches Edelmannes* (Munich: Süddeutscher Verlag, 1955), 15.
57 Zumholz, *Volksfrömmigkeit*, 440–3.
58 Karl du Prel, "Das Stigma und das 'Wunder' von Konnersreuth," *Völkischer Beobachter*, 31 August 1927.
59 Monatsbericht der Regierung (Februar 1938), *Die kirchliche Lage in Bayern*, 192.
60 "Therese Neumann: die stigmatisierte von Konnersreuth, Archiv für publizistische Arbeit," 24 December 1942, Bundesarchiv Berlin-Lichterfelde, NS 5-VI 17682 (Bestand deutsche Arbeitsfront).
61 Feldmann, 90–1.
62 Der Vorstand des Bezirksamts Tirschenreuth an die Bayerische Politische Polizei, 3 August 1935, StaAm BT 4169.
63 Ibid.
64 Toni Siegert, e-mail to the author, member of the historical commission for the beatification of Therese Neumann, 28 September 2013.
65 Andreas Kotulla, *"Nach Lourdes!" Der französische Marienwallfahrtsort und die Katholiken im Deutschen Kaiserreich, 1871–1914* (Munich: M Meidenbauer, 2006), 317–19; Eduard Aigner, *Die Wahrheit über eine Wunderheilung von Lourdes* (Frankfurt: Neue Frankfurter Verlag, 1908).
66 Eduard Aigner, *Zehn Jahre Konnersreuth* (Berlin: A. Bock Verlag, 1939), 86–92.
67 Eduard Aigner, "Zehn Jahre Konnersreuth," *Das Schwarze Korps*, 3 March and 10 March 1938.
68 "Erinnerungen," 126–8, Fürstlich Waldburg-Zeil'sches Gesamtarchiv, Nachlass Fürst Erich von Waldburg-Zeil.
69 Georg Wunderle to Cardinal Pacelli, 18 December 1936, PdAW, NL Wunderle.
70 Eduard Aigner, "Zehn Jahre Konnersreuth," *Das Schwarze Korps*, 10 March 1938.

71 "Bericht über die Ereignisse eines dreiwöchentlichen Aufenthaltes in Konnersreuth im Mai 1944 von Dr E. Aigner, Freiburg, PdAW, NL Wunderle.
72 Max Jordan, "Therese Neumann, Stigmatized Peasant Woman, Interviewed," *Arkansas Catholic*, 11 May 1945; Feldmann, 92–4; Spiegl 62–3.
73 Thomas Brodie, "The German Catholic Diaspora in the Second World War," *German History* 33, no. 1 (2015): 80–99.
74 AEK Gen I 4.30,1: Banneux.
75 Zumholz, *Volksfrömmigkeit*, 451.
76 Ibid., 20, 299, 325–7, 469.
77 Ibid., 21–5, 451.
78 Ibid., 327, 342, 488.
79 *Führer durch die Gebetsstätte der Unbefleckt empfangenen Mutter vom Sieg in Wigratzbad* (Wigratzbad: Selbstverlag des Vereins Maria v. Sieg e.V., 1977); Maunder, *Our Lady of Nations*, 103–6.
80 For more about von Galen, see Griech Polelle, *Bishop von Galen*; Joachim Kuropka, ed., *Clemens August Graf von Galen: Neue Forschungen zum Leben und Wirken des Bischofs von Münster* (Münster: Verlag Regensburg, 1993).
81 Peter Löffler, ed., *Bischof Clemens August Graf von Galen: Akten, Briefe und Predigten 1933–1946*, 2 vols. (Paderborn, Munich, Vienna, and Zurich: F. Schöningh, 1996); Predigt von Galens, 7 June 1942, Nr. 369; Die Reichsbahn Köln teilte dem Generalvikariat Münster am 15. Mai 1942; Nr. 369, SD-Bericht vom 23. Juli 1942, 949–52, Nr. 369.
82 Löffler, Bericht der Gestapoleitstelle Münster, 7 July 1942, Nr. 370.
83 Polizei und Sicherheitsdiensstellen- Geheime Staatspolizei-Polizeistelle Köln- Katholische Kirche, Betrifft: Pilgerfahrten zur Klosterkirche 'Marianwald' b/ Heimbach (Eifel), 7 July 1943, Hauptstaatsarchiv Düsseldorf (HStAD) RW 34–3.
84 Hans-Dieter Arnzt, ed., *Kriegsende 1944/1945: Zwischen Ardenne und Rhein* (Euskirchen: Kümpel Verlag, 1984), 144–7.
85 Betrifft: Weihe der Stadt und des Bistums Aachen an die Gottesmutter am 23.5.1943, 8 May 1943; Betrifft: Weihe der Diözese Aachen an die Gottesmutter, 1 June 1943; Betrifft: Weihe der Diözese Aachen an die Gottesmutter. Bericht über die Feierlichkeiten im Dom zu Aachen am 23.5.1943, 1 June 1943, all in HStAD RW 35–9.
86 See Christoph Allroggen, "Ein Marsch durch die Hölle," in *Priester in Uniform: Seelsorger, Ordensleute und Theologen als Soldaten im Zweiten Weltkrieg*, ed. Hans Jürgen Brandt (Augsburg: Pattloch Verlag, 1994), 41.
87 Betrifft: Stimmung im kath. Klerus, 26 May 1944, HStAD RW 35–9.

88 Betrifft: Konfessionelle Greuelpropaganda, 16 June 1943, HStAD RW 35–9.
89 Kettenbriefe, 1941–44, EAM NL Faulhaber 5950.

6. Marian Apparitions during the Early Federal Republic

1 Sandra Simdars-Swartz, *Encountering Mary: Visions of Mary from La Salette to Medjugorje* (Princeton, NJ: Princeton University Press, 1991); Paula M. Kane, "Marian Devotion since 1940: Continuity or Casualty?" in *Habits of Devotion: Catholic Religious Practice in Twentieth-Century America*, ed. James M. O'Toole (Ithaca, NY and London: Cornell University Press, 2004), 89–129; Maunder, *Our Lady of Nations*, 122–35.
2 From 1937–54 the Virgin Mary appeared four times in Bavaria, four times in the Rhineland, two times in the Palatinate, once in the Emsland, and once in the Swabian region of Württemberg. Monique Scheer, *Rosenkranz und Kriegsvisionen: Marienerscheinungskulte im 20. Jahrhundert* (Tübingen: Tübinger Vererinigung für Volkskunde, 2006), 18–19, 169–70.
3 Scheer, *Rosenkranz und Kriegsvisionen*; Cornelia Gösku, *Heroldsbach: Eine verbotene Wallfahrt* (Wurzburg: Echter, 1991).
4 Monica Black, "Miracles in the Shadow of the Economic Miracle: The 'Supernatural '50s' in West Germany," *Journal of Modern History* 84, no. 4 (December 2012): 833–60.
5 Mitchell, *The Origins of Christian Democracy*, 86–99; Michael Phayer, *Pius XII, the Holocaust, and the Cold War* (Bloomington and Indianapolis: University of Indiana Press, 2008).
6 Wilhelm Damberg, *Abscheid von Milieu*; Ruff, *The Wayward Flock*.
7 Mitchell, *Origins of Christian Democracy*, 77–85; Adam Seipp, *Strangers in a Wild Place: Refugees, Americans, and a German Town, 1945–1952* (Bloomington, IN: University of Indiana Press, 2013).
8 Rey, "Marketing the Goods of Salvation."
9 Till van Rahden, "Clumsy Democrats: Moral Passions in the Federal Republic," *German History* 29, no. 3 (2011): 485–504.
10 Göksu, 30–6, 39, 45, 47, 60; Johann Baptist Walz, *Die Protokolle von Augenzeugen zu den 'Muttergottes-Erscheinungen' von Heroldsbach-Thurn. Von Anfang an bis zum 2. Römischen Dekret*, Band I, (Mönchengladbach, 1958), 28–9.
11 Scheer, 207–45.
12 Göksu, 41.
13 Ibid., 68–70.
14 For more on the culture of this borderland in Bavaria, see Yuliya Komska, *The Icon Curtain: The Cold War's Quiet Border* (Chicago and London: University of Chicago Press, 2015).

15 For more on the concept of popular theologians, see Maunder, *Our Lady of the Nations*, 109–21.
16 Walz, *Die Protokolle*, 30–4.
17 Fritz Müller, Offener Brief an Seiner Heiligkeit Papst Pius XII, 1952, and "Hoffentlich hält der Westfale stand!" AEK Gen II 31,6a 1: Heroldsbach.
18 Fritz Müller, Maria weint….!/ Katholischer Existenzialismus? 15 January 1954, AEK Gen II 31,6a 2: Heroldsbach Teil II.
19 Band I "Niederschrift" 6 October 1950, BHSAM, Justizministerium (MJu) 23795 Vorgänge in Heroldsbach, Alle Vorgänge.
20 "Heroldsbacher Geschäfte mit mystischen Blut," *Passauer Neue Press Niederbayerische Zeitung* (PNP) Ausgabe 5, 7 January 1957; Black, "Miracles in the Shadow of the Economic Miracle," 849, 853.
21 Faulkner Rossi, 115–17, 232–9.
22 Breuer, 195; Ruff, *The Wayward Flock*, 144–51; Tobias Dietrich, *Konfession im Dorf. Westeuropäische Erfahrungen im 19. Jahrhundert* (Cologne: Böhlau, 2004).
23 "Der Skandal von Heroldsbach: Sensationelle Enthüllungen über die Hintergrunde einer Massenpsychose," *8. Uhr Blatt: Die Illustrierte Abendzeitung*, 30 September 1950, BHSAM, MJu 2379, Vorgänge in Heroldsbach, Alle Vorgänge, Band I-III.
24 Wunderbare Erscheinungen, 1.1.1952–21.12.1959, II. Teil., AEK Gen II 31.6,4; Gösku, *Heroldsbach*, 13–23, 24–9, 36–7, 62–5, 75–8, 81–7.
25 Bishop Otto Kolb to Muench, 19 June 1953, The American Catholic History Research Center and University Archives (CUA), Aloisius Muench Papers, Box 42, Folder 28: Surveys, Bamberg 19, 1947–54.
26 Der Oberstaatsanwalt bei dem Landgricht Bamberg an den Herrn Generalstaatsanwalt in Bamberg, 30 July 1952, BHSAM MJu 23795.
27 "Tumult an Wallfahrtsort," *Neue Illustrierte*, 25 October 1950, 8.
28 Landpolizei Ober- und Mittelfranken Bezirksinspektion Forchheim an die Oberstaatsanwaltschaft beim Landgericht Bamberg, 25 September 1951, BHSAM, MJu 23795.
29 Der Direktor der Nervenklinik der Universität München, 10 October 1954, BHSAM, MuJ 23797 Walter Dettmann; "Der Eilzug nach Bamberg," *Der Spiegel*, vol. 6, 2 February 1955, 9–10, www.spiegel.de.
30 "Der Skandal von Heroldsbach: Sensationelle Enthüllungen über die Hintergrunde einer Massenpsychose," *8. Uhr Blatt: Die Illustrierte Abendzeitung*, 30 September 1950; and Der Oberstaatsanwalt bei dem Landgericht Bamberg an den Herrn Generalstaatsanwalt bei dem Oberlandsgericht, 6 October 1950, both in BHSAM, MJu 23795.

31 Bayerische Landpolizei-Landpolizeiinspektion Forchheim an die Landpolizeidirektion Ober- und Mittel Franken, 21 May 1953, BHSAM, MJu 23796.
32 Werner Blessing, "'Deutschland in Not, wir im Glauben…' Kirche und Kirchenvolk in einer katholischen Region 1933–1949," in *Von Stalingrad zur Währungsreform. Zur Sozialgeschichte des Umbruchs in Deutschland*, ed. Martin Broszat, Klaus-Dietmar Henke, and Hans Woller (Munich: Oldenbourg, 1988), 17.
33 Scheer, 227–45.
34 "Die vergewaltigte Demokratie" and "Heroldsbacher Prozess oder viel Lärm um nichts" *Der Bote von Heroldsbach*, 10 September 1952, BHSAM, MJu 23795; Staatsanwaltschaft bei dem Landgericht Nürnberg-Fürth an das Schöffengericht Nürnberg, 1 April 1953, MJu 23796.
35 Fritz Müller, Generalangriff für Heroldsbach: Entweder Reden oder verdammt werden, 1952, AEK Gen. II 31.6a; "Das Lied des Obergefreiten: Marien-Erscheinungen," *Der Spiegel*, 17 September 1952, 8–9; Rainer Moltmann, *Reinhold Heinen (1894–1969) Ein christlicher Politiker, Journalist und Verleger* (Düsseldorf: Droste, 2005), 189–190.
36 Scheer, 208–9.
37 Mark Edward Ruff, *The Battle for the Catholic Past in Germany, 1945–1980* (Cambridge: Cambridge University Press, 2017), 83.
38 Der Oberstaatsanwalt bei dem Landgericht Bamberg, 27 July 1953, BHSAM, MJu 23796.
39 Frank Biess, *Homecomings: Returning POWs and the Legacies of Defeat in Postwar Germany* (Princeton, NJ and Oxford: Princeton University Press, 2006), 56–8, 98–109.
40 Kaufmann, 97–113.
41 Ute Poiger, *Jazz, Rock, and Rebels: Cold War Politics and American Culture in a Divided Germany* (Berkeley, Los Angeles, and London: University of California Press, 2000), 72–9; Ruff, *Wayward Flock*, 58–77; Frank Biess, "Survivors of Totalitarianism: Returning POWs and the Reconstruction of Masculine Citizenship in West Germany," in *The Miracle Years: A Cultural History of West Germany, 1949–1968*, ed. Hannah Schissler, 57–82.
42 "Schlagerei auf dem Heroldsbacher Erscheinungshügel," *PNP* 116, 26 July 1955 and "Berganhänger werden politisch," 127, 17 August 1953, p. 8; Der Direktor der Nervenklinik der Universität München, 10 October 1954, BHSAM, MJu 23797.
43 Staatsanwaltschaft bei dem Landgerichte Nürnberg-Fürth an das Schöffengericht Nürnberg, 1 April 1953, BHSAM, MJu 23796.
44 "Heller Schein in gelben Laub," *Der Spiegel*, 44, 27 October 1949, 31–2.

45 Der Oberstaatsanwalt bei dem Landgericht Bamberg an Generalstaatsanwalt bei dem Oberlandesgericht, 10 January 1952, BHSAM, MJu 23795.

46 Der Oberstaatsanwalt bei dem Landgerichte Bamberg an Generalstaatsanwalt bei dem Oberlandesgericht, 10 January 1952; Der Oberstaatsanwalt bei dem Landgericht Bamberg an den Herrn Generalstaatsanwalt in Bamberg, 15 February 1952, both in BHSAM, MJu 23795; "Opfergroschen rollten in unbekannte Kanäle," *Die Neue Zeitung* 19 February 1952, EAM NL Faulhaber 5955: Heroldsbach, Privatoffenbarungen, Marienerscheinungen.

47 Maunder, *Our Lady of the Nations*, 132–4.

48 Dr Scholler an Pilger Druckerei Speyer, 29 May 1952, Bistumsarchiv Speyer (BaS) BO NA 23/10 1/49: Fehrbach; Gösku, *Heroldsbach*, 114–15.

49 Ein Fehrbacher an Seine Exzellenz den Hochwürdigsten Herrn Bischof von Speyer Dr Josef Wendel, 16 September 1950, AEK Gen. II 31.6,1.

50 Schriftleitung *Der christliche Pilger: Bistumsblatt für die Diözese Speyer*, 10 August 1950; Abschrift, Dr Fritz Nees, Rechtsanwalt Mainz, 1951, both in BaS, BO NA 23/10 1/49.

51 Scheer, 200–1.

52 Ein Fehrbacher an Seine Exzellenz den Hochwürdigsten Herrn Bischof von Speyer Dr Josef Wendel, 16 September 1950, AEK 31.6,1.

53 "Anhänger von Fehrbach," Heinrich Kuntz (Fehrbach) an Bischofl. Ord. Speyer, 23 July 1950; "Andere Diöseze und Fehrbach," Kath. Pfarramt Murg (Baden) an Bischofl. Ordinariat Speyer, 32.11.1951; Fehrbach Rosa Haber, Anna Klein, et. al. an Bischofl. Ordinariat, September 1950, all in BaS, BO NA 23/10 1/49.

54 Maria Höhn, *GIs and Fräuleins: The German-American Encounter in 1950s West Germany* (Chapel Hill and London: University of North Carolina Press, 2002), 22–5, 116–17.

55 "Anhänger von Fehrbach," Robert Vath an Bischolfl. Ordinariat, September 1950, BaS, BO NA 23/10, 1/49; Scheer, 202.

56 Geschwister Peter (Helene Peter and Frau Knappo) an Hochw. Herr Böhm, St. Ingbert/Saar, 16 February 1952; Abschrift, Dr Fritz Nees, Rechtanwalt in Mainz, 1951, both in BaS, BO NA 23/10, 1/49.

57 Anton Sittl to Cardinal Frings, 16 September 1951, AEK 31.6,1.

58 Josef Locher an den Vorsitzenden der Fuldaer Bischofskonferenz 1951, Seine Eminenz den Hochwürdigsten Herrn Kardinal Frings von Köln, 11 June 1951, AEK 31.6,1.

59 M J-H. an Hochw. Bishofl. Ordinariat, Fehrbach, 15 October 1952, BaS, BO NA 23/10, 1/49.

60 Rosa Haber, Anna Klein, et al. an Bischofl. Ordinariat, September 1950; Kath. Pfarramt Eußerthal-Pfalz an Hochw. Bischof, betrf. Bekehrung H. Mangold in Fehrbach, 25 April 1951; An das katholisches Pfarramt Fehrbach, 17 January 1952, both in BaS, BO NA 23/10 1/49 Fehrbach.
61 Höhn, *GIs and Fräuleins*.
62 Das Erzbischöfliche Generalvikariat, Generalvikar Teusch an Erzbistum Köln, 5 September 1952; Generalvikar Teusch an den Hochwürdigen Herren Dechanten der Dekanate Bensberg, Neunkirchen, Wipperfürth, Gummersbach und Remscheid mit der Bitte um baldige Weitergabe an alle Welt- und Ordensgeistliche Ihres Dekanates, 10 September 1952; Bericht über die Vorgänge in Nieder-Habbach am Montag, den 8. September 1952, Direktor Dabiels, Bensberg, 9 September 1952; "Tausende Warteten auf eine 'Erscheinung:' Habbach, der Ort, der plötzlich von Menschen überfullt war," *Kölner Stadt-Anzeiger*, 9 Septemerb 1952, 8; "Viele sagten: Ich habe das Zeichen gesehen! 5000 bei der Marienerscheinung in Habbach- Nur Ziganke sah hl. Maria," *WNP*, 9 September 1952, all in AEK Gen. II 31.6,4.
63 Robert Moeller, *War Stories: The Search for a Usable Past in the Federal Republic of Germany* (Berkeley: University of California Press, 2001).
64 Bericht über die Vorgänge in Nieder-Habbach am Montag, den 8. September 1952, Bensberg, Direktor Daniels, AEK Gen. II 31.6,4; "Das Lied des Obergefreiten," *Der Spiegel*.
65 Pfarramt Rodalben, 17 January 1952, Bericht über A. Wafzig und. S. Ransberger; Kathol. Pfarramt Rodalben an Herr Bischof, 14 December 1951; S. Ransberger an Bischof Josef Wendel, Teilprotokol über die Erscheinungen, 1 February 1952; Scheer, 392, all in BaS BO NA 23/10 2/51: Rodalben.
66 Polizeiverwaltung/Rodalben, 1 July 1952; Augenzeugenbericht über die Vorgänge in Rodalben, Rheinpfalz bei Pirmasens von Pater Augustinus a S. Maria (Wolfgang Kimmel) O.C.D.; Augenzeugen Bericht über die Vorgänge in der Nacht vom 1. auf 2. Juli 1952 in Rodalben, Rheinpfalz von P. Gebhard Heyder O.C.D., all in BaS BO NA 23/10 2/51.
67 S. Ransberger an Bischof Josef Wendel, 1 February 1952; Bischöfl. Ordinariat an Provinzialat der Unb. Karmeliten, Munich, 18 August 1952; Anton Fischer an Bischof Dr Isidor Emmanual Speyer, 6 August 1954, all in BaS BO NA 23/10 2/51 Rodalben.
68 For a description of Johannes Maria Höcht, another former concentration camp survivor turned apparition activist, see Scheer, 372–84.
69 Kolpingsfamilie, 21 January 1953, BaS BO NA 23/10 2/51.
70 Aktennotiz, 27 October 1952, BaS BO NA 23/10 2/51.
71 Blackbourn, *Marpingen*, 30–1.

72 "Erscheinungen um jedem Preis?" *Der christlicher Pilger: Bistumsblatt für die Diözese Speyer*, 25 May 1952, BaS BO NA 23/10 2/51; "Anhänger von Fehrbach," Dr Fritz Nees (Rechtsanwalt Mainz) an den Herrn Schriftleiter des Bistumsblattes *Der christlicher Pilger*, 31 May 1952, BaS BO NA 23/10 1/49.
73 Scheer, 144–60.
74 Peregrinatio Mariae durch das Erzbistum Köln-Berichte und Korrespondenzen über Vorbereitung, Durchführung und Wirkungen, Bericht über den Verlauf der Peregrinatio Mariae in der Erzdiözese Köln im Marianischen Jahr 1954, AEK Seelsorgeamt Heinen (SH) 104.
75 Maria an Hochwürdigste Herr Erzbischof, 14 May 1950, AEK Gen. II 31.6,1.
76 "Aufruf zum geistlichen Kreuzzug!" Fritz Homberg August 1946, AEK Gen. II 31.6,2.
77 Peregrinatio Mariae durch das Erzbistum Köln- Allgemeine Korrespondenzen A-K, An die *Katholische Kirchenzeitung des Erzbistums Köln*, 12 September 1953, AEK SH 102.
78 Peregrinatio Mariae das Erzbistum Köln- Berichte und Korrespndenzen über Vorbereitung, Durchführung und Wirkungen, Fatimatag in Brühl, no date, but probably May 1954, AEK SH 104.
79 Fatimatag in Brühl, May 1954; Düsseldorf St Maximillian, 17–18 May 1954, both in AEK SH 104.
80 Früchte des marianischen Jahres und deren Erhaltung, no date, no author, AEK SH 104.
81 Solingen-Wald, 31 May–1 June 1954, AEK SH 105.
82 Remscheid, St. Suibertus, 4–5 June 1954, AEK SH 104.
83 Bezirksschulrat to Cardinal Frings, 4 September 1954, AEK SH 102.
84 Mülheim/Ruhr St. Mariä Geburt, 12–14 June 1954, AEK SH 105.
85 Solingen-Gräfrath, no date, AEK SH 105.
86 Mit der Pilgerfahrt quer durch Deutschland von P. Karl Pfister MSJ, AEK SH 103.
87 "Stadt und Dekanat Euskirchen hören die Botschaft von Fatima," AEK SH 104.
88 "Unsere Liebe Frau von Fatima auf Pilgerfahrt in 'Der Weinberg,'" by Josef Steundebach, OMI, AEK SH 104.
89 Mülheim/Ruhr, 7–8 June 1954, AEK SH 105.
90 Bezirksschulrat an Kardinal Frings, 4 September 1954, AEK SH 102.
91 "Mit der Pilgerfahrt quer durch Deutschland," by P. Karl Pfister MSJ, AEK SH 103.
92 "Botschaft von Fatima für Erzdiözese Köln: Kardinal Frings predigte am Vorabend des 1. Mai vor katholischen Arbeitern," *Kölnische Rundschau*, 1 May 1954, AEK SH 105.

93 Heinen to Rektor Wilhelm Antins in Alzen, 3 February 1955, AEK SH 102.
94 Pfarramt Leverkusen-Wiesedorf, 24 August 1954, AEK SH 105.
95 Robert Moeller, *Protecting Motherhood: Women and the Family in the Politics of Postwar West Germany* (Berkeley: University of California Press, 1993); Elizabeth Heineman, *What Difference Does a Husband Make? Women and Marital Status in Nazi and Post-War Germany* (Berkeley: University of California Press, 2003); Höhn, *GIs and Fräuleins*.
96 Rey, "Marketing the Goods," 337–8.

7. Between Catholic Traditionalism, Cold War, and Economic Miracle

1 Julia Edwards, "Pilgrims See Phenomenon of Stigmata," *Stars and Stripes Europe Edition (SSEE)*, vol. 2, nr. 112, 27 March 1948, 1.
2 Therese Neumann, Dr. jur. Herrn Mersmann an Erzbischof Buchberger in Regensburg, April 1953, AEK, Gen. II 31.9, 1; "10,000 Menschen in Konnersreuth: Eigener Bericht," *Frankfurter Allgemeine Zeitung (FAZ)*, 28 March 1959; "Thousands Visit Home of Therese Neumann and Witness Phenomenon on Good Friday," *New York Times (NYT)*, 27 May 1948.
3 Max Jordan, "Therese Neumann and Prophecies," *The Guardian: The Official Organ of the Diocese of Little Rock*, 9 March 1951, 4, http://arc.stparchive.com/; "Resl von Konnersreuth lebt," *Mittelbayerische Zeitung (MZ)* Ausgabe 93, 21 November 1947, 5, http://digipress.digitale-sammlungen.de.
4 Scheer, 372–84.
5 Johannes Maria Höcht, "Sturmrufe Mariens an die bedrohte Welt," *Konnersreuther Lesebogen (KL)* Nr 2/3, 1949; "Atomkrieg oder- Umkehr? Drohende Weltlage und Sturmrufe der Gnade," 4, 1949.
6 Johannes Maria Höcht, "Wundmale, Kreuzopfer und wesentliches Christentum," *KL* 2/3, 1949; "Der Einbruch der übernaturlichen in unserer Zeit," 1, 1949; "Karfreitag in Konnersreuth," 2:10, May 1950.
7 Mitchell, *Origins of Christian Democracy*, 76–125.
8 Dr jur. Herrn Mersmann an Erzbischof Buchberger, 3 April 1952, AEK, Gen. II 31.9, 1; Luise Rinser, *Die Wahrheit über Konnersreuth. Ein Bericht* (Frankfurt: Fischer, 1953), 173–4.
9 Adalbert Albert Vogl, *Therese Neumann: Mystic and Stigmatist, 1898–1962* (Rockford: Tan Books and Publishers, 1987), 103.
10 Graef, 153.
11 Steiner, *Therese Neuman*. 66–73; Rinser, *Die Wahrheit*, 140–50; Noreen von Zwehl, *America Salutes Therese Neumann. Testimonials of WWII Servicemen* (Staten Island, NY: Publisher, 1999); Helmut Witetschek, *Pater Ingbert Naab, O.F.M. Cap. (1885–1935). Ein Prophet wider den Zeitgeist* (Munich:

Schnell und Steiner, 1985), 42–5; Zumholz, "Die Resistenz," 221-34; Erwein Freiherr von Aretin, "Therese Neumann von Konnersreuth," *Passauer neue Presse (PNP)*, 6 November 1946.

12 "Die Therese prophezeit nicht," *Der Spiegel*, 30 August 1947; Max Jordan, "Therese Neumann and Prophecies," *Guardian*, 9 March 1951; "Resl von Konnersreuth lebt," *MZ* 93, 21 November 1947, 5.

13 "Eine Klarstellung betr. Konnersreuth," *KL* 18, 1950, 2.

14 Werner Kraus, "Vor 25 Jahren began eine wundersame Passion," *Süddeutsche Zeitung (SZ)* Nr. 82, 10 April 1951, 3, Archiv für Christlich-Soziale Politik (ACSP), Nachlass (NL) Josef Müller, S78.

15 Surveys of the Church in Germany, Dioceses Regensburg, 1950–4, CUA Munech Papers, Box 44, Folder 7.

16 Steiner, *Therese Neumann*, 73.

17 Von Zwehl, 53; Steiner, *Therese Neumann*, 66–73.

18 "Wounds Stop Bleeding; Mystic Too Ill for Easter Vistors," *Pacific Stars and Stripes* 8 April 1954, 2; Max Jordan, "Therese Neumann Injures Stigmata on Hands, Suffers Lung Bleeding in Fall– Improves," *Guardian*, 8 September 1950, 8; Placid Jordan, OSB, "Crowd on Hand to see suffering of Stigmatic," *Guardian* 26 April 1957, 1; "Ostertage brachten wieder Rekordreiseverkehr," *PNP* 73, 31 March 1959.

19 Luise Rinser, *Die Wahrheit über Konnersreuth;* Luise Rinser, "Die Wahrheit über Konnersreuth," *KL* 5:9, September 1953, 125–6.

20 Rößler, 7.

21 Naber to Faulhaber, 9 March 1932, EAM NL Faulhaber 5945/3.

22 Reverend F. Thomas, *The Mystery of Konnersreuth: Facts, Personal Experiences, Critical Remarks* (Los Angeles: Kessinger Legacy Reprints, 1940), 138.

23 Elizabeth Marable Brennan, *Visits to Theresa Neumann* (New York: Paulist Press, 1936), 17–21; Paula Kane, "Stigmatic Cults and Pilgrimage: The Convergence of Private and Public Faith," in *Christian Homes: Religion, Family, and Domesticity in the 19th and 20th Centuries*, ed. Patrick Pasture and Tine van Osselaer (Leuven: Lueven University Press, 2015), 105–25; Thomas Tweed, *America's Church: The National Shrine and Catholic Presence in the Nation's Capital* (New York and Oxford: Oxford University Press, 2011), 73–8.

24 Graymoor to Faulhaber, 24 September 1936, NL Faulhaber 5946/1, Father General Francis; "Therese Neumann, Famous Stigmatist, is Interviewed; Refused Food Tickets," *Guardian*, 22 December 1939, 2.

25 Msgr. Thos. J. Prendergast, "1st American Chaplain to Meet Mystic, Theresa Neumann, Visits in Little Rock," *Guardian*, 26 October 1945, 7; Max

Jordan, "Therese Neumann and Prophecies," *Guardian* 9 March 1951, 4; Vogl, 64–5, 71–3.

26 Gerd Horton, *Radio Goes to War: The Cultural Politics of Propaganda during World War II* (Berkeley: University of California Press, 2003), 30–1; Ken Cuthberstson, *A Complex Fate: William L. Shirer and the American Century* (Montreal and Kingston: McGill-Queen's University Press, 2015), 152.

27 Ruff, *The Battle for the Catholic Past*, 140, 144, 147; Max Jordan, *Beyond All Fronts: A Bystander's Notes on This Thirty Years' War* (Milwaukee, WI: Bruce, 1945), 302.

28 Max Jordan, "Therese Neumann, Stigmatized Peasant Woman, Interviewed," *Guardian*, 11 May 1945, 3; Max Jordan, "Ecstatic Visions Ascribed to Stigmatic," *Guardian* 29 October 1949,

29 Suzanne Brown-Fleming, *The Holocaust and Catholic Conscience: Cardinal Aloisius Muench and the Guilt Question in Germany* (South Bend, IN: University of Notre Dame Press, 2006).

30 Jordan to Muench, 4 December 1950, CUA Muench Papers, Box 12, Folder: Clergy and Religious: Priests, U.S., Placid (Max) Jordan, Rev, 1946–50.

31 Graef, 42.

32 Jordan to Muench, 3 July 1951, CUA, Muench Papers, Folder 15; Max Jordan, "Arguments Proposed in Konnersreuth Case Reflect Only One Side, Writer Finds," *Guardian*, 8 June 1951, 5; Max Jordan, "Reviews of Konnersreuth Book Take Author's Own Theories as Proven Fact, Writer Says," *Guardian*, 15 June 1951, 5.

33 Rev Francis Lally to John Hall, 1951; John McHale to Frank Hall, 16 June 1951, both in CUA, National Catholic News Service (NCNS) Records, Box 27, Folder 15: Therese Neumann.

34 "Coverage of Konnersreuth Controversy Brings Praise," 29 July 1951; George Fangauer to Frank Hall, 22 September 1951, Fangauer, "The Case of Therese Neumann," 1951, all in CUA, NCNS Records, Box 27, Folder 15: Therese Neumann.

35 John Ross-Dugan to Msgr. Carrol, 13 June 1951, CUA, NCNS Records, Box 27, Folder 15.

36 Julia Edwards, "Pilgrims See Phenomena of Stigmata," *SSEE* 2:112, 1–2; "Americans Flock Bedside of Therese Neumann," *Guardian*, 23 March 1951, 8.

37 Msgr Thos. J. Prendergast, "Twenty Years without Water," *Guardian*, 28 November 1947, 5; Msgr Thos. J. Prendergast, "1st American Chaplain to Meet Mystic, Theresa Neumann, Visits in Little Rock," *Guardian*, 26 October 1945, 7.

38 Von Zwehl, 52–8, 82, 90; "Furlough Facts,"*SSEE*, 24 February 1951, 4.

39 Vogl, *Therese Neumann*, 71–8.
40 Von Zwehl, 65–77.
41 "Devout, Ailing Visit the Maid of Konnersreuth,"*SSEE*, 18 April 1949, 7.
42 Von Zwehl, 51, 68, 97.
43 Ian Connor, "The Churches and the Refugee Problem in Bavaria 1945–1949" *Journal of Contemporary History* 20 (1985): 399–421.
44 Guttenberg, 260–1.
45 Siwek, 35; Spiegl, 68.
46 Von Zwehl, 47; Vogl, 64–5.
47 "Therese Neumann Calls Prophecies Attributed to her Fabrications; Baroness Tells of her Denial," 5 March 1951, NCWC Service, CUA, NCNS Therese Neumann Box 27, Folder 15.
48 "Yanks Aid Village Congregation," *SSEE* Friday, 1 November 1957, 8; "Stigmatic's Plea Brings Army Help," *Guardian*, 6 December 1957, 8.
49 Vogl, 64–5.
50 "Ein 'Fliegergruss' für Therese Neumann," *PNP* 69, 11 June 1952, 3.
51 Baroness Elisabeth Guttenberg to Frank A. Hall, 26 January 1951, CUA, NCNS Box 19 Folder Baroness Elisabeth Guttenberg, 1951; Max Jordan, "Therese Neumann, Stigmatized Peasant Woman, Interviewed," *Guardian*, 11 May 1945, 3.
52 "Erklärung," 27 January 1946, ACSP, Nachlass Ferdinand Neumann.
53 "CSU-Abgeordneter Neumann kritisiert Parteikollegen," ACSP, NL Neumann.
54 Friedolin Goetz (Freising) to F Neumann, 31 August 1948; Fritz Vonficht to F Neumann, 18 May 1946, both in ACSP, NL Neumann.
55 Anton Schuller to Muench, 9 September 1946; John F. Orzel, Office of the Catholic Chaplain, 7 October 1946 to Muench, 7 October 1946; Anny Schuller to Muench, 25 November 1946; Anny Schuller an Muench, 10 December 1946, all in CUA, Muench Papers, Box 8, Folder 2, Correspondence with Kemnath officials.
56 Therese Neumann to Josef Müller, 12 December 1946, ACSP, NL Müller S78.
57 Josef Müller, *Bis zur letzten Konsequenz. Ein Leben für Frieden und Freiheit* (Munich: Süddeutscher Verlag, 1975), 322–4, 329; Mark Riebling, *Church of Spies: The Pope's Secret War against Hitler* (New York: Basic Books, 2015); Friedrich Hermann Hettler, *Josef Müller ("Ochsensepp"), Mann des Widerstandes und erster CSU-Vorsitzender* (Munich: Stadtarchiv Munich, 1991), 274–80.
58 Graham Ford, "Constructing a Regional Identity: The Christian Social Union and Bavaria's Common Heritage, 1949–1962," *Contemporary European History* 16, no. 3 (August 2007): 277–97.

59 Thomas Schlemmer, *Aufbruch, Krise und Erneuerung. Die Christlich-Soziale Union 1945 bis 1955* (Munich: R. Oldenbourg Verlag, 1998), 269–80.
60 Dr Alois Hundhammer to F. Neumann, 25 August 1947; Alois Hundhammer to Naber, 1 September 1947, both in CSU Archive, NL Ferdinand Neumann; "Therese Neumann bedauert," *PNP* 69, 2 September 1947, 4.
61 "Redaktur wegen Beleidigung Hundhammer verurteilt," *PNP* 260, 10 November 1964; "Alois Hundhammer," *Der Spiegel* 17, 22 April 1964, 126.
62 Schlemmer, 262.
63 "Wer ist schuldig?" *Der Spiegel* 16, 13 April 1955; "Der Spiegel berichtete" *Der Spiegel* 8, 20 February 1957, and 40, 3 October 1956; "Zeugen verwickeln sich in Widersprüche," *PNP* 200, 22 November 1956; "Neue Verhandlung in Trausteiner Weinschieberprozess," *PNP*, 10 June 1959; "Meineidsanklage im Weinschieberprozess untermauert," *PNP* 195, 16 November 1956, 3; "Ehemaliger Polizeipräsidents des Meineids angeklagt," *PNP* 109, 13 May 1958.
64 Josef Hanauer, *Konnersreuth als Testfall. Kritischer Bericht über das Leben der Therese Neumann* (Munich: Manz Verlag, 1972), 197–206.
65 Mark E. Spicka, "Gender, Political Discourse, and the CDU/CSU Vision of the Economic Miracle, 1949–1957," *German Studies Review* 25, no. 2 (May 2002): 305–32.
66 Graef, 153.
67 Spiegl, 63–5; Vogl, 107–9, Steiner, *Therese Neumann*, 96–9.
68 "Wer ist Schuldig?" *Der Spiegel*; "Therese Neumann," *Der Spiegel* 45, 6 November 1957.
69 Spiegl, 65–6, Steiner, *Therese Neumann*, 98–100.
70 Spicka, "Gender, Political Discourse, and the CDU/CSU Vision."
71 Heineman, *What Difference Does a Husband Make*?
72 Siwek, 57.
73 Meiwes, *"Arbeiterinnen des Herrn*.
74 Spiegl, XV; Connelly, 211–16; Ruff, *The Battle for the Catholic Past*, 145.

Conclusion

1 Kimba Allie Tichenor, *Religious Crisis and Civic Transformation: How Conflicts over Gender and Sexuality Changed the West German Catholic Church* (Waltham, Mass: Brandeis University Press, 2016).
2 Judith Samson, "EU Criticism in Two Transnational Marian Anti-Abortion Movements," in *Gender, Nation, and Religion in European Pilgrimage*, ed. Willy Jansen and Catrien Notermans (Surrey, England: Ashgate, 2012), 71–88.

3 "Kardinal beim Kaffeeplausch.," Onetz, September 7, 2016, www.onetz.de.
4 Detlef Pollack and Olaf Müller, "Churchliness, Religiosity, and Spirituality: Western and Eastern European Societies in Times of Religious Diversity," in *What the World Believes: Analyses and Commentary on the Religion Monitor 2008*, ed. Bertelsmann (Gütersloh: Bertelsmann Stiftung, 2009), 399–416; Detlef Pollack, Olaf Müller, and Gert Pickel, "The Religious Landscape in Germany: Secularizing West – Secularized East," in *The Social Significance of Religion in the Enlarged Europe: Secularization, Individualization, and Pluralization*, ed. Detlef Pollack, Olaf Müller, and Gert Pickel (Surrey, England: Ashgate, 2012).
5 Georg Schwager, personal interview, 13 June 2013.
6 Chris Maunder, "Mapping the Presence of Mary: Germany's Apparition Sites," *Journal of Contemporary Religion* 28, no. 1 (2013): 79–93.
7 Schneider, *Maria und Lourdes*, 1.
8 Helmut Zander, "Maria erscheint in Sievernich. Plausibilitätsbedingungen eines katholischen Wunders," in *Wunder: Poetik und Politik des Stauens im 20. Jahrhundert*, ed. Alex C.T. Geppert and Till Kösller (Berlin: Suhrkamp, 2011), 146–76; Albert Schäffer, "Heroldsbach: Keine Tränenwunder- nur Wasser," *FAZ*, 30 November 2007.
9 Hape Kerkeling, *I'm Off Then: Losing and Finding Myself on the Camino de Santiago* trans. Shelley Frisch (New York: Free Press, 2009), 9.
10 Mark Landler, "A Pilgrimage Tale (Not Chaucer's) Amuses and Inspires," *NYT*, 8 March 2008; Ronald Reng, "Hat Hape Kerkeling die Jakobsweg ruiniert?" *SZ Magazin* 52, 2007.

Bibliography

Archival Materials

Archiv für Christlich-Soziale Politik (ACSP)

Nachlass (NL) Josef Müller
Nachlass (NL) Ferdinand Neumann

Bayerisches Hauptstaatsarchiv München (BHSAM)

Außenministerium (MA) 104527: Therese Neumann von Konnersreuth, 1927–1933
Bayerische gesandschaft Päpstlicher Stuhl 1919
Justizministerium (MJu) 23795–23797 Vorgänge in Heroldsbach, Alle Vorgänge

Bayerische Staatsbibliothek München (StaabiM)

Ana 338 Nachlass Johann Westermayr
Ana 445 Nachlass Friedrich Ritter von Lama

Bischöfliches Zentralarchiv Regensburg (BZR – Access granted to archival copies in the personal collection of Maria Anna Zumholz)

Ordinariatsarchiv, (OAR) Bestand Therese Neumann (THN)

Bistumsarchiv Speyer (BaS)

BO NA 23/10 1/49: Fehrbach
BO NA 23/10 2/51: Rodalben

Bistumsarchiv Trier (BAT)

Abt. 90, Nr. 100–199, Die Heilige Wallfahrt 1933

Bundesarchiv Berlin-Lichterfelde

NS 5-VI 17682 Bestand deutsche Arbeitsfront

Erzbischöfliches Archiv München (EAM)

Nachlass (NL) Kardinal Michael Faulhaber. 5945–5949 Therese Neumann
5950 Kettenbriefe, 1941–1944

Fürstlich Waldburg-Zeil'sches Gesamtarchiv

Nachlass Fürst Erich von Waldburg-Zeil, "Erinnerungen,"

Historisches Archiv des Erzbistums Köln (AEK)

Gen. I 4.30,1, Banneux
Gen. I 31.6,1, Wunderbare Erscheinungen, 1852–1935
Gen. II 31.6,1–4, Wunderbare Erscheinungen, 1945–1959
Gen. II 31,6a 1–2, Heroldsbach
SH 102–121: Marianisches Jahr 1954, Peregrinatio Mariae

Klosterarchiv Neviges (KaN)

28: Wallfahrtschronik, 1919–1940
461: *Hardenberger Wallfahrtsnachtrichten*, 1934–1935
500: Pilgerstatistik, 1913–1929
501: Pilgerstatistik, 1954–1962
516: Einzelne Pilgerprozessionen

NRW – Hauptstaatsarchiv Düsseldorf (HStAD)

RW 34–3, Polizei- und Sicherheitsdienstellen: Geheime Staatspolizei-Staatspolizeistelle Köln- Berichte von Vertrauensleuten über Kirchenangelegenheiten 1934–1945: Katholische Kirche, 1943–1945
RW 35–8, Polizei- und Sicherheitsdienststellen: Geheime Staatspolizei-Staatspolizei Aachen- Berichte von Vertrauensleuten über Kirchenangelegenheiten 1941–1944: Kirchen
RW 35–9, Polizei- und Sicherheitsdienststellen: Geheime Staatspolizei-Staatspolizei Aachen- Berichte von Vertrauensleuten über Kirchenangelegenheiten 1941–1944: Katholische Kirche

Provinzarchiv der deutschen Augustiner, Würzburg (PdAW – Access granted to archival copies in personal collection of Maria Anna Zumholz)

Nachlass (NL) Georg Wunderle

Staatsarchiv Amberg (StaAm)

Regierung der Oberpfalz, Kammer des Innern 13038: Die Stigmata der Therese Neumann von Konnersreuth
Bezirksamt Tirschenreuth (BT) 4169: Therese Neumann von Konnersreuth, 1926–1953

The American Catholic History Research Center and University Archives (CUA)

Aloisius Muench Papers
National Catholic News Service (NCNS) Records

Interviews

Toni Siegert, 22 June 2013.
Georg Schwager, 13 June 2013.

Periodicals

Aachener Nachtrichten
Das Schwarze Korps
Der Gerade Weg (GW)
Der Spiegel
Frankfurter Allgemeine Zeitung (FAZ)
Kirchenzeitung für das Erzbistum Köln (KZK)
Konnersreuther Lesebogen (KL)
Mittelbayerische Zeitung (MZ)
Münchener Neuste Nachtrichten (MNN)
Münsteranische Morgenpost (MM)
New York Times (NYT)
Pacific Stars and Stripes
Passauer neue Presse (PNP)
Stars and Stripes Europe Edition (SSEE)
Süddeutsche Zeitung (SZ)
The Catholic Herald
The Guardian: The Official Organ of the Diocese of Little Rock /Arkansas Catholic
Völkischer Beobachter

Primary Published Materials

Aigner, Eduard. *Die Wahrheit über eine Wunderheilung von Lourdes.* Frankfurt: Neue Frankfurter Verlag, 1908.

– Aigner, *Zehn Jahre Konnersreuth*. Berlin: A. Bock Verlag, 1939.
Aretin, Erwein Freiherr von. *Das bayerische Problem*. Munich: J. Lindauerische Universitätsbuchhandlung, 1924.
– *Krone und Ketten: Erinnerungen eines bayerisches Edelmannes*. Munich: Süddeutscher Verlag, 1955.
– *Die Sühneseele von Konnersreuth*. Edited by Karl Otmar Freiherr von Aretin. Munich: Verlag Siegfried Hacker, 1956.
Arntz, Hans-Dieter, ed. *Kriegsende 1944/45: Zwischen Ardenne und Rhein*. Euskirchen: Kümpel Verlag, 1984.
Barbara Weigand Gesellschaft, e.V. *Offenbarungen an Barbara Weigand*. Band 7, Juni 1908–September 1923, Nr. 899–1155. Schippach: Barabara Weigand Gesellschaft, 2002.
Birven, Henri. *Abbé Vachère: Ein Thaumaturg unserer Zeit*. Brandenburg: J. Wiesike, 1928.
Brandt, Hans-Jürgen, ed. *Priester in Uniform: Seelsorger, Ordensleute und Theologen als Soldaten im Zweiten Weltkrieg*. Augsburg: Pattloch, 1994.
Brennan, Elizabeth Marable. *Visits to Theresa Neumann*. New York: Paulist Press, 1936.
Deutsch, Josef. *Ärztliche Kritik an Konnersreuth! Wunder oder Hysterie?* Lippstadt: C. Jos. Laumanns, 1938.
– *Konnersreuth in Ärztlicher Beleuchtung*. Paderborn: Bonifacius, 1932.
Die Seherin von Konnersreuth: Berichte über Therese Neumann, Separatabdruck aus dem Tagblatt Die Neue Zeitung. Vienna, 1927.
Ernst, Robert. *Die Seherin aus dem Ruhrgebiet*. Stein am Rhein: Christiana-Verlag, 1988.
Feilding, Everard. *Sittings with Eusapia Palladino and Other Studies*. Hyde Park, NY: University Books, 1963.
Führer durch die Gebetsstätte der Unbefleckt empfangenen Mutter vom Sieg in Wigratzbad. Wigratzbad: Selbstverlag des Vereins Maria v. Sieg e.V., 1977.
Galen, Clemens August Graf von. *Bischof Clemens August Graf von Galen: Akten, Briefe und Predigten 1933–1946*. Edited by Peter Löffler. 2 vols. Paderborn and Munich: F. Schöningh, 1996.
Gerlich, Fritz. *Die Stigmatisierte Therese Neumann von Konnersreuth, Erster Teil, Die Lebensgeschichte der Therese Neumann*. Munich: Kösel & Pustet, 1929.
Graef, Hilda C. *The Case of Therese Neumann*. Westminster, MD: The Newman Press, 1951.
Guttenberg, Baroness Elisabeth von. *Holding the Stirrup: A Bavarian Noblewoman's Adventurous Tale of Great Lords, Lofty Castles, the Decline of the Aristocracy, and the Plot to Assassinate Hitler*. Post Falls, ID: Lepanto Press, 1953.
Heermann, H. *Um Konnersreuth*. Paderborn: Bonifacius Druckerei, 1932.

Jordan, Max. *Beyond All Fronts: A Bystander's Notes on This Thirty Years' War.* Milwaukee: Bruce, 1945.

Kerkeling, Hape. *I'm Off Then: Losing and Finding Myself on the Camino de Santiago.* Translated by Shelley Frisch. New York: Free Press, 2009.

Kirchliches Handbuch für das katholische Deutschland. Cologne: J.P. Bachem Verlag, 1916–67.

Lama, Friedrich Ritter von. *Further Chronicles of Therese Neumann.* New York and Milwaukee, WI: Bruce, 1931.

– *Therese of Konnersreuth: A New Chronicle.* Milwaukee: Bruce Publishing, 1935.

– *Therese Neumann: A Stigmatist of Our Day.* New York and Milwaukee: Bruce, 1929.

Morsey, Rudolf, ed. *Fritz Gerlich- ein Publizist gegen Hitler. Briefe und Akten 1930–1934.* Paderborn: Ferdinand Schöningh, 2010.

Müller, Josef. *Bis zur letzten Konsequenz. Ein Leben für Frieden und Freiheit.* Munich: Süddeutscher Verlag, 1975.

Naab, Ingebert. *Ist Hitler ein Christ?* Munich: Verlag Zeichenring, 1931.

Naber, Joseph. *Tagebücher und Aufzeichnungen über Therese Neumann.* Munich and Zurich: Verlag Schnell & Steiner, 1987.

Priller, Georg. *Anna Maria Goebel, die Stigmatisierte von Bickendorf (Eifel).* Tirschenreuth: E. Kohl, 1928.

Radlo, Peter. *Trug oder Wahrheit. Neues über Konnersreuth.* Karlsruhe: Badenia, 1938.

Rinser, Luise. *Die Wahrheit über Konnersreuth. Ein Bericht.* Frankfurt a.M: Fischer, 1953.

Rößler, Max. *Therese Neumann von Konnersreuth.* Würzburg: Verlag Wilhelm Naumann, 1989.

Salzmann, A.M., ed. *Therese Neumann: die Stigmatisierte von Konnersreuth, persönliche Eindrücke und Berichten von Augenzeugen.* Dessau: Martin Salzmann Verlag, 1929.

Siwek, Paul. *The Riddle of Konnersreuth: A Psychological and Religious Study.* Translated by Ignatius McCormick. Milwaukee, WI: Bruce Publishing, 1953.

Spiegl, Anni. *The Life and Death of Therese Neumann of Konnersreuth.* Eichstätt: Carmelites of Regensburg, 2002.

Spieker, Josef. *Mein Kampf gegen Unrecht in Staat und Gesellschaft: Errinerungen eines Kölner Jesuiten.* Cologne: J.P. Bachem, 1971.

Steiner, Johannes. *Therese Neumann: A Portrait Based on Authentic Accounts, Journals, and Documents.* New York: Alba House, 1967.

Teodorowicz, Josef. *Mystical Phenomena in the Life of Theresa Neumann.* London and St Louis, MO: Herder, 1945.

Thomas, Rev. F. *The Mystery of Konnersreuth: Facts, Personal Experiences, Critical Remarks.* Los Angeles, CA: Kessinger Legacy Reprints, 1940.

Verweyen, Johannes Maria. *Das Geheimnis von Konnersreuth: Ein Augenzeuge berichtet und deutet die rätselhaften Vorgänge.* Stuttgart: Süddeutsches Verlagshaus, 1932.

Vogl, Adalbert Albert. *Therese Neumann: Mystic and Stigmatist, 1898–1962.* Rockford, IL: Tan Books and Publishers, 1987.

Walz, Johann Baptist. *Die Protokolle von Augenzeugen zu den 'Muttergottes-Erscheinungen' von Heroldsbach-Thurn. Von Anfang an bis zum 2. Römischen Dekret,* Band I. Mönchengladbach, 1958.

Witry, Michael Theodor. *Die Resl: Medizinisches aus Konnersreuth.* Saarbrücken: Saarbrücker Druckerei, 1934.

Wunderle, Georg. *Die Stigmatisierte von Konnersreuth: Tatsachen, Eindrücke, Erwägungen.* Eichstätt: Schriftenreihe des Klerusblattes, 1927.

Ziegler, Walter, ed. *Die Kirchliche Lage in Bayern nach den Regierungspräsidentenberichten 1933–1943 IV, Regierungsbezirk Niederbayern und Oberpfalz,* IV. Mainz: Mattias-Grünewald-Verlag, 1973.

Zwehl, Noreen von. *America Salutes Therese Neumann. Testimonials of WWII Servicemen.* Staten Island, NY: The MAN Foundation, 1999.

Secondary Published Materials

Allen, Ann Taylor. *Feminism and Motherhood in Germany, 1800–1914.* New Brunswick, NJ: Rutgers University Press, 1991.

– "Religion and Gender in Modern German History: A Historiographical Perspective." In *Gendering Modern German History: Rewriting Historiography,* edited by Karen Hagemann and Jean H. Quartert, 190–207. New York: Berghahn, 2006.

Altermatt, Urs. *Katholizismus und Moderne. Zur Sozial- und Mentalitätsgeschichte der Schweizer Katholiken im 19. und 20. Jahrhundert.* Zurich: Benzinger, 1989.

Anderson, Margaret Lavinia. "Interdenominationalism, Clericism, Pluralism: The *Zentrumsstreit* and the Dilemma of Catholicism in Wilhelmine Germany." *Central European History* 21 (1990): 350–78.

– "Piety and Politics: Recent Work on German Catholicism." *The Journal of Modern History* 63 (1991): 681–716.

Arbeitskreis für kirchliche Zeitgeschichte (AKKZG), Münster. "Katholiken zwischen Tradition und Moderne. Das katholische Milieu als Forschungsaufgabe." *Westfälische Forschungen* 43 (1993): 588–654.

Baumann, Ursula. "Religion, Emancipation, and Politics in the Confessional Women's Movement in Germany, 1900–1933." In *Borderlines: Genders and Identities in War and Peace, 1870–1930,* edited by Billie Melman, 285–306. New York and London: Routledge, 1998.

Baumanns, Hans Leo. "Die Aachener Heiligtumsfahrt 1937: Ein sozialgeschichtlicher Beitrag zur katholischen Volksopposition im III. Reich." Dissertation: Rheinisch-Westfälischen Technischen Hochschule Aachen, 1968.

Bergen, Doris. "German Military Chaplains in World War II and the Dilemmas of Legitimacy." *Church History* 70, no. 2 (June 2001): 232–47.

Berger, Peter L. "Further Thoughts on Religion and Modernity." *Society* 49 (2012): 313–16.

Biess, Frank. *Homecomings: Returning POWs and the Legacies of Defeat in Postwar Germany.* Princeton, NJ and Oxford: Princeton University Press, 2006.

Black, Monica, and Eric Kurlander, eds. *Revisiting the "Nazi Occult": Histories, Realities, and Legacies.* Rochester, NY: Camden House, 2015.

Black, Monica. "Miracles in the Shadow of the Economic Miracle: The 'Supernatural '50s' in West Germany." *Journal of Modern History* 84, no. 4 (December 2012): 833–60.

Blackbourn, David. *Class, Religion, and Local Politics in Wilhelmine Germany: The Center Party in Württenburg before 1914*. New Haven, CT: Yale University Press, 1980.

– *Marpingen: Apparitions of the Virgin Mary in Nineteenth-Century Germany.* New York: Knopf, 1994.

– *Populists and Patricians: Essays in Modern German History*. London: Allen & Unwin, 1987.

Blaschke, Olaf, and Frank-Michael Kuhlemann, eds. *Religion im Kaiserreich: Milieus-Mentalitäten-Krisen*. Gütersloh: Chr. Kaiser, 1996.

Blessing, Werner. *Staat und Kirche in der Gesellschaft. Institutionelle Autorität und mentaler Wandel in Bayern während des 19. Jahrhunderts*. Göttingen: Vandenhoeck & Ruprecht, 1982.

Breuer, Thomas. *Verordneter Wandel? Der Wiederstreit zwischen nationalsozialistischen Herrschaftsanspruch und traditionaler Lebenswelt im Erzbistum Bamberg*. Mainz: Mattias-Grünewald Verlag, 1992.

Bridenthal, Renate, Atina Grossmann, and Marion Kaplan, eds. *When Biology Became Destiny: Women in Weimar and Nazi Germany.* New York: Monthly Review Press, 1984.

Brodie, Thomas. "The German Catholic Diaspora in the Second World War." *German History* 33, no. 1 (2015): 80–99.

Broszat, Martin. "Resistenz und Widerstand: Eine Zwischenbilanz des Forschungsprojekts." In *Bayern in der NS-Zeit*, vol. IV, edited by Broszat, 686–705. Munich and Vienna: Oldenbourg, 1981.

Broszat, Martin, Klaus-Dietmar Henke, and Hans Woller, ed. *Von Stalingrad zur Währungsreform. Zur Sozialgeschichte des Umbruchs in Deutschland.* Munich: Oldenbourg, 1988.

Brown, Callum. *The Death of Christian Britain: Understanding Secularization 1800–2000*. London and New York: Routledge, 2001.

Brown-Fleming, Suzanne. *The Holocaust and Catholic Conscience: Cardinal Aloisius Muench and the Catholic Guilt Question in Germany*. South Bend, IN: University of Notre Dame Press, 2006.

Burton, Richard D.E. *Holy Tears, Holy Blood: Women, Catholicism, and the Culture of Suffering in France, 1840–1970*. Ithaca, NY: Cornell University Press, 2004.

Cary, Noel. "The Making of the Reich President, 1925: German Conservatism and the Nomination of Paul von Hindenburg." *Central European History* 23, no. 2/3 (June/September 1990): 179–204.

– *The Path to Christian Democracy: German Catholics and the Party System from Windthorst to Adenauer*. Cambridge, MA: Harvard University Press, 1996.

Connelly, John. *From Enemy to Brother: The Revolution in Catholic Teaching on the Jews, 1933–1965*. Cambridge, MA: Harvard University Press, 2012.

Connor, Ian. "The Churches and the Refugee Problem in Bavaria 1945–1949." *Journal of Contemporary History* 20 (1985): 399–421.

Cramer, Douglas J."'To Avoid a New Kulturkampf': The Catholic Workers' Associations and National Socialism in Weimar-era Bavaria." *Journal of Church and State* 41, no. 4 (Autumn 1999): 739–60.

Cucchiara, Martina. "The Bonds that Shame: Reconsidering the Foreign Exchange Trials against the Catholic Church in Nazi Germany, 1935/36." *European History Quarterly* 45, no. 4 (2015): 689–712.

Cutherbertson, Ken. *A Complex Fate: William L. Shirer and the American Century*. Montreal and Kingston: McGill-Queen's University Press, 2015.

Damberg, Wilhelm. *Abschied von Milieu? Katholizismus im Bistum Münster und in den Niederlanden 1945–1980*. Paderborn: F. Schöningh, 1997.

– *Der Kampf um die Schulen in Westfalen 1933–1945*. Mainz: Mattias-Grünewald, 1986.

– *Moderne und Milieu, 1802–1998*. Münster: Dialogverlag, 1998.

Dierker, Wolfgang. *Himmlers Glaubenskrieger: Der Sicherheitsdienst der SS und seine Religionspolitik, 1933–1941*. Paderborn: F. Schöningh, 2002.

Dietrich, Tobias. *Konfession im Dorf. Westeuropäische Erfahrungen im 19. Jahrhundert*. Cologne: Böhlau, 2004.

Doney, Skye. "Brown and Black Boundaries: Nazism and German Catholicism in the Summer of 1933." *Catholic Historical Review* (forthcoming 2017).

– "The Sacred Economy: Devotional Objects as Sacred Presence for German Catholics in Aachen and Trier, 1832–1937." *International Journal of Religious Tourism and Pilgrimage* 1, no. 1 (2014): 62–71.

Evans, Ellen Lovell. *The German Center Party, 1870–1933: A Study in Political Catholicism*. Carbondale and Edwardsville: Southern Illinois University Press, 1981.

Faulkner Rossi, Lauren. *Wehrmacht Priests: Catholicism and the Nazi War of Annihilation*. Cambridge, MA: Harvard University Press, 2015.

Feldmann, Christian. *Wahn oder Wunder? Die Resl von Konnersreuth- wie sie wirklich war*. Regensburg: MZ Buchverlag, 2010.

Ford, Graham. "Constructing a Regional Identity: The Christian Social Union and Bavaria's Common Heritage, 1949-1962." *Contemporary European History* 16, no. 3 (August 2007): 277–97.

Forster, Marc. *The Counter-Reformation in the Villages: Religion and Reform in the Bishopric of Speyer, 1560–1720*. Ithaca, NY: Cornell University Press, 1992.

Friedländer, Saul. *The Years of Extermination: Nazi Germany and the Jews, 1939–1945*. New York: Harper, 2006.

Geppert, Alex C.T., and Till Kössler, eds. *Wunder: Poetik und Politik des Stauens im 20. Jahrhundert*. Berlin: Suhrkamp, 2011.

Gösku, Cornelia. *Heroldsbach: Eine verbotene Wallfahrt*. Wurzburg: Echter, 1991.

Griech-Polelle, Beth A. *Bishop von Galen: German Catholicism and National Socialism*. New Haven, CT and London: Yale University Press, 2002.

Gross, Michael B. "*Kulturkampf* and Unification: German Liberalism and the War Against the Jesuits." *Central European History* 30 (1997): 545–66.

– "The Strange Case of the Nun in the Dungeon, or German Liberalism as a Convent Atrocity Story." *German Studies Review* 23 (2000): 69–84.

– *The War against Catholicism: Liberalism and the Anti-Catholic Imagination in Nineteenth-Century Germany*. Ann Arbor: University of Michigan Press, 2004.

Großbölting, Thomas. "Religion, Individuum und Gesellschaft. Ein Versuch zur Erklärung des religiösen Wandels in den 1960er Jahren." *Schweizerische Zeitschrift für Religions- und Kulturgeschichte* 107 (2013): 389–406.

– *Der verlorene Himmel. Glaube in Deutschland seit 1945*. Göttingen: Vandenhoek & Ruprecht, 2013.

Großbölting, Thomas, and Klaus Große Kracht. "Religion in der Bundesrepublik Deutschland. Eine Einleitung." *Zeithistorische Forschungen/Studies in Contemporary History*, online edition, 7, no. 3 (2010): www.zeithistorische-forschungen.de.

Große Kracht, Klaus. *Die Stunde der Laien? Katholische Aktion in Deutschland im europäischen Kontext 1920–1960*. Paderborn: F. Schöningh, 2016.

Hall, David D., ed. *Lived Religion in America: Toward a History of Practice*. Princeton, NJ: University of Princeton Press, 1997.

Hanauer, Josef. *Konnersreuth als Testfall. Kritischer Bericht über das Leben der Therese Neumann*. Munich: Manz Verlag, 1972.

– *"Konnersreuth" eine ewige Lüge*. Regensburg: Eigenverlag, 2002.

– *Der Schwindel von Konnersreuth: Ein Skandal ohne Ende?* Regensburg: Eigenverl. der verf., 1989.

Hanks, William F. "Pierre Bourdieu and the Practices of Language." *Annual Review of Anthropology* 34 (2005): 67–83.

Harris, Ruth. *Lourdes: Body and Spirit in the Secular Age*. New York: Penguin, 1999.

Hastings, Derek. *Catholicism and the Roots of Nazism: Religious Identity and National Socialism*. Oxford and New York: Oxford University Press, 2010.

Haun, Gerhard. *Die Wallfahrt nach Neviges*. Wuppertal: Frohn, 1981.

Heal, Bridget. *The Cult of the Virgin Mary in Early Modern Germany: Protestant and Catholic Piety, 1500–1648*. Cambridge: Cambridge University Press, 2007.

Heilbronner, Oded. *Catholicism, Political Culture, and the Countryside: A Social History of the Nazi Party in the Countryside*. Ann Arbor: University of Michigan Press, 1998.

– "From Ghetto to Ghetto: The Place of German Catholic Society in Recent Historiography." *The Journal of Modern History* 72 (2000): 453–71.

Heineman, Elizabeth. *What Difference Does a Husband Make? Women and Marital Status in Nazi and Post-War Germany*. Berkeley: University of California, 2003.

Henkelmann, Andreas. *Caritasgeschichte zwischen katholischem Milieu und Wohlfahrtsstaat. Das Seraphische Liebeswerk (1889–1971)*. Paderborn: F. Schöningh, 2008.

Hettler, Friedrich Hermann. *Josef Müller ("Ochsensepp"), Mann des Widerstandes und erster CSU-Vorsitzender*. Munich: Stadtarchiv Munich, 1991.

Herzog, Dagmar. *Sex after Fascism: Memory and Morality in Twentieth-Century Germany*. Princeton, NJ: Princeton University Press, 2005.

Hockerts, Hans Günter. *Die Sittlichkeitsprozesse gegen die katholische Ordensangehörige und Priester 1936/1937. Eine Studie zur nationalsozialistischen Herrschaftstechnik und zum Kirchenkampf*. Mainz: F. Schöningh, 1971.

Höhn, Maria. *GIs and Fräuleins: The German-American Encounter in 1950s West Germany*. Chapel Hill: University of North Carolina Press, 2002.

Horstmann, Johannes, and Antonius Liedhegener, eds. *Konfession, Moderne und Milieu: Konzeptionelle Positionen und Kontroversen zur Geschichte von Katholizismus und Kirche im 19. und 20. Jahrhundert*. Schwerte: Katholische Akademie Schwerte, 2001.

Horton, Gerd. *Radio Goes to War: The Cultural Politics of Propaganda during World War II*. Berkeley: University of California Press, 2003.

Houlihan, Patrick J. *Catholicism and the Great War: Religion and Everyday Life in Germany and Austria-Hungary, 1914–1922*. Cambridge: Cambridge University Press, 2015.

Jarausch, Konrad H., and Michael Geyer. *Shattered Past: Reconstructing German Histories*. Princeton, NJ: Princeton University Press, 2003.

Jones, Larry E. "Catholic Conservatives in the Weimar Republic: The Politics of the Rheinish-Westphalian Aristocracy, 1918–1933." *German History* 18 (2000): 60–85.

– "Franz von Papen, the German Center Party, and the Failure of Catholic Conservatism in the Weimar Republic." *Central European History* 38, no. 2 (June 2005): 191–217.

– *Hitler versus Hindenburg: The 1932 Presidential Elections and the End of the Weimar Republic.* Cambridge: Cambridge University, Press, 2015.

Jonas, Raymond. *The Tragic Death of Claire Ferchaud and the Great War*. Berkeley: University of California Press, 2005.

Kane, Paula. "'She Offered Herself Up': The Victim Soul and Victim Spirituality in Catholicism." *Church History* 71, no. 1 (March 2002): 80–119.

– *Sister Thorn and Catholic Mysticism in Modern America.* Chapel Hill: University of North Carolina Press, 2013.

– "Stigmatic Cults and Pilgrimage: The Convergence of Private and Public Faith." In *Christian Homes: Religion, Family, and Domesticity in the 19th and 20th Centuries*, edited by Patrick Pasture and Tine van Osselaer, 105–25. Leuven: Leuven University Press, 2015.

Kaufmann, Doris. *Frauen zwischen Aufbruch und Reaktion. Protestantische Frauenbewegungen in der ersten Hälfte des 20. Jahrhunderts*. Munich, 1988.

– *Katholisches Milieu in Münster 1928–1933*. Düsseldorf: Schwan, 1984.

Kaufmann, Suzanne. *Consuming Visions: Mass Culture and the Lourdes Shrine.* Ithaca, NY: Cornell University Press, 2005.

Kershaw, Ian. *Popular Opinion and Political Dissent in the Third Reich: Bavaria 1933–1945*. Oxford: Oxford University Press, 1983.

Klein, Gotthard. *Der Volksverein für das Katholische Deutschland, 1890–1933: Geschichte, Bedeutung, Untergang*. Paderborn: F. Schoningh, 1996.

Köhler, Joachim. "Ausbruch aus dem katholischen Milieu? Katholikinnen und Katholiken in Württemberg 1918 bis 1933." In *Württembergs Protestantismus in der Weimarer Republik*, edited by Rainer Lächele and Jörg Thierfelder, 122–39. Stuttgart: Calwer, 2003.

Kösters, Christoph. "'Fest soll mein Taufbund immer steh'n...'- Demonstrationskatholizismus im Bistum Münster 1933–1945." In *Zwischen Loyalität und Resistenz*, edited by Rudolf Schlögl and Hans-Ulrich Thamer. Münster: Aschendorff, 1996, 158–84.

– *Katholische Verbände und moderne Gesellschaft: Organizationsgeschichte und Vereinskultur im Bistum Münster, 1918–1945*. Paderborn: F. Schöningh, 1996.

Komska, Yuliya. *The Icon Curtain: The Cold War's Quiet Border.* Chicago and London: University of Chicago Press, 2015.

Koonz, Claudia. *Mothers in the Fatherland: Women, the Family, and Nazi Politics.* New York: St Martin's Press, 1988.

Kotulla, Andreas. *"Nach Lourdes!" Der französische Marienwallfahrtsort und die Katholiken im Deutschen Kaiserreich, 1871–1914*. Munich: M Meidenbauer, 2006.

Krieg, Robert. *Catholic Theologians in Nazi Germany*. New York: Bloomsbury, 2004.

Kurlander, Eric. "Hitler's Monsters: The Occult Roots of Nazism and the Emergence of the Nazi 'Supernatural Imaginary.'" *German History* 30, no. 4 (2012): 528–49.

Kuropka, Joachim, *Clemens August Graf von Galen: Menschenrechte-Widerstand-Euthanasie-Neubeginn*. Münster: Verlag Regensburg, 1998.

– *Zur Sache- das Kreuz! Untersuchungen zur Geschichte des Konflikts um Kreuz und Lutherbild in den Schulen Oldenburgs, zur Wirkungsgeschichte einen Massenprotests und zum Problem nationalsozialistischer Herrschaft in einem agrarisch-katholischen Region*. Vechta: Vechtaer Druckerei und Verlag, 1987.

Kuropka, Joachim, ed. *Clemens August Graf von Galen: Neue Forschungen zum Leben und Wirken des Bischofs von Münster*. Münster: Verlag Regensburg, 1993.

– *Grenzen des katholischen Milieus- Stabilität und Gefährdung katholischer Milieus in der Endphase der Weimarer Republik und der NS-Zeit*. Münster: Aschendorff, 2013.

Laycock, Joseph P. *The Seer of Bayside: Veronica Lueken and the Struggle to Define Catholicism*. Oxford and New York: Oxford University Press, 2014.

Lepsius, M. Rainer. "Parteiensystem und Sozialstruktur. Zum Problem der Demokratisierung der deutschen Gesellschaft." In *Wirtschaft, Geschichte und Wirtschaftsgeschichte*, edited by Wilhelm Abel, 371–93. Stuttgart: G. Fischer, 1966.

Leugers, Antonia. "'Du hast alles vereint: Seele und Geiste und Körper.' Kardinal Faulhaber und seine Freundin." *Rottenburger Jahrbuch für Kirchengeschichte* 35 (2016): 173–211.

Lewy, Günter. *The Catholic Church and Nazi Germany*. New York: McGraw-Hill, 1964.

Liedhegener, Antonius. *Christentum und Urbanisierung: Katholiken und Protestanten in Münster und Bochum 1830–1930*. Paderborn, Munich, Vienna, and Zurich: F. Schöningh, 1997.

– "Gottessuche, Kirchenkritik und Glaubenstreue unter Münsters Katholiken in den Krisenjahre der Weimarer Republik. Untersuchungen zur katholischen Deutungskultur anhand einer frühen pastoraltheologischen Meinungsfrage." *Westfälische Forschungen* 47 (1997): 323–76.

Loth, Wilfried. *Katholiken im Kaiserreich: Der politische Katholizismus in der Krise des wilhelminischen Deutschlands*. Düsseldorf: Droste, 1984.

Marhoefer, Laurie. *Sex and the Weimar Republic: German Homosexual Emancipation and the Rise of the Nazis*. Toronto: University of Toronto Press, 2015.

Maunder, Chris. "Mapping the Presence of Mary: Germany's Apparition Sites." *Journal of Contemporary Religion* 28, no. 1 (2013): 79–93.

– *Our Lady of Nations: Apparitions of Mary in Twentieth-Century Europe*. Oxford: Oxford University Press, 2016.

McCartin, James P. *Prayers of the Faithful: The Shifting Spiritual Life of American Catholics*. Cambridge, MA: Harvard University Press, 2010.

McLeod, Hugh. *Secularization in Western Europe, 1848–1918*. New York: St Martin's, 2001.

Meiwes, Relinde. *"Arbeiterinnen des Hernn": Katholicshe Frauenkongregationen im 19. Jahrhundert*. Frankfurt: Campus, 2000.

Melman, Billie, ed., *Borderlines: Genders and Identities in War and Peace, 1870–1930*. New York and London: Routledge, 1998.

Menke, Martin R. "Misunderstood Civic Duty: The Center Party and the Enabling Act." *Journal of Church and State* 51, no. 2 (Spring 2009): 236–64.

Mitchell, Maria. *The Origins of Christian Democracy: Politics and Confession in Modern Germany*. Ann Arbor: University of Michigan Press, 2012.

Moeller, Robert. *Protecting Motherhood: Women and the Family in the Politics of Postwar West Germany*. Berkeley: University of California Press, 1993.

– *War Stories: The Search for a Usable Past in the Federal Republic of Germany*. Berkeley: University of California Press, 2001.

Moltmann, Rainer. *Reinhold Heinen (1894–1969) Ein christlicher Politiker, Journalist und Verleger*. Düsseldorf: Droste, 2005.

Morsey, Rudolf. *Die deutsche Zentrumspartei, 1917–1923*. Düsseldorf: Droste, 1966.

– *Der Untergang des politischer Katholizismus*. Stuttgart and Zurich: Belser, 1977.

Muller, Dirk H. *Arbeiter-Katholizismus-Staat: Der Volksverein fur das katholische Deutschland und die katholischen Arbeiterorganisationen in der Weimarer Republik*. Bonn: Dietz, 1996.

Olenhusen, Irmtraud Götz von, ed. *Frauen unter dem Patriarchat der Kirchen: Katholikinnen und Protestantinnen im 19. und 20. Jahrhundert*. Stuttgart: Verlag W. Kohlhammer, 1995.

– *Wunderbare Erscheinungen: Frauen und katholische Frömmigkeit im 19. und 20. Jahrhundert*. Munich: F. Schöningh, 1995.

Orsi, Robert. *Between Heaven and Earth: The Religious Worlds People Make and the Scholars Who Study Them*. Princeton, NJ: Princeton University Press, 2005.

– *The Madonna of 115th Street: Faith and Community in Italian Harlem, 1880–1950*. 2nd ed. New Haven, CT and London: Yale University Press, 2002.

Osselaer, Tine van. "Sensitive but Sane: Male Visionaries and their Emotional Display in Interwar Belgium." *Low Countries Historical Review* 127, no. 1 (2012): 127–49.

Osselaer, Tine van and Thomas Buerman. "Feminization Thesis: A Survey of International Historiography and a Probing of Belgian Grounds." *Revue d'histoire ecclésiastique* 103 (2008): 497–544.

O'Sullivan, Michael E. "An Eroding Milieu? Catholic Youth, Church Authority, and Popular Behavior in Northwest Germany during the Third Reich, 1933–1938." *Catholic Historical Review* 90, no. 2 (April 2004): 236–59.

– "From Catholic Milieu to Lived Religion: The Social and Cultural History of Modern German Catholicism." *History Compass* 7, no. 3 (2009): 837–61.

– "West German Miracles: Catholic Mystics, Church Hierarchy, and Postwar Popular Culture," *Zeithistorische Forschungen/ Studies in Contemporary History* 6 (2009): 11–34.

O'Toole, James M., ed. *Habits of Devotion: Catholic Religious Practice in Twentieth-Century America*. Ithaca, NY and London: Cornell University Press, 2004.

Pasture, Patrick, Jan Art, and Thomas Buerman, eds. *Gender and Christianity in Modern Europe: Beyond the Feminization Thesis*. Leuven: Leuven University Press, 2012.

Patch, Jr, William L. *Heinrich Brüning and the Dissolution of the Weimar Republic*. Cambridge: Cambridge University Press, 1998.

Paul, Gerhard, and Klaus-Michael Mallmann. *Milieus und Widerstand: Eine Verhaltensgeschichte der Gesellschaft im Nationalsozialismus, Widerstand und Verwiegerung im Saarland, 1935–1945*. Bonn: Dietz, 1995.

Phayer, Michael. *The Catholic Church and the Holocaust, 1930–1965*. Bloomington: Indiana University Press, 2000.

– *Pius XII, the Holocaust, and the Cold War*. Bloomington and Indianapolis: University of Indiana Press, 2008.

Plötzl, Walter. "Wallfahrten gegen das Hakenkreuz." In *Festgabe für Heinz Hürten zum 60. Geburtstag*, edited by Hedwig Dickerhof, 441–55. Frankfurt am Main, 1988.

Poiger, Ute. *Jazz, Rock, and Rebels: Cold War Politics and American Culture in a Divided Germany*. Berkeley, Los Angeles, and London: University of California Press, 2000.

Pollack, Detlef. *"Säkularisierung – ein moderner Mythos?" Studien zum religiösen Wandel in Deutschland*. Tübingen: Mohr Siebech Verlag, 2003.

Pollack, Detlef, and Olaf Müller, "Churchliness, Religiosity, and Spirituality: Western and Eastern European Societies in Times of Religious Diversity." In *What the World Believes: Analyses and Commentary on the Religion Monitor 2008*, edited by Bertelsmann, 399–416. Gütersloh: Bertelsmann Stiftung, 2009.

Pollack, Detlef, Olaf Müller, and Gert Pickel. "The Religious Landscape in Germany: Secularizing West – Secularized East." In *The Social Significance of Religion in the Enlarged Europe: Secularization, Individualization, and Pluralization*, edited by Detlef Pollack, Olaf Müller, and Gert Pickel. 95-120 Surrey, England: Ashgate, 2012.

Rahden, Till van. "Clumsy Democrats: Moral Passions in the Federal Republic." *German History* 29, no. 3 (2011): 485–504.

– "Demokratie und väterliche Autorität. Das Karlsruher 'Stichentscheid'-Urteil von 1959 in der politischen Kultur der frühen Bundesrepublik." *Zeithistorische Forschungen/Studies in Contemporary History*, online edition 2 (2005), Nr. 2, www.zeithistorische-forschungen.de.

Riebling, Mark. *Church of Spies: The Pope's Secret War against Hitler*. New York: Basic Books, 2015.

Rey, Terry. "Marketing the Goods of Salvation: Bourdieu on Religion." *Religion* 34 (2004): 331–43.

Roos, Julia. *Weimar through the Lens of Gender: Prostitution Reform, Woman's Emancipation, and German Democracy, 1919–1933*. Ann Arbor: University of Michigan Press, 2010.

Ruff, Mark Edward. *The Battle for the Catholic Past in Germany, 1945–1980*. Cambridge: Cambridge University Press, 2017.

– *The Wayward Flock: Catholic Youth in Postwar West Germany, 1945–1965*. Chapel Hill: University of North Carolina Press, 2005.

– "Integrating Religion into the Historical Mainstream: Recent Literature on Religion in the Federal Republic of Germany." *Central European History* 42 (2009): 330–1.

Sack, Birgit. *Zwischen religiöser Bindung und moderner Gesellschaft: katholicshe Frauenbewegung und politische Kultur in der Weimarer Republik (1918/19–1933)*. Münster: Waxmann, 1998.

Sailer, Joachim. *Eugen Bolz und die Krise des politischen Katholizismus in der Weimarer Republik*. Tübingen: Bibliotheca Academica Verlag, 1994.

Samson, Judith. "EU Criticism in Two Transnational Marian Anti-Abortion Movements." In *Gender, Nation, and Religion in European Pilgrimage*, edited by Willy Jansen and Catrien Notermans, 71–88. Surrey, England: Ashgate, 2012.

Schallenberg, Gerd. *Visionäre Erlebnisse: Visionen und Auditionen in der Gegenwart. Eine psychodynamische und psychopathologische Untersuchung*. Augsburg: Pattloch, 1990.

Schäfer, Michael. *Fritz Gerlich 1883–1934. Publizistik als Auseinandersetzung mit den 'Politischen Religionen' des 20. Jahrhunderts*. Munich: Dissertation, 1998.

Schank, Christoph. *"Kölsch-Katholisch" Das katholische Milieu in Köln 1871–1933*. Cologne, Weimar, and Vienna: Böhlau Verlag, 2004.

Scheer, Monique. *Rosenkranz und Kriegsvisionen: Marienerscheinungskulte im 20. Jahrhundert*. Tübingen: Tübinger Vereinigung für Volkskunde, 2006.

Schildt, Axel, Detlef Siegfried, and Karl Christian Lammers, eds. *Dynamische Zeiten: Die 60er Jahre in den beiden deutschen Gesellschaften*. Hamburg: Christians, 2000.

Schlager, Claudia. *Kult und Krieg: Herz Jesu-Sacré Coeur- Christus Rex im deutsch-französischen Vergleich 1914–1925*. Tübingen: Tübingen Verein für Volkskunde, 2011.

Schlemmer, Thomas. *Aufbruch, Krise und Erneuerung. Die Christlich-Soziale Union 1945 bis 1955*. Munich: R. Oldenbourg Verlag, 1998.

Schlisser, Hanna, ed. *The Miracle Years: A Cultural History of West Germany, 1949–1968*. Princeton, NJ: Princeton University Press, 2001.

Scholder, Klaus. *The Churches and the Third Reich*. 2 vols. Frankfurt am Main: SCM Press, 1977.

Schönhoven, Klaus. *Die bayerische Volkspartei 1924–1932*. Düsseldorf: Droste Verlag, 1972.

Schloesser, Steven. *Jazz Age Catholicism: Mystic Modernism in Postwar Paris, 1919–1933*. Toronto: University of Toronto Press, 2005.

Schmidt, Ute. *Zentrum oder CDU: Politischer Katholizismus zwischen Tradition und Anpassung*. Opladen: Westdeutscher Verlag, 1987.

Schmidtmann, Christian. *Katholische Studierende 1945–1973: Ein Beitrag zur Kultur- und Sozialgeschichte der Bundesrepublik Deutschland*. Paderborn: F. Schöningh, 2005.

Schneider, Bernard. "Feminisierung der Religion im 19. Jahrhundert. Perspektiven einer These im 19. Jahrhundert." *Trierer Theologische Zeitschrift* 111, no. 2 (2002): 123–47.

– *Maria und Lourdes. Wunder und Marienerscheinungen in theologischer und kulturwissenschaftlicher Perspektive*. Münster: Aschendorff, 2008.

Schnellenberger, Barbara. *Katholische Jugend und Drittes Reich: Eine Gescichte des Katholischen Jungmänerverbandes 1933–1939 unter besonderer Berücksichtigung der Rheinprovinz*. Mainz: Matthias-Grünewald, 1975.

Schwartz, Hans-Peter. *Adenauer, Der Aufstieg: 1876–1952*. Stuttgart: Deutsche Verlags-Anstalt, 1986.

– *Adenauer, Der Staatsmann: 1952–1967*. Stuttgart: Deutsche Verlags-Anstalt, 1991.

Seipp, Adam. *Strangers in a Wild Place: Refugees, Americans, and a German Town, 1945–1952*. Bloomington, IN: University of Indiana Press, 2013.

Simdars-Swartz, Sandra. *Encountering Mary: Visions of Mary from La Salette to Medjugorje*. Princeton, NJ: Princeton University Press, 1991.

Smith, Helmut Walser, ed. *Protestants, Catholics, and Jews in Germany, 1800–1914*. Oxford and New York: Berg, 2001.

Sneeringer, Julia. *Winning Women's Votes: Propaganda and Politics in Weimar Germany*. Chapel Hill: University of North Carolina Press, 2002.

Soergel, Philipp. *Wondrous in his Saints: Counter-Reformation Propaganda in Bavaria*. Berkeley and Los Angeles: University of California Press, 1993.

Sperber, Jonathan. *The Kaiser's Voters: Electors and Elections in Imperial Germany*. Cambridge: Cambridge University Press, 1997.

– *Popular Catholicism in Nineteenth-Century Germany*. Princeton, NJ: Princeton University Press, 1984.

Spicer, Kevin. *Hitler's Priests: Catholic Clergy and National Socialism*. Dekalb, IL: Northern Illinois University Press, 2008.

Spicka, Mark E. "Gender, Political Discourse, and the CDU / CSU Vision of the Economic Miracle, 1949–1957." *German Studies Review* 25, no. 2 (May 2002): 305–32.

Stambolis, Barbara. *Libori: Das Kirchen- und Volksfest in Paderborn*. Münster: Waxmann, 1996.

– *Religiöse Festkultur: Tradition und Neuformierung katholischer Frömmigkeit im 19. und 20. Jahrhundert- Das Liborifest in Paderborn und das Kilianifest in Würzburg im Vergleich*. Paderborn: F. Schöningh, 2000.

– "Wallfahrtsfrühling im Dritten Reich: Überlegungen zu Religiosität und Resistenz unter dem Nationalsozialismus." In *Religion und Gesellschaft im Deutschland des 19. und 20. Jahrhunderts. Studien zur neuren Geschichte und Westfälische Landesgechichte*, edited by Ludger Grevelhorster, 159–70. Vierow bei Greifswald: SH-Verlag, 1995.

Steigmann-Gall, Richard. *The Holy Reich: Nazi Conceptions of Christianity, 1919–1945*. Cambridge and New York: Cambridge University Press, 2003.

Steinert, Johannes-Dieter. "Gnadenbild und Hakenkreuz: Die Wallfahrt nach Kevelaer." In *Verfolgung und Widerstand im Rheinland und Westfalen 1933–1945*, edited by Anselm Faust, 77–88. Düsseldorf: W. Kohlhammer, 1992.

– *Kevelaer: Eine niederrheinische Region zwischen Kaiserreich und Dritten Reich*. Kevelaer: Butzo & Bercker, 1988.

Sun, Raymond C. *Before the Enemy is Within Our Walls: Catholic Workers in Cologne, 1885–1912*. Boston, MA: Humanities Press, 1999.

– "Catholic-Marxist Competition in the Working-Class Parishes of Cologne during the Weimar Republic." *Catholic Historical Review* 83, no. 1 (1997): 20–43.

– "'Hammer Blows': Work, the Workplace, and the Culture of Masculinity Among Catholic Workers in the Weimar Republic." *Central European History* 37, no. 2 (2004): 245–71.

Tichenor, Kimba Allie. *Religious Crisis and Civic Transformation: How Conflicts over Gender and Sexuality Changed the West German Catholic Church*. Waltham, MA: Brandeis University Press, 2016.

Tweed, Thomas. *America's Church: The National Shrine and Catholic Presence in the Nation's Capital*. New York and Oxford: Oxford University Press, 2011.

Verter, Bradford. "Spiritual Capital: Theorizing Religion with Bourdieu against Bourdieu." *Sociological Theory* 21, no. 2 (2003): 150–74.

Wehler, Hans-Ulrich. *The German Empire*. New York: Berg, 1973.

Welter, Barbara. "The Feminization of American Religion: 1800–1860." In *Clio's Consciousness Raised: New Perspectives on the History of Women*, edited by Mary S. Hartman and Lois Banner, 137–57. New York: Harper & Row, 1974.

Weichlein, Siegfried. *Sozialmilieus und politische Kultur in der Weimarer Republik, Lebenswelt, Vereinskultur, Politik in Hessen*. Göttingen: Vandenhoeck & Ruprecht, 1996.

Wiesemann, Falk. *Die Vorgeschichte der nationalsozialistische Machtübernahme in Bayern 1932/1933*. Berlin: Dunker und Humbolt, 1975.

Wiethaus, Ulrike. "Bloody Bodies: Gender, Religion, and the State in Nazi Germany." *Studies in Spirituality* 12 (2002): 189–202.

– *German Mysticism and the Politics of Culture*. New York: Peter Lang, 2014.

Witetschek, Helmut. *Pater Ingbert Naab, O.F.M. Cap. (1885–1935). Ein Prophet wider den Zeitgeist*. Munich: Schnell und Steiner, 1985.

Wolffram, Heather. *Stepchildren of Science: Psychical Research and Parapsychology in Germany, c. 1870–1939*. New York and Amsterdam: Editions Rodopi, 2009.

Zalar, Jeffrey. "'Knowledge is Power': The Borromausverein and Catholic Reading Habits in Imperial Germany." *Catholic Historical Review* 86, no. 1 (January 2000): 20–46.

Ziemann, Benjamin. *Encounters with Modernity: The Catholic Church in West Germany*, 1945–1975. Translated by Andrew Evans. New York and Oxford: Berghahn, 2014.

– *War Experiences in Rural Germany, 1914–1923*. Translated by Alex Skinner. Oxford and New York: Berg, 2006.

Zumholz, Maria Anna. *Volksfrömmigkeit und katholisches Milieu. Marienerscheinungen in Heede 1937–1940 im Spannungsfeld von Volksfrömmigkeit, nationalsozialistischem Regime und kirchlicher Hierarchie*. Cloppenburg: Verlag Runge, 2004.

Index

German and European Studies

General Editor: Jennifer J. Jenkins

1 Emanuel Adler, Beverly Crawford, Federica Bicchi, and Rafaella Del Sarto, *The Convergence of Civilizations: Constructing a Mediterranean Region*
2 James Retallack, *The German Right, 1860–1920: Political Limits of the Authoritarian Imagination*
3 Silvija Jestrovic, *Theatre of Estrangement: Theory, Practice, Ideology*
4 Susan Gross Solomon, ed., *Doing Medicine Together: Germany and Russia between the Wars*
5 Laurence McFalls, ed., *Max Weber's 'Objectivity' Revisited*
6 Robin Ostow, ed., *(Re)Visualizing National History: Museums and National Identities in Europe in the New Millennium*
7 David Blackbourn and James Retallack, eds., *Localism, Landscape, and the Ambiguities of Place: German-Speaking Central Europe, 1860–1930*
8 John Zilcosky, ed., *Writing Travel: The Poetics and Politics of the Modern Journey*
9 Angelica Fenner, *Race under Reconstruction in German Cinema: Robert Stemmle's Toxi*
10 Martina Kessel and Patrick Merziger, eds., *The Politics of Humour: Laughter, Inclusion, and Exclusion in the Twentieth Century*
11 Jeffrey K. Wilson, *The German Forest: Nature, Identity, and the Contestation of a National Symbol, 1871–1914*
12 David G. John, *Bennewitz, Goethe,* Faust: *German and Intercultural Stagings*
13 Jennifer Ruth Hosek, *Sun, Sex, and Socialism: Cuba in the German Imaginary*

14 Steven M. Schroeder, *To Forget It All and Begin Again: Reconciliation in Occupied Germany, 1944–1954*
15 Kenneth S. Calhoon, *Affecting Grace: Theatre, Subject, and the Shakespearean Paradox in German Literature from Lessing to Kleist*
16 Martina Kolb, *Nietzsche, Freud, Benn, and the Azure Spell of Liguria*
17 Hoi-eun Kim, *Doctors of Empire: Medical and Cultural Encounters between Imperial Germany and Meiji Japan*
18 J. Laurence Hare, *Excavating Nations: Archaeology, Museums, and the German-Danish Borderlands*
19 Jacques Kornberg, *The Pope's Dilemma: Pius XII Faces Atrocities and Genocide in the Second World War*
20 Patrick O'Neill, *Transforming Kafka: Translation Effects*
21 John K. Noyes, *Herder: Aesthetics against Imperialism*
22 James Retallack, *Germany's Second Reich: Portraits and Pathways*
23 Laurie Marhoefer, *Sex and the Weimar Republic: German Homosexual Emancipation and the Rise of the Nazis*
24 Bettina Brandt and Daniel Purdy, eds. *China and the German Enlightenment*
25 Michael Hau, *Performance Anxiety: Sport and Work in Germany from the Empire to Nazism*
26 Celia Applegate, *The Necessity of Music: Variations on a German Theme*
27 Richard J. Golsan, and Sarah M. Misemer, eds., *The Trial That Never Ends: Hannah Arendt's* Eichmann in Jerusalem *in Retrospect*
28 Lynne Taylor, *In the Children's Best Interests: Unaccompanied Children in American-Occupied Germany, 1945–1952*
29 Jennifer A. Miller, *Turkish Guest Workers in Germany: Hidden Lives and Contested Borders, 1960s to 1980s*
30 Amy Carney, *Marriage and Fatherhood in the Nazi SS*
31 Michael E. O'Sullivan, *Disruptive Power: Catholic Women, Miracles, and Politics in Modern Germany, 1918–1965*

www.ingramcontent.com/pod-product-compliance
Lightning Source LLC
LaVergne TN
LVHW090150080826
844660LV00013B/742/J

* 9 7 8 1 4 8 7 5 0 3 4 3 7 *